WOMEN AND WAR

This volume explores how art and artifacts can tell women's stories of war—a critical way into these stories, often hidden due to the second-tier status of reporting women's accomplishments. This unique lens reveals personal, cultural, and historically noteworthy experiences often not found in records, manuscripts, and texts.

Nine stories from history are examined, from the mythical Amazons of Ancient Greece to a female prisoner of war during World War II. Each of the social, political, and battlefield experiences of Penthesilea, Artemisia, Boudica, the feminine cavaliers, the Dahomey Amazons, suffragists, World War I medical corps, and a World War II prisoner of war are intertwined with a particular work of art or an artifact. These include pottery, iconographic images, public sculpture, stone engraving, clothing, decorative arts, paintings, and pulp art. While each story stands alone, brought together in this volume they represent a cross-sectional reflection on the record of women and war. The chapters cover not only a diverse range of women from around the globe – the African continent, the Hispanic territory of Europe, Carian and Ancient Greece and Rome, Iran, Great Britain-Scotland-ancient Caledonia, Western Europe, and North America—but also a diverse choice of artwork and artifacts, eras, and the nature of the wars being fought.

This book will be of value to those interested in gender across history and its interplay in the field of war.

Dr. Mary Raum is a tenured professor of national security affairs at the United States Naval War College, where she created and has been teaching the history of women in war and combat courses for 15 years. She earned a Bachelor of Arts in art history from Cambridge University, holds several art history certifications, and has a dual Ph.D. in Engineering and Public Affairs. Dr. Raum was the legacy Swanee Hunt Academic Chair for Women Peace and Security and served in that role for a decade.

WOMEN AND WAR

Stories from the Amazons to the Greatest Generation through Art and Artifacts

Mary Raum

LONDON AND NEW YORK

Designed cover image: Hebert, Pierre-Eugene-Emile, circa 1860/1872. Amazon Preparing for

Battle (Queen Antiope or Hippolyta? Or Armed Venus, cast bronze, National Gallery of Art,

Washington, D.C. West Building, Ground Floor Gallery 3, Accession Number 1987.25.1

Courtesy National Gallery of Art, Washington. *National Gallery of Art Washington D.C. CC0 Public Domain*

First published 2025
by Routledge
4 Park Square, Milton Park, Abingdon, Oxon OX14 4RN

and by Routledge
605 Third Avenue, New York, NY 10158

Routledge is an imprint of the Taylor & Francis Group, an informa business

© 2025 Mary Raum

The right of Mary Raum to be identified as author of this work has been asserted in accordance with sections 77 and 78 of the Copyright, Designs and Patents Act 1988.

All rights reserved. No part of this book may be reprinted or reproduced or utilised in any form or by any electronic, mechanical, or other means, now known or hereafter invented, including photocopying and recording, or in any information storage or retrieval system, without permission in writing from the publishers.

Trademark notice: Product or corporate names may be trademarks or registered trademarks, and are used only for identification and explanation without intent to infringe.

British Library Cataloguing-in-Publication Data
A catalogue record for this book is available from the British Library

Library of Congress Cataloging-in-Publication Data
Names: Raum, Mary, author.
Title: Women and war : stories from the Amazons to the Greatest Generation through art and artifacts / Mary Raum.
Other titles: Stories from the Amazons to the Greatest Generation through art and artifacts
Description: Abingdon, Oxon ; New York, NY : Routledge, 2025. | Includes bibliographical references and index. | Contents: Storytelling with Ceramics Penthesilea, Queen of the Amazons -- Anachronism and Iconography as Artifact : Artemisia I of Persia, Admiral & Queen of the Anatolian Region of Caria -- Stylized Public Sculpture : Boudica Queen of the British Celtic Iceni Tribe -- Stone Engraving Order of the Hatchet : The Feminine Cavaliers of the Torch in Tortosa -- Uniforms as Artifacts : The Dahomey Warriors of West Africa -- Decorative Arts Medals as Artifacts Suffragism : The Women's Civil War 1840-1921 -- Portraiture as a Historical Record : Mable Annie St Clair Stobart and the Serbian Women's Sick and Wounded Convoy Corps -- Painting as Social Commentary : Drs Flora Murray and Louisa Garrett Anderson & the Endell Street Hospital -- Pulp Art : Prisoner of War, Chief Navy Nurse, Marion Olds.
Identifiers: LCCN 2024029248 (print) | LCCN 2024029249 (ebook) | ISBN 9781032523804 (hbk) | ISBN 9781032523750 (pbk) | ISBN 9781003406372 (ebk)
Subjects: LCSH: Women in war--History. | Women in war--History--Sources. | Women soldiers--Biography--Sources. | Women in combat--History--Sources. | Women and war--History--Sources. | Art and war.
Classification: LCC UB416 .R37 2025 (print) | LCC UB416 (ebook) | DDC 355.0082--dc23/eng/20240809
LC record available at https://lccn.loc.gov/2024029248
LC ebook record available at https://lccn.loc.gov/2024029249

ISBN: 978-1-032-52380-4 (hbk)
ISBN: 978-1-032-52375-0 (pbk)
ISBN: 978-1-003-40637-2 (ebk)

DOI: 10.4324/9781003406372

Typeset in Sabon
by KnowledgeWorks Global Ltd.

This book is dedicated to seven amazing women.
Suzy Ghuarani, MD
Lynn Handleman
Penelope Harrell
Elizabeth Hemmerdinger
Elena Mastors, Ph.D.
Kathleen McDonald, MD
Donna Nicely

CONTENTS

List of Figures		*ix*
Acknowledgments		*xiv*
	Introduction	1
1	Storytelling with Ceramics: Penthesilea, Queen of the Amazons	9
2	Artistic Iconography: Artemisia I of Persia, Admiral, and Queen of the Anatolian Region of Caira	27
3	Stylized Public Sculpture: Boudica Queen of the British Celtic Iceni Tribe	49
4	Stone Engraving: Order of the Hatchet: The Feminine Cavaliers of the Torch of Tortosa	74
5	Uniforms as Artifacts: The Dahomey Warriors of West Africa	93
6	Decorative Arts Medals as Artifacts: Suffragism: The Women's Civil War 1840–1921	140

viii Contents

7 Portraiture as a Historical Record: Mable Annie
St. Clair Stobart and the Serbian Women's Sick and
Wounded Convoy Corps   190

8 Painting as Social Commentary: Drs. Flora Murray
and Louisa Garrett Anderson and the Endell Street
Hospital   220

9 Pulp Art: Prisoner of War, Chief Navy Nurse, Marion Olds   251

Epilogue   *281*
Bibliography   *289*
Art and Art Periods Addendum   *314*
Index   *322*

FIGURES

1.1 Penthesilea and Achilles on Exekias Pottery. © Author   9

1.2 Statue of Phidias in gold and ivory in Olympia's main temple covered with paintings and precious stones. © Creative Commons CC 1.0 Universal Public Domain Dedication Wikimedia Commons   11

1.3 15th Century illustration of Penthesilea as one of the nine female worthies. © PICRYL Public Domain Media Search Engine Wikipedia   12

1.4 Marble block from the Frieze of the Temple of Apollo Amazons Fighting the Greeks. © CC BY-SA 2.0 Deed | Attribution-ShareAlike 2.0 Generic | Creative Commons https://www.flickr.com/photos/carolemage/14073518379/in/photostream/   13

2.1 Guillaume Rouille's profile portrait of Artemisia. © Public Domain Mark 1.0   27

2.2 A profile carving of Xing Xerxes. © CC BY-SA 4.0 Legal Code | Attribution-ShareAlike 4.0 International | Creative Commons Category: Xerxes I – Wikimedia Commons   29

2.3 and 2.4 Map of the Achaemenid Empire under Cyrus the Great. © CC BY-SA 4.0 Deed | Attribution-ShareAlike 4.0 International | Creative Commons File: Persian empire-history-818×490.jpg – Wikimedia Commons   29

x Figures

2.5 Two fleets of Greek triremes fighting in close quarters. © Reuse of PD-Art Orientation UK This work was published in 1882 and is no longer under copyright Cassell's Illustrated Universal History: OLLIER, Edmund: Free Download, Borrow, and Streaming: Internet Archive p. 349   30

2.6 Ciaran coin of a helmeted female with hair in sakkos wearing a rosette earring. © GNU Free Documentation License, Version 1.2 CNG-Ancient Greek, Roman, British Coins (cngcoins.com)   42

2.7 Ciaran coin of a kneeling winged female. © CC BY-SA 2.5 Deed | Attribution-ShareAlike 2.5 Generic | Creative Commons File:CARIA, Kaunos. Circa 470–450 BC.jpg – Wikimedia Commons   43

3.1 Statue of Boudica and her daughters by Thomas Thornycroft in London. © CC BY 2.0 Deed | Attribution 2.0 Generic | Creative Commons Category: Boadicea and Her Daughters – Wikimedia Commons   49

3.2 Nineteenth-century children's bookplate of Boudica and her daughters. © CC0 Creative Commons CC-PD Mark File: Pictures of English History Plate IV – Boadicea and Her Army.jpg – Wikimedia Commons   57

3.3 Map showing the Iron Age tribes of Great Britain. © CC BY-SA 3.0Deed Attribution-Share Alike 3.0 Unported Creative Commons File:Britain.circa.540.jpg – Wikipedia   59

3.4 Nineteenth-century illustration of Boudica in Iceni Dress. © Creative Commons Attribution-Share Alike 4.0 International   61

3.5 Map showing the major cities attacked by Boudica during her revolt. © Creative Commons Attribution-Share Alike 4.0 International File: Map of the Boudican Revolt.svg – Wikipedia   63

4.1 Stone carving the emblem of the Order of the Hatchet. © Released by originator worldwide File: TortosaOrdeAtxa.JPG – Wikipedia   74

4.2 Architectural diagram showing the layout of the Cathedral of Tortosa. © GNU Free Documentation License, Version 1.2 Attribution-Share Alike 4.0 International, 3.0 Unported, 2.5 Generic, 2.0 Generic and 1.0 Generic license File: Catedral tortosa224.jpg – Wikipedia   76

4.3 Illuminated manuscript of women participating in a castle siege. © Creative Commons Attribution-Share Alike 4.0 International license. https://commons.wikimedia.org/wiki/File:Seige.jpg   80

5.1	A female Dahomey warrior at a tribal spectacle taking a battle stance. © Out of print book taken from the original source. A mission to Gelele, king of Dahome: with notices of the so-called "Amazons," the grand customs, the yearly customs, the human sacrifices, the present state of the slave trade, and the Negro's place in nature: Burton, Richard Francis, Sir, 1821–1890.	93
5.2	Dahomey Amazons with trophy heads after a battle. © World Cat Search ebook Electronic Reproduction.	98
5.3	She-Dong-Hong-Beh as the leader of the Dahomey Amazons. © Public domain. Dahomey and the Dahomans; being the journals of two missions to the king of Dahomey, and residence at his capital, in the years 1849 and 1850: Forbes, Frederick E. (Frederick Edwyn).	110
5.4	Illustration from a French magazine of the Battle of Dogba. © Gallica Digital Library and is available under the digital ID btv1b6938782f. This image from the Bibliothèque nationale de France (BnF) is a reproduction by scanning of a bidimensional work that is now in the public domain.	115
5.5	Picture postcard of the costumes and utensils of a Dahomey veteran tribe. © Creative Commons CCO License File: The célébration at Abomey (1908). The veteran amazones (AHOSI) of the Fon king Béhanzin, Son of Roi Gélé.jpg – Wikipedia.	125
5.6	Two Dahomey Amazons wearing a band of iron crowned with two antelope horns symbolizing power, strength, and flexibility. © Creative Commons CC0 1.0 Universal Public Domain Dedication ("CCO 1.0 Dedication") https://picryl.com/media/amazons-or-female-warriors-of-dahomey-4ce5f2.	127
6.1 and 6.2	A suffragette valor medal for force-feeding and imprisonment with a portcullis on the top (Figure 6.1) and hunger strike medallion on the bottom (Figure 6.2). © CC BY SA 3.0 Attribution share alike 3.0 unported Violet Ann Bland Medal (cropped).jpg – Wikimedia Commons.	140
6.3	Primary groups in the suffrage movement. © Author.	144
6.4	and 6.5 A chromolithograph spoofing the differences between suffragettes (Figure 6.4) and remonstrants (Figure 6.5) entitled "Find the Group in Favor of Woman's Suffrage". © Public domain media usage CC0.	146

xii Figures

6.6 Mrs. Helen Appo Cook, Organizer and President of the Colored Women's League of Washington, D.C. © Public domain. Published (or registered with the U.S. Copyright Office) before January 1, 1929. PD US expired. Helen Appo Cook from TheColoredAmerican DC 4 June1898, p. 2 – Helen Appo Cook – Wikipedia. 151

6.7 A suffragette being force-fed by two women and a man. © Public domain. PDM 1.0 Deed | Public Domain Mark 1.0 Universal | Creative Commons. 167

6.8 Votes for women poster advertising the story of William Ball. © Public domain. Flickr by LSE Library at https:// flickr.com/photos/35128489@N07/22896718036. 171

7.1 George James Rankin's painting, Lady of the Black Horse, showing Mable Stobart Leading Serbian Troops through the Montenegrin Mountains during The Great Retreat. © Public domain. Evidence reported by judyjordan for item flamingswordinse00stobrich on November 6, 2007. 190

7.2 Mable Stobart with the commander of the Schumadia Division repitiching a tent. © Public domain under the terms of the Project Gutenberg License. 201

7.3 Cover of War Illustrated highlighting Mable Stobart's volunteer work in Serbia. © Public Domain All issues of the British WW1-era magazine The War Illustrated Jul–Dec 1915 Internet Archive HTML5 Uploader 1.6.4 Scanned and cropped by self from original document. 203

7.4 Mable Stobart's flying field hospital train leaving for the front. © Public domain under the terms of the Project Gutenberg. 205

8.1 The Francis Dodd painting of an operation at the Endell Hospital showing Drs. Lousia Garrett, Flora Murray, and W. Buckley. © Public domain File: An Operation at the Military Hospital, Endell Street – Dr. L Garrett, Dr. Flora Murray, Dr. W Buckley Art.IWMART4084.jpg – Wikipedia. 220

8.2 Dame Rachel Crowdy, Principal Commander of the VAD by Austin Osman Spare. © Public domain. File: Dame Rachel Crowdy, the Principal Commander of the VADs (Art. IWM ART 3205).jpg – Wikimedia Commons. 239

8.3 Pastel image of a nurse in indoor uniform at Endell Hospital drawn by Austin Osman Spare. A nurse in a white lab coat. © Public domain. HMSO has declared that the expiry of Crown Copyrights applies worldwide. File: A Nursing Orderly (indoor) – Endell Street Military Hospital, London Art.IWMART2853.jpg – Wikimedia Commons. 240

| | Figures | **xiii** |

8.4 Pastel drawing of a nurse at Endell Street in outdoor uniform drawn by Austin Osman Spare. © Public domain. HMSO. File: A Nursing Orderly (Outdoors), Endell Street Military Hospital, London (Art. IWM ART 2854).jpg – Wikimedia Commons. 241

9.1 Cover of *Sensation* magazine in which Marion Olds story appeared. A blonde nurse and a pilot holding a gun in a crouched position. © Roger Mansell, Palo Alto, CA. Public domain. File: News From the Past – JAP ATROCITIES AROUSE NATION (mansell.com). 251

9.2 Left to right Doris Yetter, Leona Jackson, Lorraine Christansen, and Marion Olds near Zensuji Prison Camp, Japan. © Sponsored by the Roger Mansell group, Palo Alto, CA. Public domain. File: The Research Center (mansell.com). 263

ACKNOWLEDGMENTS

Writing a book is a community effort and requires many cheerleaders. Thank you to Lynn Handleman and her service dog, Yarrow, for the hours spent walking and discussing chapter content. She can probably recite the entire book. Her support was constant and unrelenting. For Dr. Elena Mastors, your insight into the publishing community was invaluable and set me on the right course. Dr. Terrence Roehrig's insights into publishing an academic work were exceptional, and the final product would not have moved forward without his input. To the research and resource librarians and experts at the United States Naval War College, Gina Brown, Isabel Lopes, Julie Zecher, and Carolyn Wilk, and their hours of background work in aiding me in the research materials that guided the final product were instrumental to the quality content derived for each chapter. The enjoyment of discussing ideas will always be appreciated deeply. The endless support of the staff in the electives department over the years was why the subject matter of the history of women and war received its due inclusion into the curriculum. Faces have changed many times within this entity, and all have been advocates, with one constant over many years: Patty Duch.

Disclaimer

The views expressed in this publication are those of the author and do not necessarily reflect the official policy or position of the Naval War College, Department of the Navy, Department of Defense, or the U.S. government.

INTRODUCTION

When civilian psychiatric pediatric nurse Monika Schwinn stepped off the plane in Vietnam, she never expected that three and a half years of her life would be spent in prisoner-of-war (POW) camps along the Ho Chi Minh Trail. The only woman. Alone, often spending time in solitary confinement, and always closer to death than alive. Monika's father had died in World War II and was never recovered, a captive in the brutal northern Russian POW camp system. She would never have believed such a scenario would enter her own life. Her last internment was at the "Hanoi Hilton," formally named Hao Lo, the prison for political dissidents and the torture of American military hostages before she was repatriated to her homeland and flown back to Lebach, West Germany. Her brother had kept her apartment ready for her since the day she had been categorized as missing, knowing that if anyone would survive, it would be his sister, Monika. Schwinn's story, *We Came to Help*, was published in several languages and details her treatment as a female prisoner. In her living hell, she was considered less than an animal by North Vietnamese captives because "she was a woman." POWs recall their date of loss vividly but celebrate their repatriation day. Monika Schwinn: Date of Loss: 27-Apr-69; Status in 1973 (Returnee March 5) is what is written in her POW record.

A series of ongoing swirling events buffeted her jungle survival and infiltrated their way into the ups and downs of how she was treated. Richard Nixon had inherited the protracted war on winning the presidential election four months before Monika was captured. Nixon then ordered what was labeled a secret menu of calculated B-52 bombings of Cambodia. The Paris peace talks were deteriorating into a propaganda theater by the North Vietnamese and Americans. In 1971, Prince Norodom Sihanouk of Cambodia

DOI: 10.4324/9781003406372-1

2 Women and War

toppled, increasing instability in the region. A theater offensive was ordered, and the South Vietnamese crossed into Cambodia and Laos in early 1971. The following year, the United States instigated a reinforcement of massive air force and naval engagements in Indochina and Guam. Finally, in January 1973, the Democratic Republic of Vietnam and the United States initiated a peace agreement. On the Ho Chi Minh trail and the land around it, the United States and its allies dropped 7.5 billion tons of bombs, and a total of 2.8 million combat missions were conducted. The Women Strike for Peace members struck outside the United Nations in New York City, and college campuses erupted with anti-war sentiment.

Monika's colleague, and later medical doctor Bernhard Diehl, was the only other of a group of a total of five volunteer Maltesers that were captured on the same day and survived captivity. The three other missionary workers are a footnote "killed in captivity." *We Came to Help* is a chronology of alternating male and female voices of two individuals experiencing the same circumstances. Monika left Germany as a peacekeeper, a volunteer who would give medical aid to both sides of the conflict as a Catholic Aid Service Worker.

West Germany's Indochina foreign policy followed no solidarity or combat philosophy. US President Lyndon Johnson publicly chastised the German government and attempted to pressure them into supporting the war. Chancellor Ludwig Erhard reacted by limiting the country's inclusion to humanitarian support under the notion of "medicine instead of ammunition," and he approved the anchoring of the hospital ship *Helgoland* off the cities of Saigon and Danang for six years with the mission to treat the war wounded and sick. The year was 1966, and Schwinn was 24 years old. Monika was based inland in Vietnam, primarily nursing wounded babies, children, and mothers. Her other working partners, a few women and Diehl, went on an afternoon outing. They were in their nursing uniforms with the red and white Maltese emblem with its four "V" arrowhead-shaped concave quadrilateral sewn on the left chest. She had bought a camera and wanted to take photos of daily life in the rice paddies and beautiful southern Vietnamese terrain, its wildlife, and people. The group had unknowingly crossed into North Vietnamese territory and was captured by a villager at gunpoint. From that point forward, her life detoured from being a children's nurse to an enemy captive. Her forced walking route up the Ho Chi Minh trail, the military supply route running from North Vietnam through Laos and Cambodia to the South Vietnamese territory – involved time spent in both brick and mortar and jungle internment camps. Daily, guerillas moved several tons of military supplies along the main artery and hundreds of trails, footpaths, and roadways. Monika was used as a human shield made to march in front of the armed Viet Cong to trip any wired explosives.

I was researching female POWs for a new curriculum in the history of women in war and combat for a military college when I learned of

Monika's story. At that time, there were next to no resources that detailed noncombatant or military women's roles in civil or armed conflict environments that could be used as solid curriculum representations. I had to rely on men's stories of military accomplishment and, in POW research, the men's stories of imprisonment to glean the slightest references to female exploits. One evening, while reading Vietnam POW US Army Chief Warrant Officer Frank Anton's book *Why Didn't You Get Me Out*, the author mentioned a female nurse who had resided with him in a military jungle camp. I sat and reread the two or three sentences over and over to prove to myself that, yes, in fact, there had been a Western woman interned in the jungles at the height of the Vietnam War. She was a professional and not Vietnamese and was treated as if she were a combat enemy. In Anton's camp, Monika would come face to face with the infamous US defector Bobby Garwood, would be starved and given no medical treatment for rampant jungle diseases, given indoctrination lessons, and cared for and watched die; one of the other female nurses who quickly succumbed mentally, emotionally, and physically to the tortuous environment.

Why wasn't such a woman and others of equal incredible experiences part of every military history curriculum? The answer was simple: nobody thought the female storyline was important. This knowledge led me to develop an elective course on women's history and armed conflict. The idea was met with stark incredulity. The individuals who blockaded the attempt with comments meant to dissuade such an idea are long gone. I was told, "*No man* would ever take this course," and "We don't want this *women's stuff* in here." Getting the course online took two years of fighting and some courageous supporters. Such resistance left me shocked, and from that point forward, I researched, probed, and prodded into the nooks and crannies of existing literature to learn about the lives and careers of the obscure females who were left out of a stilted and backward 21st-century viewpoint of females in battle and its supportive structures. The first outing was three male and two female students putting to rest the idea that men were uninterested in women's war stories.

I was fortunate to meet Monika in her home in Lebach and interview her with the phenomenal assistance of German translator Ursula Doerr. In the hours the three of us spent drinking tea, eating German cuisine and Vietnamese food, and looking out her window into her beloved garden, I listened to her story of love, dedication, fierce independence, strength, and resilience. At one point in the conversations, Monika mentioned that she had her last POW uniform in the attic. I asked far too eagerly if I might see it. The reticence was palpable. "Perhaps," she said, "it was washed, pressed, starched, and packed away." I had not yet built enough trust to become part of such an intimate and personal remembrance.

4 Women and War

Bringing the uniform into the airiness of the kitchen and garden scene could dredge up memories better left in the past. Artifacts such as POW clothing meld with stories about a person's soul, represent significant life events, call out essential bridges crossed in life, and represent acts of personal strength. Their physicalness makes them all the starker as storytelling items because of their touchable dimensionality. Physical items prove that something did occur when written documentation is unavailable. Monika surprised me during a follow-up day of interviews when she disappeared into the living room and returned with a set of POW pajamas. There was a tunic and pants made with coarse, oddly gray material that had originally been white and sandals made of old tires. One of the sandals had a broken strap, and these, she said, were given to her only near the end of her internment.

The four items were like none I had experienced in museums or with friends sharing their life's relics. These articles were alive. Heavy bleaching had been unable to remove the grayness of constant wear, sweat, sickness, blood, injury, and filth. Yet the rubber and cloth had endured as participants in Monika's life. She had cared for the items well, almost evoking the feeling of their being a shrine to her survival. Razor-sharp creases had been stitched down the middle of each leg, sewn by Monika in painstaking redundancy. A single stitch at a time with a dull needle. She had done this because, even though she was a prisoner, there was no need to look sloppy. Both the top and bottoms were starched. The creases and careful ironing showed that her troubling story had not dissuaded her from believing in her self-worth and value even in the most horrendous circumstances. The color of the cloth is what struck me hardest. I was staring at not just any color but the color of survival. Pants and tunics told the story of strength, resilience, and perseverance – each having literally been with Monika through hell and her return to civilization. She brought to Ursala's and my attention that no number was printed on the left upper chest area, which was reserved for male internees only. Women didn't get numbers because they didn't matter.

From that intense experience of coming in contact with a strong woman, storytelling, and physical artifacts, my interest in their combined essence moved me to locate other physical representations in artistic renderings and physical items that could tell stories of women, war, and conflict. There were far fewer written representations about women, so physical items were valuable for relating their exploits where other resources were lacking. This approach has become a part of my war history curriculum for many years. I even require students to go to a museum and discover an item that chronicles women and conflict. Students come back together and relate to others their interpretation of the item's meaning to them personally and its importance to the annals of war.

Over the years, my artifact and art research have put me into contact with many examples that have emerged from many sources, including pottery, clothing, jewelry, paintings, carvings, statues, music, and poetry. Physical items represent a three-dimensional truth of an event or person. Perhaps the intrigue with this approach is due to my advanced studies in engineering, being a practicing artist, ravenous museumgoer, and a recent graduate with two diplomas in art history from Cambridge University. What I find striking about using art and artifacts as a basis for study is that their creation involves additional storylines of the prior and post-eras in which the women lived. In effect, using physical and visual representations engenders a more complete picture of the events surrounding their achievements before, during, and after their lifetimes. Who created the artifact, what medium they used, and why they wanted to replicate a female's story are testaments about changing generational perceptions of fighting women. Art and artifacts can be touched and viewed for long periods, allowing an observer to formulate a deeper connection to an individual and an event. Each example proves that heroines, Amazons, fighters, peacemakers, and volunteers have been integral to the timeline of global strife.

About the Book

If history were taught in the form of stories, it would never be forgotten.
Rudyard Kipling

Nine stories connected within physical artifacts and art and women's roles in war and conflict were chosen for inclusion in this book. The timeframe of coverage of the nine representations is vast, beginning with the Greek Amazonian myth and concluding in the timeframe of World War II. Chosen from earlier times are the fabled ground fighter Penthesilea, Queen of the Amazons; Artemisia I, the sea admiral serving under King Xerxes; and Boudica, the Queen of the British Celtic Iceni Tribe and her revolt against Roman invaders. From the Middle Ages is the story of the Feminine Cavaliers of the Torch of Tortosa who fended off the Moors during the Crusades. Following these periods are the 19th-century Dahomey warriors of West Africa and the 20th-century women's civil rights fight to become equal citizens under the law. Two World War I stories about the Serbian Women's Sick and Wounded Convoy Corps and the all-female World War I military hospital on Endell Street are representative of women's first formal inclusion into the front and behind-the-lines spheres of modern warfare. The book ends with a story of a World War II POW. In order of appearance, connections are made between women or a woman and a black figure amphora piece of pottery, iconographic images, stylized public sculpture, stone engraving, uniforms, decorative arts, portraiture as both historical record and social commentary, and pulp art.

6 Women and War

In Chapter 1, the mythical goddess Penthesilea's life and warrior spirit in fighting her nemesis Achilles in the fabled Trojan Wars are uncovered using a black attic amphora believed to have been fashioned by the Greek artisan Exekias. Fables surrounding ancient Amazons and their current status in the annals of war are explained. Chapter 2 relates the story of Queen Artemisia I of Ciara, who was a rarity in the annals of war for being a fighting admiral. An accurate likeness of the navalist does not exist, as has often been the case with long-ago artistic embodiments of women. This is why an explanation of Artemisia occurs through iconographic imaging specimens found on coins and the most replicated image of her from the prominent humanist bookseller Guillaume Rouille in his 16th-century compilation of portrait types. Chapter 3 presents Boudica, the Queen of the Iceni tribe in Britain, who fought the Romans in 60 AD. The backdrop to her legend is the bronze sculptural group *Boudicea and her Daughters*, created by British sculptor Thomas Thornycroft in the 19th century. Chapter 4 is placed in the times of siege warfare on the European continent when a group of mixed-race Catalonians defended their castle against a Muslim onslaught at the Battle of Tortosa in Spain. A carved stone dedicated to the Order of the Hatchet, which was conferred upon them by Count Ramon Berenguer IV, is the connecting artifact that assists in illustrating their honorific battle, which occurred during the Second Crusades.

Chapter 5 recounts the brutality and ferocity of the Dahomey Amazons of Western Africa from the late 19th century. The concept of enclothed cognition, the symbolic meaning and physical wearing of attire, is employed as an exploratory means of integrating their battle uniforms with reports of their fighting lives. Once colonialism depleted the warriors, their battle livery was transfigured into costume attire to be consumed as exotica in exhibitions around Europe and North America. Chapter 6 shifts away from the military battlefield onto the front lines of civil unrest during the first wave of suffragism in North America and Europe in the late 18th and early 19th centuries. Imprisonment and hunger strike medals created by the militant arm of suffragists became important relics of women's sense of urgency and the tremendous physical and emotional lengths they were willing to endure to gain equality before the law. Categorical denominations of suffragists, suffragettes, anti-suffragists, and pacifists portray the history and infighting among movement participants and the advances and contractions that occurred because of personal values of the role women should play in society. Chapters 7 and 8 link suffragism to two military medical stories about Mabel St. Clair Stobart and the hospital team of Drs. Flora Murray and Louisa Anderson. Both examples are two of the first times in the annals of modern war in the West that women served in large groups near or behind the front lines with formal military ranks. Integral to each chapter is the art of portraiture. Chapter 7 views the painting *The Lady of the Black Horse*, composed by artist Geroge James Rankin, as an accurate historical record of a wartime woman on the battlefield. The painting, *An Operation at the Military Hospital, Endell Street – Dr. L Garrett, Dr. Flora Murray, and Dr. W Buckley* by Francis Dodd in Chapter 8 is a testament to the inaccuracies that can occur in presenting professional women in a realistic light. Chapter 9 reveals the story of US Chief Navy Nurse Marion Olds, who was captured on Guam by the Japanese in the Pacific during World War II. The domain of pulp art helps tell of the changes in customs for presenting images of military women in more sexualized forums.

Each woman faced conflict for distinct reasons. Penthesilea from ancient Greek mythology represents the fable of the female warrior ethos. A remarkable twist regarding the allegory of the Amazonian woman is that what was deemed only a parable proved true through modern scientific research. Artemisia I is an unusual instance of a female naval phenom who fought with King Xerxes at the Battle of Salamis. Boudica was the personification of a fierce leader of her people when she stood against the Roman legions as an indigenous queen, charioteer, and hand-to-hand combatant. The Battle of Tortosa is an account of women who took over what was primarily a male responsibility to fend off siege attacks by others and stood as intermediaries in the fight for their homeland. They fought Muslim hoards when the men left to fight in the Second Crusades. The African Dahomey Amazons are reminders of the fierceness and bravery required in the brutal kingdom and colonial wars in West Africa. Their tale is also one of enslavement, abolitionism, and becoming stage participants in exotica shows in a racist 19th-century environment.

The first wave of suffragism is essential to the annals of women and war. One of the critical connections derived from the fight for emancipation was how suffragist philosophy and newly formed organizational skills directly impacted their struggle to serve as Western military professionals during World War I. These fights for women's equality taught participants how to politicize, raise money, and create support mechanisms when none existed within formal channels. The battle for suffragism shifted on the eve of World War I when women began to organize large military medical groups. Three women who successfully fought for inclusion into the military were Mable St. Clair Stobart and the team of doctors Flora Anderson and Louisa Garret Anderson.

All three served with military ranks: Stobart in the Serbian Army and Anderson and Murray with the British Medical Corps. Stobart left her homeland when the British military refused her services. The Serbian Army saw an immediate value in her idea for medical aid on the front and promoted her to Major. Dr. Anderson and Dr. Murray eventually gained acceptance for their ideas through regulated British army structures, even though they had to prove themselves in France first. Their all-female 573-bed hospital on

8 Women and War

Endell Street in London performed over 7000 operations and treated 26,000 wounded personnel. The offbeat, bold, and audacious field of pulp art is directly linked to US Navy Nurse Marion Olds, who was captured by the Japanese when they overtook Guam. Her story illustration on the cover of the magazine *Sensation* became the springboard for discussing the sexualization of the military woman.

A Note to Educators

For educators, those looking for inclusivity will find this in the choice of artwork and artifact, the era, the global region, and the nature of the wars being fought. Key characters come from the African continent, the Hispanic territory of Europe, Carian and Ancient Greece and Rome, Iran, Great Britain-Scotland-ancient Caledonia, Western Europe, and North America. Conflicts were diverse relative to locale and type. There are references to the mythical hand-to-hand combat battles of the ancient Greeks, a sea battle in Ancient Cyprus, chariot and field fighting of the Iceni ethnic group, siege warfare and the Crusades, knight's orders, bush regiments of Africa, modern warfare legionnaires, front- and rear-line medical units, street fighting for a civil war for equal rights, and captivity.

Battles that intersect with the primary protagonists are the storied Trojan War, the sea battle at Salamis, the Battle of Wattling Road, the Second Crusades and Battle of Tortosa, the First and Second Dahomeyan Wars, the Civil War Battle of the Suffragettes in Great Britain and the United States, the Balkan Wars, the fight by the Edinburgh Seven to attend medical school, World War I, and the Battle of Guam during World War II. Women came from different military backgrounds. Various women were cavalry; others were charioteers, fought in hand-to-hand combat, or were female artillerymen. The civil war for equality in the eyes of the law relegated women to becoming streetfighters in their hometowns. Ages also differed, with the youngest, the Dahomey Amazons, who began training at ages five to seven, and the oldest, Marion Olds, in her fifties when she was captured and interned as a POW.

Chapters may be utilized as singular units of study or merged as a single course of reflection on the record of women and war. At the end of each chapter is a list of supplemental readings, a question set related to the reading, and a second question set entitled "Modern Take." "Modern Take" queries attempt to incite parallels and differences between the nine histories and current affairs. Suggested optional activities are varied and involve visiting museums, linking to virtual websites, and reading poetry. Other educational tools are selecting a piece of art and describing its content, context, style, and meaning of color and shape; watching films and videos; searching a family genealogy; creating artistic symbols of renderings of events; and conducting an interview.

I hope that you enjoy the book.

1
STORYTELLING WITH CERAMICS

Penthesilea, Queen of the Amazons

FIGURE 1.1 Penthesilea and Achilles on Exekias Pottery.
© Author

Art meets math and the golden ratio

Greek society relied on the golden ratio or golden mean, represented by the numeric value of phi, as a quantitative guideline for creating exquisite architectural designs, everyday objects, and artwork. Phi was first recorded in Euclid's *Elements* and was expressed arithmetically as 1.618, executed to an infinitely long series of numbers.[1] Through observation, people of the Greco culture discovered that proportion existed naturally in the solar system, flora, fauna, and the human body. It was believed that applying the golden ratio would lead the architect or artist toward a divine sharing of the continuum of excess and deficiency in their work.[2]

The irrational number's namesake, Phidias, a Greek sculptor, painter, and architect, was most remembered for creating the *Statue of Zeus*, the sky and thunder god of ancient Greek religion. Zeus ruled a dozen mythical beings and was believed to guide life, control the natural world, and instigate events in people's lives. Athena, Ares, Hermes, and Hera were the goddesses of war and reason, the god of war and courage, an officer of arms of all gods, and the overseer of women's lives.[3] Demetra, Hephaestus, Artemis, and Poseidon administered food harvests, the gift of fire, the world of animals and hunting, sea storms, and earthquakes. Dionysus and Apollo inspired the making of wine, art, and literature and were called upon through prayer for healing, youth, and beauty. Lore declared that this group of immortals resided on Mount Olympus, a fitting spot for deities, as the geographic formation was located near the Aegean Sea, towering above the landscape to a pinnacle of 10,000 feet.[4]

Completed in 430 BC, Phidias's ivory and gold rendering of *Zeus* was believed to have been designed with phi as a guide to its construction. It was commissioned by the peoples of northwest ancient Elis, who were custodians of the Olympic Games and known for their superior equine breeding skills. Mediterranean pilgrims worshiped the forty-foot-high *Zeus* and traveled to luxuriate in its presence. Due to its notoriety and grandeur, Phidias's sculpture was considered one of the seven wonders of the ancient world alongside the Great Pyramid of Babylon, the Temple of Artemis, the Mausoleum at Halicarnassus, the Colossus of Rhodes, and the Lighthouse of Alexandria.[5] Taking eight years to complete, the statue must have been stunning. Zeus sat upon a cedarwood throne whose features were fashioned using silver, copper, glass, ebony, enamel, paint, and jewels. The widely traveled Greek geographer, historian, and military officer Pausanias recounted in one of his ten books that the carved god's head had a garland of olive shoots, and in his right hand was a winged Nike made of ivory and gold. In the left hand was a scepter topped with an eagle, and on Zeus's feet were sandals coated with gold leaf.

On the base of the statue was a composition of the Amazon Penthesilea dying on the Trojan battlefield in the arms of Achilles, painted by Phidias'

FIGURE 1.2 Statue of Phidias in gold and ivory in Olympia's main temple covered with paintings and precious stones.

© Creative Commons CC 1.0 Universal Public Domain Dedication Wikimedia Commons

brother Penaeus.[6] Depictions of her have been found across an extensive geographic range as far out as 528 miles at the Etruscan city of Vulci, on the Tyrrhenian Sea northwest of Rome, the port city of Thessaloniki, Greece, on the Thermaic Gulf of the Aegean Sea, and Attica in eastern central Greece. The goddess' image also appeared in 14th-century French manuscripts as a female knight in European costume and in a 15th-century folio as one of the seven female worthies, showing that interest in her exploits had not waned for centuries.[7]

Her likeness of being slayed by Achilles became a popular theme to duplicate, and she appeared in carved reliefs on coffins. She was painted on Attic red-figure pottery bowls, wine vessels, kylix, and skyphos cups.[8] A motive of Penthesilea was discovered at the 3rd century BC Temple of Aphrodisias in western Anatolia, Turkey, and another 3rd century stone detail of a Roman

12 Women and War

FIGURE 1.3 15th Century illustration of Penthesilea as one of the nine female worthies.

© PICRYL Public Domain Media Search Engine Wikipedia

sarcophagus fighting with Achilles. Penthesilea was presented again in a battle with Achilles in the 5th century BC southern Italian Lucanian red-figure bell-krater, a large vessel used to dilute wine and water. In the same period, a carved marble high relief at the Temple of Apollo lying in the mountains of Arcadia and three carved narratives of Amazons were placed among 23 storytelling panels. In the first, they were shown charging the Greek army. On another was the scene of Achilles' murder of Penthesilea, and a third depicted the truce between the Greeks and the Amazons.

On a shrine created by artisans of Euboea, the second-largest island geographically next to Crete, wounded Amazons who had fought in the mythic battle for Athens in the 4th century AD were portrayed. Her image continued to be reinterpreted in sculptures and mosaics in ancient Rome after their defeat of the Greek empire.

FIGURE 1.4 Marble block from the Frieze of the Temple of Apollo Amazons Fighting the Greeks.

© CC BY-SA 2.0 Deed | Attribution-ShareAlike 2.0 Generic | Creative Commons https://www.flickr.com/photos/carolemage/14073518379/in/photostream/

Lore places the two protagonists on the battlefield during the Trojan War, in which Penthesilea fought on the side of Troy. As a warrior, the Amazonian queen was respected for her daring, weapon skills, and intelligence. One of her three sisters, Hippolyta, another famous female Amazon fighter in Greek mythology, was said to have been gifted a girdle by her father, Ares, the god of war, which gave the sibling supreme powers. Myths about Hippolyta are varied and are usually tied to the legend of the ninth of twelve labors of penance of Hercules, where Penthesilea fights against the strong man to free her sister from captivity after he abducts her. Another story recounts that Penthesilea accidentally murdered her sister while hurling a spear at a stag on a hunting expedition. Remorseful of the accident, she avenged Hippolyta's name in a battle against the Trojan forces.

The Roman poet Virgil referenced Penthesilea in the *Aeneid*, characterizing her as a fury, leading the crescent-shielded ranks of the Amazons, blazing amid her thousands with a golden belt bound below her naked breast as a maid clashing with men.[9] Author Pliny the Elder credited Penthesilea with developing the battle-ax as a weapon. A more detailed biographical verse of her larger-than-life personality is found in *Ethiopic*, the seventh *Epic Trojan Cycle*, and was attributed to a legendary but unproven poet, Arctiines of Miletus. *The Fall of Troy Book 1* and *Book 14* style her as an Indo-European Thracian woman from an area in southern Russia, Serbia, and Western Turkey. The Amazons embodied ferocious courage and independence in their physical prowess and agility, riding and archery skills, and dexterity in combat arts. They undertook military raids and expeditions that stretched to the frontiers of the ancient world. The Greek epic poet Quintus Smyrnaeus wrote in his missive about the fall of Troy the story of a dozen Amazonian women who followed Penthesilea into battle. Among the group were the fair Clonie, the dark-eyed Harmotome, and the glorious spear thrower, Thermidors.[10]

General agreement surrounding the ancient storytelling of Penthesilea is that during the Trojan War, the queen and several of her warrior champions rose in support of the wise Priam, father of 50 sons and 50 daughters who served as the last king of Troy.[11] As the Amazons entered the city, they slew all soldiers in their path, with Penthesilea meeting her match in Achilles, the most stalwart of all warriors among soldiers of the army of Agamemnon. Styled as the lord of ashen spears with a might so great that it overpassed even the august Penthesilea, his fierce antagonistic attack felled her.[12]

In another adaptation, Penthesilea faces Achilles and kills him in battle, only to have Zeus, the father of all gods, bring him back to life to fight again. Upon being resurrected, Achilles' self-image, now sunk low by a woman's success against him, searched for Penthesilea on the battlefield.[13] Achilles' glorious feats were weighed down by his overwhelming fury toward others and oversized ego. Filled with rage for her mastery over him, he sought her out among all the soldiers to kill and rape her. As Achilles made his death thrust with his sword, he looked into his enemy's eyes and fell in love with the goddess. In remorse, he tenderly held her as she bled to death. In a rare show of concern unbecoming a Greek warrior, Achilles carried Penthesilea from the battlefield and was ridiculed for this unmanly act of penitence. Auintus Smyraneaus recounted this death scene as one in which Achilles's heart was wrung with love's remorse for having slain a thing so sweet.[14] As the strongest warrior and hero of the Greek army pondered her dying, he resolved that he might have taken the flawless, divinely tall, and fair woman home as a queenly bride.[15]

The story of Penthesilea through the eyes of Potter Exekias

Between the beginning of the 6th and the end of the 4th century BC, black-and-red-figure vase decorating techniques were used in Athens to embellish fine pottery. In the black-figure vase painting, ornamental motifs were applied with a slip that turned dark during firing, and the background was left with the complexion of the reddish-brown clay. In contrast, the ornamental themes on red-figure vases endured as the clay color, with the background being painted with a light slurry that turned black when fired in a kiln. Silhouettes were achieved by carefully incising drawings with pointed hand tools before placing them in a furnace that exposed the pottery beneath. Post oven, the articles could be highlighted using opaque yellow, white, and red hues. White was used to denote female flesh, with men's skin being black.[16]

Around the 7th to 5th centuries BC, black-figure ceramic artists began to sign their works for the first time, leaving a legacy of their styles and known locales from which the pottery had been exported. Trade pots with customized scenes of Greek mythology were most admired and sought after. Artist Exekias was among the most distinguished of the black-figure potters and was noted for his splendid horses, scenes of Ajax the Great, and compositions of mythical stories.[17] A favorite shape of the Athenian artisan was the storage amphora jar with a narrow neck and vast body. His proficiency and precise draftsmanship across a range of clay vessels and his talent for creating exquisite patterning around lips, bases, and handles, and the delicate characterizations on the fashions worn by his chosen mythical characters showed a height of sensitivity, dignity, and solemnity no other potter had been capable of achieving. Exekias used a three-phase firing process at temperatures of 800–950 degrees Fahrenheit to obtain sophisticated pigmentation and experimented with painting techniques using red slip. One of the most significant transformations in the style that stimulated the entire realm of clay art was Exekias' aptitude for depicting a moment immediately occurring just before or after an action. This real-time viewpoint forever changed the habit of artists in their depiction of storylines, which, up to that point, merely marched around rather than lived upon the pottery.[18]

Evidence of applying the ancient concept of the golden ratio can be seen in the placement of the patterns and the construction on one of the most beautiful of his 12 pieces still known to exist, the amphora decorated with the allegory of Achilles slaying the immortal Penthesilea.[19] Achilles bears down on the goddess in full armor, his massive muscles tense for the kill as he plunges his spear into her throat. The queen wears a high-crested helmet and a cheekpiece with a serpent relief from her cervix to her forehead. Dressed in a short chiton with a leopard skin overlay, she fights Achilles off with a sword and shield. Blood gushes from her wound. On the reverse side of the amphora, used for storing spirits, is a scene of Dionysus, the god of wine and ecstasy, and his son Oenopion, a vintner.[20]

16 Women and War

It would not have been easy to frame this scene on a curved surface. Art had yet to reach a phase where the difficulties of presenting events in three dimensions had been overcome.[21] The hero and heroine were portrayed in a show of emotional attraction for one another. Exekias deliberately froze the moment at which Achilles realized he loved the woman he had just slain. The fading body of Penthesilea, the point where Achille's spear hits her in a death thrust, and the muscular structure of his body with his back foot planted on the battlefield in a show of furious physical force were among the first presentations by an artist endeavoring to reproduce a live scene. In a 1915 article by a noted professor of classical archeology and scholar of ancient painting, Mary Swindler shared her thought that the subject of Penthesilea was treated so regularly after the period of Exekias by a single red attic-style potter between 450 and 470 BC that she named the person the Penthesilea Master.[22] This later ceramicist added to the shades of earlier counterparts by using dark coral red, light red, and tints of brown, yellow-white, and gold, adding even more depth and appeal to the design of the ancient fable.

Jay Hambidge and 20th-century revival of the golden mean

Twenty-four centuries after these extraordinary objects were fabricated by Exekias, Canadian-born American artist Jay Hambidge aimed to shed light on the use of the golden ratio and divine proportions in the designs of Greek pottery in his two books, *The Greek Vase* and *The Elements of Dynamic Symmetry*.[23] In the early 1900s, the artist and designer studied classical art. He traveled through Greece after abandoning his wife and four children and partnering with his mistress, model, singer, and actress Mary Crovatt. He concentrated his investigations on the Parthenon, the Temple of Apollo at Bassae, Zeus at Olympia, and Athena at Aegina.[24]

The shape and style of the Penthesilea and Achilles pot enthused the author and theorist. He called it superb among all clay vessels, which led him on a quest for a scientifically based concept of harmony. He became convinced that the secret to its loveliness was in the Grecian's thoughtful use of a law of natural design, which took on the form of balanced proportions in their art, architecture, temples, and theaters, and labeled this phenomenon dynamic symmetry. His analysis was based upon the writings of a collection of great minds from the 5th century BC to the 18th century.[25] Explorations were made of Pythagoras's geometry, Euclid's, and Italian Leonardo Bonacci's and Luca Pacioli's Fibonacci number sequences and statistics and accounting frameworks, polymath Leonardo da Vinci's principles of linear perspective, horizon lines and vanishing points, and Kantian philosophy. Hambidge also applied algebraic and geometric notions of square root – two, three, and five rectangles; phyllotaxis patterns occurring naturally in plant life; and Bernoulli's Law of Fluid Dynamics. Formulas were also borrowed from the systems of the mathematical duplication of cubes and the computations of the roots of lines and conic sections.[26]

Hambidge argued that Exekias exploited the golden ratio by placing elements of Achilles and Penthesilea on the amphora. Among his dizzying set of mathematical applications, an attempt was made to show that the proportions of the two bodies of the male god and the Amazonian woman and the length of the head, torso, and legs were closely allied. All decorative aspects, whether the mouth rim at the top, the fillet area at the base, or the body of the amphora to the sides of the main scene, were shown to have purposeful symmetry. The war weapons of the two fighters came to an exacting cross-point near their heads. This same 'X' was found below the weapons when crossing the left and right legs, with Achilles' leg bearing the weight of his antagonistic fury and Penthesilea sinking to earth as her enemy overtook her. Replicated were opposing patterns of red and black in the armor and shields of both warriors. The whorl borrowed from nature and a standard rendering in the golden ratio of Greek art appeared in Achilles' uniform. It was duplicated skillfully on vast swaths away from the main scene. The round shape of Achilles' eye is intimately reproduced upon the armor of Penthesilea and appears as an apotropaic design element at the base of the amphora.

Eventually, the calculations and wide array of scientific and arithmetic formulations found among the quantitatively based suppositions would be questioned. Peers censured the approach, but others found the principles intriguing, even if they could be more mathematically sound. American classical art historian Rhys Carpenter of Bryn Mayr College avowed the scheme of dynamic symmetry was ingenious but ambiguous and the theory a priori improbable.[27] Beyond academia, the contents of *The Elements of Dynamic Symmetry* became popular among artists in their photography and painting techniques.[28]

Hambidge shared his hypotheses with students in the lecture halls of Yale and Harvard, and he was recognized as an influencer in the revival of the golden mean in design methods.[29] Tiffany and Company based a jewelry collection and a set of their decorative vessels on his suppositions, and Chrysler Corporation used his tenants to design a line of automobiles.[30] Artistically, the conjectures of Hambidge influenced painting across a continuum from realism to abstractionism. American painter George Wesley Bellows, known for his boxing and tenement scenes; illustrator and neoclassical imagery painter Maxfield Parish; and abstract emotionalism painter Mark Rothko's color variations all employed elements of dynamic symmetry in their work. In the late 1980s, the Hambidge system of aesthetics became part of the training modules in the academic and industrial design programs at Georgia Tech and Ohio State University.[31]

18 Women and War

The importance of myth

Myths are more than stories. They function as a moral compass, reinforcing a variety of positive vices such as loyalty, humility, and integrity, as well as harmful imperfections such as arrogance and cruelty.[32] They illustrate roles played by individuals in society and connect histories of momentous events, highlighting lessons to be learned about humankind. They persist and flourish only when they provide an enduring purpose. In the case of Penthesilea, the fable functioned as a parable of attributes deemed acceptable by male fighters, such as achieving honorable death in battle, the cowardice of men on the battlefield, and a cautionary tale that all heroic beings had weaknesses.[33] The myth was also a statement about gynocracy, the rule and leadership of a government or event by a woman or women, showing that cultural margins existed for them under the framework of masculine control.[34] This is particularly evident in the story where Penthesilea wins her fight against Achilles and is not allowed to be the victor, as Achilles is resurrected rather than left to die at the hands of a female protagonist. If viewed through a less complicated lens, the story may be considered an interpretation that a woman could withstand the horrors of war and be successful as a leader and fighter of cavalry and foot soldiers on the front lines of battle.

Poet and writer Robert Graves, a World War I veteran who saw front-line action as a captain in the Welch Fusiliers and was severely wounded during the bloodiest day in history for the British Army at the Somme Offensive, published an autobiographical account of his experiences in the trenches entitled *Goodbye to All That* and a mythography, *The Greek Myths*.[35] Graves speculated on the process of iconotropy, the study of visual images and symbols used to explain the truth and fiction of artistic representations of others.[36] From this investigation came his line of reasoning about the period in Greek history when society was highly matrilineal. Graves decided the Greeks had evolved a hypothetical cult image of women due to misogynistic pressures from the influence of beliefs emanating from the etymology of patriarchal tribes of the Pelasgians who occupied Greece before the 12th century BC.[37]

Graves pronounced all myths as having two primary functions.[38] The first was to answer the children's awkward questions, such as who made the world? How will the world end? Who was the first man? Where do souls go after death? The second function of myth was to justify an existing social system and account for traditional rites and customs.[39] Myths, believed Graves, could represent faith and optimism and narrate culturally based accounts of people and events of the past. As metaphors, they symbolized the limits of good and evil in civilization.[40]

His in-depth research on the intrepid Penthesilea shifted what had become a primary deduction by Byzantine scholars: that the prospect of a female fighter was a ridiculous fairytale.[41] Penthesilea's story impacted the World War I veteran so profoundly that he drafted a poem detailing her profuse wounds, her despoiling at the hands of Achilles, and the reactions of those on the battlefield observing her demise.[42] Her legend was a guidepost regarding the social and corporeal norms that early 20th-century society had attached to women's physical and emotional ability to fight and endure war. Graves suggested it was credible that the concept of the woman warrior was not as oblique as modern society had advanced. The battle-hardened soldier's post-World War I research reinvigorated the idea that a female heritage existed of women participating in combat and that their role had been considered essential and believable enough to have been passed down through generations until their stories were usurped by skepticism and deletion from historical accounts.

Amazonian research 20th and 21st centuries

A research paper produced in the mid-1990s at Louisiana State University surmised that the interpretation of the Amazon myth as a positive model for women did not occur until Christine de Pizan, a medieval court writer for King Charles VI of France and other royal household members, addressed the subject in her allegorical biographical catalog, *City of Ladies*.[43] It was not the combativeness of the Amazons she embraced but their lineage of possessing a noble spirit. Framed in the format of a dream vision, her elegy was a direct criticism of the widespread popularity of the storyline in *Romance of the Rose*, written by two successive authors, Guillaume de Lorris and Jean de Meun, in the 1230s and the 1270s and known for its flagrant and unjustified chauvinist viewpoint of women as either romanceable objects for sexual pleasure or their viciousness, which became a standard interpretation of the roles women were expected to play in society. Pizan also relied upon the content in *Lamentations of Matheolus*, a tirade against women and marriage, to formulate her rejoinder.[44]

In the story, three personified virtues, Reason, Rectitude, and Justice, arrive during a dream in female form to tell the narrator that God has chosen her to rectify the misinformation found in *Lamentations* and *Romance*.[45] The Dreamer is directed to build a city to house a group of creditable heroines. As the building commences, each virtue schools her on the accomplishments of great women in the arts, philosophy, and war. Within Part I, chapters sixteen through twenty, is a conversation with Lady Reason, an allegorical administrator who oversaw the construction of the unblemished city of ladies.[46] Amazon Scythian queen Tomyris and Hippolyta were incorporated into the dialog upon the demise of Penthesilea's mother, Orthya, a female spirit of sea waters. The other Amazons in the plot crown Penthesilea as their new ruler. It was through Penthesilea's military savvy, reason, judgment, and ability to defeat male-centric nations in times of war that the kingdom of Amazonia expanded in power and endured for eight centuries.[47]

Over time, male historians, for the most part, conveyed that the Amazon idea was not designed to enhance women but to serve the needs of its masculine creators in various ways.[48] These functions tended to be of three manners.[49] They used the Amazon image to provoke cowardly men into action to fight, as a cautionary anecdote to women who might rebel against conventional roles, or as proof that women could be successful fighters and mighty warriors.[50] Now agreed upon is that Amazonian dissolution resulted from an alarming level of societal acceptance for overbearing male attitudes of what roles women should perform, male schemes for what it meant to be feminine, and male manipulations of historical works that completely ostracized the women's narrative.[51]

Historical patterns of the woman warrior as either pretend or delusional have been slowly killed off. Excavations of 20th and 21st centuries prove a disconnect between women's concrete roles in wars in the past millennia and what the public had been consistently taught about their experiences.[52] Nomadic societies existed between 900 and 200 BC in the modern region of Crimea, where women held successful leadership roles in battle. These women lived in Sarmatia, Libya, Egypt, and Syria, near the Black Sea and in areas north and east of the Mediterranean on the vast steppes of Eurasia.[53] Many held pivotal roles in their societies and were not subjugated to the segregated domestic labor-filled lives like other women of their generation.[54]

Writings from the Romans have survived, validating the sovereign warrior status held by Scythian women. Within ancient journals is a procession of female kings and generals captured during the Roman triumph over the ruthless emperor, Mithridates VI, who sought to dominate Asia Minor. Ancient Greek writer and geographer Herodotus referenced the Iranic queen Tomyris, who defeated Cyrus the Great. He also reported that women shared power equally with their men among the civilized and righteous Issedonians, the ancient people of Central Asia residing along one of these people's trade routes.[55]

Mockery about women as fighters has lessened in recent decades, and with this changing conviction has come an increased interest in proving if the Amazon were a reality. New scientific and anthropologic research has brought intriguing data demonstrating that the Amazonian fighter is not a myth.[56] Archeological digs verify that women resembling Penthesilea, her sister, Hippolyta, or other great combatants known for their physical strength, cunning, and battle intelligence did exist. In Russia, unearthed burial sites of the Eastern Iranic equestrian nomadic warriors have identified 300 skeletons of female fighters through DNA testing. They were 10–45 years old with combat wounds or weaponry embedded in their bones.[57]

Most burial sites unearthed since the end of the 20th century, dating to the 5th and 4th centuries BC, authenticate the idea that there was an Amazonian cadre of fighters. Skeletal analyses of steppe nomad graves spread across territories from Turkey to Russia and objects buried within them have revealed that of over 1000 graves, an impressive 37 percent were warrior women. Remains had injurious wounds, which could only have occurred during violent one-on-one combat.[58]

It is now understood that girls received extensive training at an early age in military tactics, and their lives centered around horses. Each was taught to defend their domain and hunt. Available relics point to their living in small tribes, wearing trousers, smoking stimulants and hallucinogens, and fighting on horseback with bows and arrows. Various weapons from digs include daggers with forked arrowheads, spears, and battle campaign horseback riding equipment. Certain women's bodies were buried and posed in equestrian positions with their steeds.[59]

Scientific evidence needed to emerge to offset the male historicism that women could not be fearless in battle or serve nobly and with valor and loyalty as fellow soldiers. Adrian Mayor, author of *The Amazons: Lives and Legends of Warrior Women*, affirmed the truth about the Amazon in war. 'We have about 1,300 or so images of Amazons fighting. Only about two or three of them gestured for mercy. So, they are shown to be extraordinarily courageous and heroic. And I think that's the Amazon spirit.'[60]

Notes

1 Mario Livio. The Golden Ratio: The Story of Phi, the World's Most Astonishing Number, Broadway 1st Ed, October 29, 2002. NYC, NY.

2 Vladimir J. Konečni. "The 'Golden Section' as Aesthetic Idea and Empirical Fact." *Visual Arts Research* 30, no. 2 (2004): 75–86. http://www.jstor.org/stable/20715354.

3 Gisela M. A. Richter. "The Pheidian Zeus at Olympia." *Hesperia: The Journal of the American School of Classical Studies at Athens* 35, no. 2 (1966): 166–70. https://doi.org/10.2307/147305.

4 Jan N. Bremmer and Andrew Erskine (eds). *The Gods of Ancient Greece: Identities and Transformations*. Edinburgh University Press, 2010. http://www.jstor.org/stable/10.3366/j.ctt1r236p.

5 James K. Smith. "The Temple of Zeus at Olympia." *Memoirs of the American Academy in Rome* 4 (1924): 153–68. https://doi.org/10.2307/4238521.

6 Robert Hannah. "An Astean Ancestry: Sources for Multi-Level Compositions." *Mediterranean Archaeology* 2 (1989): 65–71. http://www.jstor.org/stable/24666624.

7 G. M. Sifakis. "'Iliad' 21.114-119 and the Death of Penthesilea." *Bulletin of the Institute of Classical Studies* no. 23 (1976): 55–57. http://www.jstor.org/stable/43646137.

8 J. D. Beazley. "Achilles and Polyxene: On a Hydria in Petrograd." *The Burlington Magazine for Connoisseurs* 28, no. 154 (1916): 137–39. http://www.jstor.org/stable/860265.

9 Virgil. *Aeneid*, Book 1 LCL 63:296–97, Loeb Classical Library, VIRGIL, Aeneid I Loeb Classical Library (loebclassics.com).

10 Quintus Smyrnaeus. *The Fall of Troy, Book 1 (4)*. (173) Translation from A. S Way [40], Quintus Smyrnaeus, The Fall Of Troy Book 1 – Theoi Classical Texts Library.

Lee Fratantuono. "The Penthesilead of Quintus Smyrnaeus: A Study in Epic Reversal." *Wiener Studien* 129 (2016): 207–31. http://www.jstor.org/stable/24752775.

11 Ibid. Smyrnaeus

12 Ibid. Smyrnaeus

13 "Greek Legends and Myths, Penthesilea Greek Mythology," Penthesilea in Greek Mythology – Greek Legends and Myths. Accessed 12/27/2023.

14 Opcit. Smyrnaeus

15 Ibid. Smyrnaeus

16 John H. Oakley. "Greek Vase Painting." *American Journal of Archaeology* 113, no. 4 (2009): 599–627. http://www.jstor.org/stable/20627620.

Gisela M. A. Richter. "Red-and-Black Glaze." *Nederlands Kunsthistorisch Jaarboek (NKJ)/Netherlands Yearbook for History of Art* 5 (1954): 127–36. http://www.jstor.org/stable/24705257.

17 H. A. Shapiro. "Old and New Heroes: Narrative, Composition, and Subject in Attic Black-Figure." *Classical Antiquity* 9, no. 1 (1990): 114–48. https://doi.org/10.2307/25010923.

18 John Boardman. "Exekias." *American Journal of Archaeology* 82, no. 1 (1978): 11–25. https://doi.org/10.2307/503793.

19 Opcit. Smyraneus (173). Also, for this section, see Rotondo, M. "The Golden Ratio: In harmony with the Universe," ART IMHO, The weird blog of Mirta Rotondo. Web. 05/20/2014. Mirarotondo.com/blog.

20 Dietrich von Bothmer., "Greek Vase Painting: An Introduction." *The Metropolitan Museum of Art Bulletin* 31, no. 1 (1972): 3–9. https://doi.org/10.2307/3259006.

21 Susan Woodford and Margot Loudon. "Two Trojan Themes: The Iconography of Ajax Carrying the Body of Achilles and of Aeneas Carrying Anchises in Black Figure Vase Painting." *American Journal of Archaeology* 84, no. 1 (1980): 25–40. https://doi.org/10.2307/504392.

22 Mary Hamilton Swindler. "The Penthesilea Master." *American Journal of Archaeology* 19.4 (October 1915): 398–417. The series, *Bilder Griechischen Vasen* volume 10, edited by Hans Diepolder (1936), is devoted to the Penthesilea-Maler.

23 Jay Hambidge. *Landscape Architecture* 11, no. 1 (1920): 47–49. http://www.jstor.org/stable/44661871.

24 Jay Hambidge. *Dynamic Symmetry the Greek Vase*, New Haven, CT: Yale University Press (1920).

25 "The Annual Report of the Museum for 1921." *Museum of Fine Arts Bulletin* 20, no. 117 (1922): 9–10. http://www.jstor.org/stable/4169804.

26 Opcit. Hambidge. Humphrey Milford. "*Dynamic Symmetry; the Greek Vase.*" Oxford University Press, 1920. p. 27. Accessed 9/18/2021. Dynamic symmetry is a proportioning system and natural design methodology described in Hambidge's books. The system uses dynamic rectangles, including root rectangles based on ratios such as $\sqrt{2}$, $\sqrt{3}$, $\sqrt{5}$, the golden ratio ($\phi = 1.618...$), its square root ($\sqrt{\phi} = 1.272...$), and its square ($\phi2 = 2.618...$), and the silver ratio. Mark Hambidge Brewer (Great grandchildren of Jay Hambidge). 2017. E-mail 01/19/2017 as

referenced in Jay Hambidge: Illustrator, writer, mathematician (mirtarotondo.com)

27 Rhys Carpenter. "Dynamic Symmetry: A Criticism." *American Journal of Archeology*, 25, no. 1 (Jan–Mar 1921): 18–36.

28 H. J. McWhinnie. "Influences of the Ideas of Jay Hambidge on Art and Design." *Computers Math. Applic* 17, no. 4–6 (1989): 1001–8.

29 Gisela M. A. Richter. "Dynamic Symmetry from the Designer's Point of View." *American Journal of Archaeology* 26, no. 1 (1922): 59–73. https://doi.org/10.2307/497635.

30 The Hambidge Center. "History," History – The Hambidge Center Also see: Eliot Wigginton. "Mary Hambidge," reprinted by Foxfire, The Hambidge Center, Rabun Gap, GA, History – The Hambidge Center.

31 Jay Hambidge. Norman Rockwell Museum, Illustration History, Jay Hambidge – Illustration History.

32 "What Is Myth? Myths and Heroes, Four Myths, Myths & Archetypes, What Is a Myth?" Educational Broadcasting Corporation, PBS, 2005, In Search of Myths & Heroes. What is a Myth? | PBS

33 E. O. James. "The Nature and Function of Myth." *Folklore* 68, no. 4 (1957): 474–82. http://www.jstor.org/stable/1258206.

34 Cynthia Eller. "Matriarchy and the Volk." *Journal of the American Academy of Religion* 81, no. 1 (2013): 188–221. http://www.jstor.org/stable/23357881.

35 Graves was an experienced fighter, having served in World War I as a captain in the Royal Welch Fusiliers. He became widely known for his biography, *Goodbye to All of That*, which described his vivid recollections of events leading up to the Somme Offensive and his observations about trench warfare and the use of gas on his comrades. He expressed through second-hand accounts the massacres of the Allies' killing of German prisoners of war. He also related his observations about how war wounds and physical and mental experiences caused neurasthenia, a mechanical weakness in the nerves commonly referred to as shell shock or war neurosis.

36 Weisinger, Herbert. "'A Very Curious and Painstaking Person' Robert Graves as Mythographer." *Midwest Folklore* 6, no. 4 (1956): 235–44. http://www.jstor.org/stable/4317604.

37 G. E. Dimock Jr. Review of *Robert Graves and Greek Mythology*, by Robert Graves. *The Hudson Review* 8, no. 3 (1955): 449–55. https://doi.org/10.2307/3847942.

38 Robert Graves. "Greek Myths and Pseudo Myths." *The Hudson Review* 8, no. 2 (1955): 212–30. https://doi.org/10.2307/3847680.

39 Robert Graves. *The Greek Myths*. UK: Penguin Books, 1955. Graves, Robert, Analecta 3 Robert Graves – Penthesilea. http://self.gutenberg.org/articles/penthesilea. Accessed 5/12/2020. Taken from Penguin Books, combined edition *The Greek Myths*. ("REVIEW: Greek Mythology – Ms. C McMahon – Google Sites") ("Top 25 Quotes By Robert Graves (of 101) | A-Z Quotes")

40 F. Carter Philips. "Greek Myths and the Uses of Myths." *The Classical Journal* 74, no. 2 (1978): 155–66. http://www.jstor.org/stable/3296798

41 Graves related that Penthesilea was killed by Achilles, who fell in love with her at her death by his hand. Achilles then slew one of his soldiers, Thersites, for jeering at him because he showed compassion on the battlefield. What follows is a feud fought for the death of Thersites. Thersites' cousin, enraged by the death, ties Penthesilea's corpse to his chariot, drags it in public, and then tosses it to the river gods. The corpse is retrieved and given an appropriate burial by Achilles or the Trojans.

C. M. Bowra. *The Sewanee Review* 64, no. 3 (1956): 498–507. http://www.jstor.org/stable/27538559.

24 Women and War

42 For the complete poem, see Michael Longley, (ed) Graves, Robert, *Selected Poems*, 05 July 2018. Faber and Faber.
43 Joan M. Ferrante. *Tulsa Studies in Women's Literature* 2, no. 2 (1983): 244–47. https://doi.org/10.2307/463727.
44 Alexander H. Schutz. "'The Lamentations of Matheolus' and the Basic Tempo of Villon's Testament." *Studies in Philology* 47, no. 3 (1950): 453–59. http://www.jstor.org/stable/4172936.
45 Cynthia Ho. "Communal and Individual Autobiography in Christine de Pizan's 'Book of the City of Ladies.'" *CEA Critic* 57, no. 1 (1994): 31–40. http://www.jstor.org/stable/44377130.
46 Laura Rinaldi Dufresne. "Christine de Pizan's 'Treasure of the City of Ladies': A Study of Dress and Social Hierarchy." *Woman's Art Journal* 16, no. 2 (1995): 29–34. https://doi.org/10.2307/1358572.
47 J. L. Myres. "Homeric Art." *The Annual of the British School at Athens* 45 (1950): 229–60. http://www.jstor.org/stable/30096756.
48 Valeri I Guliaev. "Amazons in the Scythia: New Finds at the Middle Don, Southern Russia." *World Archaeology* 35, no. 1 (2003): 112–25. http://www.jstor.org/stable/3560215.
49 Candace Slater. "Visions of the Amazon: What Has Shifted, What Persists, and Why This Matters." *Latin American Research Review* 50, no. 3 (2015): 3–23. http://www.jstor.org/stable/43670307.
50 Walter Duvall Penrose. "Postcolonial Amazons: Female Masculinity and Courage in Ancient Greek and Sanskrit Literature, November 2016. Oxford Academic, pp. 1–22. htps://doi.org/10.1093.
51 Andrew Kahn, and Rebecca Onion. "Is History Written About Men, by Men? SLATE, Jan 6, 2016, Popular history: Why are so many history books about men, by men?" (slate.com)
52 V. I. Guliaev. "Amazons in the Scythia: New Finds at the Middle Don, Southern Russia." *World Archeology* 35, no 1 "The Social Commemoration of Warfare" (Jun. 2003): 112–25.
53 "Introducing the Scythians," The British Museum Blog, Introducing the Scythians – British Museum Blog. Accessed 9/25/2021.
54 Valeri I. Guliaev. "Amazons in the Scythia: New Finds at the Middle Don, Southern Russia." *World Archaeology* 35, no. 1 (2003): 112–25. http://www.jstor.org/stable/3560215.
55 *Delphi Complete Works of Herodotus*. Delphi Classics, 2013.4.26.21.205-14 *Mithridatic Wars*, 17.116-17.
56 For additional information on this subject, see Timothy A. Kohler, Michael E. Smith, Amy Bogaard, Gary M. Feinman, Christian E. Peterson, Alleen Betzenhauser, Matthew Pailes, Elizabeth C. Stone, Anna Marie Prentiss, Timothy J. Dennehy, Laura J. Ellyson, Linda M. Nicholas, Ronald K. Faulseit, Amy Styring Jade Whitlam, Mattia Fochesato, Thomas A. Foor, Samuel Bowles. "There were more significant post-Neolithic wealth disparities in Eurasia than in North America and Mesoamerica." *Nature* (2017); DOI: 10.1038/nature24646
57 Data gathered from 63 archaeological sites showed that disparities among the sexes mounted with the rise of agricultural trade and the expansion of a business model that required the protection of resources and movement outside the immediate community to conduct commerce. Kohler noted that early types of "inequality have a lot of subtle and potentially pernicious effects on societies." The more trade required to attain wealth from the land and commit to commerce to sell agricultural output, the more tightly defined women's roles became. Women stayed behind instead of traveling to harvest, oversee, store their natural resources, and protect buildings and progeny. This is the ancient beginnings of the dichotomy

of the stay-at-home female and the intrepid role of the male as the venturesome businessman and warrior.

58 Derek Hawkins. "Amazons were long considered a myth. These discoveries show warrior women were real." *The Washington Post* December 31, 2019. "New Russian Gravesite Proves Amazon Warrior Women Were Very Much Real." *J Cassady Rosenblum produced and edited this interview for broadcast with* Todd Mundt. Serena McMahon *adapted it for the web. This segment aired on January 14, 2020. Radio Station, Boston, MA, WBUR Jan 14, 2020,* Anna Curtenius Roosevelt, "The Rise and Fall of the Amazon Chiefdoms." *L'Homme* 33, no. 126/128 (1993): 255–83. Accessed 12/19/2020. http://www.jstor.org/stable/40589896.Jo Whalley, On the Bravery of Women: The Ancient Amazon and Her Modern Counterparts URI: http://hdl.handle.net/10063/1696 2010 Victoria University of Wellington Gaukhar Z. Balgabayeva, Sergey V. Samarkin, Elizaveta V. Yarochkina, Aigul B. Taskuzhina, Aigul B. Amantaeva, Svetlana V. Nazarova. "The Role of Women in Military Organization of Nomads." *International Journal of Environmental and Science Education*, 11, no. 12 (2016): 5273–81. Foreman A. The Amazon Women: Is There Any Truth Behind the Myth? *Smithsonian Magazine* (April 2014). Adrienne Mayor. *The Amazons: Lives and Legends of Warrior Women across the Ancient World.* Princeton University Press, 2014. Ana Gabriela Macedo. "From The Amazon to the Flaneuse – Women at the Turn of the Century." pp. 63–70 pdf. Accessed 12/19/2020. Universidade do Minho Robert Schmiel. "The Amazon Queen: Quintus of Smyrna, Book 1." *Phoenix* 40, no. 2 (1986): 185–94. Accessed 12/19/2020. doi:10.2307/1088511.

59 Simon Worrall. "Amazon Warriors Did Indeed Fight and Die Like Men Archaeology shows that these fierce women also smoked pot, got tattoos, killed – and loved – men." *National Geographic* (October 28, 2014). *Amazon Warriors Did Indeed Fight and Die Like Men – History.* https://www.nationalgeographic.com/history/article/141029-amazons-scythians-hunger-games-herodotus-ice-princess-tattoo-cannabis

60 Adrienne Mayor. *The Amazons: Lives and Legends of Warrior Women across the Ancient World.* Princeton University Press, 2014. https://doi.org/10.2307/j.ctt7zvndm.

Additional Resources

A.S. Way (trans). *Quintus Smyrnaeus the Fall of Troy*, Loeb Classic Library, Vol 19. London: William Heinemann, 1913.

Dietrich von Bothmer. *Amazons in Greek Art, Oxford Monographs on Classical Archeology*, 1st edition. Oxford: Clarendon Press, January 1, 1957.

John Davidson Beazley. *Development of the Attic Black-Figure*, Revised edition. Berkeley: University of California Press, 1986. http://ark.cdlib.org/ark:/13030/ft1f59n77b/

Margaret Franklin. "Boccaccio's Amazons and Their Legacy in Renaissance Art: Confronting the Threat of Powerful Women." ("Boccaccio's Amazons and Their Legacy in Renaissance Art – JSTOR") *Woman's Art Journal* 31, no. 1 (2010): 13–20. Accessed 12/19/2020. http://www.jstor.org/stable/40605235

Patrick J. Geary. *Women at the Beginning, Origin Myths from the Amazons to Virgin Mary.* Princeton, NJ: Princeton University Press, February 19, 2006.

Sophie Bourgault and Rebecca Kingston (eds). *Christine de Pizan, The Book of the City of Ladies and Other Writings.* Indianapolis, IN: Hackett Publishing, 2018.

26 Women and War

Questions

Why is the Amazon an essential story in the history of women in war and combat?

Why are Amazon myths like that of Penthesilea only acceptable to societies as being true once scientific evidence proves their validity?

What other types of artifacts besides pottery from ancient periods tell stories of the Amazons?

Modern take

Is the Amazonian ideal a complementary means of labeling female combatants of the 21st century? Why or why not?

Why are most artistic portrayals of Amazonian characters produced in the 21st century over-sexualized? What does this say about current viewpoints on females in combat generally?

Activities and discovery

Create an image of Penthesilea using the description found in The Fall of Troy.

Research other Amazon stories from non-Western cultures. How do they differ from the Western notion of Penthesilea?

2
ARTISTIC ICONOGRAPHY

Artemisia I of Persia, Admiral, and Queen of the Anatolian Region of Caira

FIGURE 2.1 Guillaume Rouille's profile portrait of Artemisia.
© Public Domain Mark 1.0

DOI: 10.4324/9781003406372-3

28 Women and War

Artemisia I and Xerxes I

Rather than *presenting* the world, icons *represent* it.

(Sander Gilman)

The story of Artemisia I, queen of the Greco region of Halicarnassus in the district of Caria in southwest Anatolia, descended from many different ancient literary tales. The queen was mentioned in Plutarch's 2nd-century AD *Parallel Lives* and essay, *On the Malice of Herodotus,* criticizing Carian Herodotus' prejudices and misrepresentations of historical events. Polyaenus's *Stratagems in War* commented upon Artemisia's actions during the largest naval battle in antiquity at Salamis as her being a gallant fighter, and she appeared in the 9th-century writings of Photius, a church leader of Constantinople, as a legendary fictionalized character who heard oracle commands. Within the Roman empire, Latin writer and historian Justin wrote of her in his 2nd-century *History of the World* as being a foremost leader, having inherited manly boldness in her dauntless actions and undertakings. Artemisia was believed to have been married to a local politician and had a son, Pisindelis, whose tyrannical rule lasted until he abandoned the throne in the mid-400s BC.[1]

The lives of Persian ruler Xerxes I, who formulated a massive military incursion across Greece and Artemesia I, became closely intertwined during the sea battle of Artemisium in August of 480 BC and the Battle of Salamis, which occurred in September of the same year. King Xerxes was a brutal expansionist, born the son of a daughter of Cyrus the Great and whose father, Darius I, stabilized the empire by building a road system and creating a centralized political administration and a cadre of regional governors to administer land holdings.

By the time Xerxes became ruler, his father's Iranian Achaemenid Empire had covered the territory from Anatolia and Egypt and crossed western and central Asia and northern India.

Xerxes amassed an enormous land and sea fighting force. He commanded up to 300,000.

Persian fighters at the height of his rule and his armada numbered about 400 triremes comprised of warships from several regions, including Lycian, Ionian, Carian, Phoenician, and Egyptian territories.

One or more supply carriers sailed with every two triremes, bringing the total number of naval vessels to above 1000 or more.[2] Fast and agile, the war galleys were propelled using three banks of oars, one rower per oar with a mere 34–38 inches of space to operate. Triremes were noted for their speed, which made them sound like forward scouts for observation in convoys off the littoral areas near the rocks and cliffs of the water regions the Persian King had conquered.[3]

Artistic Iconography 29

FIGURE 2.2 A profile carving of Xing Xerxes.

© CC BY-SA 4.0 Legal Code | Attribution-ShareAlike 4.0 International | Creative Commons Category: Xerxes I – Wikimedia Commons

FIGURE 2.3 and 2.4 Map of the Achaemenid Empire under Cyrus the Great.

© CC BY-SA 4.0 Deed | Attribution-ShareAlike 4.0 International | Creative Commons File: Persian empire-history-818×490.jpg – Wikimedia Commons

30 Women and War

FIGURE 2.3 and 2.4 (*Continued*)

FIGURE 2.5 Two fleets of Greek triremes fighting in close quarters.

© Reuse of PD-Art Orientation UK This work was published in 1882 and is no longer under copyright Cassell's Illustrated Universal History: OLLIER, Edmund: Free Download, Borrow, and Streaming: Internet Archive p. 349

The armada was a mixture of navies subjugated by force, with many of the flotillas coming together primarily by free will. Dynastic Cretan ruler Kybernis led a large contingent of 50 Lycian ships in the Achaemenid fleet. Herodotus described the entourage as wearing torso and shin armor with goat skins on their shoulders and carrying bows of cornelian cherry wood with arrows without feathers, daggers, and short swords with curved blades.[4] The Phoenicians, who were celebrated master mariners for their navigation skills, ship-building prowess, inventors of the keel, placing battering rams on bows, and use of caulking to seal water from invading the holds of watercraft, became the primary entity under which the other nationalities organized.[5]

Many boats within the mixed entourage were crewed by good fighting stock, such as the Egyptian-trained native marines. In contrast, the Lycians had garnered maritime fighting reputations as mercenaries.[6] The strengths of the diverse fleet were its courageous personnel and its robust knowledge of seamanship. Weaknesses of the hybridization of nationalities were the numerous divisions arising in command from the patchwork of continental participants and the use of the ramming bow as a primary means of over-coming adversaries. Reliance upon smashing into an enemy was practical in larger water spaces but of little consequence when foes were trained as archers, close-quarter fighters, and in boarding tactics. It is in this powerful hybridized military arm of Xerxes's navy that Artemisia, queen of the ancient region of Halicarnassus, brought a fleet of five ships to fight with the king's naval armada at the 480 BC battles against the Greek city-states.[7] Modern research states that her fleet comprised as many as 70 vessels across the Carian region.[8]

Artemisia as an iconographic image

No accurate likenesses of Artemisia I exist. She has been characterized visually in various styles of artwork for centuries. She is often confused with Artemisia II, a naval leader who reigned after her death from 377 to 353 BC.[9] In 1868, German painter Wilhelm von Kaulbach staged Artemisia I as a robed archer wearing a diaphanous white frock fighting off the bow in a highly romanticized allegorical mele of ethereal skies, terrestrial and aquatic scenes of fighting Greeks and Persians and escaping, disrobed, and murdered female citizenry. In the upper left corner, Xerxes beacons from a stalwart rock throne toward the scene unfolding below his high perch.[10] An 18th-century Victorian English school print had in its content a portrait of Artemisia with her Victorian bodice sliding off her shoulders with one hand to her breast, clasping a handkerchief as she gazes into a sumptuous metal drinking cup.[11]

The queen was also denoted as a nun-like character in monk's robes and as an archer in a print of a small rowboat in front of a Viking naval fighting force. Most of these illustrations were placed within the pages of historical lore.

One of the most reprinted of the queen's likenesses appeared as a woodcut print in Guillaume Rouille's *Handbook of Images of the Renowned*, published in 1553 in Lyon, France.[12] Using this type of creative license to portray a woman in history is standard, with each generation attempting to make the character part of their era, leaving little room for the exact remembrance of the protagonist. These transitions from reality result in the person's image becoming a less-than-truthful embodiment of themselves.[13]

Historically, physical artifacts of women have often been based upon their creator's ideologies and beliefs, resulting in imprecise physical, emotional, and cultural stereotypes.[14] Mistruths about female warriors have been particularly rife due to the prevalence of ostracizing their feats through a predominantly male-driven lens.[15] Jumbled among their portrayal of insanity or as sexualized objects, there seemed to be a need to align them with a form of motherly or wifely nurturing.[16] Thankfully, other historians left stories for future generations highlighting warrior women as normalized with common human faults and their strengths, showing them to be talented in pursuing various roles during national conflict.[17]

The iconographic figures of Artemisia lack accurate detail to establish a precise role as queen and admiral in the ancient world.[18] A more realistic expose of her character can be discovered through cross-referencing females from her region of the world and the timeframe in which she lived. One way to do this is to look at ancient coins from the same geographic area on which noble females were struck. Coins are some of the only physical evidence that ancient women had power or held leadership roles and displayed images of goddesses or power brokers and political leaders in their own right.[19]

Observing the profile and accouterments found on the coin impressions can be used to answer a set of questions that may lead to a greater understanding of what a royal woman from Caria may have looked like. What type of person does each item seem to present? Are there any symbolic elements from the coinage that may aid in understanding what their status may have been or the roles they may have played in society? Next, compare the coins to the mid-16th-century book print by Rouille. What makes the illustration and the coin features of females different physically? What materials are the coin and the print made from? Can any surmise be made about the era in which each may have been created? The coins and the print are all profiles of women, but the fashion of head adornments is drastically different, and what can be seen of their style of dress at the neckline is different. Facial features are dissimilar, and their hairstyles are inconsistent with one another. Results from answering these queries help understand whether the motifs pinpoint a person's social standing, civil or private lives, and ethnic backgrounds.[20]

German-born Erwin Panofsky, an eminent supporter of iconology in the 1930s and a top influencer in art history in the 20th century, established a three-step approach to art and artifact identification, which is still in use today.[21] The first was to recognize the apparent elements of the piece. In this case, the etching, coins, busts, and portrait-like profiles of women are from somewhere other than the current 21st century. Second, compare the art or artifact to an existing text or oral tradition that may assist in creating an association between the real Artemisia and a simulacrum of her. Ancient written sources for comparison attest to the existence of the queen of Caria, including the Gallo-Roman historian Pompeius Trogus' 1st-century BC account in *Philippic History* describing her virile courage.[22] Third, Panofsky recommended attaching an intrinsic meaning to the information gleaned from the first two steps as to whether what is being observed represents a precise picture of an individual or event. What was required was the creation of a subjective or emotional value about the artifact and the sensations each item provoked. Perhaps the printed illustration rouses a feeling of stoicism, the winged female, a sense of victory and athletic movement, and the coin a sentiment that here is a fashionable and not a commonly dressed woman. Currency portraits were often of famous individuals, national leaders, royalty, or members of families and not images of the lower classes. Those women who did appear on coins came from a higher stratum of society.[23]

Applying the three-step approach triggers additional questions. Which object seems the oldest and why? What is the difference between a print and a coin? When was printing and the use of woodcuts, etchings, engravings, and lithography first available, and when were the first coins struck? What symbols help recognize the person as being a woman? What styles are evident in each woman's clothing? How do their hairstyles and coverings relate to a viewer relative to nationality or century? Can a supposition be made that one woman seems more Caucasian and the others are more likely to have roots outside Western Europe? If so, what leads to this thought?

Few displays of women existed from the Achaemenid period of Xerxes and Artemisia. Persian women were seldom memorialized in sculptures, stone carvings, or in the more prolific minor arts.[24] No woman appeared among the numerous human forms found on the stone tapestries of Pasargadae, the capital of the Achaemenid Empire, and the ruins of the five palaces at Persepolis, nor were any women ensconced in high-ranking tombs and ceremonial complexes. Minor features left to posterity of women's dress were one of the only avenues to draw associations with Artemisia I.[25] It is proven that women wore chitons, tunics that fastened at the shoulder, which often resembled those worn by their spouses. It has also been disclosed that royalty or court women wore variations of these robes from those of lower social status.[26]

Turning to the period's prose, poets depicted them wearing Persian wraps or Doric garments made from woolen fabric slit on both sides from the hips with clasps attached at both shoulders.[27] Materials were handwoven and styled using a variety of colorations of red, indigo, green, ochre, and purple, derived

34 Women and War

from Murex shells, pomegranates, walnuts, saffron, and red flowering shrubs.[28] Artemisia, being geographically from the Greek monarchical city-state of Halicarnassus and island territory of the Achaemenid satrapy of Ciara, may have meant her clothing and headdress were of a nature that combined fashion influences.[29] Unlike other regions that omitted females in their architectural carvings and statues, the Mausoleum at Halicarnassus, though built by Artemisia II, who succeeded Artemisia I, had an Amazonomachy frieze showing women in hand-to-hand combat with the Greeks.[30] Their cultural roots were tied to the customs and traditions of the Greek Amazonian fighters.

Because the queen oversaw an island and coastal region in the Mediterranean, it should be no surprise that she was a skilled navalist and owned and operated several triremes and other ships. These would have been equipped with grappling hooks to catch enemy craft and two mangonels that threw stones and flammable projectiles. As a fighting admiral, it is unlikely she wore soft, flowing apparel in command of her fleet. The physicality of fighting on a deck at close quarters would have meant the queen was properly uniformed to withstand the brutalities of the naval environment.[31] Since helmets had been staples used in the region by combatants since the third millennium, it is to be expected she wore such headgear or that, in line with Herodotus' accounts of male military uniforms of the Persians, she may have sported a soft cap called a tiara when not in battle.[32]

Herodotus's recollections of Artemisia

Herodotus' *Histories*, written in the 5th century BC, is where the most thorough story of Artemisia I resides.[33] Known primarily as a talented geographer, the great traveler had a tireless curiosity about past societies. He was nonprejudicial and meticulous in his summaries of the Greeks and their enemies. Herodotus was one of only a few ancient historians whose narrative illustrated powerful females as a natural occurrence in Dorian society and attempted to distinguish fact from fantasy in their exploits.[34] Fourteen of nearly 400 women noted in Herodotus' writings were "independent agents in the public sphere" or those making "decisions unconstrained by the opinions or power of male realities."[35] Descriptions of women were rational and goal-seeking, and he did not "find acts of violence and vengeance especially deplorable" in them.[36]

In its final form, the lengthy nine-book treatise held three sections devoted to Xerxes I and his attempts to avenge a defeat he had sustained at the Battle of Marathon by annexing Greece into the Achaemenid Empire. Developed from living memory, travels, and empirical observations, Herodotus held verbal recitations of his narrations in front of street crowds. The naval battle came to represent a crucial moment in the ongoing demise of the Xerxes Empire's regional domination. Herodotus' story of Artemisia gave credibility to her role as a seagoing commander.

Artemisia is first mentioned in chapter ninety-nine of *Book Seven*, which began by tracing Xerxes's decision to invade Greece with additional commentary regarding the king's land and naval expeditions. The section also cataloged events undertaken by the Persian army and navy forces, reports on the alliance of Greek states at the Battle of Thermopylae, and recounted how the Greeks reacted to the infiltration.[37] Artemisia appeared again in chapters sixty-eight, sixty-nine, eighty-seven, and eighty-eight of *Book Eight*, which covered the naval battle at Artemisium, the retreat of the Greek fleet, the precursors to the naval battle at Salamis, its aftermath, and the Persian withdrawal.[38]

The queen was introduced in *Book Seven* as an excellent marvel for her willingness to go out on an expedition against Hells (Greece), taking up the reigns of her kingdom upon her husband's death.[39] Her fearlessness was noted by exclaiming that she was not pressured into committing to the sea battle, but participating was her choice, having followed Xerxes' army with youthful spirit and manliness.[40] Herodotus tells his reading audience that this naval warrior, businesswoman, and politician also faced the challenge of being a widower with a young boy. Like most characters in the *Histories*, Artemisia's lineage is recited, which adds to understanding her background. Her father served as a provincial governor within the monarchical Persian loyalist Halicarnassian culture. Her mother was from Cretan stock, whose people had deep roots as sailors and were notable riotous mercenary seamen. From 50 to 100 AD, biblical storytelling from the pastoral epistles of the New Testament, where the Book of Titus is located, strongly marks her mother's culture as being liars, thieves, self-indulgent, and promiscuous pirates.[41]

The battles of Artemisium and Salamis

The Greeks and Persians had been involved in long clashes for years. Greek leaders began forming themselves into city-states, an evolution that turned them toward creating a democratic society. Two of their most prominent power bases were in Athens and Sparta. Before Xerxes's naval battle, Anatolian king Croesus and Cyrus the Great had overrun the Hellenic territories of Lydia and Mesopotamia to the west. Cyrus later defeated Croesus and formed the geopolitical Achaemenid Empire, which ruled the Mediterranean for over two centuries. Darius the Great, a nephew of Cyrus the Great, began winning territories to the north and east on the continent of Europe. Greek community leaders along the western coastline of the former Lydia began to revolt against Darius' intrusions and received military support from the Athenians for their efforts. The Persians sent one of their naval fleets to quell the rebellious Hellenic leaders, and they retook the area in 494 BC.[42]

In 492 BC, Darius launched a campaign against Greece as retribution for their mutinous activities against the Persian leadership.[43] The Greeks and

36 Women and War

their allies reformed and beat the Persians in the Battle of Marathon in 490 BC. As Darius turned his sights toward Egypt to quell an insurrection there, the Western Greek territorial leaders used the time to form another alliance with Sparta and Athens. Xerxes began a new offensive in 480 BC and moved the land army toward the Macedonian border. At the same time, the Persian navy performed flanking maneuvers. With this move by Xerxes, the Greeks had to be concerned about a potential conquest on two fronts. A 300 trireme navy under Athenian command closed off the Straits of Artemisium against the Persian forces, evolving into three days of naval engagements. The Persian Navy was much larger, with a thousand triremes, but the contingent was hit by a severe storm at the end of the summer on the east coast of the Greek mainland, resulting in high losses of 30 percent of their ships.[44]

In an entrapment maneuver, the Persians sent 200 of their remaining force around the large coastal island of Euboea. Another storm shipwrecked this contingent. On shore at Thermopylae, the Greeks succumbed to the outflanking maneuvers of the vast southward advancing army of Xerxes, and the Greek politician and general Themistocles withdrew his forces to Salamis. One of the general's primary advocacies had been to rebuild a strong Athenian Navy and a calculated push to build 200 triremes in the interim period before Salamis would become integral to stopping the next Persian onslaught. Themistocles gathered reinforcements from 21 cities, each bringing from one to 180 vessels to the fight, enlarging the Greek navy to approximately 400 ships.[45] Xerxes came to the battle of Salamis with massive supplies and forces that outnumbered the Greeks at least two to one. His navy entered the harbor with Phoenicians on the right, Ionians on the left, and Asia Minor Greeks in the center, forming a diamond pattern.

The Greek navy moved back toward land in an imitated retreat. Xerxes ordered naval forces to move forward but stumbled miserably when it was discovered the straits were too narrow for the larger, heavier Persian triremes to maneuver, and the ships bunched together. Now unable to shift direction, Themistocles ordered a counterattack just as the winds changed in his favor. The Greeks dominated in their boarding actions against the Persian triremes. Several important, experienced Persian commanders were killed in the fray, leaving the navy without higher leadership. Xerxes lost 300 ships and limped out of the harbor in disarray. The juggernaut had ceased, and he retreated to Asia Minor, left the army in northern Greece for the winter, and reconcentrated his efforts in stabilizing Persia.[46]

My men have behaved like women, my women like men

Herodotus' translations disclose that Artemisia was politically astute, comfortable at sea in battle, and wise in the global and local network of events impacting her and Xerxes' reign and people. Due to her years around the water, she was deeply entrenched in the methods and manners required to govern and fight in coastal territories. Herodotus was complimentary about the effects of the queen upon political maneuvering.

> Of the other lower officers, I shall make no mention since no necessity is laid on me, but I must speak of a certain leader named Artemisia, whose participation in the attack upon Hellas, notwithstanding that she was a woman, moves my special wonder... her brave spirit and manly daring sent her forth to the war when no need required her to adventure...she gave to Xerxes sounder counsel than any of his other allies...the five triremes which she furnished to the Persians were, next to the Sidonians, the most famous ships in the fleet.[47]

The war council to which Herodotus referred occurred when Xerxes called together the members of his military tribunal and asked them whether he should engage the Hellenes at Salamis. *Book Seven* depicts several influencers Xerxes considered integral to his decision-making. The king sought advice from Demaratus, the ex-king of Sparta, on the nature of the Greeks' fighting abilities. Tetramnestos, King of Sidon, served as chief advisor on naval matters. Two additional primary advisers were his uncle Artabanus, who served as vizier, akin to the role of state minister, and as head bodyguard. Mardonius, Xerxes' cousin and one of his father's most trusted generals, advised the king to punish the Greeks, citing their racial inferiority, inability to cooperate, and lack of skill in choosing battle sites. The kings of Thessalia from the north and Pisistratids from the region of the Ionian Sea and Gulf of Messenia also encouraged him to invade. Xerxes's brother, Achaemenes, who was in command of the Egyptian contingent of the fleet, made recommendations in favor of the battle. Still, the brothers were at loggerheads about most kingdom decisions due to a confrontational attitude regarding their inheritance of formal titles. A chresmologue, or compiler of prophecies and forger named Onomacritus, was also involved in Xerxes's decisions and fed him phony oracles, encouraging an invasion.[48]

All those gathered at the tribunal except for Artemisia replied in favor of an attempted conquest.[49] Undeterred by being a minority voice, the queen stood firm and outlined to the king why his idea was both political and military suicide. The Carian admiral's retorts showed knowledge of current events, who the major international players were, and their strengths. Artemisia's commentary signaled that she had a propensity for long-term strategic thinking. In straightforward terms, she advised Xerxes to spare his ships and not risk battle because the enemy was just as expert and fine in seamanship as his navy.[50] Artemisia asked the king why he

38 Women and War

should risk inviting peril on the sea since he had already proven himself master of Athens and Hellas. She continued by pointing out that nobody could resist his advances, proven by his ability to resist their treacherous acts against him.

Artemisia became direct, "Now learn how I expect affairs to go with your adversaries," then spoke in strategic terms, "If you are not over-hasty to engage with them by sea but will keep your fleet near the land, then whether you stay as you are or march forward towards the Peloponnese's, you will easily accomplish all for which you have come here."[51] The naval queen's opinion was that the Hellenes would not withstand Xerxes' onslaught for very long. She trusted the king could "part them asunder and scatter them to their several homes."[52] Artemisia had also heard that food was becoming scarce for the enemy, and an attack was prepared and awaiting him should he land forces.[53] A decision made in haste would defeat the King's naval forces and land army.

The Queen of Ciara next played to the King's ego, indicating that subterfuge within his ranks could cause him distress.

> This, too, you should remember, O king; good masters are apt to have bad servants and bad masters good ones. Now, as you are the best of men, your servants must need to be a sorry set. These Egyptians, Cyprians, Cilicians, and Pamphylians, who are counted in the number of your subject allies, of how little service are they to you![54]

Herodotus derided the table of advisors as full of self-conceit with a penchant for valuing ingratiation over truth to power.

> As Artemisia spoke, they who wished her well were greatly troubled concerning her words, thinking that she would suffer some hurt at the king's hands because she exhorted him not to risk a battle." Those who were jealous within the ranks of her and hated her due to the favor shown of her by the King and his allies they, on the other hand, who disliked and envied her, favored as she was by the king above all the rest of the partners, were pleased with her taboo announcements as they expected her forthrightness would result in her death.[55]

Instead of being chastised by Artemisia's commentary, Xerxes affirmed his pleasure for the Queen's frankness. Even so, he proceeded with the order to attack by sea, saying he would remain an eyewitness to the naval combat by placing himself on a high outcrop overlooking the water. Artemisia readied five triremes and was placed in command of the ships from Halicarnassus, Cos, and Nisyros, including the Calyndian craft of King Damasithymus. She moved forward to lead from the bow. Caught in the Greek feint of retreat and unable to move, in a hit-and-run gambit with renditions stating that she was notorious for raising the staff of an enemy as a ploy to confuse her nationality, the queen gave orders to ram the trireme into King Damasithymus' ship. Observing the feint, the Greeks judged she was one of their own and did not attack. Herodotus implied that the Queen had perhaps committed an injustice, asserting, "Everything, it is said, conspired to prosper the queen—it was especially fortunate for her that not one of those on board the Calyndian ship survived to become her accuser."[56] Herodotus commented further about this quick-thinking ruse,

> In the first place, she saved her life by the action and was enabled to escape from the battle; while further, it fell out that in the very act of injuring the king, she raised herself to a greater height than ever in his esteem.[57]

At the point of impact of Artemisia's vessel into Damasithymus' ship, the bystanders surrounding the king seated on the hillock declared, "See, master, how well Artemisia fights and how she has just sunk a ship?" Xerxes asked if it was Artemisia's doing, and they answered, "Certainly, for they knew her ensign." Xerxes, in reply to the remarks made to him, retorted, "My men have behaved like women, my women like men!"[58] The Macedonian writer of *Strategems*, Polyaenus, who included among his prose for the Roman emperors Lucius Verus and Marcus Aurelius how to woo a tyrant's daughter and how to force a relative to give you money, recorded Xerxes as having said, "O Zeus, surely you have formed women out of man's materials, and men out of woman's."

Positive and negative viewpoints about Artemisia arose, and it was unclear whether the admiral queen's fortitude at the moment gave her credibility as an expert strategist or an ignominious marauder.[59] Herodotus also reported that machinations had been rumored to have occurred between the Queen and Damasithymus before they left port to join the fight. Diamasithymus was the commander of the only Calyndain ship and a brigadier and king of Calyndos in Caira. The two quarreled when anchored in Hellespont, but what about is not related. The Calyndain king's ship was under the command of Artemisia at the time she sunk him. "I am not able to say whether she did this by intention or whether the Calyndian ship happened by chance to fall in her way," indicated Herodotus. Perhaps she had run afoul of his contrarian strategy to send the queen to her demise. What is understood is that the Greeks were closing in on Artemisia, and Damasithymus was blocking the Cairan admiral from taking effective action.[60]

40 Women and War

After the disastrous sea battle, Xerxes called another war council. Herodotus wrote:

> "He convened a meeting of Pesians, and while listening to their advice, it occurred to him to invite Artemisia to see what she would suggest…when she came, he dismissed everyone else."[61] Then, he sought the queen's opinion of what strategy should be followed next.

The queen replied that she believed Xerxes should pull back. She recommended that Mardonius, the Achaemenid general and nephew of King Darius I, be given the troops he had asked for. She believed that, whether Mardonius was to win or lose, Xerxes would come out on top due to the prosperity of his kingdom. A Greek win would not be so important a victory because the loss of Mardonius was merely the loss of one of King Xerxes' enslaved people.[62]

Xerxes withdrew from Greece and left Mardonius to fight the remainder of the campaign.

Following the naval battle, the Greeks put up a bounty of 10,000 drachmas for anyone who could kill or capture Artemisia, and they wrote in vitriolic terms about her regal position and power at sea. Greek physician Thessalus, the son of Hippocrates, spoke of Artemisia in a derogatory way, calling her a cowardly pirate.[63] Ancient writings claim a marble statue in her name was erected in the agora, a public open space for assemblies, in Sparta. Another anecdote has Xerxes acknowledging the navalist for excelling above all officers in his naval fleet, recognizing her heroic acts, sending Artemisia a suite of Greek armor, and presenting her craft's captain with an honorary distaff and spindle. In a more personal and intimate vein, there was also an account that Xerxes, upon defeat, sent for Artemisia and requested she oversee the flight of his illegitimate sons away from the area due to trust in her abilities and confidence in her decision-making.

Rouille, Artemisia, and iconography

Guillaume Rouille's *Handbook* alphabetically contained 240 individuals from diverse periods, with a short historiography of each and a woodcut print of their faces. Chosen for inclusion were gods, sculptors from the 7th century, biblical and mythical kings and queens, and the obscure sons, daughters, and wives of authentic and fictional characters. Trojan warriors, poets, high priests, and prophets were also incorporated into the volume. Nationalities represented were diverse, with portrayals of Franks, Italians, Israelites, Czechs, and Spartans.

Artemisia's inclusion was singular for two reasons. First, she was picked from among potentially all those women protagonists before the Renaissance book had been written. Second, it was remarkable that her story resonated with the wealthy illustrator and businessman of Lyon, France, 1100 years after her death. Rouille was generous in including many women in his biographies. Examples were Asenath, a high-born aristocrat from Egypt found in the Book of Genesis; Glaphyra, a princess and courtesan of the Turkish region of Cappadocia; Jezebel, the first wife of the Prophet of Mohamed, Caleb's daughter from the Book of Corinthians and Athaliah the only woman in the Hebrew Bible and queen of Judah. Artemisia's inscription, roughly translated, stated she was the wife of Maufoli, was beautiful, and worthy of being numbered within the spectacles of the worlds being praised by many different men.[64] Maufoli was the wife of Artemisia II, not Artemisia I, a substantiation that the two women have been readily confused throughout historical accounts. This means the print can be erased as a potential one of Artemisia I, who reigned around 480 BC.

The exploits of Artemisia I show that she was a fearless personality, an influential admiral of the sea, and an astute politician. The use of Rouille's and others' depictions of the queen as a nun, Viking, and Victorian woman in books of lore are examples of her being presented in an iconographic light. Over centuries, she has been artistically placed in the wrong period, in inappropriate geographical settings, wearing erroneous clothing, and being confused with Artemisia II. What can be stated is that her home of Halicarnassus was a Greco-Carian city in the ancient region of Caria founded by the Dorian Greeks of the Peloponnese. She was wealthy, and during her lifetime, the area was recognized for having spawned the father of history and investigative researcher Herodotus and for its prosperity as an urban trade center.[65]

Regarding how the queen may have looked, it is most likely that she had brown hair and brown eyes since DNA research has determined that three-quarters of the region's population fit this description. Also, people of the territory had an average height of about five and a half feet.[66] Using the coinage from the timeframe of her life and knowledge about how females robed themselves, it is probable that as a queen, she would have worn colorful and not white diaphanous clothing and sported jewelry due to her wealth and societal status.

Two imprinted coins may give further detail of the physical treatment of what the queen may have resembled. From the region of the Ancient Ionian Greek city of Anatola in the timeframe of 570–494 BC is what is believed to be a royal woman wearing a rosette earing, her hair gathered under a *sakkos*.[67] Another has a Nike-like female in a combined kneeling stance significant in ancient renderings of victory.

Even if Roulle's Artemesia is not Artemisia I, the woman shown as styled in the *Handbook* is presented with the facial features of an Anglophile. She sports a European hairstyle and dress collar. So, even if she is supposed to be Artemisia II, the rendering is a questionable one of the females living in ancient Caira in the lifetimes of the two women. It is imaginable that the obverse of the 6th-century coin from Kaunos, the ancient city of Caira, or the female figure running and holding the staff of Hermes and a victory wreath is symbolic of the character of the females of the region in which Artemisia lived, fought, and ruled.

Hermes staff symbolized the inviolability of peace, heraldry, and ambassadorship, and the wreath represented triumph and military victory. A correct portrayal of Artemisia will likely never become known unless new ancient texts are found that relate to her story. Artemisia is one of many women in the annals of war who are presented as a future generation who would like to envision them. Passing down such images of powerful women is sometimes the only means of knowing they existed. Even though not entirely correct and unreliable in interpretation, these representations suggest that even if only

FIGURE 2.6   Ciaran coin of a helmeted female with hair in sakkos wearing a rosette earring.

© GNU Free Documentation License, Version 1.2 CNG-Ancient Greek, Roman, British Coins (cngcoins.com)

Artistic Iconography 43

FIGURE 2.7   Ciaran coin of a kneeling winged female.

© CC BY-SA 2.5 Deed | Attribution-ShareAlike 2.5 Generic | Creative Commons File:CARIA, Kaunos. Circa 470–450 BC.jpg – Wikimedia Commons

figurative, the strong navalist and stateswoman who arose to support Xerxes at Salamis continued to resonate with audiences across successive cultures and generations as a story worth repeating.

Notes

1 Plutarch, *Parallel Lives of Noble Grecians and Romans*, MBS Library Micro Book Studio. Plutarch PARALLEL LIVES OF NOBLE GRECIANS AND ROMANS (documentacatholicaomnia.eu).
   Plutarch. "Moralia. On the Malice of Herodotus," Loeb Classics Library. LCL 426 PLUTARCH, Moralia. On the Malice of Herodotus | Loeb Classical Library (loebclassics.com).
   Polyaenus. *Strategims* Book 8(b) Chapters 26–71. Adapted from the translation by R. Shepherd (1793) Attalus, Polyaenus: Stratagems – Book 8 (b) (attalus.org).
   Justin's History of the World, Extracted from Trogus Pompeius. Translated by John Selby Watson (1804–84), (G. Bell 1876) a work in the public domain placed online by Roger Pearce at Tertullian.org. ToposText.
   "Pisindelis," *Encyclopedia, Science News & Research Reviews*, Academic Accelerator. Pisindelis: Most Up-to-Date Encyclopedia, News & Reviews (academic-accelerator.com).

2 W. W. Tarn. "The Fleet of Xerxes." *The Journal of Hellenic Studies* 28 (1908): 202–33. https://doi.org/10.2307/624607. p. 2.
3 H. T. Wallinga. "The Trireme and History." *Mnemosyne* 43, no. 1/2 (1990): 132–49. http://www.jstor.org/stable/4431893.
4 Herododotus. *LacusCuritus* Book VII: Chapters 57–137. Loeb Classic Library, 1922, LacusCurtius • Herodotus – Book VII: Chapters 57-137 (uchicago.edu).
5 Gil Gambash. "Servicing the Mediterranean Empire: Non-State Actors and Maritime Logistics in Antiquity." *Mediterranean Studies* 25, no. 1 (2017): 9–32. https://doi.org/10.5325/mediterraneanstu.25.1.0009.
6 William A. P. Childs. "Lycian Relations with Persians and Greeks in the Fifth and Fourth Centuries Re-Examined." *Anatolian Studies* 31 (1981): 55–80. https://doi.org/10.2307/3642758.
7 G. Aperghis. "Athenian Mines, Coins and Triremes." *Historia: Zeitschrift Für Alte Geschichte* 62, no. 1 (2013): 1–24. http://www.jstor.org/stable/24433621.
8 Op cit. Tarn.
9 E. D. Carney. "Women and Dunasteia in Caria." *The American Journal of Philology* 126, no. 1 (2005): 65–91. http://www.jstor.org/stable/1562184.
10 Robert Koehler, "Painting of the Nineteenth Century in Germany." *Fine Arts Journal* 34, no. 11 (1916): 579–608. https://doi.org/10.2307/25587423. pp. 585–88.
11 "Artemisia of Caria-English School," MYARTPRINTS.CO.UK. "Artemisia I of Caria, a Greek queen of the ancient Greek city-state of Halicarnassus, Almay Artemisia I of Caria, a Greek queen of the ancient Greek city-state of Halicarnassus Stock Photo – Alamy Queen Artemisia in the naval battle of Salamis, ancient Greece, heroine, Persians, Greeks, warships, sailing ships, sea, boat, crossbow, shooting Stock Photo – Alamy Forty-six unique images of Artemisia of Caria may be found on the Stock Photos and Images page Artemisia of caria hi-res stock photography and images – Alamy.
12 Natalie Zemon Davis. "Publisher Buillaume Rouille, Businessman and Humanist," in R. J. Schoeck, ed., Editing Sixteenth Century Texts (Toronto: University of Toronto Press, 1966), 72–112. Available on (99+) Natalie Zemon Davis. "Publisher Guillaume Rouillé, Businessman and Humanist," in R. J. Schoeck, ed., Editing Sixteenth-Century Texts (Toronto: University of Toronto Press, 1966), 72–112 | Natalie Zemon Davis בר – Academia.edu
13 R. L Kesler. "The Idealization of Women: Morphology and Change in Three Renaissance Texts." *Mosaic: A Journal for the Interdisciplinary Study of Literature* 23, no. 2 (1990): 107–26. http://www.jstor.org/stable/24780630.
14 Gudrun Schubert. "Women and Symbolism: Imagery and Theory." *Oxford Art Journal* 3, no. 1 (1980): 29–34. http://www.jstor.org/stable/1360176.
15 Jennifer Marion. "Historic Heteroessentialism and Other Orderings in Early America," *Signs*, 34, no. 4 (2009) 981–1003.
16 Sander L. Gilman. "Black Bodies, White Bodies: Toward an Iconography of Female Sexuality in Late Nineteenth-Century Art, Medicine, and Literature." *Critical Inquiry* 12, no. 11985. http://www.jstor.org/stable/1343468, pp. 204–205.
17 Margaret W. Conkey, and Janet D. Spector. "Archaeology and the Study of Gender." *Advances in Archaeological Method and Theory* 7 (1984): 1–38. http://www.jstor.org/stable/20170176.
18 Rosaria Vignolo Munson. "Artemisia in Herodotus." *Classical Antiquity* 7, no. 1 (1988): 91–106. https://doi.org/10.2307/25010881.
19 Mary T. Boatright, "Imperial Women on Coins and in Roman Cult," *Imperial Women of Rome: Power, Gender, Context* (NY 2021; online edition, Oxford Academic, 17 June 202), https://doi.org/10.1093/oso/9780190455897.003.0005.
20 "Classical Numismatics Discussion, Ancient Women," Forum Ancient Coins Member's Coin Gallery, Ancient Women – Classical Numismatics Discussion – Members' Coin Gallery (forumancientcoins.com).

21 Keith Moxey. "Panofsky's Concept of 'Iconology' and the Problem of Interpretation in the History of Art." *New Literary History* 17, no. 2 (1986): 265–74. https://doi.org/10.2307/468893.

22 Thornton C. Lockwood. "Artemisia of Halicarnassus: Herodotus' Excellent Counsel." *Classical World: A Quarterly Journal on Antiquity* 116 (2023): 147–72.

23 María Isabel Rodríguez López. "Victory, Triumph and Fame as the Iconic Expressions of the Courtly Power." *Music in Art* 37, no. 1/2 (2012): 9–23. http://www.jstor.org/stable/24420190.

24 Pierre Brulé, and Antonia Nevill. *Women of Ancient Greece*. Edinburgh University Press (2003). http://www.jstor.org/stable/10.3366/j.ctt1r25hx.
Lloyd Llewellyn-Jones. "In and Out of Imagination: Locating the Women of Achaemenid Persia," Cardiff University Lecture Series, Iran Heritage Foundation Prof. Lloyd Llewellyn-Jones: 'Locating the Women of Achaemenid Persia' (youtube. com).

25 Bernard Goldman. "Women's Robes: The Achaemenid Era." *Bulletin of the Asia Institute* 5 (1991): 83–103. http://www.jstor.org/stable/24048288, pp. 83–86.

26 Ibid. Goldman. Also see Georgina Thompson. "Iranian Dress in the Achaemenian Period: Problems Concerning the Kandys and Other Garments." *Iran* 3 (1965): 121–26. https://doi.org/10.2307/4299565.

27 Aeschylus. *The Persians* (produced 472 BC) The Internet Classics Archive | The Persians by Aeschylus (mit.edu).

28 "An Introduction to Achaemenid Military Equipment's" CAIS Circle of Ancient Iranian Studies, Achaemenid Military Equipments | CAIS© (cais-soas.com). Accessed 11/18/2022.

29 *Encyclopedia Iranica*. "Clothing ii. In the Median and Achaemenid periods," CLOTHING ii. Median and Achaemenid periods – Encyclopaedia Iranica (iranicaonline.org). Accessed 11/18/2022.

30 William B. Dinsmoor. "The Mausoleum at Halicarnassus: I. The Order." *American Journal of Archaeology* 12, no. 1 (1908): 3–29. https://doi.org/10.2307/496853.

31 Kaveh Farrokh. *Shadows in the Desert: Ancient Persia at War*. Osprey Publishing, pp. 68–69.

32 Llewellyn-Jones, Lloyd, Sue Blundell, Douglas L. Cairns, Andrew Dalby, Glenys Davies, Aideen M. Hartney, Daniel Ogden, et al. *Women's Dress in the Ancient Greek World*. Edited by Lloyd Llewellyn-Jones. Classical Press of Wales (2002). https://doi.org/10.2307/j.ctv1n3581n.

33 See W. W. Tarn for alternative explanations. "The Fleet of Xerxes." *The Journal of Hellenic Studies* 28 (1908): 202–33. https://doi.org/10.2307/624607.
Thornton C. Lockwood. "Artemisia of Halicarnassus: Herodotus' Excellent Councel" (Forthcoming in *Classical World* accepted for publication 06/2021). LOCAOH-7 (philarchive.org).

34 Nearly 400 of his passages include women, queens, and priestesses. All of which are involved in a wide range of complex roles and events. Of those women presented, forty were referenced as family members, mothers, daughters, or sisters; sixty-seven were professionals. Only seven were not priestesses. See Carolyn Dewald. "Biology and Politics: Women in Herodotus' Histories." *Pacific Coast Philology* 15 (October 1980): 11–18.

35 Carolyn Dewald and John Marincola (eds). *The Cambridge Companion to Herodotus*, UK: Cambridge University Press (2006).

36 Ibid. Dewald.

37 For a complete summary of topics covered in Book 7, Herodotus: Book Seven (reed.edu).

46 Women and War

38 For a complete summary of topics covered in Book 8, Herodotus: Book Eight (reed.edu).
39 A. D. Godley (translation). *The Histories of Herodotus, A Translation by A. D. Godley*, Scribe Publishing (2018). Book 7, Chapter 99 Herodotus, The Histories, Book 7, Chapter 99 (tufts.edu).
40 Ibid. Godley. Also see Penrose, Walter Duvall, Chapter 4: "Greek and Persian Warrior Queens: Herodotus Artemisia in Ethnic Perspective." https://doi.org/10.1093/acprof:oso/9780199533374.003.0005. pp. 152–183 Oxford Academic.
41 B. Al. "Cretan Religion in Relation to Greek Religion." *Mnemosyne* 12, no. 3 (1944): 208–22. http://www.jstor.org/stable/4427070.
   Anna Lucia D'Agata, and Antoine Hermary. "Ritual and Cult in Crete and Cyprus from the Third Millennium to the First Millennium BC: Towards a Comparative Framework." *British School at Athens Studies* 20 (2012): 273–88. http://www.jstor.org/stable/23541213.
42 Gunther Heilbrunn, and Paul Anthony Rahe. "Meet the Spartans." *The National Interest*, no. 152 (2017): 83–92. https://www.jstor.org/stable/26557432.
43 Jack Martin Balcer. "The Persian Wars against Greece: A Reassessment." *Historia: Zeitschrift Für Alte Geschichte* 38, no. 2 (1989): 127–43. http://www.jstor.org/stable/4436101.
44 W. W. Tarn. "The Fleet of Xerxes." *The Journal of Hellenic Studies* 28 (1908): 202–33. https://doi.org/10.2307/624607.
   Thomas R. Martin, *Ancient Greece*. Yale University Press (2013). http://www.jstor.org/stable/j.ctt32bm98.
45 Athens 180 ships, Chalcis 20 ships, Sicyon 15 ships, Ambracia 7 ships, Leucas 3 ships, Cythnus 1 ship, Siphnus 1 ship, Corinth 40 ships, Megara 20 ships, Epidaurus 10 ships, Troezen 5 ships, Hermione 3 ships, Ceos 2 ships, Serifos 1 ship, Aegina 30 ships, Sparta 16 ships, Eretria 7 ships, Naxos 4 ships, Styra 2 ships, Melos 2 ships, Croton 1 ship.
46 Arther Ferrill. "Herodotus and the Strategy and Tactics of the Invasion of Xerxes." *The American Historical Review* 72, no. 1 (1966): 102–15. https://doi.org/10.2307/1848172.
47 Paul Halsall. *Ancient History Sourcebook: Herodotus, Artemisia at Salamis*, 480 BCE, VII 99, VIII 68, VIII 69, VIII 87, VIII 88. From Herodotus *The History*, George Rawlinson (trans.) (New York: Dutton & Co. 1862.) Scanned by: J. S. Arkenberg, Department of History, Cal State Fullerton, updated 21 January 2020.
48 Book 7 Xerxes: Decision and preparation to invade Greece, The Expedition Begins, Catalogue of Persian Forces, The Voyage to Greece of Xerxes' army and fleet, Reactions of the Greeks to Xerxes' Invasion, Greeks not a Salamis: Gelon of Syracuse, the Corcyraeans and the Cretans. The Approach to Thermopylae, the Battle of Thermopylae, the Aftermath of Thermopylae. Perseus Digital Library, Gregory R. Crane, Editor-in-Chief Tufts University. Herodotus: Book Seven (reed.edu).
   Pericles B. Georges. "Saving Herodotus' Phenomena: The Oracles and the Events of 480 B.C." *Classical Antiquity* 5, no. 1 (1986): 14–59. https://doi.org/10.2307/25010838.
49 William W. Goodwin. "The Battle of Salamis." *Harvard Studies in Classical Philology* 17 (1906): 75–101. https://doi.org/10.2307/310311.
50 Ibid.
51 Ibid.
52 Ibid.
53 Ibid.
54 Ibid.
55 Ibid.
56 Op cit. Halsall, VII 69.

57 Op cit. Herodotus Book 8.87 Polyaneus, *Strategems* English translation, Attalus, Polyaenus: Stratagems – translation (attalus.org).
58 Ibid. Halsall, VII 69.
59 Jonas Grethlein. "How Not to Do History: Xerxes in Herodotus' 'Histories.'" *The American Journal of Philology* 130, no. 2 (2009): 195–218. http://www.jstor.org/stable/20616180.
60 Op cit. Herodotus Book 8.87.
61 Herodotus VII.101.
62 Herodotus VIII.101–102 Holly Haden. "Foreign Women on the Ancient Mediterranean Sea," undergraduate research scholars' thesis. Texas A& M University. May 2016. HAYDEN-DOCUMENT-2016.pdf (tamu.edu). Accessed 3/23/2022.
63 Ellen Lloyd. "Artemisia I of Caria-Pirate Queen and Ally of Xerxes I was Loyal to no-one Except Herself," March 4, 2019. AncientPages.com. Accessed 6/2023.
64 Ibid. Herodotus. Herodotus VIII.101–102 Holly Haden. "Foreign Women on the Ancient Mediterranean Sea," undergraduate.
65 Joshua J. Mark. "Halicarnassus," World History Encyclopedia, September 2, 2009. Halicarnassus – World History Encyclopedia.
66 Dienekes Pontikos. "Racial Type of the Ancient Greeks: A Racial Analysis of the Ancient Hellenes, How did the Greeks physically look like compared to modern Greeks?" May 30, 2019. Racial Type of the Ancient Greeks: A Racial Analysis of the Ancient Hellenes (greecehighdefinition.com).
67 Agnes Baldwin. "Symbolism on Greek Coins." *American Journal of Numismatics (1897–1924)* 49 (1915): 89–194. http://www.jstor.org/stable/43589909. W. Greenwell, and Canon Greenwell. "On Some Rare Greek Coins." *The Numismatic Chronicle and Journal of the Numismatic Society* 10 (1890): 20–32. http://www.jstor.org/stable/42679615.

Additional Resources

Barry Strauss. *The Battle of Salamis, The Naval Encounter That Saved Greece and Western Civilization*, New York: Simon and Schuster, June 29, 2004.
Erwin Panofsky. *Meaning in the Visual Arts*, Chicago: University of Chicago Press, 1983.
Guillaume Rouille. *Handbook of the Images of Renown*, Public Domain Internet Archive.org, Lausanne: University of Lausanne, 1553. Google-idf5FDAAAAcAAj.
Herodotus. *The History*. George Rawlinson (trans.), New York: Dutton & Co., 1862. Available on Internet Archive, "Full Text of Herodotus Volume I https://archive.org/stream/herodotus00herouoft/herodotus00herouoft_djvu.txt
Richard Popplewell Pullen and Charles Thomas Newton. *Halicarnassus: The History and Legacy of the Ancient Greek City and Home to One of the Seven Wonders of the World* (1861), Sacramento: Creative Media Partners, 2015.
Richard Stoneman. *Xerxes A Persian Life*, New Haven; London: Yale University Press, August 15, 2015.

Questions

What makes Artemisia important in the history of women in the Navy?

What were the crucial talents Artemisia exhibited as a military leader? Did she have any weaknesses?

48 Women and War

Why is knowledge about the art of iconography essential to understanding the portrayal of women's history in war?

Modern take

What roles do women perform in the modern navies of the world? What types of vessels are women assigned to? What qualifications are required to serve? How long are sea assignments?

What is the modern Navy like for females?

Who are some of the topmost female officers and enlisted personnel? What are their backgrounds?

How have international naval academies changed relative to allowing women to enter?

Activities and discovery

Watch the 2014 film 300 Rise of an Empire. *How is Artemisia portrayed? Does the film precisely reflect the personality and exploits of Artemisia I? What iconographic elements can you discover?*

Hundreds of women have appeared on coins throughout history. Unearth examples from numismatic history sites. Why are coins important as artifacts, and who were the women pictured on them?

What other iconographic images can you find in sculpture and art that relate to a story about a woman in the history of women and war? How does the version differ from what would be considered a factual rendition of the times they lived and fought?

Research modern female naval admirals. What hurdles did they have to overcome to succeed? Why did they become navalists and not air or ground fighters?

3
STYLIZED PUBLIC SCULPTURE
Boudica Queen of the British Celtic Iceni Tribe

FIGURE 3.1 Statue of Boudica and her daughters by Thomas Thornycroft in London.

© CC BY 2.0 Deed | Attribution 2.0 Generic | Creative Commons Category: Boadicea and Her Daughters – Wikimedia Commons

DOI: 10.4324/9781003406372-4

Sculpting with bronze

> The three women could be seen riding in a scythe-wheeled war chariot pulled by two thundering steeds. Standing ten feet high, with her arms outstretched and her spear clasped firmly in one hand, the warrior queen Boudica would have cut a fearsome silhouette.
>
> (Martha Vandrei, 2014)

Monuments and statues are important as symbolic or literal artistic representations of cultural heritage or take on the form of historical signposts commemorating people or events. They have the power of mass communication to relate achievement and the projection of societal values. Relative to war and combat, statues may be fashioned to remember those who fought and died in battle and to craft a space for communal reflection or to honor a significant turning point won or lost. Their three-dimensional configurations are presentations of physical rhetoric, a form of empowerment to be viewed by future generations long after the occasion they are meant to embody has passed. Globally, the balance of females in public sculpture honoring heroines and their successes is marginal at only two percent of the total compared to males.[1] Artisans who build monuments and statuary, particularly those who may receive commissions for publicly displaying their objects, must be able to fabricate something that moves a multifaced audience and be resilient enough to follow through on a project that will take several years to complete. Sculptors must be thick-skinned relative to the many negative and positive opinions announced as the piece takes shape and is placed in a public space.[2]

The political, artistic, and sociological story behind the statue of Boudica, located in London, England, is just as fascinating as her often repeated story in the annals of women and warfare. She was revered as the Queen of the British Celtic Iceni tribe for having led an uprising against the conquering forces of the Roman Empire in 60 AD. A bronze effigy in her honor sits atop a plinth beside the Victoria Embankment next to Westminster Bridge and the House of Parliament near the River Thames in London, England. Boudica stands upright in a flowing garment with a spear in her right hand and her left arm raised.[3] Her daughters with bared breasts crouch in the chariot, one to either side of their warrior mother. None of the women hold the reins of the biga as the frenetic horses thunder forward. A spirit of freedom and a skillful fighter is innate to the statue's composition.[4] A line from 18th-century poet William Cowper's 1792 *Boadicea, An Ode*, is inscribed on the side, "Regions Caesar never knew, thy posterity shall sway," meaning Boudica's country will grow greater than Rome.[5] It is Cowper's queen, armed with thunder and clad with wings, now residing on a populous London byway that became late 19th-century sculptor Thomas Thornycroft's magnum opus.[6]

How large, publicly displayed bronze sculptures like *Boudica* come alive requires a long and arduous series of subtractive and additive processes. Techniques used to complete a statue like that of Boudica are carving, casting, modeling, and assembly. Carving is a subtractive process where the sculptor purposefully removes parts of stone, metal, wood, or other hard material using handheld instruments to uncover a three-dimensional image. Chiseling or engraving is then used to enhance the composition.[7] Casting, modeling, and assembly are additive sculptural practices. In casting, the sculptor first constructs a mold or skin of their vision, then pours melted-down materials, usually bronze, into the form once completed. Modeling is primarily done with clay, but other malleable materials may be employed. Often, in modeling, a skeletal framework is used as a structural guide for the artist. Assembly sculptures may be of any material, including metal, glass, tile, wood, garbage, cement, or plastic, which can be combined to generate a three-dimensional shape. Sculptures can be historically accurate or stylized according to the era in which they are made. Rather than precisely replicating a story or person, they may be nonrepresentational, leaving it to the observer to place a value or idea upon what they are viewing. Bronze casting, the method that Thornycroft employed to shape his Boudica, can be traced to 5000 BC and the geographic regions of China and the Mediterranean. These early methods entailed hammering riveted metal sheets to produce rudimentary images of people and animals. With an increased understanding of more complex technological, engineering, and materials sciences, creating bronze statuary shifted toward using lost cast waxing.[8]

Boudica emerged after years of effort and a thorough multistage progression of steps.[9] First, Thornycroft and his working assistants created an original design. Then, an armature or skeleton for the final rendition was built. The textures that generated the dimensionality that the artist desired on the final product were conceived, and then several molds were made of separate pieces to be welded together. Wax was poured into the molds and chased, where imperfections were removed in the casting and air bubbles expunged. Wax casting could require up to four separate coatings. After the casts were completed, spruing followed, where channel rods were strategically placed to release air and gases during heating. Sculpture parts were then returned to a foundry so that molten metal could be poured into each section of the empty shell. To melt bronze, temperatures of 2000 degrees Fahrenheit needed to be reached.[10] Resultant wax forms would then get dipped multiple times in a fine-ceramic fluid called slurry. Once completely dry, the shells were placed in a kiln where the wax could be drained from strategically located pour holes. After cooling, molds were broken apart with sledgehammers and removed. Sections were then welded back together with pneumatic tools. At this phase, particularly on a sculpture the size of Boudica, additional artisans

52 Women and War

and workers were brought in to assist in detailing the piece. The last step was creating the desired patina using propane torches and painting sections with oxides and nitrates.

The Thornycroft artisans

Thomas Thornycroft specialized in equestrian statuary and subcontracted primarily with the royal family and Parliament. His background included farming and engineering, and he sometimes assisted his shipbuilder son, John Isaac, a naval architect and proprietor of a fast steamboat company.[11] Mary, his wife, one of the most successful sculptors in Britain, taught art to one of the royal princesses and had seven children: Hamo, John Isaac, Helen, Theresa, Frances Sarah, Anne, and Alyce.[12] Hamo became a renowned sculptor. Theresa became a sculptor and painter. Helen was a painter and watercolorist, as was her sister, Mary Alyce, who exhibited at the autumn exhibition of modern pictures in oil and watercolors in 1892 at the Walker Art Gallery in Liverpool.[13] The Thornycroft daughters were expected to attend London's premiere art academies and seek employment. This familial support of female children was exceptional for the period and was not representative of standard social conventions that kept young women out of college.[14] Daughters with professional mother artists like Mary encountered less opposition inside and outside the home for resisting Victorian norms to become wage earners. Coming from a family of talented sculptors, they also had the advantage of receiving parental direction in locating patronages and becoming skilled at dealing with a discerning clientele and the business aspects of art.[15]

Mary's popularity with the royals never waned due to her portraits' quality, elegant attitude, and decorative style. In 1846, she completed nearly one statue every two months and produced seven sculptures for Prince Albert.[16] Her salaried position and consistent royal commissions became the primary monetary support for the family. In an age when a middle-class male professional earned a salary of from 100 to 150 pounds a year, her sculptures were occasionally sold individually for 100 pounds or more. Even at these prices, her fees remained below the sums given to male artists. Her royal busts, fragments, and sculptures still reside in the Royal Collection in London.[17]

Thomas Thornycroft's principal interests were in the mechanics of sculpting and creating large-scale sculptural projects. Mary's income allowed him to pursue his art, for he did not readily receive commissions, and the nature of his expansive ideas was time-consuming to complete. Other than *Boudica*, Thomas became most known for his equestrian statues of Queen Victoria and Prince Albert, the figure of Charles I located in Westminster Hall, and one of the corner groups of statuary, *Commerce*, which was part of the complex at the Albert Memorial erected in Hyde Park by Victoria after her husband's death at the age of 42.[18]

Thornycroft's *Boudica* and a mounted rider statue of the queen were completed on the supposition that the royal family would eventually fund his efforts. Still, he never received a formal commission from the royals. The association with the monarchy would never be as personal or prolific as Mary's. Had he not been married to a favorite of the Prince Consort and Queen, he would likely have had to concentrate on engineering or more rudimentary creations and conventional markets to remain a full-time artist. Mary believed in her husband's abilities, and her abundant output to meet patrons' requests kept the family secure. She considered her constant creativity a price worth paying to allow Thomas to spend his time on large, speculative projects.[19]

Prince Albert moved to have Boudica immortalized in bronze after he saw Thornycroft's life-size statue of "his Drina" riding side-saddle on her Arabian stallion that was completed to be shown at the first World's Fair in 1851 at the London Great Exhibition of the Works of Industry of All Nations.[20] The massive plate glass and cast-iron exhibition hall covered 990,000 square feet and hummed with people excited to participate in the 14,000 exhibits. Two-thirds of Britain's population attended the trade fair, and receipts totaled 18 million pounds. Science and technology, clothing and textiles, glass, arboretums, machinery, and architecture were displayed, advertising the bourgeoning trades behind the wealth-making industrial revolution.[21] It was the perfect venue for the Queen's likeness. When the enthusiastic Victorian visitors entered the main hall, the first thing they saw was their Victoria towering above them dressed in a plumed hat and long flowing skirt, sitting sidesaddle on top of a magnificent steed legging up as if in an eventing arena, her right hand lightly holding her riding crop.[22]

Victoria admired the statue, but critics did not appreciate Thomas' innovative representation of the young sovereign in contemporary riding clothes and was lambasted as too modern. London's oldest and most widely read and influential newspaper, *The Times*, berated it as exceedingly anatomical. It was Thornycroft's technique that the press did not like. He had a naturalistic artistic eye, and his creations fell on the creative continuum between realism and everyday naturalism rather than the prudish classical romanticism associated with Victorian-era art.[23]

Once Thornycroft's vision of the queen was unveiled, and perhaps the comparator responsible for the scathing reviews of the middle-class Cheshire engineer was Italian-born aristocrat Baron Carlo Marochetti, who was commissioned to create a statue memorializing the queen's 1849 visit to Glasgow. The final product was not revealed until 1854, three years after the London Exhibition, but it was in the process of being created and of newsworthy importance. The baron had deep ties with the French Royal family and secured the British monarchy's support through his Italian family. In rapid succession, he received backing for 15 projects, including the royal couple's private tomb effigy.

54 Women and War

Marochetti, unlike Thornycroft, who never became intimate with the royals, was complimented by the queen as agreeable, pleasing, and gentlemanlike – three traits that Thornycroft was never described as having had.

The Glasgow statue presented an entirely different mood than the more non-conformist style of Thornycroft. An air of formality permeated the design. The queen sat erect, a crown on her head, and the stallion, unlike the compact Arabian thoroughbred with its high tail carriage and charm used in the Exhibition piece, was of an Irish Draught type known for its size, strength, and use in ceremonial duties. Neoclassical in style and resembling the ancient sculptural masterpieces of Greece and Rome, it lacked the presence and emotion captured in Thornycroft's adaptation. Marching around the base were relief inlays depicting the details of the queen's venue during her visit, including her entourage on tour with religious dignitaries at the Crypt of Glasgow Cathedral. Greek Corinthian columns were placed at each corner of the rectangular marble pedestal.[24]

The *Edinburg Evening Post* and the *Glasgow Courier* exhibited a love-and-hate relationship with the Italian artist's style. The *Courier* positively expounded on Marochetti's ability to balance the queen's proportion to her steed without dwarfing her feminine figure. The *Post* review did not admire the result, stating the effort was clipped and affective in style and expression, calling his rendering pinched and meager. It was also noted that "their" queen seemed as if she were dressed for a salon rather than the outdoors. Criticism was also leveled on the horse being posed as if moving forward with a raised fore and aft leg rather than standing still.[25]

In 1870, a second statue of Queen Victoria by Thornycroft was unveiled riding side saddle as a complimentary piece for Prince Albert that had been placed in Queen Square, Wolverhampton, in 1866. The queen's likeness was flaunted as "the piece that made his name."[26] She sat atop her royal steed in a voluminous draped skirt, wearing a plumed hat as she had in the Exhibition and Marochetti pieces.[27] Under the riding saddle was a ceremonial blanket. Across her breast, she wore the sash of St. George and was holding what looked to be a small scepter but was a riding crop.

Thornycroft and his search for the real Boudica

Thomas's letters to mentor and educational sponsor, W.B. Dickinson, a surgeon and numismatist, left a legacy of the artist's relationship with the royal house. The letters serve as windows into the past that describe the convulsions Thornycroft faced as a creator in a public arena.[28] During the construction of *Boudica*, Thomas wrote to Dickinson about the problematic tensions between him and Albert, the Prince Consort. Thornycroft complained he was plagued by persistent royal meddling of his sponsor, particularly when Albert pronounced that Boudica's chariot should be equivalent to a royal throne upon wheels.[29] The prince even suggested the sculpture contained a third charging beast and wanted the final product placed in Hyde Park. The noble's ideas, wrote Thornycroft to Dickinson, "would absolutely condemn, nay destroy my composition."[30]

Discussions occurred between the artist and the imperial critic about the value he placed upon realism versus the prince's poetic desires of romanticizing his wife through the image of Boudica.[31] Thornycroft was unwilling to assent to royal interpolations, and he researched classical writings of Julius Caesar's *Gallic Wars* for correctness. He intended not to incorporate a Victorian image but to complete something historically accurate and correspond with qualities he could ascertain from ancient accounts of period weaponry.[32] Knowing the content of these letters and Thornycroft's creative approach proves *Boudica* did not have a straightforward association with Victorian Imperialism, nor was it done to replicate the Victorian monarchy, as many stories passed down have noted.[33]

Boudica had long been a subject of interest to the nation.[34] Her chronicle was revived often. Around 1613, *Bonduca* was written by John Fletcher, a more productive playwright than William Shakespeare, who teamed several times with dramatist Francis Beaumont and satirist Philip Messenger. *Bonduca* was performed in 1613 by the acting troupe The King's Men, the top company of performers of the era who were organized under a royal Letters Patent. Twenty-one characters were portrayed, three of which were Boudica and her two daughters. There were druids and several Roman officers and commanders whose prose was a mix of political allegory and colonialist rhetoric of the 17th century – scenes centered around the two military camps of the Romans and Boudica's people. The Queen of the Iceni was a gloating leader who asked her youngest daughter to kill herself when she was unable to fend off a Roman attack. The older of the two daughters gave a grandiose soliloquy of sacrifice. Both mother and older daughter commit suicide, after which the remainder of the play is a series of exchanges among the Roman soldiers and their moving on to new conquering agendas.

Baroque music composer Henry Purcell produced the opera *Bonduca or the British Heroine* in 1695 based on the 1619 play *The Tragedy of Bonduca* by collaborative playwrights Francis Beaumont and John Fletcher.[35] They produced 55 plays together. One of the musical numbers in the opera was *Britons Strike Home!* Sometimes referred to as Britain's first anthem on par with *Rule Britania. Britain's Strike Home!* embraced the allegory of Boudica and the druids in its repeating stanza, *Briton's Strike Home! Fight! Fight and record. Fight! Fight and record yourselves in druids song. Revenge, Revenge your country's wrong.*[36] The melody became popular during the conflict from the 1700s to the early 20th century to represent national identity and call to arms. Trendy in British theater, it was often played using winds and strings.[37] The melody served as a rousing national theme during the Seven Years War, as a campaign tune in the 1830s, and played as a diplomatic instrument in 1914 at a concert to show Britain's solidarity with Belgium. Troops during the Third Anglo Mysore War in 1791 sang the song; it was sung in the House of Commons in 1797, at the Battle of the Gut of Gibraltar in 1801, at the Battle of Trafalgar in 1805, and was used as a toast to the Army and Navy in the 1700s. The cavalry regiment, the 13th Light Dragoons, who served in the Napoleonic and Crimean Wars and World War I, carried squadron standards incorporating phrasing from Purcell's lyrics.[38]

The account of Boudica was resurrected again in 1782 when William Cowper published *Boadicea: An Ode*. Cowper's poem was written with the American War of Independence in mind as a cautionary warning to the upstart imperial rebels. The closing stanza reads, "Ruffians, pitiless as proud, Heav'n awards the vengeance due; Empire is on us bestow'd/Shame and ruin wait for you."[39] In 1864, Queen Victoria's poet laureate, Alfred Lloyd Tennyson, put Boudica front and center in his six-stanza elegy, *Boadicea*.[40] She is presented in this poem as standing loftily charioted, brandishing a dart in her hand and throwing "rolling glances lioness-like with a fierce volubility, burning with anger."[41] The poetic and artistic dyad of episodes with Queen Victoria being described in popular media as a Boudica namesake led to a generalization of an idea that the "tremendous anti-imperialist rebel of the Iceni tribe from the first century was identifiable with the royal head of the late 18th century British Empire."[42] In addition to the poem and statue's influences, the name Boudica was touted as embracing the Celtic word, 'bouda,' meaning victory. It did not take much to derive a non-credible association of her name with the feminine royal equivalent, Queen Victoria.[43] Prince Albert became engrossed in these modern perceptions of the lore of Boudica. He saw a bridge between her strength and fortitude and his intimate knowledge of Queen Victoria's character.[44] At Albert's encouragement, Victoria supported her husband's idea for a statue of the Iceni queen but never came through with formal monetary backing for Thornycroft to conduct the project.[45]

Thornycroft's realistic bent sent him in search of information about the Queen of the Iceni tribe. He was led to Caesar's documentation in the *Gallic War, IV 33*, which traces seven years of military campaigns. Through such readings, Thornycroft discovered a comparable idea of the demeanor and qualities of the era in which Boudica lived. In researching the queen's life and times, he may have come across battlefield descriptions of ancient Briton's like:

In chariot fighting, the Britons began by driving all over the field hurling javelins, and generally, the terror inspired by the horses and the noise of the wheels were sufficient to throw their opponents' ranks into disorder. Then, after making their way between the squadrons of their cavalry, they would jump down from the chariot and engage on foot… they attained such proficiency that even on a steep incline, they were able to control the horses at full gallop and check and turn them in a moment.[46]

Boudica was considered a gifted fighter aboard a chariot, so it is fitting that the research conducted by Thornycroft was used in her final representation. Many illustrations of Boudica and her daughters exist in young adult books from the 19th century, when Thornycroft designed his statue.

A further detailed historical investigation led the sculptor to reject Prince Albert's vision of having a queen-like dais instead of a period-correct war machine. Thornycroft preferred the larger Roman version and not the less dynamic chariot of the tribes of Britain. Part of this was due to a desire to put three female characters aboard, which could be viewed by the public without blocking any aspect of their bodies. In one correspondence, he described how deeply he had meditated on the emotional state the mother and her daughters would have been in during their fight with the Roman soldiers.

FIGURE 3.2 Nineteenth-century children's bookplate of Boudica and her daughters.

© CC0 Creative Commons CC-PD Mark File: Pictures of English History Plate IV – Boadicea and Her Army.jpg – Wikimedia Commons

58 Women and War

He wanted the queen to show majestic fury and vehemence in her movement. He also wanted a public reaction of excited sympathy when they viewed the Iceni queen's two daughters cleaving to her garment.[47] During a visit by an art critic to review the ongoing process of creating *Boudica*, Thornycroft received redemption for the harsh censure he had endured in making the statue of Victoria at the Chrystal Palace. A reporter called *Boudica* the most successful attempt in a historical sculpture of this barren time, representing the hope of better things and better days for art, which…is sadly degenerate.[48] The artist's soul had won the day over a meddling public and prince. Thornycroft had kept *Boudica* from becoming a contrived celebration of Victoria's reign.[49]

Completing the statue took 29 years, beginning in 1856 and ending in 1885, and it was not erected until 1902, one year after Queen Victoria's death. Thornycroft died before the 6000 pounds sterling could be secured for the bronze essential for filling the molds. Eventually, his naval engineer son, John Isaac, reached an agreement to secure backing in Parliament, and a committee was formed to raise money to complete the statue through subscription fundraising. John Webb Singer, who owned a large foundry for statuary and ecclesiastical products in Somerset, finished the bronze pouring process for 2000 British pounds.[50] Even after this occurred, no site was made available for erecting the statue, and it would take four more years before permanent placement was finalized on the spot near the Thames on the north side of Westminster Bridge near Portcullis House.

Boudica's realm

Before the Romans set their objective on assimilating the peoples of Britain and pillaging their resources, the Celts had evolved into a strong and economically affluent society due to their ability to design and create items from ferrous materials. Boudica came to power as queen during this prolific era within the Iceni culture upon the death of her husband, Prasutagus. Two daughters of the king and queen are mentioned in historical records and remain unnamed. Many Celtic tribes were agriculturally based and housed in hill forts and open farms or villages. Tribes were organized into three tiers. At the apex were nobility, a king, queen, or chieftain, under which were tradespeople, and then at the bottom were those who tilled the land. Political unity was not shared between the many tribes, and interfighting occurred often.

Druid priests oversaw religious practices, and tribes were polytheists, worshiping many gods and goddesses. Prominent deities were Dana – The Primordial Goddess of Nature, Dagda – The Cheerful Chief of gods, Aengus the Youthful God of Love, Lugus – The Courageous Warrior God, Mórrígan –

Stylized Public Sculpture 59

FIGURE 3.3   Map showing the Iron Age tribes of Great Britain.

© CC BY-SA 3.0Deed Attribution-Share Alike 3.0 Unported Creative Commons File:Britain. circa.540.jpg – Wikipedia

The Mysterious Goddess of Fate, Brigid – The 'Triple' Goddess of Healing, and Belenus – The Effulgent Sun God. Religion was practiced in natural settings, usually in the woods or fields near residences. Romans viewed this type of nature-driven worship as barbaric even though they honored multiple deities, such as Jupiter. Roman military commanders would praise Jupiter, the sky god, after winning a battle.[51]

During the 1st-century BC Roman conquests, archeologists numbered the ancient tribes of Boudica's world to about 27.[52]

Little is known of several of the tribes, but anthropologists have put together background materials on others. The Venicons of the northeast were a group that was never permanently occupied by the Romans, and they were one of the very few people in Britain who cremated and placed their dead in stone-lined graves. The Votadini were a vast tribe divided into several smaller communities located in the upper central east region of the United Kingdom, which is now part of southeast Scotland. They lived in hillforts. In northern England, the Brigantes were the most prominent tribe territorially and were led by Queen Cartimandua for three decades, from 43 to 68 AD.

60 Women and War

Roman historian Tacitus' writings relay that she was a powerful and influential leader, was pro-Roman, and made many covenants with the Holy Empire. The Trinovantes inhabited the northern Thames estuary and established the tribal capital of Camulodunum around 20 BC. They were separated from Boudica's Iceni to the north by wooded regions. To the west of the Iceni lay the Catuvellanui, who led the resistance to Julius Caesar's first expedition to Britain in 54 BC.

Unlike most Iron Age peoples, the Iceni developed a formalized monetary and financial structure. They minted coins and were known to have gathered and stored gold treasure. They also designed and fought with metal weapons. The tribe relied on numerous tradespeople employed as bronze smiths or as leather workers, carpenters, potters, enamellists, and brewers. A series of archeological digs unearthed Icenian golden torcs, interwoven neck, and arm jewelry. A grouping of gold, silver, and copper alloy jewelry known as the Snettisham hoard was uncovered in the late 1940s, pointing to the value placed upon personal adornment and creating items that displayed Iceni status and wealth. There have been other hordes of decorated bronze chariot fittings, which were also a means of conspicuous display.[53] As queen of the Iceni, Boudica would have had many of these neck and arm rings, and her chariot would have been decorated to a degree equal to her status.

Boudica and the Iceni as related by Tacitus and Cassius Dio

Two descriptions from Tacitus' *Histories*, Book XIV Chapters 29–37, and Cassius Dio's 80-volume *Roman History* Epitome of Book 62 Chapter LXII are essential documentations of the character and battle savvy of Boudica and her uprising against the Roman usurpation of her people around 60 AD.[54] Cassius Dio's style and descriptions of her revolt are more derogatory toward the British and go to much more extraordinary lengths in describing the matrilineal side of the Celts in demeaning ways. The story is jaded from the side of the Romans overtaking the Iceni and is a blatant attempt at perpetuating a Roman legacy.

Tacitus' rendition of the Iceni uprising came from versions told to him by Agricola, his father-in-law, who was a Roman Italo-Gallic general who led military troops during much of the Roman conquest of Great Britain and served under Governor General Gaius Suetonius Paulinus. Due to the intimacy of the familial connections of a critical general and the fact that Tacitus's writings occur closer to the British rebellion, Tactius' story may be considered a more probable truth-telling of the situation. On the other hand, Cassius was a Roman politician who spoke Greek and Latin and held several official posts, and his father was a prominent senator, counsel, and governor. Cassius rarely cited sources and is believed to have borrowed from the ideas of Greek historian Thucydides. Subjective experiences as a politician were relied upon rather than being concerned with historical accuracy. His tale was created from a mix of literature and public documents. Criticism for errors and distortions is common, but he claimed to have read everything about the Romans available in his lifetime. He argued that no Roman or non-Roman reading his material would have difficulty with his storyline due to his presentation of essential facts. *Roman History* was written chronologically into 80 volumes, and it took a decade to gather research and another 12 years of writing to complete.[55]

Tacitus and Cassius Dio described the druids as people dedicated to superstitions and barbarous rites. Tacitus professed that they stain their altars with prisoners' blood, glut themselves with their enemies' blood, and use men's entrails to explore the gods' will. They were warlike people living in common refuge with no military talent, were averse to taking prisoners, and did not want to exchange captives or reserve them for slavery. These British despised all the laws of war, which were of savage valor and vengefulness. Cassius reported that the druids in their temple were heard using foreign

FIGURE 3.4 Nineteenth-century illustration of Boudica in Iceni Dress.
© Creative Commons Attribution-Share Alike 4.0 International

jargon mingled with laughter, outcries, lamentations, and groans.[56] Cassius left a visual description of Boudica: "In stature, she was very tall, in appearance most terrifying, the glance of her eyes was most fierce, and her voice was harsh; a great mass of the tawniest hair fell to her waist, around her neck was a large golden necklace; and she wore a tunic of diverse colors over which a thick mantle was fastened with a brooch."[57]

Additional details of Boudica were that she was of royal lineage. Cassius scoffed, she "was possessed of far greater intelligence than often belongs to women."[58]

Reasons for Boudica's revolt are several, according to the two ancient historians.[59] From Tacitus comes the tale that Prasutagus, the King of the Iceni and husband to Boudica, had a long reign and amassed great wealth. He was determined to leave half of all he owned to his two daughters and Emperor Nero to provide tranquility for his family and kingdom. Nero's death obliterated the political alliance between the Iceni and Rome. In the chaos after Nero's death, Rome's military generals began elbowing for power, and in one year, three men became leaders, all of whom were brutally murdered. In this political upheaval, the Iceni were enslaved and made to pay a head tax on their subjugation. The Romans ravaged the islanders, pillaged Prasutagus's homes, and seized his lands. The king's royal familial relations were reduced to slavery. The Romans drove the druids out of Camulodunum, the site of the Brythmi-Celtic fortress and capital of the Trinovantes and Catuvellaun tribes. To continue the insult, the invaders erected a temple in honor of Claudius on the druid site, a place of deep meaning to the Iceni.

Cassius Dio designated three economic reasons as the cause for the Celtic uprising.[60] The fourth Roman emperor, Claudius, on giving Briton's money with no expectation of repayment, is said to have told them to suddenly return it with threats of retribution if the order was not followed. The Procurator of Roman Britain, Catus Decianus, demanded the Iceni pay back the money Claudius had given them. Seneca the Younger, who had lent the islanders 40 million sesterces they had not wanted, called in this loan and resorted to severe measures to extract it.[61]

After the death of her husband, Boudica aggressively and openly opposed these acts of the barbaric treatment of her people, the lies of Roman Emperor Nero for not keeping the peace, and the order from Italy for the reclamation of vast sums of money. Tacitus reported that the Romans disgraced Boudica with cruel tripes, and she was publicly flogged for defending her people's rights. According to Cassius, the brutal lashing left Boudica's body permanently seamed with ignoble stripes. Her two daughters were tied to wooden supports and brutally raped as she was made to watch. The horrific physical treatment enraged Boudica to seek revenge for her daughters.[62]

Camulodunum, Verulamium, and Londinium

The Iceni queen set forward and amassed a quarter to a third of a million troops from the varying tribes, receiving significant support from the Trinovantes. With her followers organized, she burned and sacked Camulodunum (Colchester), Londinium (London), and Verulamium (St Albans).

The fierceness with which she conducted these battles was staggering. Tacitus depicted the tri-city rout against the Romans in the following way. The Trinovantes and neighboring states joined, and they pledged themselves together. In Camulodunm, the Celts overpowered the Romans with a general assault, laid waste with fire and sword, and took the temple by storm. No Roman citizen in the city escaped the rage of the barbarians. In Londinium and Verulamium, all Romans were put to the sword and were attacked with fury, killing at least 70,000 Roman allies. Cassius adds greater detail to the event.

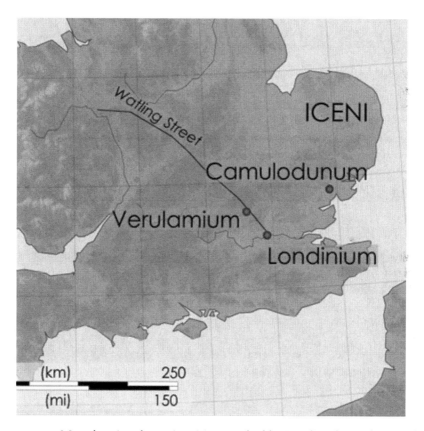

FIGURE 3.5 Map showing the major cities attacked by Boudica during her revolt.

© Creative Commons Attribution-Share Alike 4.0 International File: Map of the Boudican Revolt.svg – Wikipedia

64 Women and War

The Romans were subjected to every form of outrage, and the most bestial atrocities occurred. All the noblest and most distinguished women were hung up naked and then had their breasts cut off and sewed to their mouths to appear as if they were eating them. The women were impaled on sharp skewers run lengthwise through their entire bodies, after which sacrifices, banquets, and wanton behavior in celebration occurred in their sacred places.

The Iceni queen had successfully beaten back the most powerful army in the world. Cassius and Tacitus, however, do not justify her military success due to her superior warrior spirit but due to the misfortunes of the Romans. Tacitus claimed that the Roman colony at Camulodunum fell because the area was exposed and was an easy mark for the Iceni. He also mentions an omen as proof of their potential demise. At Camulodunum, the Hellenic statue of victory fell from its base without apparent cause, with its face toward the ground signifying an inauspicious event. Mentioned also were the actions of several Roman military leaders. Bad luck had been perpetuated by the bad judgment and cowardice of three military officers in succession. After seeing the carnage, Catus, the procurator of Roman Britain, fled the area. General Petilius Ceralis marched to relieve Camulodunum but was routed by the druids who cut his infantry to pieces, "fleeing in a fit of fatal rashness along with his cavalry to backline entrenchments."[63] The Camp Prefect, the third most senior officer of the Roman legion, Poenius Postumus, ignored Suetonius Paulinus's call to put down the rebellion. In a story that has not been corroborated, he supposedly succumbed to guilt for his actions and died by his sword.

Boudica's success was due to her gifted and ruthless hit-and-run tactics. Her approach was to confuse the more formally organized Roman enemy before they could respond in force. She effectively weakened the adversaries through raids, harassment, and skirmishes, achieving a supreme psychological effect on their morale. Her ultimate battle on Wattling Road would pit her strengths of numbers, fierceness, hand-to-hand combat, and chariot fighting against a more formal, highly trained national army with modern weaponry.

Suetonius was unperturbed by the actions of Catus and Cerialis and marched his already weary troops to Londinium. Cassius's story divulges that Paulinus feared the desperation and numbers of the enemy and was inclined to postpone a battle until a more convenient season. His troops were also growing short on food, but Boudica's wins had pressed him to act contrary to his judgment. Since the Roman army was scant compared to Boudica's, the general decided to reorganize his 14th legion, the veterans of the 20th legion, and auxiliaries to form an army of about 10,000 men. Next, he determined not to wait but to meet the Iceni head-on. Forming the center was his legion with the light-armed troops stationed in reserve, and the cavalry was posted in the wings. He chose a spot to best pit his regiment against the Iceni queen's hoards. He marched along the great arterial Wattling Road, from modern-day Dover to London to St. Albans. Here, he located an area encircled with woods, narrow at the entrance, and sheltered in the rear by thick forest. The locale would allow him to avoid a British ambush and force Boudica's troops into a frontal assault rather than giving them the mandatory space to adhere to their slash, burn, and regroup tactics.

The Iceni, claimed Tacitus, arrived at the battlefield and "appeared as an incredible multitude," with "no regular line of battle, detached parties, and loose battalions." They were, he conveyed, "a frantic transport bounding with exultation and so sure they were of victory, they brought their wives and wagons to survey the scene of action and to behold wonders of British valor."[64] Boudica arrived, "riding in front of her hoards on her war chariot, then assigned her troops to their stations."[65] The queen's line was so long that Suetonius would not have been able to extend his troops the entire length of hers even if he had placed his men only one deep.

Boudica's battle speeches

Tacitus sets the scene before the carnage begins, with Boudica giving a speech from her war chariot and her two daughters next to her. She moves through the ranks, ranting and relaying that "she was the meanest among them." Boudica began her oration: The Romans are arrogant, with no filter as to whom they may decimate, including the elderly and virgins. Our cause, as Briain's, is public liberty and revenge for my two daughters' being beaten and raped. Our strengths, she informs the hoard, are our motive to avenge Roman indignations, numbers, pride, and warlike spirits. She concludes with an ultimatum: We either conquer or die with glory.

Cassius Dio claims two separate orations made by Boudica. The first is a short message entitled "An Address to Her Army." The second is an agonizingly long diatribe of four dense paragraphs that project Roman sociological and political thoughts that no druid would have uttered. In this instance, Boudica is represented as a pseudo-Roman orator, as if standing before a group of citizens in a public square waxing upon historical references to two Egyptian Queens, Nitocris, believed to have been the last pharaoh of the sixth dynasty of Egypt, and Semiramis, queen regent of the Assyrian empire.[66] He also references Julius Caesar, Nero, Caligula, Messalina, and Agrippina as images alluded to in her speech.

In her first rally, Boudica is placed on the battlefield, grasping a spear as a prop to induce terror in the Romans. Her oratory begins. It is time to renew Britain's birthright of freedom. Poverty, she claims, is better with no master than to have wealth through being Roman enslaved people. The queen reminds her troops of the oppressive taxation they have been forced to meet.

66 Women and War

Then, Boudica stated that all Romans were weak because they had to protect themselves with breastplates, helmets, greaves, palisades, walls, and trenches and hide behind their mail suits. Needing such protections shows a Roman level of fear toward the Britons. The enemy's feebleness is exhibited in their inability to live without shade or covering and their requirement for sustenance in the form of kneaded bread, wine, and oil. In comparison, Britain's robust animalistic strength comes from using tents, not walls and tribal shields. Grass and root are their bread, and their deep regional knowledge is their ally. She concludes, let us show them that they are hares and foxes trying to rule over dogs and wolves.[67]

Cassius revealed in a second speech that Boudica claimed that Nero may be a man, but he is, in fact, "a woman," proved by his singing, lyre playing, and beautification of his person. Further, the Iceni leader is made to have said Romans should not be considered men. They enjoyed effeminate practices like bathing in warm water, eating artificial dainties, drinking unmixed wine, anointing themselves with myrrh, or sleeping on soft couches with boys for bedfellows. Sporus, a young boy Nero favored, whom he castrated and then married, is also referenced. Boudica pronounces that her men and women are versed in the art of war, with the latter possessing the same valor as brothers and husbands. Then, she speaks woman to woman with Andrastre, the Iceni war goddess, to seek her favor. This second discourse ends with Boudica's proclamation, "May this mistress Domitia-Nero no longer reign over her people or her men, let the wench-Nero sing and lord it over the Romans for they deserve to be the slaves of such a woman after having submitted to her for so long."[68]

The final battle according to Tacitus and Cassius

Tacitus' narrative has the Romans advancing with ferocity and discharging darts at random, rushing forward as a wedge with the auxiliary troops following with equal ardor. The cavalry bore down on Boudica's forces with pikes. The cornered Iceni attempted to flee to the rear but were obstructed by the wagons of Celtic families, who had gathered as spectators in complete confidence that they would win. Tacitus testifies that there is a scene of dreadful carnage. Over 80,000 British and 400 Romans lay dead. No sex, animal, or age are spared.[69]

Cassius's more romanticized version of the last battle has Suetonius and Boudica approaching each other, "the barbarians with much shouting mingled with battle songs."[70] In high order, the Romans silently throw their javelins. Boudica advances. The Romans rushed forward at a signal and charged the druids at full speed.[71] Boudica's troops fought everywhere at once, assailing the Romans in a rush of chariots. Riders overthrew foot soldiers, and foot soldiers struck down mounted riders. Roman troops formed in close order and advanced to meet the chariots – the British scattered others.[72] A band of druids continued to fight in close quarters, with the Roman archers routing them. Others stayed back, dodging their shafts at a distance. All, said Cassius, was ongoing not in one spot but among all three Roman divisions at once. The enemies contended with the same animated zeal and daring for a long time. But late in the day, Rome prevailed, slewing many at the wagons near the forest edge and capturing many. This story ends with the Iceni escaping to fight another day.[73]

There is no accurate information about what happened to Boudica after the battle on Wattling Road. Tacitus's last reference to her was that she was so full of remorse at the loss to the Romans that she fell upon her sword and expired on the spot. Cassius's Boudica fell sick and died, was mourned deeply, and was given a costly burial. The druids scattered to their homes. Others were assimilated into Roman society. Urban legend places her final resting place in Birdlip in Gloucestershire, Stonehenge, Norfolk, and London's Hampstead area. Another myth is that her burial spot is under a train platform at King's Cross Station in London.[74]

The Queen of the Iceni tribe's revolt seriously unhinged Roman rule in 60–61 AD. She exemplifies a woman who could serve in fierce hand-to-hand combat and was a talented charioteer. Tacitus's and Cassius's interpolations and judgments of Iceni's last revolt paint vivid depictions of Boudica and the Celtic people. Both historians formulated their stories critically, using chronicles from past annals and, in Tacitus's case, from a father-in-law who had served and led in the Battle of Britain. While their renditions rely on rumor, philosophy, or gossip, the Queen of the Iceni story would have vanished without their depictions. The statue Thomas Thornycroft completed of her is a fitting memory of a fierce, heroic figure of freedom for the United Kingdom. Her legacy, cast in bronze, was no easy feat for Thornycroft with the meddlesome inputs by the prince consort and the public's opposing viewpoint of his naturalistic approach to sculpting. Because of Thornycroft's desire to replicate Boudica as a fierce Iceni queen instead of a Victorian hieroglyph, he left behind for future generations an enduring symbol of a female warrior who continues to live on as a champion for her nation.

Notes

1 Statues for Equality, Statues for Equality – Statues for Equality.
2 MASSON-BERGHOFF, Aurélia (ed). *Statues in Context: Production, Meaning and (Re)Uses*. Vol. 10. Peeters Publishers, 2019. https://doi.org/10.2307/j.ctv1q26tr1.
    Waldemar Cudny, and Hakan Appleblad. "Monuments and Their Functions in Urban Public Space." *Norwegian Journal of Geography*, 73:2019 Issue 5 (03 Jan 2020): 273–89 https://doi.org/10.1080/00291951.2019.1694976
3 ...*My Beautiful Queen...*, https://villaniarmando.wordpress.com/2016/03/11/my-beautiful-queen/.

68 Women and War

4 "Boudicea-Boudicca," War Memorial Register, Imperial War Museums, Boadicea – Boudicca | War Imperial War Museums (iwm.org.uk).

5 The complete poem, written in 1780 and published in 1782 from *The Complete Poetical Works of William Cowper*, H. S. Milford (ed). London: Henry Frowde, 1905 310–1. Online William Cowper. "Boadicea. An Ode." (luminarium.org). Accessed 12/20/2020.
BOADICEA: AN ODE

6 Lily Johnson. "Boadicea and Her Daughters, Statue," History Hit, Boadicea and Her Daughters Statue – History and Facts | History Hit 23 March 2021.
Martha Vandrei. "A Victorian Invention? Thomas Thornycroft's 'Boadicea Group' And The Idea Of Historical Culture In Britain." *The Historical Journal* 57, no. 2 (2014): 485–508. http://www.jstor.org/stable/24529056.

7 Charles Wheeler. "English Sculpture: Style and Materials." *Journal of the Royal Society of Arts* 93, no. 4695 (1945): 398–409. http://www.jstor.org/stable/41362159.
"How to Make a Bronze Sculpture with Photos," https://www.laurelpeterson-gregory.com/blog/how-to-make-a-bronze-sculpture/ Accessed 6/15/2020.

8 Collette Hemmingway, Heilbrunn Timeline of Art History Essays, "The Technique of Bronze Statuary in Ancient Greece," Department of Greek and Roman Art, The Metropolitan Museum of Art, October 2003. The Technique of Bronze Statuary in Ancient Greece | Essay | The Metropolitan Museum of Art | Heilbrunn Timeline of Art History (metmuseum.org). Accessed 12/28/2020.
Kunst and Ambiente, Manufactory for Bronze Sculpture and Statues, "Manufacturing of our Bronze Statues," Dresden, Manufacturing of our Bronze Statues – Art Bronze Sculptures (art-bronze-sculptures.com).

9 Title History of the Boadicea group [by T. Thornycroft] erected 1902 [on the Victoria embankment], Thomas Thornycroft, Compiled by L. Priddle, 1902.

10 For an excellent description and history of the lost wax method, see "The Bronze Casting Process, Lost Wax" Modern Arts website 2020–2021 Bronze Casting Process – lost wax – ModernArts (modernsculpture.com). Accessed 12/30/2020.

11 Elfrida Thornycroft, and Thomas Thornycroft. "Bronze and Steel. The Life of Thomas Thornycroft, Sculptor and Engineer, King's Stone Press, 1932.

12 For an excellent article about Mary Thornycroft's life work and relationship with her husband, see Penny McCracken. "Sculptor Mary Thornycroft and Her Artist Children." *Woman's Art Journal*, no 2 (Autumn, 1996–Winter 1997): 3–8. https://www.jstor.org/stable/1358460. Accessed 12/29/2020.

13 "Mapping the Practice and Profession of Sculpture in Britain and Ireland 1851–1891." Alice Thornycroft – Mapping the Practice and Profession of Sculpture in Britain and Ireland 1851–1951 (gla.ac.uk). Accessed 5/11/2022.

14 Ibid. p. 6. Also see David Thistlewood. "Social Significance in British Art Education 1850–1950." *Journal of Aesthetic Education* 20, no. 1 (1986): 71–83. https://doi.org/10.2307/3332313.

15 Ibid. p. 7.

16 Royal Collection Trust Collection Mary Thornycroft (1809–95), Mary Thornycroft (1809–95) – Albert Edward (1841–1910), Prince of Wales, as Winter (rct.uk).
Debra N. Mancoff. *Woman's Art Journal* 11, no. 1 (1990): 42–45. https://doi.org/10.2307/1358388.

17 Mary Thornycroft. "Twenty-nine Related Objects." The British Museum, Mary Thornycroft | British Museum.

18 The Victorian Web, "Thomas Thornycroft (1815–1885)," Thomas Thornycroft (1815–1885) (victorianweb.org).

Stylized Public Sculpture **69**

19 Sotheby's Website. https://www.sothebys.com/en/buy/auction/2020/european-art-paintings-sculpture/thomas-thornycroft-young-queen-victoria-on. Accessed 6/15/2020.
20 "Thomas Thornycroft, 1815–1885, British, Queen Victoria on Horseback, 1853." Yale Center for British Art, Queen Victoria on Horseback – YCBA Collections Search (yale.edu).
21 Anonymous, "Official descriptive and illustrated catalogue/Great Exhibition of the Works of Industry of All Nations, 1851; by authority of the Royal Commission," Spicer Brothers, London, UK, 1851, Smithsonian Libraries and Archives Digital Library https://archive.org/details/officialdescrip1grea.
22 Ed King. "The Crystal Palace and Great Exhibition of 1851." British Library Newspapers. Detroit: Gale, 2007.
23 Martha Vandrei. "A great deal of historical claptrap: Heroine of Empire," *Queen Boudica and Historical Culture in Britain: An Image of Truth*, The Past and Present Book Series (Oxford, 2018; online edn, Oxford Academic, 19 July 2018). https://doi.org/10.1093/oso/9780198816720.003.0006. Accessed 12/27/2023.
24 A list of Marochetti's works can be located Baron Carlo (Charles) Marochetti (1805–1867) (victorianweb.org).
   Philip Ward-Jackson. "Expiatory Monuments by Carlo Marochetti in Dorset and the Isle of Wight." *Journal of the Warburg and Courtauld Institutes* 53 (1990): 266–80. https://doi.org/10.2307/751351.
25 The Victorian Web, 15 February 2020 "Queen Victoria, Glasgow," by Baron Marochetti (victorianweb.org) quoting Ray McKenzie. *Public Sculpture of Glasgow*. Liverpool: Liverpool University Press, 2002, and Benedict Read, *Victorian Sculpture*. New Haven & London: Yale University Press, 1982.
26 Quote from Bob Speel. "Sculpture in Queen Square, Wolverhampton," Sculpture in Queen Square, Wolverhampton – Bob Speel's Website. Accessed 3/24/2022.
27 Royal Collection Trust, "Baron Carlo Marochetti (1805–67)-Prince Albert 1849," Baron Carlo Marochetti (1805–67) – Prince Albert (rct.uk).
28 Henry Moore Institute, "Papers of the Thornycroft Family, 1824–1978," 1986.4–1986.4 Collection – 41 boxes Henry Moore Institute Archive – Search Results (henry-moore.org) & Papers of the Thornycroft Family – Archives Hub (jisc. ac.uk).
   Andrea Garrihy. "Falling heads, raised arms and missing persons: Thornycroft Studio Practice." *Sculpture Journal* 15, no. 1 (June 2006) Gale Academic Onefile, Falling heads, raised arms and missing persons: Thornycroft studio practice – Document – Gale Academic OneFile.
29 Martha Vandrei. "A Victorian Invention? Thomas Thornycroft's 'Boadicea Group' and the Idea of Historical Culture in Britain." *The Historical Journal* 57, no. 2 (June 2014): 485–508 (p. 496).
30 Ibid. p. 496.
31 Ibid.
32 Ibid.
33 Ibid. p. 497.
34 This section compiled using "Britain's First 'National Anthem Embraced Boudica and Druids," University of Exeter, September 18, 2018, September – Britain's first 'national' anthem embraced Boudica and druids – University of Exeter.
35 Nina Budabin McQuown. "'Britain-Gulf': *Bonduca* and the English Earth." *Restoration: Studies in English Literary Culture, 1660–1700* 40, no. 2 (2016): 23–42. https://www.jstor.org/stable/26419402.
36 Robert Gale Noyes. "Conventions of Song in Restoration Tragedy." *PMLA* 53, no. 1 (1938): 162–88. https://doi.org/10.2307/458410.

37 Stephen Conway. "War and National Identity in the Mid-Eighteenth-Century British Isles." *The English Historical Review* 116, no. 468 (2001): 863–93. http://www.jstor.org/stable/579195.

38 Opcit. Britain's First National Anthem.

39 Luminarium.org. "William Cowper Boadicea: An Ode written 1780, published 1782." William Cowper. "oadicea. An Ode." (luminarium.org). Accessed 3/25/2022.

40 See: Alfred Lord Tennyson, Boadicea, translation on poemhunter.com Boadicea Poem by Alfred Lord Tennyson – Poem Hunter. Accessed 12/30/2020.

41 "Boudica Poem by Alfred Lord Tennyson," Poem Hunter. Boadicea – Boadicea Poem by Alfred Lord Tennyson (poemhunter.com). Accessed 3/24/20220.

42 Graham Webster, *Boudica: The British Revolt against Rome AD 60* NY: Routledge, 1999.

43 "Poets and every conceivable type of writer, politician, public speaker, and artist took their cue from William Cowper's *Boadicea, an Ode*, and with the re-emergence of her name in the 1864 publication by Tennyson, fused Boudicca and Britannia into a benevolent maternal figure who had suffered and been martyred in the attempt to retain a national identity and now personified humane, idyllic imperialism."
Martha Vandrei. "Queen Boudica, A Life in Legend, A pagan queen, an unruly woman and a valiant warrior avenging her daughters: Coudica has lived a varied afterlife in British history. Why is the ancient queen of the Iceni such an enduring figure?" 18 Sep 2018 Queen Boudica, A Life in Legend | History Today.

44 Elanor M. Vannan. "The Queen of Propaganda: Boudica's Representation in Empire." *The Arbutus Review* 12, no. 1. https://doi.org/10.18357/tar121202120187

45 Rachel L. Chenault. "The Celtic Queen Boudica as a Historiographical Narrative." *The Gettsburg Historical Journal* 19, no. 6 (September 2020). The Celtic Queen Boudica as a Historiographical Narrative (gettysburg.edu).

46 The British War Chariot quoted as being from *Gallic War, IV.33.* https://penelope.uchicago.edu/~grout/encyclopaedia_romana/britannia/boudica/chariot.html. Accessed 6/16/2020.

47 Ibid. p. 497.

48 Martha Vandrei. "A Victorian Invention? Thomas Thornycroft's 'Boadicea Group' And The Idea Of Historical Culture In Britain." *The Historical Journal* 57, no. 2 (2014): 485–508. http://www.jstor.org/stable/24529056.

49 Ibid. p. 497.

50 "Casting the World, The Story of J. W. Singer & Sons, Frome," Rook Lane Arts trust project, National Lottery Heritage Fund, 2019. Casting the World – The Story of J. W. Singer & Sons, Frome (rooklanearts.org.uk).

51 *The Gods and Goddesses of Ancient Rome | National ...*, https://www.national-geographic.org/article/gods-and-goddesses-ancient-rome/.

52 01: Caledones 02: Taexali 03: Carvetii 04: Venicones 05: Epidii 06: Damnonii 07: Novantae 08: Selgovae 09: Votadini 10: Brigantes 11: Parisi 12: Cornovii 13: Deceangli 14: Ordovices 15: Corieltauvi 16: Iceni 17: Demetae 18: Catuvellauni 19: Silures 20: Dubunni 21: Dumnonii 22: Durotriges 23: Belgae 24: Atrebates 25: Regni 26: Cantiaci 27: Trinovantes.

53 "Ancient History in Depth: Native Tribes of Britain, BBC BBC – History – Ancient History in depth: Native Tribes of Britain, 2014. Accessed 9/13/2023.

54 Most of the rhetoric in this section is paraphrased from two sources. The Annals of Tacitus, published in Vol 5 of the Loeb classical library edition of Tacitus, 1937. Tacitus Annals, Book XIV pp. 153–73. LacusCurtius • Tacitus, Annals – Book XIV Chapters 29-39 (uchicago.edu). Accessed 1/1/2021.

Cassius Dio's work was published between 211–233 AD, and Tacitus wrote *Histories* sometime around 116 AD, five decades after Boudica's ultimate battle against the Romans on Wattling Road. His rendition of the Iceni revolt came from versions told by Agricola, his father-in-law, who was a Roman Italo-Gallic general who led military troops during much of the Roman conquest of Great Britain and served under Governor General Gaius Suetonius Paulinus. Due to the intimacy of the familial connections of a key general and the fact that Tacitus's writings occur closer to the timeframe of the Briton revolt, his story may be considered a more probable truth-telling of the situation. Cassius was a Roman politician holding several political offices, spoke Greek and Latin, and his father was a prominent senator, counsel, and governor. Cassius rarely cited his sources and is believed to have borrowed from the works of the Greek historian Thucydides and relied on his personal experience rather than historical accuracy, literature, and public documents to formulate his prose. Descriptions are criticized for errors and distortions, but he claimed to have read everything about the Romans available in his lifetime.

Reproduction of Roman History published by Cassius Dio published in volume VIII of the Loeb Classical Library edition, 1925. Epitome of Book 62, LXII, various pages 61–171. Cassius Dio – Epitome of Book 62 (uchicago.edu). Accessed 1/1/2021.

55 Earnest Cary (translator). *Dio's Roan History on the Basis of the Version of Herbert Baldwin Foster, In Nine Volumes*. London William Heinemann 1925. Dio's Roman history, with an English translation by Earnest Cary, PH.D., on the basis of the version of Herbert Baldwin Foster, PH.D. In nine volumes (archive.org).

56 Jessalynn Bird, Brittany Blagburn, and Marirose Osborne (eds). Adapted from the translation of Tacitus, *Annals*, bk. 14, posted by Bill Thayer at https://penelope. uchicago.edu/Thayer...nals/14b*.html.

57 Cassius Dio, Epitome of Book LXII, Loeb Classic Library, DIO CASSIUS, Roman History | Loeb Classical Library (loebclassics.com).Accessed 3/24/2022.

58 Boudica (Boudicca), Roman Britain from Caesar's expedition in 55 BC to the advent of the Saxons in AD 449. Encyclopedia Romana, University of Chicago, n.d. Boudica (uchicago.edu).

59 Caitlin C. Gillespie. 'Introduction', *Boudica: Warrior Woman of Roman Britain*, Women in Antiquity (New York, 2018; online edn, Oxford Academic, 21 June 2018). https://doi.org/10.1093/oso/9780190609078.003.0001. Accessed 12/27/2023.

60 Lindsay Moynihan. "Gender in Celtic Britain: Boudicca's Uprising through the Eyes of Tacitus and Dio." *Janus* (October 25, 2021). Gender in Celtic Britain: Boudicca's Uprising through the Eyes of Tacitus and Dio (umdjanus.com).

61 "The Revolt of Boudica According to Cassius Dio," Classics and Ancient History Warwick Classics Network, The Revolt of Boudica according to Cassius Dio (warwick.ac.uk).

62 John C. Overbeck. "Tacitus and Dio on Boudicca's Rebellion." *The American Journal of Philology* 90, no. 2 (1969): 129–45. https://doi.org/10.2307/293422.

   L. A. du Toit. "Tacitus and The Rebellion of Boudicca." *Acta Classica* 20 (1977): 149–58. http://www.jstor.org/stable/24591531.

63 Opcit. Cassius Dio.

64 Ibid.

65 Ibid.

66 Nitocris was mentioned in Herodotus's (*Histories* ii–100), which may be the source for Cassius' inclusion. Austrian-British scholar Gwendolyn Leick said, "This woman achieved remarkable fame and power in her lifetime and beyond.

72 Women and War

According to contemporary records, she had considerable influence at the Assyrian court."

67 Animism was inherent to the British culture. They believed dogs were keen-scented, good at hunting, guarding, and healing, and the fox was wise and cunning and knew the forest better than anyone else.

68 Op cit. Cassius.

69 "The Revolt of Boudica According to Tacitus," Classics and Ancient History Warwick Classics Network, The Revolt of Boudica according to Tacitus (warwick.ac.uk).

70 Ibid.

71 "The Revolt of Boudica According to Cassius Dio," Book LXII, Text from the Loeb edition translated by J. Jackson and accessed via Lacus Curtius. Warwick Classics and Ancient History Warwick Classics Network, The Revolt of Boudica according to Cassius Dio (warwick.ac.uk). Accessed 12/28/2021.

72 Ibid.

73 Cassius, as did Tacitus, noted a significant reason for the carnage of the Britons was their wagon train full of animals and family members placed on a hillock behind their line of battle. As the druids attempted a retreat, the wagon train became a death wall, blocking any means of an exit.

74 Scott Wood. "Is Boudica Buried in London?" The Londonist blog. Is Boudica Buried In London? | Londonist n.d.

Additional Resources

Elfida Thornycroft. *Bronze, and Steel: The Life of Thomas Thornycroft Sculptor and Engineer*, South Yorkshire, UK: Trefoil Books, reprinted 1982.

Publius Cornelius Tacitus. *Tribes of Ancient Britain, and Germany*. (Ed) Bob Carruthers, Barnsley: Pen and Sword Books, 2013.

Richard Hingley and Christina Unwin. *Boudica: Iron Age Warrior Queen*, London: Hambledon Continuum; New edition, August 21, 2006.

Questions

How much should ancient writings be trusted? What is their value to the historical narrative?

What is the Iron Age? What is remarkable about this period in history? Who were the other Iron Age female military leaders? What insights do artifacts such as torcs give about how people lived in the past?

Could Boudica and her troops be considered military insurgents? What strengths did the Iceni bring to the fight? What were their primary weaknesses?

What other examples of female war and combat statuary are stylized and iconic rather than accurate relative to the people or era they represent?

Modern take

How does knowledge about Boudicca's ability to fight and lead in lethal combat change the 21st-century viewpoint that women do not have the physical or mental capabilities to be front-line combatants?

What legacy does the story of Boudica leave for 21st-century women's rights and dignity?

What forms of brutality are still occurring against women worldwide in combat zones?

What recent International Criminal Courts have tried and convicted countries for using rape as a weapon of war? What amendments have been created by the United Nations and Geneva Conventions regarding the use of sexual violence in war?

Activities and discovery

Read Tennyson's poem, Boudicca. *Do you believe his poem is a positive or negative statement about the Queen?*

Interview an artist who specializes in sculpting. What methods do they employ? What themes or subjects interest them?

Watch Warrior Queen, *Bill Anderson III Director, PBS Studios, ASIN: B00009MEKC January 6, 2004, 1:30. What was lacking in Boudica's strategy? What inferences had she made about the enemy? How does this glamorized version differ from the reality of the Queen's environment?*

Review the Journals of a Time Traveler website "The Iceni, their land, their people – Iron Age Britain," The Iceni, their land, their people – Iron Age Britain – Journals of a Time Traveler (posthaven.com). What stories do the wearable and other artifacts tell about Boudicca's society?

4
STONE ENGRAVING

Order of the Hatchet: The Feminine Cavaliers of the Torch of Tortosa

FIGURE 4.1 Stone carving the emblem of the Order of the Hatchet.
© Released by originator worldwide File: TortosaOrdeAtxa.JPG – Wikipedia

DOI: 10.4324/9781003406372-5

Stone carving

Stone carving and sculpting are the oldest known forms of artistic expression. These ancient artifacts, in the form of cave drawings and hand-carved wall art using simple tools, ingeniously used naturally formed rock as a canvas. Dating to prehistory, Stone Age art is divided into three periods known as the Paleolithic, Mesolithic, and Neolithic periods, covering the years from 30,000 BC to 3000 BC, each era requiring a unique form of decoding to determine if the art was a form of creativity or an essay about daily or seasonal events. Petroglyphs, figurines, pictographs, and stone arrangements, known as megalithic art, served ritual, religious, or symbolic functions.[1] There were also stone-carved beads used as personal adornments. During the Holy Roman Empire, stone sculpture became popular for leaving a permanent legacy of people in portrait busts, as memorials to historical and mythological events on building reliefs, and as decorative motifs on religious structures.

A high point was reached in stone carving's popularity during the Romanesque art period of 1000–1300 AD.[2] In Spain, the trend reached its zenith in the cities of Leon, Madrid, and Santiago de Compostela. One of the more admired examples of Spanish stone-carved edifices from the Romanesque period is the Benedictine monastery Abbey of Santo Domingo de Silos, located in the northern portion of the country. Intricate, colorfully painted limestone sculptures of religious events formed part of the pillars of the Benedictine monastery.[3] Many stone-carved scenes and relief panels were entwined within the internal and external components of the edifice. In the lower cloister on each side of a capital pillar were carved female figures, half human, half bird. Referred to as sirens, these beings were believed to be life-threatening temptresses. Other carved forms were dragons, centaurs, and mermaids. Saint Bernard of Vlairvaux, cofounder of the Knights Templar remarked the carvings were so plentiful and of such astonishing variety that "one would rather read in the marble than in books and spend the whole day wondering at every single one of them than in the mediating on the law of God."[4]

Gothic-style masonry emerged in Spain and flourished through nine stylizations from the 12th to the 15th centuries.[5] Primary locales of stonework are found in religious buildings. One architectural illustration from this period is the Cathedral of St. Mary of Tortosa in Catalonia, Spain, an outstanding example of Catalan Gothic architecture.[6] Its Chapel of Our Lady of the Ribbon has a shrine constructed with pink jasper from Tortosa and imported fine marble. There are many stone archways, quatrefoil columns, carved stones, and panels throughout the basilica-shaped building, arranged around three naves and lateral chapels.[7]

Close by in the surrounding hillsides are a large group of cave paintings, some of which are of high technical quality, picturing naturalistic deer, archers, and goats.[8]

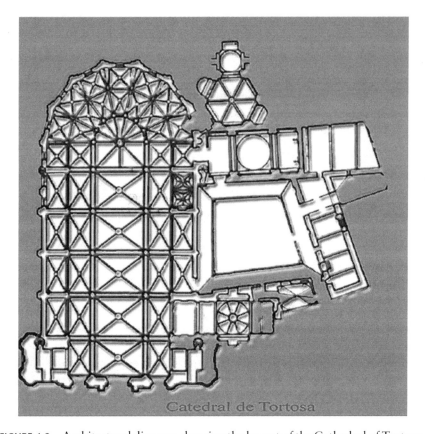

FIGURE 4.2 Architectural diagram showing the layout of the Cathedral of Tortosa.

© GNU Free Documentation License, Version 1.2 Attribution-Share Alike 4.0 International, 3.0 Unported, 2.5 Generic, 2.0 Generic and 1.0 Generic license File: Catedral tortosa224.jpg – Wikipedia

The rock engraving of The Order of the Hatchet of the Feminine Cavaliers of the Torch of Tortosa is embedded in a low wall within the cathedral's cloister, where monks would have performed daily exercises, studied, and meditated.[9] The carving was not created until sometime in the 1300s, two centuries after the occurrence of the event it honors. The town of Tortosa lies to the northeast near the Ebro River and was occupied by the Moors in 714 until Roman Catholic Ramon Berenguer IV, Count of Barcelona, led the military blockades of Lisbon and Tortosa in 1148 to extricate the invaders. The river was strategically vital as it flowed for nearly 600 miles in a southeasterly direction, culminating on the Mediterranean coast midway between Barcelona and Valencia. Quarries were readily available near the city surrounded by the Cardo Massif mountains for access to carving and building materials and had existed along the eastern coast of Spain off the Mediterranean and

Balearic Seas since Roman expansionism.[10] In the area where the Cathedral sits, various rock types would have been available, including the blue-silver granite found to the north and lighter-colored limestones and sandstones to the south and central regions.[11]

Stone is a brittle surface requiring much resistance to human intervention to change its shape and is available in different tones and consistencies. Before the discovery of metal tools, stone carving was accomplished using an abrasive technique.[12] Hard stones like carbonite were rubbed against softer limestone and granite, with water used to carry away debris. With the coming of the Bronze and Iron Ages, the evolution of metal carving tools allowed for more intricate artistic stone renderings and making art for art's sake. Compared to abrasion, this more formalized carving took physical strength, a steady hand, and talent in chisel cutting.[13]

Hammers of different weights, mallets, sharpeners, rasps, pointed, round-ended, toothed, and splitting chisels were designed specifically for stone artisans to create more elaborate interpretations of humans, animals, historical scenes, and mythological stories. New research has uncovered that women worked alongside men on construction sites as day laborers, assisting bricklayers and stone masons.[14] In the 1300s, they dug trenches for a city wall in the town of Seville and, in Toledo, and were hired to gather lime and work on roofs. "Tax records from Paris during the years 1296-1313 reveal the existence of two female masons, a tiler and a plasterer."[15] In her publication, *The Treasury of the City of Ladies*, Christine de Pizan, a 15th-century French writer, stated that craftswomen should learn all the managerial skills to oversee the running of shops and supervise employees when their husbands were afield or not paying attention.[16]

Masons and imagers completed the engravings. The craft of carving and etching eventually became so popular, marketable, and desirable that apprenticeships for master artisans were formed within schools and guilds, which served as training facilities and ensured professional networking, patronage, and salaries for those selected as members. To graduate with the title of expert craftsman, the students had to execute original work highlighting their talents. Stone artisans in this period rarely left their signatures on their work, nor were they recorded in historical documents. [17] Therefore, it is unsurprising that no formal references exist for those who may have carved the *Order of the Hatchet*.

In Spain, where the stone carving honoring the female cavaliers is found, the work of artisans was overseen by mason's federations. Initially, these were religiously based but eventually expanded to become business entities that protected the quality of work and instituted fee schedules for creating stone sculptures or etchings. Spain had guilds in Barcelona, Catalan, Valencia, and the Crown of Castile.[18] The style of the stone cutting used in the Order of the Hatchet is simple, neat, and clean. It is a flat carving outlined

78 Women and War

with a sharp implement, and the background was cut away to leave a slightly elevated image. Its character represents a decorative remembrance stone of humble embellishment in flat relief.[19] Since the rendition of the hatchet is not amateurish, it may have been that the church paid for an artisan to carve it. Perhaps one of the cathedral's monks or other religious members was assigned the duty, but this is only a supposition.

The women of Catalonia

It is obsolete to think that medieval times confined women's lives to homes, convents, and palaces.[20] While society was patriarchic, this fact did not wholly disavow women's freedoms. Examples of women who occupied roles in warfare between the 12th and 15th centuries were pretty widespread.[21] So much so that many must have had a form of customary military schooling, but it is atypical to find sources from the period detailing their involvement. Reasons for their exclusion are that the role was considered unfeminine even though their participation was frequently required due to the nature of crusading and the recurrent plays for land and resources that resulted in confrontation. Also suggested is a theme that a woman fighting reflected severely on the roles men were expected to play, so writing about their feats was an embarrassment.[22]

Crusader castles of the 12th century were built to preserve the internal order of those who served as part of the owner's fiefdom and provided a martial and police function.[23] They were no less important in politics than in administration. Castle life centered around domestic and military activity. Physically, the buildings served as a form of extravagant power. They were under constant reconstruction to provide the best possible defense against long-term and advanced threats. Knights would have used certain areas to practice their combat skills. Existence for the women would have been cold, cramped, lacking in privacy, and smelly from poor hygiene and waste systems. Female family members and vassals managed staff, the procurement of supplies, and logistics. They were given specific jobs, including spinning wool, making clothes, doing laundry, cooking, tending children, acting as teachers, and sewing. Taking immediate charge of men's affairs was expected during absences. This meant women made decisions about war and political matters.[24]

Women could follow a specific trade, teach, or become merchants. Many could ride and hunt, and they supervised the provisioning of the property and household. They could record a will and name heirs, but notations were required that male relatives had been present during the transaction. Three main classes existed: peasantry, middle classes associated with landowners and merchants, and a third tiny percentage were tied to royal domiciles. Peasant classes paid dues with wheat, wine, pork, fowl, or grain. Servitude charters could be issued to both sexes and sold with land when bought by other family circles. Exemptions could be made in specific cases. Within the middle classes, there were women active in weaver's leagues. Some directed mass in monasteries and sang funeral chants for payment. Selected women in the upper classes completed their educations, usually through private home tutoring or auditing a male sibling's lessons. At times, noblewomen became involved in political life.[25]

After Raymond Berengar succeeded in the siege of Tortosa, he allowed the Muslims and Jews to remain and granted a franchise and extensive rights to the Jewish population. He confined the Muslims to a particular quarter outside the walls of the central city, and they were given a year's reprieve to surrender their metropolitan property. In 1391, across Spain, forced conversions of the Jewish community to Christianity came into effect under the threat of death. In March 1492, King Ferdinand and Queen Isabella signed the Alhambra Decree, which banished all Jews from Spain. There was intermarrying between ethnic groups; in various regions, it was uncommon for widows to remarry if a dowry was passed down through male lines. Arab women were legally forbidden to marry Christian men but could be drawn into slavery and harems.[26]

Since the time of Troy, women have participated in siege warfare in offensive and defensive roles. Historical records show them as clever, valiant, and politically and martially inclined. Others engineered the design and building of castles. Generally, stories of sieges in Europe where women were involved were within families with a queen or queen regent whose responsibility was to take on military obligations and the oversight for their realms when their husbands or male relatives left for extended periods to fight or conduct business. If besieged, an offer might arise to the females to surrender and give safe conduct away from the property. However, this could mean imprisonment, physical abuse, and ransom. Women preferred to fight or hold out if they had secured enough stores of food and weaponry.[27] Tactics used to fend off the assailants were to pour boiling oil or water on them from the castle walls or throw rocks or other projectiles. They had little control over disease and weather, two primary detriments in their siege survivability. Ramon Berengar IV, left a multifaced population of women within the city when he returned to the field to fight during the Crusades, which mirrored the diversity of his troops. Among those who had joined with him were Genoese army personnel, Catalan knights, Hospitallers, Knights of the Holy Sepulcher, Knights Templar, Englishmen, Flemings, Normans, the army of the Aragonese from the Pyrenees valleys, and the Occitans of southern France.[28]

Stories of women on the European continent involved in sieges have been passed on through historical records and folktales.

From these accounts, assumptions may be made regarding their overall roles in this arena. There is evidence that women from the lower strata

FIGURE 4.3 Illuminated manuscript of women participating in a castle siege.

© Creative Commons Attribution-Share Alike 4.0 International license. https://commons.wikimedia.org/wiki/File:Seige.jpg

of society, not just the royal classes, engaged in warfare. No matter their social standing, they all shot, hacked, and chopped away at their enemies, were effective in fighting, and were trained in swordsmanship. One of the more humorous legends, not proven and recounted with variations, comes from Saxony in Weissenberg, Germany, when Weibertreue Castle was besieged in 1140 by Emperor Conrad III, King of Italy, and Germany during the Second Crusades.[29] Frustrated by a standstill in his efforts to overtake the edifice, Conrad vowed to kill all the men within by sword but agreed to spare the women's lives if they relented. Conrad allowed the women to carry their most valued treasure from the castle. The offer was accepted, and each woman marched out with their husband on their shoulders. The belligerent, so moved by the scene, spared the lives of everyone and set the city free. A storyline of a similar character resides in a translation of a 16th-century work by entertainer and social critic Martin Montanus. Margaret of Beverley, who traveled to the Holy Land in the 1180s and 1190s, is described by her brother, Thomas of Froidmont, in the tale of her exploits entitled *Hodoeporicon et Percale Margariet Iherosolimitane*.[30]

She helped defend Jerusalem during an attack by throwing stones from the wall and wearing a cooking pot for a helmet.[31] Another account from the 13th century relates that Dame Nicola de Lay Haye, who served as Sheriff of Lincoln Castle in Great Britain during the nation's civil war, was considered instrumental in offsetting the city's siege in 1217 led by France's Prince Louis.[32]

In the 1090s, Isabel of Conches, who is recorded in Orderic Vitalis' *Historia Ecclesiastica* circa 1075–1142, recites that "when her vassals took to war, (she) rode armed as a knight among the knights (and) showed no less courage among the cavakuers in hauberks (a coat of mail) and sergeants-at-arms than did the maid Camilla, a character in the *Aeneid*, the pride of Italy among the troops of Tunis."[33] Portrayed as a Roman queen of the Volsci, Vitalis claims that Camilla deserved to be compared to Hippolyta, Penthesilea, and other warlike queens.[34] Anna Comnena, princess and authoress of the *Alexiad*, wrote a historiography of the political and military archives of the Byzantine Empire during the reign of her father.[35] She describes the Crusades and includes the tale of Norman conqueror and adventurer Robert Guiscard's wife, Sichelgaita, who frequently accompanied her husband into military contests and campaigned alone. Sichelgaita led the 50-day siege of Trani in 1080 with the support of Barian troops. She studied medicine, stood six feet tall, and was an expert with a sword and fighting from the back of a horse.

Women could not be granted the title of Knight, but many chivalric orders admitted women who performed a significant role in protecting a homeland or castle.[36] Documented stories, usually from the upper strata of society, tell of them donning armor and directing troop movements during a war. Knights Templar Rules of 1129 note a mandate that allowed women admission to their order, and in the first decade of its existence, 1118–1128, the group permitted women's involvement in their organization. The Teutonic Order, a Catholic military society, accepted women as lay associates or membership in semireligious consortiums but were limited to performing menial and hospitaller functions.[37] At the Hospital of Saint John of Jerusalem, lay sisters served as hospital attendants and acted as devotional liturgists and as commanders. By the end of the 12th century, the Order of Saint John segregated the men from the women and moved them into female-only facilities.[38]

One of the first recorded among the hospitaller women was Adelaide, who became a member of the Hospitallers of Saint-Gilles and Trinquetaille in 1146.[39] In exchange for all her belongings, which were recorded as houses in the City of Arles in France, a plot of land, and usage of certain vessels, she was made a *soror* (sorority sister) and traveled East to the Hospital of Saint John of Jerusalem. Overall, women in the Latin East had a more remarkable ability to take on what were considered male roles than their noted contemporaries from Germany and England during the 12th century. This changed when a patriarchal attitude resurfaced toward them within Outremer, a

82 Women and War

region of Crusader states formed along the coast of the eastern Mediterranean Sea, including Jerusalem, Tripoli, Antioch, and Edessa, in the 13th century.[40]

Cavaliers and knights

To be a cavalier is to be associated with knights and chivalry, and its meaning denotes a person who may be skilled in horsemanship, fighting, and other military acts. Knights formed as fighting groups in Europe around the 9th century AD and had direct ties to the economic growth of cities and the increased desire to become land barons. Such valuable forms of wealth needed to be safeguarded from marauders. Landowners and merchants with many resources hired armed cavalry to protect their possessions. Wealthy patrons monopolized the best of the defenders, and knights received honorary gifts of property for their work. During the 9th through the 13th centuries, many knights amassed financial and physical resources, with the majority having personal or hereditary connections to nobility.[41] Count Ramon Berenguer IV aided landowners in conquering Nice from Genoa. His mother, Douce I, Countess of Provence, inherited lands that covered a third of southern France through her mother. Because of their social status and net worth, knights like Berenguer could fund the production of better weapons and armor and raise high-quality livestock used in battle. The usefulness of this hired military ended in the 1400s with the advent of organized armies and navies and technological advances in armaments, particularly with the development of guns.[42]

Knighthood was derived in one of two ways: a man could own their lands under a "knight's fee," or they were inducted into an order by those with economic and regional powers. A knight's fee was based on the size of a fiefdom with a value determined by the amount of healthy soil, forests for game and water, and whether the property contained quarries. It was mandatory to own enough land to support a knight's family, servants, and their esquires who served as knights' apprentices. Kings could gift areas directly to a knight or secondarily through a tenancy with the requirement that the occupiers were able to produce soldiers for the king's armies. For knights to maintain their status, they were to act dignified, live in a suitable but not flashy style, and maintain enough armor, horses, and other accouterments sufficient for the number of esquires under their care. There was an expectation for military service of at least 40 days out of a year, with these activities being equal to tax payments.[43]

A second means of becoming a knight was through a ceremony of induction received as praise, an accolade, or an honorarium from royalty for contests fought and won. In the Middle Ages, with the influx of Christian teachings and beliefs, becoming a knight involved an all-night vigil of self-reflection, a bath to wash away sins, a mass, and a sermon with a girding ceremony afterward. Other traditions were simple, with an embrace around the neck, gifting a gilt shoulder belt, or receiving a kiss on the left cheek or a bare-fisted box to the ear.

Codes of chivalry were to be followed by all knights and arose for two primary reasons: to keep with them in check socially and to set ground rules for military violence. Chivalrous codes were popularized in a literary record written in 1155 by the Norman poet Robert Wace in *Roman de Brut*, in which there is a good deal of information concerning the legendary King Arthur and an early reference known to Arthur's Round Table. Knights were to follow moral codes of chivalry to temper their warrior focus and fierceness. Honor, honesty, valor, loyalty, and gallantry toward all women were vital to knightly conduct. All knights were to be seated in a rounded circle so that no single member could be considered as having a position of authority while convening.[44]

> The fellowship of the Round Table was likened to the medieval military orders of the Knights Hospitallers (1113) and Knights Templar (1119), founded in the First Crusade. Each order had its own set of rules or customs, such as what color or device they could have on their shields, banners, and surcoat's outer layers of their clothes on which insignia were sewn.[45]

Elias Ashmole and The Most Nobel Order of the Garter

Elias Ashmole authored a voluminous book for Charles II, King of Great Britain and Ireland, which traced the lineage of chivalry through the 17th century. The book's title was as long as its content: *The Institution, Laws, and Ceremonies of the Most Noble Order of the Garter, Collected and Digested into One Body*.[46] The completed document was 1000 pages long and broken into 26 chapters with 189 tabs. There were descriptions of first founders and knight's companions and their successors and a variety of discussions about grand feasts, offerings for chivalrous acts in the forms of gold and silver, ceremonial orders, commissions, investitures, and many other programmatic and rules-based elements of knighthood.

Ashmole studied astrology and alchemy and was also a Freemason. Still, He was best recognized as a lover of antiquities and received an official appointment by Charles II to become the king's conservator and interpreter of genealogy and heraldic records.[47] The King wrote a forward to the book, noting that his "keeper of history" had spent 15 years putting the information together, including adornments of sculptures. His Highness expressed his "good liking" for the final product. Within this vast account of heraldry is a description of the institution, laws, and ceremony of the female order,

84 Women and War

the Most Noble Order of the Garter. A notable exception to the many men documented in the book is a passage in which Ashmole mentions Amazonians and female heroism.

> …in the close of our discourse of the Orders of Knighthood, give us leave to bring up the rear, with a memorial relating to feminine valor and of the later age (for we shall not need to instance in the Amazons of old, whose fame in arms is generally known) since some of that sex, having acquired honor and renown, by their personal courage and valiant exploits; have had bestowed on them the privilege of living after the manner and in the esteem of knights.[48]

Ashmole used as a reference to this explanation the priest and natural historian of Sicily, Joseph Micheli Marquez's *Nobel Women of Tortosa in Aragon*, which appears in his 1642 Spanish language book, *La Orden Militar Espadaa* (The Military Order of Swords). In Marquez's version, the female knights, who are also referenced as *cavalleras* and *equitissae* (horsewomen) "on hearing that the idea was being entertained on making a surrender which the women hearing of, to prevent the disaster threatening their City, themselves, and children, put on men's clothes and by a resolute sally forced the moors to raise the siege."[49] Their actions were seen as not extraordinary in this specific case as the women had been fighting for their realm off and on for a year during the Second Crusade, participating as required after Ramon Berenguer IV had left the region temporarily to fulfill military obligations that eventually led to the formation of the Crown of Aragon. The women, coming behind the retreat of Berenguer's crusaders and without fighting forces available to them, faced the Moorish army head-on as they attempted to barricade the city.

The women were a mixed population of Iberians, Muslims, and Jews who fended off the invaders using axes, stones, liquids, and all other weapons they could lay their hands upon. Other potential ammunition prevalent at the time were prisoners, manure, dead animals, and rotten corpses.[50] The credibility of these women's role in defending their homeland can be found in various European illuminated texts located in the timespan of 1000–1400.[51] Their award was described by Ashmole.

> The Earl (Berenguer) finding himself obliged, by the gallantry of the action, thought it to make his acknowledgments thereof, by granting them several privileges and immunities and to perpetuate the memory of so single an attempt, instituted an order somewhat like a military order into which were admitted only those brave women deriving the honor to their descendants and assigned them for a badge, a thing like a friars *capouche* (a long pointed hood) sharp at the top, after the form of a torch and of a crimson color to be worn upon their head clothes.[52]

In addition to the clothing, Berenguer "ordained that during all public meetings, the women should have precedence of the men," be exempted from all taxes, and their apparel and jewels left by dead husbands would be owned by them. "These women, having thus acquired this honor by their personal valor, carried themselves after the manner of military knights of those days."[53]

Sieges of Almira and Tortosa

Genoese admiral, statesman, chronicler, and diplomat Caffaro di Rustico da Caschifellone left behind papers recounting events of the First Crusade and descriptions of 12th-century Genoa where Berenguer's exploits during the Second Crusade are explained.[54] In this writing, the Count's deeds began when the Christians were captured by the Saracen peoples of Arabia, Turkey, and those who followed the religion of Islam.[55] Having been killed, imprisoned, tormented, and punished, the Christians abandoned the law of the council of government of the Muslims. They vowed to avenge what they adjudged to be the diabolical name of Muhamad. Through the eyes of Caffaro, what was purported to have occurred was an "advisement and summoning by God" through the Apostolic See in Rome. A religious parliament held six consuls, and eight "better sort of men" sat with four more men from Genoa, who had "impressive character, behavior, eloquence, sense, and leadership." These ten members ordered everyone to swear to observe peace, after which the "Holy Spirit prompted them to kiss each other in acceptance" and "both men and women rejoiced in the sight."[56]

A unanimous vote among the consul resulted in the creation of a fund for an army and the making of provisions for a military expedition to include "many weapons, fine tents, beautiful and impressive banners, towers-castella, machines, enough food to avoid any want, and all sorts of devices to capture the city."[57] Five months passed before preparations were complete. Caffaro wrote, "No army as great, fine, and well equipped had been seen or heard of in the past 100 years." Sixty-three galleys and over one hundred other vessels were sent to attack the Saracens. Three military officials were assigned to make war, 400 knights rallied, and 1000 infantry joined. The Muslim opposition sent 40,000 armed men, of which more than 5000 were killed.[58]

Raymond Berenguer entered the scene of Caffaro's story of the Crusades with a great ship of soldiers and 53 mounted knights.[59] The Count encamped near the Lena River. Christian engineers and sappers were ordered to build siege engines and towers. Cats, which were protective screens made of wood and leather mounted on wheels, were put in place to capture projectiles of the Muslims on approach near the city ramparts. Mangonels, a military device for throwing stones, other missiles, and fire weapons, were added to the mix. Christians arranged themselves into 12 companies of 1000 men each. Within three hours, Almeria and its citadel were captured. Shield money, a payout

86 Women and War

given to participants for winning against the Saracens, was high enough that the Genoese Council retained 60,000 lire distributed communally among those who fought. The remainder of the money was divided between the men of the galleys and other ships. One thousand men were left to guard the city. The others departed and arrived in Barcelona "unharmed" and were met by its inhabitants "in glory and triumph."[60]

The navies wintered around the Catalonia region to regroup and prepare for the next fight, which was to occur in Tortosa, which had been chosen by the Moors as a frontier city of the Caliphate of Cordoba and turned into a Moorish capital. Caffaro describes the Christian preparation for hostilities. Wood was selected from the forests to build towers and machines. Envoys were sent to Genoa, Italy, to urge men to join. By July, they were ready, and the seafaring entourage entered the Ebro. Here, they held a parliament to select banner bearers and reconnoiter the situation to determine tactics.

It was decided by democratic agreement to station half of the Genoese's soldiers, counts, and knights below the city next to the river. Others pitched their tents above the town. English knights and many other foreigners stationed themselves near a mill on the river. One rogue group attempted to move forward to attack without permission of the hybrid parliament. Another counsel was hastily held, and the conveners probed the men's rashness at acting alone. This resulted in an ancillary agreement that all future movement would occur only through universally determined permissions. Two towers were erected, and heavy battle machines were moved near the city's bulwarks. Ravines on the upper side were filled with wood, stones, and earth to assist in moving equipment nearer the enclosures.

A contentious fight broke out among the diverse Christian war parties as they attempted to prepare for the onslaught.[61] Again, the council intervened, proclaiming all work be fulfilled with "knights, foot soldiers, rich and poor," and all to come together daily "and labor as one." Preparations continued, and a significant net of ropes intended to capture enemy projectiles was placed along two sections of the ravine. The Saracens replied to this movement of the Christians by hurling stones weighing 200 pounds at their besiegers, inflicting temporary damage to the Genoese tower. At this point in the story, Caffaro tells of all the Knights of Barcelona, who did not have the funds to stay and fight, dispersing from the area and leaving 20 of their group behind as a show of support.[62]

The engagement drug on for five months. Morale sunk during the stalemate, and more meetings were conducted to boost knightly esprit de corps, with the men swearing not to abandon the city and to fight the Muslim enemy "night and day more fiercely than was their Christian custom." Mangonels throwing stones and burning objects eventually penetrated the town. Terrified by the deadly peril of the catapults, the Muslims sent envoys to seek a truce of 40 days. They then handed over

100 Saracen fighters of rank as a means of barter to lessen the seriousness of their plight. An unconditional surrender finally occurred on the last day of December during the Vigil of St. Silvester to celebrate the pope's role in assisting martyred Christians during the reign of Roman Emperor Constantine.

Count Berenguer left Tortosa believing it was safely ensconced as a Christian domain. He continued his quest by battling and overcoming the Moors in Fraga, Lleida, and Mequinenza further along the Erbo and Segre Rivers. The Moors viewed Berenguer's exit as an opportunity to regroup and counterattack the city. Without any military means of backing them, the women in the town put up a fierce fight using war hatchets, stones, and any means of projectiles and defensible weapons they could secure. Stirred by their successful town defense, Count Berenguer bestowed upon them the chivalric Order of the Hatchet. Female soldiers had given their lives to the cause of reclaiming the Holy Land, and the Order recognized their piousness, mercifulness, generosity, bravery, and loyalty to their lord and companions.[63] Unlike many male orders passed from generation to generation, those women awarded the Order of the Hatchet do not seem to have been able to stake a hereditary line of honor to their female family members, and the Order completely disappears from local histrionics.

Notes

1 Simon Burns-Cox. "History of Stone Carving, in Creativity, Design, Development, Inspiration, Uncategorized," Blog. April 28, 2020, History of Stone Carving – Simon Burns-Cox (simonburnscox.co.uk). Accessed 1/4/2022.
2 J. D. Mc Guire. "On the Evolution of the Art of Working in Stone." *American Anthropologist* 6, no. 3 (1893): 307–20. http://www.jstor.org/stable/658313.
3 "The Deposition, Relief ca 1100," Victoria and Albert Museum, The Deposition | V&A Explore The Collections (vam.ac.uk).
4 As quoted from "Feminae: Medieval Women and Gender Index, Heraldic sirens on a capital," Feminae: Medieval Women and Gender Index, University of Iowa Libraries, 2014 Feminae: Details Page (uiowa.edu).
5 Frederick B. Deknatel. "The Thirteenth Century Gothic Sculpture of the Cathedrals of Burgos and Leon." *The Art Bulletin* 17, no. 3 (1935): 243–389. https://doi.org/10.2307/3045586.
6 Josep Lluís i Ginovart, and Agustí Costa Jover. "Design and Medieval Construction: The Case of Tortosa Cathedral (1345–1441)." *Construction History* 29, no. 1 (2014): 1–24. http://www.jstor.org/stable/43856060.
7 "The Cathedral and the Permanent Exhibition," Tortusa Turisme, n.d. The Cathedral and the permanent exhibition – tortosaturisme.
8 Laura Fernandez Macias. "Artsoudscapes in Catalonia: Exploring its Rock Art," September 14, 2020, Artsoundscapes in Catalonia: Exploring its rock art – Artsoundscapes (ub.edu).
9 Ibid. I. Ginovart.
10 Anna Gutiérrez M. Garcia. "The Exploitation of Local Stone in Roman Times: The Case of North-Eastern Spain." *World Archaeology* 43, no. 2 (2011): 318–41. http://www.jstor.org/stable/41308500. p. 320. Also see: J. Luis I. Ginovart,

A. Costa-Jover, S. Coll-la & R. Miralles-Jori. "Non-invasive techniques for the assessment of masonry structures: Experiences in the Pillars of a Gothic apse," *Structural Analysis of Historical Constructions-Anamnesis, Diagnosis, Therapy, Controls*, Van Balen and Verstrynge (eds), London: Taylor and Francis Group, 2016. p. 2

11 Anna Gutiérrez Garcia-M. "The Exploitation of Local Stone in Roman Times: The Case of North-Eastern Spain." *World Archaeology* 43, no. 2 (2011): 318–41. http://www.jstor.org/stable/41308500.

12 "The Stone Age, Prehistoric Art," Lumencandela, The Stone Age | Boundless Art History (lumenlearning.com). Accessed 1/4/2022.

13 Stone Sculpture History, Types, Materials, Techniques: Famous Stone Statues, Reliefs. Stone Sculpture: History, Types, Materials, Techniques (visual-arts-cork.com). Accessed 1/8/2021.

14 "Women Workers Could be Found on the Medieval Construction Site, Study Finds," Medievalists.net, 2024 Women workers could be found on the medieval construction site, study finds – Medievalists.net.

15 Ibid.

16 Ibid.

17 Ricardo Cordoba. "Guild Authorities in Late Medieval Spain." In *Craftsmen and Guilds in the Medieval and Early Modern Periods*, Eva Jullien and Michel Pauly (Eds), Franz Steiner Verlag, Stuttgart, 2006. pp. 77–92.

18 Opcit. Cordoba.

19 Julia De Wolf Addison. *Arts and Crafts in the Middle Ages: A Description of Mediaeval Workmanship in Several Departments of Applied Art, Together with Some Account of Special Artisans in the Early Renaissance* original publication date 1908. Release Date: April 19, 2006 [eBook #18212]. Project Gutenberg Ebook Arts and Crafts in the Middle Ages E-text prepared by Robert J. Hall & Chapuis, Julien. "Late Medieval German Sculpture: Materials and Techniques." In *Heilbrunn Timeline of Art History*. New York: The Metropolitan Museum of Art, 2000. http://www.metmuseum.org/toah/hd/grmn_2/hd_grmn_2.htm (October 2002).

20 "Women and the Crusades," Women and the Crusades (knighttemplar.org) OPCCTS – *The Knights Templar of North America*.

21 Sarah Ifft Decker. *The Fruit of Her Hands: Jewish and Christian Women's Work in Medieval Catalan Cities*. Penn State University Press, 2022. https://doi.org/10.5325/jj.5233100.

J. F. Verbruggen in Rogers, Clifford J., Kelly Devries, and John France (eds). *Journal of Medieval Military History* Vol. IV, no. 4. Boydell & Brewer, 2006. http://www.jstor.org/stable/10.7722/j.ctt81ntp.Chapter 8. "Women in Medieval Armies," (pp. 119–136). https://www.jstor.org/stable/10.7722/j.ctt81ntp.10.

22 Elizabeth den Hartog. "Defending the Castle Like a Man, On Belligerent Female Ladies." *Journal of Nobility Studies Virtus* Vol. 27 (2020), Creative Commons, University of Groningen Press. https://doi.org/10.21827/virtus.27.79-98.

23 R. C. Smail. "Crusaders' Castles of the Twelfth Century." *Cambridge Historical Journal* 10, no. 2 (1951): 133–49. http://www.jstor.org/stable/3021083.

24 Ibid. Smail.

25 Michelle Armstrong-Partida, Alexandra Guerson, and Dana Wessell Lightfoot (eds). *Women and Community in Medieval and Early Modern Iberia*. University of Nebraska Press, 2020. https://doi.org/10.2307/j.ctv10vkzqx.

26 Jonathan Ray. *The Sephardic Frontier: The "Reconquista" and the Jewish Community in Medieval Iberia*. First Ed. Cornell University Press, 2006. http://www.jstor.org/stable/10.7591/j.ctt7v6p8.

Thomas W. Barton. *Victory's Shadow: Conquest and Governance in Medieval Catalonia*. Cornell University Press, 2019. http://www.jstor.org/stable/10.7591/j.ctvfc54nx.

27 Ibid. Barton.
28 Barton C. Hacker. "Women and Military Institutions in Early Modern Europe: A Reconnaissance." *Signs* 6, no. 4 (1981): 643–71. http://www.jstor.org/stable/3173736.
29 "The Women of Weinsberg and other legends of Aarne-Thompson-Uther type 875 translated and/or edited by D. L. Ashliman," 2009–2011. The Women of Weinsberg (The Wives of Weinsberg): Folktales of Type 875* (pitt.edu).
30 Susan Signe Morrison. "Margaret of Beverley (c.1150–c.1214/15): Fighting Crusader." In *A Medieval Woman's Companion: Women's Lives in the European Middle Ages*, 74–82. Oxbow Books, 2016. https://doi.org/10.2307/j.ctvh1dnb3.13.
31 Ibid. Footnoted p. 91. Schmidt, '"Peregrinatio Periculosa" Thomas Von Froidmont über die Jerusalemfahrten seiner Schwester Margareta', in: U. J. Stache, W. Maaz, and F. Wagner (eds), Kontinuität und Wandel: Lateinische Poesie von Naevius bis Baudelaire. Franco Munari zum 65. Geburtstag (Hildesheim, 1986), 461–85.
32 Richard. 'The Matron's Tale: Nicola de la Haye and the Defence of England', *Tales from the Long Twelfth Century: The Rise and Fall of the Angevin Empire* (New Haven, CT, 2016; online edn, Yale Scholarship Online, 22 Sept. 2016), https://doi.org/10.12987/yale/9780300187250.003.0010. Accessed 12/27/2023.
33 Trudy Harrington Becker. "Ambiguity and the Female Warrior: Vergil's Camilla," University Libraries, ElAnt v4n1 – Ambiguity and the Female Warrior: Vergil's Camilla | Virginia Tech Scholarly Communication University Libraries (vt.edu).
34 Opcit. Footnoted. p. 79.
   Marjorie Chibnall. *The Ecclesiastical History of Orderic Vitalis, Vol. 2, Books III and IV*, Clarendon Press, 1991.
35 Paul Halsall. "Medieval Sourcebook: Anna Comnena: The Alexiad," Fordham University Sourcebooks, 20 Nov 2023 Internet History Sourcebooks: Medieval Sourcebook (fordham.edu).
36 Natasha R. Hodgson. "Women in the History of Crusading and the Latin East." In *Women, Crusading and the Holy Land in Historical Narrative*, 25:36–52. Boydell & Brewer, 2007. http://www.jstor.org/stable/10.7722/j.ctt81mst.11.
   Natasha R. Hodgson. "Conclusion." In *Women, Crusading and the Holy Land in Historical Narrative*, 25:236–45. Boydell & Brewer, 2007. http://www.jstor.org/stable/10.7722/j.ctt81mst.16.
37 WilliamUrban. "The Teutonic Knights and Baltic Chivalry." *The Historian* 56, no. 3 (1994): 519–30. http://www.jstor.org/stable/24448704.
38 M. M. Bom. (2012). The Lay Sisters of Saint John of Jerusalem. In: Women in the Military Orders of the Crusades. The New Middle Ages. Palgrave Macmillan, New York. https://doi.org/10.1057/9781137088307.
39 Myra Struckmeyer. "Female Hospitallers in the Twelfth and Thirteenth Centuries, Dissertation University of North Carolina, Chapel Hill, 2006. Female_hospitallers_in_the_twelfth_and_thirteenth_centuries.pdf
40 Gordon M. Reynolds. "Cross purposes: Frankish Levantine perceptions of gender and female participation in the crusades, 1147–1254," Master's Thesis University of Canterbury, 2017 Cross purposes: Frankish levantine perceptions of gender and female participation in the crusades, 1147–1254 – Medievalists.net.
41 Crouch David, and Jeroen Deploige. "Taking the Field: Knighthood and Society in the High Middle Ages." In *Knighthood and Society in the High Middle Ages*, edited by David Crouch and Jeroen Deploige, 1–26. Leuven University Press, 2020. https://doi.org/10.2307/j.ctvbtzmj5.5.
   Eljas Oksanen. "Knights, Mercenaries and Paid Soldiers: Military Identities in the Anglo-Norman Regnum." In *Knighthood and Society in the High Middle Ages*, edited by David Crouch and Jeroen Deploige, 71–94. Leuven University Press, 2020. https://doi.org/10.2307/j.ctvbtzmj5.8.

90 Women and War

42 Lynn H. Nelson. "The Kings of Aragon." In *The Chronicle of San Juan de La Pena: A Fourteenth-Century Official History of the Crown of Aragon*, 16–40. University of Pennsylvania Press, 1991. http://www.jstor.org/stable/j.ctv512w38.7.
   Lynn H. Nelson. "The Kings of the Crown of Aragon." In *The Chronicle of San Juan de La Pena: A Fourteenth-Century Official History of the Crown of Aragon*, 53–104. University of Pennsylvania Press, 1991. http://www.jstor.org/stable/j.ctv512w38.9.
43 Ibid. Nelson.
44 Claude C. H. Williamson. "Chivalry." *The Irish Monthly* 47, no. 552 (1919): 330–39. http://www.jstor.org/stable/20505321.
45 Jimmy Joe. Timeless Myths, 1997. https://www.timelessmyths.com/author/twtpi/
46 William Jewell. The Golden Cabinet of True Treasure (London: John Crosley, 1612; Ann Arbor: Text Creation Partnership, 2011). http://name.umdl.umich.edu/A04486.0001.001.
47 C. H. Josten. "Elias Ashmole, F.R.S. (1617–1692)." *Notes and Records of the Royal Society of London* 15 (1960): 221–30. http://www.jstor.org/stable/531041.
48 Opcit. Jewell.
49 Elias Ashmole, Hollar Wenceslaus, and William Sherman. "The institution, laws and ceremonies of the most noble order of the garter collected and digested into one body by Elias Ashmole," Chapter III Section III The Feminine Cavaliers of the torch in Tortosa, University of Michigan, The institution, laws & ceremonies of the most noble Order of the Garter collected and digested into one body by Elias Ashmole … (umich.edu).
50 NOVA "Medieval Siege," NOVA Online | Bioterror | History of Biowarfare (non-Flash) (pbs.org).
51 See for example "A Women Defends Her Castle.jpg," Wikimedia Commons, File: A woman defends her castle.jpg – Wikimedia Commons.
52 Ibid.
53 Ibid.
54 Martin Hall, and Jonathan Phillips (translators). "*Caffaro, Genoa and the Twelfth-Century Crusades*," Chicago University Press, Ashgate, 2013.
55 The text utilized in the description is translated from *Annali Genovesi de Daffaro e de'suoi continuatori*, edited by L. T. Belgrao (Fonti per la storia d'italia, Rome 1890), 78–89 by G. A. Loud (2007) "The Capture of Almeria and Tortosa. All quotes in this section are from this work.
   Britannica, The Editors of Encyclopaedia. "Caffaro Di Caschifellone". *Encyclopedia Britannica*, 27 Jul. 2023. https://www.britannica.com/biography/Caffaro-di-Caschifellone. Accessed 12/27/2023.
   Jonathan Phillips, and Martin Hall. (eds). *Caffaro, Genoa and the Twelfth-Century Crusades*. Ashgate, 2013.
56 Brian A. Catlos. Review of *Caffaro, Genoa and the Twelfth-Century Crusades*, trans. by Martin Hall and Jonathan Phillips. *Comitatus: A Journal of Medieval and Renaissance Studies* 45 (2014): 218–19. https://doi.org/10.1353/cjm.2014.0003.
57 Ibid. Catlos.
58 Ibid. Catlos.
59 "The Capture of Almeria and Tortosa by Caffaro," University of Leeds uploads, n.d. Caffaro-Almeria.pdf (leeds.ac.uk).
60 Opcit Catlos.
61 A. J. Forey. "The Military Orders and the Spanish Reconquest in the Twelfth and Thirteenth Centuries." *Traditio* 40 (1984): 197–234. http://www.jstor.org/stable/27831153.

62 Ibid.
63 Livia Gershon. "Chivalry was Established to Keep Thuggish, Medieval Knights in Check Knights in the Middle Ages Were Heavily Armed and Prone to Violence," History Stories. Accessed 1/14/2021.

Additional Resources

Christine Sciacca. *Illuminating Women in the Medieval World*, Los Angeles: J. Paul Getty Museum, First Ed, June 20, 2017.

Gilbert West. *The Institution of the Order of the Garter. A Dramatic Poem*, London: R. Dodsley at Tylly's Head, Pall-Mall, 1742.

Helen J. Nicholson. *Women, and the Crusades*, Oxford: Oxford University Press, May 23, 2023.

Hugh E. L. Collins. *The Order of the Garter 1348–1461: Chivalry and Politics in Late Medieval England*, Oxford: Oxford University Press, July 2000.

Jonathan Phillips. *The Second Crusade: Extending the Frontiers of Christendom*, New Haven: Yale University Press, 2010.

Joseph Gies and Frances Gies. *Women in the Middle Ages: The Lives of Real Women in a Vibrant Age of Transition*, New York: Harper Collins e-books, November 30, 2010.

Michelle Brown. *Understanding Illuminated Manuscripts: A Guide to Technical Terms, Revised Edition (Looking At)*, Los Angeles: J. Paul Getty Museum, Second Ed, December 4, 2018.

Questions

Why is carving the Order of the Hatchet a defining moment in the history of women and war?

How do the women of the Order of the Hatchet differ from the story of Joan of Arc?

Why do you think the women's Order of the Hatchet was no longer handed down to subsequent females in matrilineal family trees?

Modern take

Research shows that women played critical roles in the biography of the church and religion in knightly ways. Why might their contributions have been deleted from mainstream historical records?

The current British Order of Chivalry, the Most Noble Order of the Garter, is the world's oldest surviving order of knighthood. It has both male Knights Companions and female Ladies Companions. The original "Ladies of the Garter members" were discontinued under King Henry VII in the 1400s and were

92 Women and War

never reinstituted. Queen Elizabeth II reinstated a means of women's recognition through the installation of the "Ladies Companion of the Garter" in 1987, and the first Black female was made a member in 2022. Why did it take a female monarch to reinstate such an honor? Does the fact that Queen Elizabeth II served during World War II as a colonel-in-chief of 16 British Army regiments and corps lend a level of credibility to this honorific title? What would have precluded people of color from being named until the 21st century?

What sorts of modern media portrayals exist of women parallel to the subject matter found in the Illumination art handwritten books of the medieval period?

Activities and discovery

Cartography is a form of art that relates stories of the Crusades. Locate old cartographic maps of the first, second, and third Crusades or use online interactive maps that show the movement of people to the Holy Land. What are some of the most important sites visited? Locate museum collections online, such as those housed at the Metropolitan Museum of Art, Palace of Versailles, Museum of the Order of St. John, or the Israel Museum, and explore their map collections from the Crusades period. What are the colors, symbols, and lettering styles used?

More than 3000 travelogues also give accounts of personal pilgrimages to the Holy Land. Lists of these accounts are available online. What were some of the experiences of these individuals?

Do a background investigation on the weapons and engineering used in a siege between Muslim and Christian armies during the 12th-century Crusades. Describe in detail what the fight might have looked like between the women of Tortosa and the Muslim army.

Create an artistic rendering of the women of the Order of the Hatchet using Ashmole's or other writers' descriptions or by reviewing drawings and paintings of knights in the 12th century. Create a standard (flag) that would identify the Order of the Hatchet.

Many pieces of art exist that tell stories of the Second Crusade. Find examples of Romanesque, Gothic, and Islamic art produced during this time. How do the styles of each differ?

5
UNIFORMS AS ARTIFACTS
The Dahomey Warriors of West Africa

FIGURE 5.1 A female Dahomey warrior at a tribal spectacle taking a battle stance.

© Out of print book taken from the original source. A mission to Gelele, king of Dahome: with notices of the so-called "Amazons," the grand customs, the yearly customs, the human sacrifices, the present state of the slave trade, and the Negro's place in nature: Burton, Richard Francis, Sir, 1821–1890.

DOI: 10.4324/9781003406372-6

Enclothed cognition and white laboratory coats

Victorian essayist Thomas Carlyle wrote that clothes mirror an individual's philosophy of life. "Society," he said, "was founded upon cloth."[1] As a form of media, clothing communicates status, age, sex, and cultural background. Social and historically significant periods change the meaning of apparel, tell observers and wearers about belongingness and monetary and social status, and signify critical life paths. While worn, garments have a psychological pull that may influence physical posture, motivate actions, create an internal mood in the clad person, and suggest a wearer's power or incapacities. Occupational roles are identified through clothing and distinguish one's spot in social and professional hierarchies. Clothes express the achievement of significant life events such as weddings, funerals, and festivals. On the one hand, how bodies are covered is a visual emblem of our social relationships; on the other, they are symbolic, metaphorical tokens of community and fellowship. That so many precedents can be associated with what is worn shows how important the phrase, we are what we wear, is to everyone's life.[2]

At the same time Carlyle was professing his reflections on wearable fabric, the medical field became concerned about extricating themselves from frauds and quacks who promised to cure ailments with elixirs, tonics, and salves full of questionable ingredients. Doctors wanted to distinguish themselves from charlatans and swindlers. They had spent years learning their craft in colleges and universities to receive licenses to care for those with illnesses. The Hippocratic Oath guided them to prescribe only beneficial treatments, to do no harm, and to live an exemplary occupational and personal life. Physicians decided to wear white lab coats to symbolize their skill, integrity, educational attainment, and commitment to being compassionate toward the ailing. White coats became a uniform that alerted other professionals and patients to the fact that this person now represented an entire community, not the individual wearing it.[3]

Lab coats were the subject of a study conducted in 2002 on the Evanston campus of Northwest University by Hajo Adam and his colleague, Adam Galinsky.[4] The two researchers began examining the effects on task completion and the level of sustained attention the wearer gave to their work. Three experimental role-playing groups were organized. The first group was doctors, the second was painters, and the third was a neutral or no association role formulated as a baseline. Adam and Galinsky discovered a co-occurrence between the symbolic meaning of clothing and its physical use. Clothes were shown to have profound and systematic psychological and behavioral consequences for their wearers.[5]

In 2019, Alexandra Vinson, a faculty member of the Learning Health Sciences Department at the University of Michigan, researched the meanings medical students invest in their white coats and how the values placed upon them parallel as a status symbol.[6] Wearing the coat for the first time marks a doctor's transition from classroom novice to clinician. A White Coat Ceremony indicates the conversion from student to professional in the United States. But there is an additional hurdle to be taken after this celebration. Novice doctors wear only short and not long coats. Specific social meaning is attached to the coat length. A budding clinical doctor still has not moved away from the trainee role to that of a full-fledged physician. Additional unwritten rules apply to this simple piece of clothing. It should not be worn in the classroom before the ceremony has officially occurred and not in public spaces. In fact, according to Vinson, "the coats are used as status symbols policed by peers and themselves...Status management is facilitated by and exposed by the coat as a material artifact."[7] The white lab coat example carries over into all uniformed professions as a meaningful visual resulting in psychological bonding, reduces the visual ques rampant in social differentiation, can boost morale and are important identifiers of having met requirements to attain a position of authority.

Uniforms

Wearing a military uniform just as within the profession of medicine is also bound by many rules and regulations. In many nations, military dress is barred from being worn when off duty. Costume theatrical or motion-picture production military costumes are limited to a portrayal which does not discredit the armed services. In the 21st century, US service members are forbidden from eating, drinking, smoking, or wearing headphones or earbuds when walking and in uniform.[8] Army, Navy, Air Force, Marine Corps, and Space Force members all have clothing regulations that are adhered to with strict conformity. Uniforms vary for combat, training, and formal dress. Each branch requires different iterations, with particular attention paid to the placement of headgear, medals, shoulder and front insignias, and patches that signify military officer ranks, enlisted personnel rates and specialties, and the unit to which the person is attached.

By way of illustration, wearing an Army combat camouflage uniform requires personnel to tuck in their tan or sand-colored T-shirts with outer jackets over the shirts being always closed. Berets must be positioned correctly at a specific angle, and hairstyle must not interfere with the placement of the beret. Differentiation is made in the design of clothing for officers and enlisted personnel. Officers are more broadly considered managers and leaders, and the enlisted corps are leaders in various fields of technical expertise. Several regulations have evolved as more women have entered the military as a sign of inclusivity. Of these changes, one of the more generous has been changing the acceptable hairstyles of female soldiers. Initially, the Army had rules for space between braids of cornrows or that women could not have ponytails or

96 Women and War

change their hair color. These rules have been rescinded, and highlighting and dying hair is acceptable, except that neon colors are prohibited.[9]

No matter the timeframe or what the military unit is organized to do, their attire represents a group emblem that only a cadre of specialized members can wear. The legitimacy expressed through wearing a uniform has become so crucial that legal statutes preclude any person not officially enlisted in the armed services from wearing them. The clothing signifies a prestigious right based upon the life and death responsibilities the institution has asked those in uniform to bear. Since military dress is not flashy and shows a high degree of similarity in color and style, uniforms and their rules serve as a means of differentiation from the general population. Sameness suppresses individuality in behavior and appearance. As such, what soldiers, sailors, and airpersons wear brings homogeneity and conformity to an otherwise heterogeneous group. To be dressed in military regalia implies maintaining discipline, promoting bonding, and evoking pride, fellowship, and loyalty to each other. Outsiders cannot join in wearing the specialized garb unless they have met the unique qualifications required to don the distinctive attire.[10]

The same year Adam and Galinsky's book introduced the idea of enclothed cognition, Paul Fussell's *Uniforms: Why We Are What We Wear* won the National Book Award for nonfiction. Fussell received a medal and 10,000 dollars in cash for the insightful and engaging approach regarding these singular pieces of apparel. Fussell divulged, "When cloth objects become uniforms, obligatory and regulated with implications of mass value, they are irresistibly fascinating."[11] Of all uniforms, counting those of medical professionals, business entrepreneurs, and skilled trades, the most recognizable are those attached to the roles of military rank. Fussel puts forward another intriguing idea. He makes the distinction between a uniform and a costume. The former has legitimacy backed by formal organizational rules and regulations. The latter is worn with frivolity, temporariness, and theatricality. A costume can be easily spotted due to its ability to entertain and create an aura of absurdity.[12]

Historically, military dress is one of the most well-recognized and chronicled fashions. Records of soldiers' attire exist from five thousand years ago. In the third millennium BC, fighting Sumerians wore metal helmets, cloaks, and fringed kilts.[13] Like the white doctor's coat, the length of skirts varied according to hierarchical status. Servants, enslaved people, and soldiers wore shorter versions than royalty and deities. Ancient Roman military legions required standardized dress and armor from the 1st century onward. Pieces produced in state-run factories could vary according to the province in which they were designed. Most tunics were either dyed red or remained the color of natural wool. Helmets could differ depending on the classification of the soldier. Most had a baldric worn over one shoulder to carry a sword.

Throughout the history of the empire, heavy-soled sandals were the required footwear.[14]

Other nations chose more flashy and colorful military fashion. The Landsknechts were allowed leeway in their choice of clothing due to Emperor Maximilian disavowing the Sumptuary Law that dictated a specific style and color for the mercenaries.[15] He believed they deserved special dispensation since their lives as fighting men were "short and brutish."[16] They wore flat berets decorated with talismans and brightly colored ostrich feathers. Poland's winged hussars were recognizable on the battlefield in their long, dyed feather wings tied to wooden frames, which they attached to their backs.[17] Ghillie suits that make their wearers look like shaggy bushes or spirits arising from the earth were designed by the Lovat Scouts during the Second Anglo-Boer War and modified versions are still used today as camouflage by sniper units.[18]

The Dahomey Amazons

Dahomey was a militaristic society that was constantly fighting. Their economic prowess in the region was built on the slave trade by peoples acquired through barter with interior nations of the continent or by raids. The kingdom's inhabitants reveled in cruelty and delighted in killing and torturing captives. Sometimes, they were seen caressing the skulls of those they had beheaded in battle as a rivalrous statement to excite jealousy and envy among their peers. Before heading into action, many magical and religious rituals and incantations were exercised in the belief that doing so increased strength. Protective amulets warded off failure, and most consulted tribal seers for a menu of sacrifices and rites to be observed before leaving for war or upon return from the fighting. Holding the Office of Executioner was a high honor and often went to the wealthiest members of society. Diverse cultures across wide regions were incorporated into a kingdom in 1600. The newly formed monarchy began raiding areas outside the Abomey Plateau, and 12 palaces were built to house up to 8000 people. Unification wars were declared when a king wanted to unite the Fon people of South Benin with their extended relatives and other Adja-speaking people who had migrated to the region in the 12th and 13th centuries.[19]

Other territorial wars were declared against targeted enemies of the kingdom, particularly with the Yoruba of the Oyo Empire over the control of both kingdoms' lucrative slave trade along the country's coastal territories.[20] From its beginnings, Dahomey kings and queens perpetuated enslavement, ritual human sacrifice, cannibalism, and headhunting.[21]

Dahomeyans believed in the transmigration of souls and that all people who die pass into a happier state to a land of spirits. Souls returned to earth to watch over the remaining members of their families. The rich took a few of

98 Women and War

FIGURE 5.2 Dahomey Amazons with trophy heads after a battle.
© World Cat Search ebook Electronic Reproduction.

their favorite wives and enslaved people to the afterlife. Many of the women were sacrificial, but most committed suicide.[22] All women were "daughters" or "wives" of the king.

Apprehending and enslaving people had existed in multiple forms on the Continent of Africa for centuries.[23] The system originated within the Indigenous populations and was further shaped by Roman, Islamic, and Christian views about slavery. Capturing, selling, and buying humans was particularly common along the coast. In Benin, these traditions were complex and rooted in the kingdom's political, economic, military, and social structures. Enslaved people could be bought or gifted, taken through conquest, acquired by geographic expansionism, or inherited. Royals and non-royals could enslave people. The larger the number possessed, the greater one's social status. Many came from the interior and were sold off in a custom known as "eating the country." By 1850, "the number of enslaved Africans within Africa far exceeded those in the Americas."[24] Quantitative records vary. Estimated slave exports from the Bight of Benin from 1641 to 1890 can be found in Patrick Manning's *The Uncommon Market*, which separates exported humans by the nations of Brazil, England, France, Holland, Spain, and America. Brazil was the largest exporter, totaling nearly one million people, England at 363,000, France at 279,000, Holland at 110, 000, and combined Spanish and American trade totaling 186,000.[25] The mortality rate of those traded ranged from 10 to 20 percent.[26]

The Portuguese were heavily involved in the West African slave trade in the 17th century, and the Edo tribes of Southern Nigeria were brutally entangled in capturing men, women, and children and selling them to Western buyers, providing significant economic power.[27] Internal geographic warring shifted to civil wars breaking out in the 1800s when the British imposed naval blockades on the ports of Dahomey. By this time, key exports were human captives traded with the Dutch, English, French, and Americans. Westerners brought back many stories about Dahomey's horrific viewpoint of the value of human life. One such account gave details of "a poor wretch" barely alive and not far from dead, "face swollen by the stings of insects and his whole body scarred by their bites."[28] The man had been tied tightly using vines as rope. These had sunk into his flesh. Below the waist, he had been gnawed at by a wild animal. For some distance, the spectacle repeated itself. A Dahomey guard told the traveler they were captives from a recent raid and were being punished for resisting the local leaders. A man identified only as M. de Courville on arriving at the capital was met with Amazons hurrying about wearing white outfits. "The women were handsome negresses evidently from the royal harem, and they seem to treat the dance as a compulsory duty that cannot be over too soon. Seizing a young, fine-looking woman among the dancers, the women dragged her from the platform, and before she could utter a shriek, she was beheaded, her head rolling almost to the feet of the king."[29]

To the Dahomey, female warriors were "she-soldiers," "Medusas," and "Spinster warriors." Westerners called them Amazons, and the name stuck. A small consensus exists in Western Africa that the warriors took root under Queen Hangbe in the early 1700s, serving as female bodyguards.[30] Others place their roles arising from the time of King Ghezo when, due to his male warriors' attrition to the slave trade and numerous deaths from their war-ridden culture, they were seen as a matter of necessity to keep the kingdom alive. Under King Ghezo, crusades were undertaken every three years to enlist more women, and under King Glele, his successor, a draft was made once a year. Only 50 of the original combatants was alive after the final French-Dahomeyan conflicts of the 1890s, and these had died out by 1970.[31]

It is not known precisely when female soldiers entered the military realm. At first, women were only allowed to carry banners and not fight. Most historical references center around them forming units of palace guards, or *gbetos*, which were specialists trained in big game hunting. Officially

100 Women and War

recognized as an organized unit in 1729, the women were used as a ploy to make the army appear larger. In the 1800s, the *Gulohento*, or Riflewomen, became the largest of the totality of organized regiments. Outsiders who watched the Amazon's marksmanship drills noticed that loading a Dane gun, a long-barreled flintlock musket, took only 30 seconds for the women compared to the male soldiers, who took almost a minute to complete the task.[32] Women's fighting prowess overall far surpassed that of the men. The all-women contingents jarred European visitors and explorers when they saw them paraded at the king's visitation shows and in military parades.[33]

Imposed celibacy was to have been mandatory. However, this requirement does not seem to have been overseen judiciously. Numbers also differ regarding the size of the total body of fighters. Allegedly, there were 600 until the mid-19th century, when King Ghezo increased their magnitude 100-fold. The British swashbuckling traveler Richard Francis Burton wrote that women were attracted to their military roles to obtain food supplies, tobacco, alcohol, and enslaved attendants. Many recruits found soldering a way out of poverty and an escape from the horrific maltreatment they received from men and family members. Others were captured, and there was no recourse but to join up or be murdered or sacrificed.[34]

Recruiting requirements for participating in battles were being tall, strong, and agile. Sovereigns insisted their women fight to the death and never confess defeat. Many recruits began military training at about the age of seven, were required to serve lengthy apprenticeships, and received bonuses of cowrie shells for each enemy they could kill or capture.[35] Cowries were found in the Maldives of the Indian Ocean and made their way to Western Africa through the trans-Saharan and western trade routes. Most were fair in color, with a porcelain sheen. Small, portable, and durable, they were difficult to counterfeit and could be strung on twine and easily carried en masse around the neck or arm. These attributes made the shells an excellent form of currency; they could be measured using standard weights and were valued more than gold by the Dahomey rulers.[36] Europeans began using the shells as early as the 16th century to buy natural resources, artifacts, and people.

Dahomeyan kings divided their warriors into two military units. One group, known as the right, was controlled by a type of prime minister, or *migan*, who also served as a chief advisor and royal executioner. The *mehu*, or left, was overseen by a key administrative officer who managed internal affairs. Two additional subdivisions were organized as center and reserve posts. These were further subdivided into platoons and companies. All were drilled incessantly, formed into columns, and employed the technique of countermarching. The most used tactics were frontal assaults and flanking movements.[37] There was no cavalry in Dahomey, unlike their enemies, the Oyo's, who employed horses on the field of combat. Dahomey also had no formal naval bases or vessels. However, in the 1700s, a maritime exchange was established with the coastal kingdom of Adra in southern Benin to fight the Epe monarchy on Nigeria's coast due to the negative impact Adra was having on the Dahomey slave trade.[38]

The whistling thorn

Nineteenth-century boundaries for the Dahomey area stretch like a club with the handle at the Gulf of Guinea, with the widest part to the north well to the interior. The kingdom was straddled by Togo to the west and Benin to the east and north, with the Oyo, their fiercest enemies, just east of Benin. The largest cities near the Gulf were Cotonou, Whydah, and Porto Novo. Further north and west were the kingdoms of Abomey and Allada. If an explorer were to walk from south to north, beginning at the seaport of Porto Novo, they would have passed through marshy areas, tall and short grass savanna, deciduous and broadleaf forests, and end their wandering on a vast acacia plain. Fishing occurred along the slow-moving, wide, and flat Yewa River, with its extensive basin of tributaries stretching across the entire country. Tribal groups were several, and habitations from south to north were the Azo, Fon, Adja, and Yoruba peoples, with the Fon being the largest population. Once reaching the cities of Parakou, then Natitingou to the north, there were the Fulani, Somba, and Bariba tribes. By the mid-20th century, the area's economy was based on oil palm, cotton, petroleum, and shea nuts.[39]

Benin's climate is hot and humid, very warm year-round, and has two rainy and dry seasons. Animal life is varied. There are elephants, wild pigs, crocodiles, buffalo, lions, leopards, monkeys, and antelope. The acacia bush is prolific, its thickets spreading unhindered for acres from north to south. These hearty plants can survive without water and withstand excessive hot and cold temperatures. Over 700 acacia species, mimosa, thorn tree, and wattle pea family members grow in Africa. In the slightest winds, holes chewed by ants to use the hollow thorn bases as nests make a high-pitched sound or whistle. The humming acts as an auditory signaling device for large and small game.[40] Most species are pod-bearing, create sap, and produce leaves and flowers. Giraffes, elephants, ants, and bird species have adapted to the plant's massive intertwining barbs by carefully navigating the leaves without touching the sharp spikes, which can grow up to eight inches. The spines can cut through human skin like a sharpened knife blade. When animals attempt to eat the leaves and interfere with the thorn structures, the plant activates a chemical response by releasing tannins into the air, inhibiting their digestion. A similar reaction in humans occurs when the mouth puckers after consuming a bitter drink or eating unripe fruits.[41]

Benin's women warriors rehearsed tearing through thorny acacia and were expected to show no pain or weakness at the effort. It was believed that the

102 Women and War

suffering endured aided in creating a fighter with unwavering courage. French forces during the Franco-Dahomeyan wars observed the Amazons charging thickets of acacias, prickly pears, and thorny shrubs, exiting, bruised, bleeding, and often maimed for life. Along with this insensitivity training, the women were expected to be able to torture and kill those they captured and enslaved as war booty from fighting tribes and participate in beheadings and human sacrifices. They competed in obstacle races, wrestled, and were tutored in bush survival skills and non-weapon-induced combat. Many were great elephant and alligator bow hunters – some collected snakes, believed to be immortal, for the king's snake temples.

Hours were spent practicing simulated attacks, tracking game and humans, and mimicking slash-and-kill methods with large machetes. Guns and cannons were added to their repertoire of fighting skills once Europeans began using firing weapons as tradeable items for gold, ivory, and pepper. While significant as an organizing element for naming the *Gulohento*, guns never became a primary means of fighting for the women who preferred not using weapons in close-quarters combat.[42] A 19th-century newspaper writer from the *Tribune* credited the troops with a warrior ethos so large that if they had been pitted against the Romans, they could have mounted successful resistance on their courage alone.[43] Their "unnatural ferocity" was due to subjecting the women to military drills, which embraced kicking, cuffing, beatings, and starvation.[44]

The Amazons were violent, brutal, aggressive, and relentless. European observers believed their daring and bravery in battle made them the best in Africa. Having faced an Amazon onslaught, a French artilleryman painted them as not well armed compared to the French forces, but they could swarm with furious courage, making them a dangerous foe.[45] A prejudiced comment came from the *Chicago Tribune*, "While having brutish instincts, they are described as above the ordinary intelligence of the African Black."[46] Multiple reports of their feats often appeared in print media between the early 1800s and the beginning of the 20th century. Newspapers contained valuable information in creating a picture of the characteristics of the Amazons in the form of trade reports, traveler's stories, and news of political and military strife. Essays on the women eroded after their defeat to France in the Second Dahomey-Franco War in 1894.

Four colonialists and their western images of the Dahomey

Most of the history of the Dahomey Amazons written down in English came from the experiences of outsiders involved in trade or exploration in the region.[47] Four of the most detailed journals written at the height of exploration of the region were turned into books by Scotsman John Duncan (1845–1846), Officer of the British Navy Frederic Forbes (1847–1851), army officer and cosplayer Sir Richard Francis Burton (1854–1855), and the eight-month account of living in residence in Dahomey by entomologist Sydney Barber Josiah (J. A.) Skertchly (1874).[48] Together, these men's recollections represented nearly three decades of observations. Through a Western lens, their accounts divulge much about the Dahomeyan way of life, clothing, rules and regulations, activities, royal hierarchies, festivals, trade, and war.

Each man had to compete with the Scotsman and missionary David Livingstone's 30 years of accounts of his explorations of southern, central, and eastern Africa, which began in 1841 and ended in 1873. Held in high esteem by the Royal Geographical Society, founded as a scholarly entity under the patronage of King William IV and a Royal Charter of Queen Victoria, his popularity morphed into becoming a heroic figure of the 19th century. Livingstone was also a devout abolitionist and networked with parliamentarians to end human trafficking. One year before Skertchly made his trek to the coast of West Africa, reports returned from Chief Chitambo's Village in the Kingdom of Kazembe (Zambia) that the Scottish physician had succumbed to malaria and internal bleeding from dysentery.[49] Unlike Duncan, Forbes, Burton, and Skertchly, Africa's greatest missionary gained great fame for being the first European to cross the continent from east to west, exploring Victoria Falls, the Nile River, and numerous African lakes. The other four African explorers disappeared into relative obscurity.

Born to a Scottish farming family, John Duncan joined the most senior cavalry regiment in the British 1st Regiment of Lifeguards, because he admired their discipline and uniforms. During his 16 years of service, he became proficient in drawing, painting, and mechanics. Setting his sights on professional travel, he convinced his superiors to approve an appointment as a master at arms for an expedition to Niger.[50] His responsibilities involved training soldiers and activating the defense of fortifications in times of war. In Niger, he was one of very few of the 300 men in his fighting unit to escape malarial sickness and warring attacks by native populations.[51] Attempting to assist a wounded colleague in the Cape Verde Islands from a murderous onslaught, Duncan was shot in the leg with a poison arrow.[52] He wrote, "At this time, my sufferings were extreme; part of both bones of my leg was entirely denuded of flesh a little above the anklebone."[53] Due to a delayed amputation, and since he was far removed from a military hospital and in conjunction with unremitting care by field physicians, the wound healed on its own.

It was the heyday of Victorian wanderings and colonialism, and Duncan approached the premier overseers of the Royal Geographical Society and convinced them to support his travels in 1845. He was given passage to traverse the now-known fabricated Kong Mountain range, which was believed to extend from the highlands of West Africa and end in the east at the also fictitious Mountains of the Moon, supposedly located at the source of the Nile River.[54] Kong Mountain myths began in 1798 when they were charted on

104 Women and War

maps by Scottish explorer Mungo Park, the popular red-haired Jeffersonian-looking Niger River explorer.[55] This false topography continued to appear in cartographic papers until the late 1800s. Finally, in 1887, French officer and explorer Louis-Gustave Binger proved that the mountains did not exist. Duncan's mission in and around the fabricated landmarks caused him to run out of funds quickly. Stranded, he was forced to seek support from Dahomey's King Ghezo.

Derek O'Connor, author of a biography about the globetrotter, categorized the meeting as one of the "most peculiar in African exploration history...the towering cavalryman attired in the magnificent uniform of the Lifeguards was honored by King Ghezo, the charismatic native leader. Together, they drank toasts from goblets carved out of human skulls to Queen Victoria and discussed Duncan's quest to explore further inland."[56] The meeting concluded with Duncan receiving aid from the king and being honored by Ghezo with the protective title of King's Stranger for the remainder of his journey.[57] On his return to Britain, the government and Geographical Society ignored his book *Travels in Western Africa in 1845 and 1846* because he had been born into a humble background and snootily opined he was not part of academia.[58] His observations of Dahomey retain vital descriptions of the period in which the kingdom was one of the most high-powered societies in Western Africa. Duncan deserved recognition, not ridicule, for his Westernized, though insightful narratives.

Readers would have been electrified reading about his journeys through Tangiers, Gambia, Abomey, Savay, and Torree. Bits of information appear about the Jews, Moors, superstitions, idols, and fetishes. Botanical, zoological, and geological findings were interspersed with explanations about the conduct of trade and descriptions of marketplace foodstuffs. From his visits to numerous towns, Duncan left for his reader's reports on their inhabitants and architecture. He expounded upon fashion and details of daily rituals such as shaving and circumcision celebrations. In the market town of Gregapojee, he spoke of the scenery, fish traps, traveling canoes, snake worship, tree oysters, and the character of the Brazilian migrant turned slave merchant Francisco Felix de Sousa and his horrific treatment of enslaved people. Sousa was given the full honorary title of cha-cha of Ouidah for these acts and served as the Viceroy of Ouidah in the Kingdom of Dahomey until his death at 94 in 1849.

In chapter 11, stories of the Dahomey soldiers appear. The women enter the dialogue as participants at a king's festival, where they remain at a distance, lying down and squatting until they are directed to come forward. Duncan's perception of the entire pageant was that it was undisciplined. After the regiments formed in an irregular column, a commanding officer called out junior officers who kneeled on both knees and covered their bodies and heads with a cloud of red dust. Heads were "entirely shaved, except a tuft resembling a cockade; others only shaved a breadth of two inches from the forehead to the poll."[59] Each officer was introduced individually, and commendations and rewards were given for valor for recent heroics. The regiment belonged to the king's son, and they stood with an ensign decorated with the figure of a lion. A song was sung in complement of the king. All were allowed one at a time to step forward and claim their fidelity to their ruler. This part of the ceremony took so much time Duncan claimed it to be "irksome." Next, the group arose, remaining on their knees, and posed with their muskets using two hands. Then, "all join(ed) in a general hurrah." A second contingent of Amazons tied to the king's second son also appeared. These numbered about 600. In that one day, Duncan estimated that approximately 6000 Dahomey Amazon soldiers passed before the king, with the king pausing and relating to the Scotsman the achievements of those who had done something outstanding.[60]

> Suddenly, then, they rise up, throwing the musket sharply into one hand, holding it high in the air, and simultaneously giving another hurrah. The whole then shoulder muskets and run off at full speed. Each individual runs as fast as she is able, so that it is a race with the whole regiment of six hundred women. It would surprise a European to see the speed of these women, although they carry a long Danish musket and short sword each, as well as a sort of club.[61]

Duncan's reminiscences are valuable for his shared details about how the Amazons were dressed. At this ceremony, they wore blue and white striped cotton surtout, the stripes about one and a half inches wide and being of "stout native manufacture."[62] He was surprised their livery had no sleeves but pondered that this design likely enabled their arms to be free when fighting. "The skirt or tunic reaches as low as the kilt of the Highlanders."[63] "Short trousers were worn under the surtout about two inches below the knee." A color drawing by John Forbes shows this near-exact rendering of a Dahomey Amazon from his travels in 1849 and 1850. A cartouche box or *agbwadya* forms a girdle and keeps the clothing closely fitted to the body and girded around the loins. In the box were 20 cartridges "about four times the quantity used in England, owing to the inferiority of the powder." Gunpowder was placed in a small leather cup and sprinkled into the gun without using wadding, causing any shot made to lose power. In examining these efforts, Duncan concluded that the result of the misses was due to the guns being "fired off more by chance than judgment." He closed his dialogue about the women by stating that they could endure "much fatigue" due to the constant exercise of their bodies from domestic and agricultural labor.[64]

Skertchly's foremost value in recording his travels to Dahomey was his detailed geology studies, colorations, and keen descriptions of animals and plants.

106 Women and War

He was interested in the kingdom's songs, dances, and art. His principal attention was placed upon learning about the customs of human sacrifice and women's roles in the king's exhibitions. In Skertchly's case, "amazons" was used for all women, not just those who went to war. He noted their overall "braggadocio airs" and "swagger."[65] In one sighting, he observed a troop of Amazons guarding a palm oil factory and recorded that many whom he passed in the area of the royal places who were part of the king's household corps saluted him. Such attendants were distinguished by wearing a particular badge on their clothing or caps during ceremonies. At night, female sentinels stood guard within the palace walls and were relieved every three hours, chanting while circling the perimeter until the next guard took over.[66] Others served as "maidens" during festivals, holding silver spittoons shaped like goblets or wiping the sweat from the king's "royal face, neck, and armpits with perfumed cloths."[67] Two chapters of his book were devoted to reporting the debates and trials held in the king's court of justice. At one trial, the clothing of male soldiers being indicted for poor decision-making in their actions was brought in and placed before the alleged in a ceremonious display. After this, arguments were given regarding whether the suspects were deserving of wearing the uniforms. In this instance, the king's final decision was not enslavement or death but to return their "cloth" without retribution for their behavior.[68] Women faced similar retributions and trials for not meeting their king's expectations.

Abbaraya troops, which Skertchly equated to the British Lifeguards, were dressed in blue tunics and gray petticoats that reached below the knee. Ammunition was placed in black leather cartridge boxes, and around their brows was a long fillet with an alligator or dragon. Other categories noted were the *Agbarays*, or blunderbuss-ers, and the *Nyekpleh-hentoh*, or blue knives. The first group carried short, large-caliber firearms with a flared muzzle; the other had a curved saber. The next troop, which represented the *gbeto* elephant hunters considered equal to the men's *Gan-u-nlan*, or Conquerors of All Animals, appeared during one ceremony.[69] Each was clothed in brown waistcoats and pink underskirts and wore a "profuse girdle of leather thongs which hung below their skirts."[70] Other women dressed in skirts of variegated colors wore scarlet robes with yellow lions emblazoned on them, and many tied black, indigo blue, or orange sashes at their waists.[71] During dances, women were observed dressed in silks, velvets, and chintzes with necks, shoulders, and arms daubed with a pale green pomade.[72] Various types of cloth were used for these public displays: white and black cotton, blue checked and striped calicos, white and blue velvet, and scarlet and gamboge-colored damask.[73] One fabric roof on a building in the palace square had needlework created by the Amazons of three black elephants with green ears and yellow tusks.[74]

Uniforms as Artifacts **107**

John Forbes, a commander of the Royal Naval vessel *Bonneta*, part of the West Africa Squadron, was assigned to antislavery patrol in 1849 and 1850 and was sent under orders to meet with King Ghezo.[75] His trip was arranged so that he might serve as an intermediary to discuss antislavery laws that Parliament had established and attempt to stop Dahomey from capturing and trading people. The West Africa Squadron, also called the Preventive Squadron, was created to police the coastal region of West Africa in 1808.[76] Its formation was seen as a step toward abolishing slavery after the British government passed the Slave Trade Act of 1807. The Act only barred one-half of the equation of human bondage, however, as only trading in enslaved people was made illegal and not the practice of enslavement. The legislation was difficult to enforce. Wealth derived from human trafficking on both the West and African sides of the equation outweighed slave traders' desire to cease filling their holds with what they trivialized as black gold. Initially, the program met with little progress due to understaffing. Because the Royal Navy was preoccupied with the Napoleonic Wars, only two vessels were assigned to carry out the legislated mandates.[77]

Laws governing the Western slave trade among key nations altered course many times. In 1315, the French outlawed slavery, but the behavior resurfaced with the rise in their efforts at colonial expansion. France again abolished slavery in 1794 for about five years, after which legal restrictions were dropped under Napolean's reign and then wholly abolished in 1848. Portugal was the first country to abolish slavery in their metropolitan areas by passing a bill in 1761. Still, it took political pressure from European nations to outlaw enslavement nationally in 1836. Denmark and Norway banned enslavement in 1803, but the conduct was not wholly expunged until 1848. The United States signed the Treaty of Ghent in 1814, marking the beginning of a tandem effort by the United Kingdom and the United States to pledge to work toward ending the slave trade. In 1820, the US Law on Slave Trade legally defined trading in humans as a form of piracy punishable by death.[78]

A revolt on November 7, 1841, staged by enslaved Madison Washington aboard the Richmond, Virginia-owned Johnson, and Eperson brig *Creole*, transporting 135 men, women, and children to be sold in New Orleans, Louisiana, resulted in the vessel's captain taking refuge in the Bahamas.[79] A hearing about the uprising ended with many aboard being given their freedom. Publicity from the event persuaded the US Congress to pass legislation to form a permanent African Squadron under the direction of the Navy. Orator, political activist, and the former enslaved Marylander Henry Highly Garnet praised Washington as a bright star of freedom, which took his station in the constellation of true heroism.[80] Frederick Douglass based the main character of his 1853 novella *The Heroic Slave* on Washington.[81] The US Squadron was formally disbanded in 1861, just as the Civil War began. Despite combined US and British efforts, by 1850, the increased demand for enslaved people in

108 Women and War

Latin America caused the number of human trafficking vessels to grow exponentially to the point that neither navy could stem the tide of the practice.[82] Over 90 percent of the captives were being sent to the Caribbean and South America to be used in agriculture. Death rates of the enslaved were so high in Brazil, Dutch Guiana, and the Caribbean that the regions attempting to keep pace with manual labor requirements caused the number of captives bought and sold to balloon.[83]

Experiences for the Squadron at sea were primal and unremitting. Commodore Sir George Ralph Collier, who distinguished himself during the French Revolutionary, Peninsular, and Napoleonic Wars, was sent to the Gulf of Guinea in 1818 with the 36-gun *HMS Creole* and six other vessels to ply 3000 miles of African coastline. He observed firsthand the viciousness of the trade. "No descriptors I could give would convey a true picture of its baseness and atrocity."[84] Crews suffered from yellow fever, malaria, and the violence perpetrated by slave traders in their attempts to quell their activities. Constant heat, inadequate sanitation, and the barbarous acts sailors witnessed against humans in bondage at sea were physically and mentally exhausting. Upon boarding, the naval patrol would find men, women, and children chained together, naked, lying on their backs, stored shoulder to shoulder or feet to face, and unable to move. Holds were covered with sickness and excrement. The British Act was also limited in scope owing to the fact that a vessel could not be seized unless people were physically aboard. Slavers began throwing their captives into the sea to avoid being restrained, fined, and jailed. By 1860, 1600 vessels had been seized, about ten percent of the total known to be plying the coast. A mere 150,000 Africans had been saved from the fate of enslavement, and one sailor of the West African Squadron died for every nine enslaved people freed.[85]

In 1840, the eccentric, talented, and reclusive British artist J.M.W. Turner exhibited his wrenching composition, *The Slave Ship*, at the Royal Academy of Art. The oil painting became a requiem about the events occurring off the African coast.[86] This was not the first time Turner had made a statement against enslavement. In 1828, he dedicated an engraving of his painting, *The Deluge*, to Whig politician John Josuah Proby, who was outspoken on ending slavery. *The Deluge* was based on the biblical flood and showed an apocalyptic panorama of tormented human carnage awash in a cavernous parting of the seas.[87] In *The Slave Ship*, scattered human forms are left floating in the wake of a sailing ship that has left its contraband to drown. Chained hands reach from the sea, and flailing body parts are shown half submerged in the ship's wake as the slaver recedes into the horizon. The painting's public showing coincided with increased international Abolitionism Campaigns in France, Britain, and the United States. It is believed Turner was influenced to compose the piece after reading about the 1781 incident of the slave ship *Zong* when the captain ordered 132 enslaved people to be thrown overboard. His excuses were that drinking water was running out, and by drowning them, he could collect insurance, which was paid out only if death was not due to natural causes. The incident was taken to court and deemed inconclusive, but public alarm about the atrocity aided in catalyzing the British abolitionist movement.

Captain Forbes's diaries contain his observations of women who came before the king's tribunals. In one instance, a regiment of 80 female bush-rangers advanced with three stripes of whitewash around each leg.[88] Three officers from this group swore oaths to the king: "We will always conquer or die; if we go to war, and any return not conquerors, let them die. If I retreat, my life is at the king's mercy...we are never yet known to turn our backs to an enemy."[89] When a male tribunal member attempted to address one of the women, he was told, "That woman is a fetish," a reference to her body being a vessel filled with a divine force – "You are not; you must not interfere with her."[90] Geoffrey Gorer, an English anthropologist who visited West Africa in 1934, witnessed a talisman ceremony firsthand. Although a few decades after Forbes diaries were published, Gorer's information is enlightening about these ceremonies. The women were in a trance, having had all "actions of everyday life, feeding, washing and so on, done for them." They first participated in prayers, prostrations, and the killing of a cockerel whose blood was dropped onto their big toes. They dressed alike, wearing "a cap of purple net from which hung in long strings threaded with cowries falling to the breast, so thick that they completely hid the face. Across an otherwise naked torso were slings of cowries and purple beads, and they wore ordinary skirts and anklets of cowries."[91]

Continuing with Forbes' observations of the ceremony, two colonels who bore the titles of Fire Horn and Turkey-Buzzard addressed the king next. He asked them to show Forbes their bush knives for inspection, to which Forbes noted they were "large, unwieldy, country-made articles," but their design was "well adapted for the service."[92] He also mentioned a woman named *She-Dong-Hong-Beh* as the leader of the Dahomey Amazons and drew a color likeness of her. She wore a white cap with an alligator, a cowrie necklace, and wristbands. Her muscled arms and legs extend from a blue and white striped bodice and a knee-length red, white, and blue striped skirt. Weapons were a long-barreled rifle, club, and curved scabbard. In her left hand is a decapitated male head held by the hair, blood dripping from the neck.

Additional oaths were made: "I am a wolf, the enemy of all I meet, and if I do not conquer, let me die." "I am the mother of Da Sousa," a reference to the reverence for the man who had brought wealth to the nation as a human bondage trader.[93]

More pledges were given to the king: "I long to kill an elephant for him to show my regard." "If we go to war, if we fail to catch elephants, let

FIGURE 5.3 She-Dong-Hong-Beh as the leader of the Dahomey Amazons.

© Public domain. Dahomey and the Dahomans; being the journals of two missions to the king of Dahomey, and residence at his capital, in the years 1849 and 1850: Forbes, Frederick E. (Frederick Edwyn).

us be content with flies because the king only knows where the war shall be."[94] After stating these vows, they danced, crawled away on their hands and knees, yelled, rose, and retired rapidly.[95] Then, a regiment of 300 entered the king's space carrying artifact fetishes, muskets, and standards. Fetishes of the Amazons are explained in Alfred Burdon Ellis's *The Land of the Fetish* as being made of crockery, shells, skulls, bells, and local natural products.[96] The 300 were "Joined by about two hundred in the dress of Amazons and retainers of the late cha-cha." This entourage had been mustered in 1848 and pledged themselves as young soldiers anxious to witness the glory of the king of kings.[97] One hundred sixty Amazons entered, sat down, saluted, placed their artifacts at the front, and swore battle declarations to the king. Women in the Sousa family came forward in military costumes and joined this group. After which, the cha-chas wife, adorned with 100 ounces of pure gold, stepped forward and pledged her allegiance.[98] All told, 2400 Amazons were in attendance during this documented extravaganza.

One of the most singular items in Forbes's retellings is his color sketch of a young Sarah (Aina) Forbes Bonetta in a pale blue cotton dress, wearing patent square-toed shoes with a plaid blanket folded at her side and holding a bonnet on her right arm. Aina stares at the artist with eyes that are strong and without fear. The King of Dahomey captured Aina before he "gifted" her to Forbes in 1850 on behalf of Queen Victoria. In addition to the girl, "the trade included a keg of rum, ten heads of cowries, and a 'rich country cloth.'"[99] It is unknown why the naval officer chose to interfere with her life; maybe it was abolitionist zeal or Christian ethos. He became concerned that since she had not been killed after two years of enslavement, the Dahomey king considered her high status and, therefore, she was merely awaiting the fate of becoming a human sacrifice at a future point in time. Aina was baptized on the return trip to England at the Church Missionary Society in the slave trading port of Badagry and given the Christian name Sarah Forbes Bonetta, a combination of the captain's surname and the name of his ship. The crew became attached to Sarah and called her Sally.[100]

After returning to Britain, Forbes arranged a meeting with Queen Victoria and Aina at Windsor Castle. Upon meeting the girl, Her Highness decided to serve as her education and welfare guardian. Victoria wrote in her journal: "Capt. Forbes saved her life by asking for her as a present…She is seven years old, sharp, intelligent, and speaks English. She was dressed as any other girl. When her bonnet was removed, her little Black woolly head and big earrings gave her the true negro type."[101] Also written down by the Queen was this comment, "She is a perfect genius; she now speaks English well and has a great talent for music…She is far ahead of any white child of her age in aptness of learning and strength of mind and affections."[102]

Forbes and his wife housed Sarah and took her on regular outings to visit the Queen, where she was presented at many society events and attended Princess Victoria's Wedding. In 1851, she was sent to the Church Missionary Society School in Freetown, Sierra Leon, remaining there for four years. Despite being far from London, Queen Victoria sent her presents and books. On returning to England, Sarah was placed with a family of former missionaries in Kent for six years. Her next move was to Brighton, where the Queen arranged for her to "come out" as a respected member of British society. Sarah's accomplishments made her a darling of the press, who enjoyed placing her as an opposing force to the commonly narrow-minded beliefs of the inferiority of Africans.

Upon turning nineteen, the Queen approved a marriage match with merchant James Davies, a Sierra Leon native who was the son of emancipated parents. Their marriage certificate shows the name Ina rather than Sarah. The bride-to-be wrote a letter about her upcoming betrothal, "Others would say he is a good man and though you don't care about him now, will soon learn to love him. That, I believe, I never could do. I know that the generality

112 Women and War

of people would say he is rich, and your marrying him would at once make you independent, and I say, Am I to barter my peace of mind for money? No-never!"[103] Three children later, the couple now residing in Sierra Leon, and her husband's business failing, Sarah died of tuberculosis at age 37. Living as a Petrie dish for experimentation with attitudes toward race, Sarah's life had been a different form of enslavement. She was used as an investigation by the upper classes as to whether Africans could be 'civilized' with proper British guidance.

Sir Francis Richard Burton stands out as the more egoistic of the four African adventurers. He was a prolific traveler and explored not only Africa but the continents of Asia and the Americas. His global treks allowed him to collect a vast understanding of over 20 languages and observe the unique attributes of many cultures. Burton had interests in behavior, birding, sexual practices, and ethnography. Descriptions of his trysts and the sexual organs of the local populations resulted in the categorization of his writings as scandalous. In *The Devil Drives: The Life of Richard Burton*, written by Fawn Brody, Burton claimed, "I am proud to say I have committed every sin in the ten commandments."[104]

He enlisted in the army of the East India Company, "Joining the military was fit for nothing but to be shot at for sixpence a day," he quipped.[105] Men serving under Burton substantiated his demonic ferocity as a fighter. After receiving security funds from the Royal Geographical Society, he absented himself from his military role in 1853. Then, he disguised himself under the fake persona of Haji Abdullah, dressed in a kandora and keffiyeh, and began a Muslim pilgrimage to Mecca and Media.[106] Other travels took him to Somaliland, the African Great Lakes, Zanzibar, Lake Tanganyika, the Nile River, and Constantinople, where he was recommissioned to fight in the Crimean War.

Within Burton's first volume of work on his African observations are 27 mentions of the Dahomey Amazons. All examinations of their behavior and mode of dress occurred during exhibitions and performances for visitors at festivals. He never witnessed the women during a battle. The King bestowed upon Burton the honorable title of Commandant of the Amazons.[107] Women make their first appearance in the diary during a village entertainment. From one of his interfaces is this account. Four soldieresses armed with muskets, habited in tunics and white culottes with two blue patches meant for crocodiles, appeared before the king. In command of the women was an old female in a man's straw hat, a green waistcoat, a white shirt, blue waistcloth, and a sash of white calico. A *virago*, a classification given to violent domineering women, directed the dance and song with an iron ferrule with her head shaded by an umbrella sourced from a "God's Tree," believed to control earth, fire, water, wind, and lightning.[108] Immediately near the king were other Amazons at a squat with their gun barrels bristling upwards. Amongst them were many young girls in training for military life.[109] Burton summarized his exposure to the Amazons by stating King Glele's women were his best troops, were many thousands in number, and were crueler than any men.

Helpful information is imparted regarding the structure of the women's units. Female officers corresponded to the male Commander-in-Chief and the men's second-in-command, the Matro. These roles were comparable in the female structure to the *Khe-tun-gan* and her deputy, the *Zokhenu*. Male high officials led four battalions in times of war, and the Amazons did so similarly. A female officer, known as a *Fosupo*, served as the highest-ranking chief, or *Akpadume*, and this role was replicated in the king's male right-hand chiefs. During ceremonies, the women tinkled bells and shook rattles. Mixed companies usually sat near the king as he presided over events. Many of those nearby physically to the king had been raised under his tutelage to become corps members. Not all Amazons were present at any one festival or ceremony. Many were off hunting or attacking other kingdoms in the surrounding country.

In the Dahomeyan Court, women took precedence over men. A soldier disgracing himself was called a woman as an insult. Burton felt this sentiment to be incongruous and let this be known by proclaiming, "Yet, with truly hypothetical language from ancient times recognized as Hamitic contradictiousness," the warrioresses say, "We are no longer females, but males."[110] Using the term Hamitic clearly shows Burton's level of knowledge about the area's cultures. The reference is to an independent branch of the Afro-Asiatic linguistic family that few outsiders would have been familiar with. His penchant for observation through a sexual lens led to a comment that "Whatever she-soldier is, celibacy must be one of its rules, or the troops will be in a state of chronic functional disorder between the ages of fifteen and thirty-five.[111] This was a commentary on the women's constant state of undress on the front lines, in the palaces, and in close quarters with men, which he assumed promoted sexual promiscuity. Burton substantiates his viewpoint by noting that no fewer than one hundred and fifty Amazons were found pregnant in the corps, summarizing from this numeric that chastity in the tropics was challenging to achieve.[112]

The period writings of those who experienced the Dahomey culture are vital guideposts for understanding the Amazons. Gathering more information from storytelling, which is innate to the culture in handing down history, traditions, knowledge, and lessons, should also be considered.[113] Unfortunately, there are few studies in the English language that aid in filling this gap. Not until recently have anthropologists begun to record oral histories. Inside the country, verbal exist which state that the rulers of Dahomey enrolled women soldiers to appease the spirit of Queen Tasi Hangbé, twin sister of King Akaba (1685–1708), who is said to have ruled the kingdom singlehanded between the years 1708–1711.[114] Academicians quickly point out that a queen named

114 Women and War

Hangbe is not mentioned by the *Kpanlingan*, the formally recognized bearers of verbal tradition who are given the authority to recite lineage.[115] It has been suggested that Hangbe was erased from history due to her gender and through *damnatio memoriae*, a form of condemnation of memory that allows a person to be excluded from official accounts. Some recitations claim the elders became displeased with her bacchanalian lifestyle. Oral tradition also states she and her family remained among the Abomey under King Ghezo and were provided significant remunerations to maintain a presence in the royal household. Hangbe was also portrayed as going before the council and making a speech that predicted their actions would lead to the conquest of Dahomey by Europeans. Her descendants claim seven successors have been bearers of her lineage into the present day.

Word-of-mouth recitations can be found occasionally in modern media. In a 2021 *Washington Post* article, 85-year-old Nanlehounde Houedanou was referenced for the speeches she made at community meetings about her step-grandmother, Nafivovo, a warrior and harvester of palm oil who spent time away from fighting fixing okra soup for hungry children without concern of the trouble that interfering with family life may have caused her in the community. Seventy-two-year-old Dahoui Ayebeleyi, cited in the same *Post* piece, recalled that her grandmother, Adana, loved battle and fought with her hands instead of the muskets they had been given, which took too long to load. "She'd rather be ambushing an enemy, tussling with her bare hands, and strangling people using her long fingernails, curling her hands into deadly claws."[116] On hitting puberty, Adana taught her grandchildren self-defense and believed battle imparted life lessons: patience, calm, and deliberate acts. Additional information was also imparted. Amazons used chokehold moves, fought barefoot, and wielded clubs and knives. Reapers carried three-foot-long razors to cut enemies in half.[117]

On the field of battle with the Amazons and the end of the King's Female Warriors

Colonialist adventure stories recount images of the women at their home base in celebratory or pre-battle mode. Their records do not give details of the Amazon's actions in battle. Eyewitness accounts from European soldiers must be relied upon to fill in this portion of their lives. Explanations were many. Women participated in the fight at Dogba in September of 1892 when the Fon attacked the French.

In this battle, the Amazons suffered heavy losses and halted their charges only after several hours of bloodshed. In October, the Fon attacked the French at Poguessa, where they once again suffered heavy casualties. Two days afterward, the Fon attacked the village at Adegon. Intense clashes arose in Cana, with the Dahomey being massacred by French firepower. French legionnaires

FIGURE 5.4 Illustration from a French magazine of the Battle of Dogba.

© Gallica Digital Library and is available under the digital ID btv1b6938782f. This image from the Bibliothèque nationale de France (BnF) is a reproduction by scanning of a bidimensional work that is now in the public domain.

left reports that the women were the fiercest combatants they had to battle, and the struggles occurred in close quarters using slashing weapons. Two days after the Battle of Cana, as a last effort, the king of Dahomey drove his slaves and convicts out to fight with the 1500 Amazons left in the field. After failing to turn the tide in his favor, the king razed the capital of Abomey and fled north, later turning himself over to the French government. He was banished to Martinique and then moved to Algeria.

One of the most descriptive eyewitness accounts of the Amazons was related by British Legionnaire Frederick Martyn, who served under General Alfred Amedee Dodds, the commander of French forces during the First and Second Dahomeyan Wars.[118] He published his experiences in *Life in the Legion: From a Soldier's Point of View* in 1911.[119] Part of the book's content was reported in the *New York Times* as a special edition in 1912.[120]

> The body of the enemy (Dahomeyan soldiers) that was opposed to us had not had enough and, led by a few Amazons, were coming on again.

116 Women and War

During this rush, a foolishly brave Sergeant Major got right into the midst of the Amazons, who closed round him and took him away with them. Next day, his body was found some distance away by a scouting party. It bore signs of the man being tortured to death and mutilated in a manner that cannot be described.[121]

A five-hour battle took place.

At the end of which the King's army was in full retreat. We had taken a few prisoners, including two Amazons, all of whom were shot by way of reprisal for the torture and mutilation of the Sergeant Major. Doubtless, many have believed that the Amazons were a sort of side issue with the Dahomeyan army and not much good in a fight.[122]

Martyn had encountered them many times and

Emphatically declared them the best soldiers in the enemy's army. A thing worth noting by gentlemen who opposed woman suffrage on the grounds that women are physically unable to bear arms.[123]

Next, a battalion of Amazons attacked the Senegalese Tirailleurs. These were the first Black soldiers, referred to as *laptots*, to serve France. All were trusted formerly enslaved people recruited from sub-Saharan Africa to provide security for the vessels of the French East India Company.

...Amazons attacked them and gave them a very rough time indeed. Anyone inclined to sympathize with the Amazons on account of their sex and look upon the combat between them and our men as unequal may take it from me that their sympathy would be misplaced. These young women were far and away the best men in the Dahomeyan army, and woman to man were quite a match for any of us. They were armed with Spencer repeating carbines and made much better use of them than the men made of their rifles, and for work at close quarters, they had a small heavy chopping sword or knife very much like a South American machete with which they did great execution. They fought like unchained demons and, when driven into a corner, did not disdain the use of their teeth and nails.[124]

One of them was seized and disarmed by a marine infantryman in this fight. She was so far from being beaten that she at once turned on her captor and set about biting his nose off. The man yelled out for his mother, but the lady would not leave off wearing him until she was cut down by the sword of an officer who rushed to the man's assistance. The uniform of these female warriors was a sort of kilted divided skirt of blue cotton stuff. This garment barely reached to the knees. It was supported at the waist by a leather belt which carried the cartridge pouches. The upper part of their bodies was quite nude, but the head was covered with a coquettish red fez or tarboosh into which she stuck an eagle's feather. These ladies were all exceedingly well developed and some of them were very handsome. One Amazon, in particular, was very enterprising. She deliberately advanced to within a couple of dozen paces of the officer commanding the battalion of the legion and put a bullet into his chest. The bravery and the military skill of these women soldiers filled us with admiration and we were pretty well agreed that if the whole of the Dahomeyan army had been made up of them, it would have taken a much larger force than ours to have got to Abomey.[125]

Such melees were a standard style of fighting used by the Dahomey, which relied on amassed waves of people rather than technology to overcome adversaries. Fighting at abnormally close range was part of their strategic equation. Using this formula meant that any leader overseeing the pell-mell actions would lose control, and any organized onslaught was impossible. Reliance was upon sheer physical force and large contingents of the warrior classes.[126] A further eyewitness account from the battle at Akpa testified the French forces bivouacked, and the King's army brutally attacked them in waves. The Amazons were reported as appearing on the front lines on the second day of battle, fighting ferociously. During the French Legion counterattack, they were wiped out in a bayonet charge, and an entire unit of Dahomey fighters was annihilated.[127]

Costuming the Dahomey Amazon Exotica and Baseball

They were called exotic displays, using humans from non-western cultures as exhibitable artifacts at expositions and fairs.[128] The driving force behind these exposes was to show the prowess of industrial power, new inventions, and recent scientific discoveries. Along with the buildings full of modern technological achievements were carnival-like areas called midways with rides, dime stores, cheap souvenirs, games, and vendors. Beyond the property that housed the main halls, different cultures considered bizarre by Westerners were now available to them in a constrained, theatrical environment. Inclusion criteria for exhibits aligned with the quack science of phrenology and bigoted biases about skin color, facial features, head shapes, and hair type. Significant lifestyle differences guided organizers in their choice of pageantry. Everyday routines and staged dramatic recreations in traditional attire, use of weapons, nakedness, theater plays, collective marches through the fair, and sacred rituals drew crowds of hundreds daily.

118 Women and War

The Dahomey Amazons became part of this milieu at the 1889 Paris Exposition *Universelle* and the 1890 Berlin Exposition, the London Crystal Palace Exposition in 1893, again in Paris in 1891 as an African female dance troupe at the Paris Hall of the Jardin, and the US Columbian Exposition in 1893.[129] The group became the most legendary of all the peoples exhibited in Europe and America.[130] Women warriors performed at London's Oxford Music Hall and were billed for shows at the Waverley Market and Edinburg's Christmas and New Year carnival. In 1891, 24 Dahomeyan female warriors, 16 men, and two musicians appeared at the *Jardin zoologique d Acclimation*, which Napoleon II and Empress Eugenie opened nearly 30 years earlier in 1860 as a place to acclimatize flora and fauna collected from around the globe. Sideshow creator Thomas Bruneau, responsible for organizing the most significant ethnographic exhibitions of the day, used Paris orchestral pieces and light shows to replicate the French legion's burning of the Dahomeyan capital.[131] The event appeared for the first time in 1892 and was billed as *La Prise d'Abomey*, which headlined later as *Au Dahomey*. Ten program elements comprised the pantomime. Most popular was the warrior dance by the Amazons. The overall appearance of the troupe was akin to a cabaret or burlesque show. As the real battles of the Franco-Dahomeyan war carried on, Paris became infatuated with the women, creating plays that required more Amazons to be brought to France to portray mock battles.[132]

Little is known about remuneration or the women's plight behind the stage lights. A small window into their world as travelers appeared in a one-paragraph article in the *London Chronicle* from 1903. Evidently, the Dahomey Amazon title was given to touring African women in general, as the six women called Amazons were from Sierra Leon, nearly 100 miles from the Dahomey homeland. The incident was set in a Salvation Army social hall where women's welfare was the chosen topic of the evening. Arriving as guests of Mrs. Bramwell Booth, the wife of the first Chief of Staff and the second General of the Salvation Army, the tall women, "clad in curious garb, stalked through the hall" and sat on the stage in chairs supplied for them. They had received the attention of the Protestant charitable organization to obtain wages that were in arrears, and they did not have enough money for passage to return home. Booth stated they knew nothing about fighting and "before they departed from West Africa on their European tour had followed the peaceful calling of selling bananas."[133]

Living exhibits of the period were inspired by the staging work of two Germans, Heinrich Bodinus, creator of the Cologne and Berlin Zoological Gardens, and Carl Hagenbeck, a supplier and merchant of wild animals.[134] The two-person team constructed three-dimensional dioramas with exotic animals and people in replicas of igloos and grass huts. Native plants, weapons, and domestic utensils acquired on expeditions by colonial explorers were added to the structural pieces.[135] American anthropologist and biologist

Frederic Putnam was assigned as lead curator to head and guide all human studies program elements at the Chicago Exhibition Midway and in the numerous cultural buildings.[136] It took Putnam two years to organize his sector of the fair, and he directed excursions to the Americas and Africa to gather ethnographically interesting peoples of the world and bring back unique artifacts from beyond Europe for display.[137]

In Chicago at the World's Columbian Exposition, its name referencing the 400th anniversary of Columbus's arrival to the American continent, all but one of the exhibits of ethnic minorities were relegated to the Midway Plaisance, a mile-long collection of carnival rides, food vendors, and livestock. Stories characterized the Midway as "an opportunity to descend the spiral of evolution, tracing humanity in its highest phases down almost to its animalistic origins."[138] Business manager Xavier Pene, a French national who had grown up in West Africa, brought the Fon people to the fair in Chicago.[139] His businesses were varied. He traded in ivory, ethnological artifacts, and people. Pene appears in a memorabilia photograph published for the fair, standing at the center with a male contingent of Dahomey men wearing a Wolseley-style pith helmet, wrinkled suit, and a white straggly beard growth that covers his upper chest.[140] Eight years after the Chicago fair and before the 1901 Pan American Exposition held in Buffalo, New York, he submitted a request to develop a notably narrow-minded midway concession called Darkest Africa, which was to be set up in conjunction with two other exhibits he called The Old Plantation and the Negro Exhibit.[141] The three exhibits were initially organized for the International Paris Exposition in 1900. Among Pene's stated qualifications was that he was an accredited agent of the Buffalo, New York Society of Natural Sciences and the Smithsonian Institution.[142] The Darkest Africa exhibit had a corps of native dancers who performed the King's Dance of the Dahomeyans. This followed the production staged at the Chicago World's Fair in 1893, when Xavier first acted as their agent.

The placement of the Dahomey as exhibition material at the end of the Midway was purposeful. Three segments were created: the "most evolved" cultures located first, the "half-civilized" at the center, and the "least evolved" cultures at the far end, which were the Dahomeyans and Indigenous Americans.[143] The only Black culture allowed away from the locale of the Midway in Chicago was the Republic of Haiti, which was placed near the German and Spanish buildings as part of the main exhibit called the White City.[144] American novella and short story essayist Nathaniel Hawthorne's son, Julian, ridiculed the absurdity of the situation and publicly stated, "The Midway should be named the World as Plaything with humans as landscapes and objects that invite Americans to view other cultures as toys."[145]

Twenty-five Amazons and ten male companions performed in the Chicago shows. The women carried ancient French guns and sabers, started with a roll call, sang a war song, and did a battle enactment, sword exercise, and

120 Women and War

war dance.[146] To the culturally uneducated, the Dahomey costumes were viewed as promiscuous. An advance ticket for the event shows a barefooted Black woman wearing an above-the-knee soft toga and a band with a large feather placed on her forehead. Women's styles in the West and Europe at the time embraced puff sleeves, which covered most or all of the arm, high necks, and bell-shaped skirts that hung to the ground. Expectations were that clothing would create an S-shaped curvature of the chest and hips. Covering up the body was essential to projecting proper etiquette in society. Dressing required owning numerous shoes, gloves, hats, different outerwear, and around-the-house ensembles. Added to this cacophony and expense were social rules that required other attire for morning, afternoon, and evening. A fire broke out at the village in June 1893 when the cookshop burst into flames, and the roof was set ablaze. Spectators stood agog as the scantily clad women danced on the burning building in their bare feet, others putting their bare hands and teeth to the reed shingles to pull them off and extinguish the flames.[147]

At the London exposition, 58 men and women participated in the Dahomey show and were portrayed as performing athletic feats with marvelous agility by the weekly paper *Era*. An ad for the Crystal Palace ran in the news from July through September of 1893 and was listed as top-billed acts, magnificent fireworks display every Thursday, and the famous Amazon warriors "as powerful and the greatest novelty in Europe." The Amazons shared billing with Prandi's royal Italian marionettes, French American entertainer, stage actor, and pantomimist Paul Martinetti, and Lockhart's incredible elephants. A reference to the Dahomey women in the *Pall Mall Gazette* and *The Daily Telegraph* had a decidedly colonialist flair. The regiment of women warriors was pronounced as being captured in Dahomey by the French Army by General Alfred-Amedee Dodds, who had commanded Legionnaire Frederick Martyn. Dodds was publicized as a cross-cultural phenom whose heredity was one-quarter African-Aboriginal and part-Canadian French Indigenous. His lengthy military service resume was stated as part of the promotional jargon. It was mentioned he had been successful in subjugating the Dahomey of the African Kingdoms and had fought in Senegal, Cochinchina, Casamance, and Tonkin and commanded during the Franco-Prussian War, the Boxer Rebellion, and the Second Franco-Dahomeyan War.

The Daily Telegraph heralded the Amazons, "Nothing so original has been seen in England for many a long day, including exhibitions in sorcery, sword dancing, prayer dancing, and sham fighting." Notices proclaimed they were stalwart, naked-footed, fighting women with sinewy strength and dexterity in using arms, fresh from the campaigns in Africa. A viewing of the program could be had for sixpence and one shilling.[148] *The Daily Chronicle* celebrated the sight as "A strong attraction, both for its novelty and the alacrity with which it displays the drill of a savage army." In the *London Standard*, the statement was made that the Dahomey were the "finest of the races of Africa." Another report from London called the women "grand specimens of Muscular Womanhood." At one point, their meager costumes incited the wrath of a shopkeeper who was angered by the crowds blocking his store near the theaters, attempting to glimpse the group entering and exiting their buses at the Canterbury and Oxford Music Halls. Policemen were assigned to ensure the women were "well wrapped up," and the judge overseeing the complaint determined the onlookers blocking the front of the wholesale watch and clock business should be allowed to continue their public rubbernecking.[149]

One of the most unusual anecdotes about the Dahomey Amazons occurred in 1905 when Artie Duggan, who pitched for the Chicago Blues, a branch of the National League in 1890, moved to Africa to work as a civil engineer on a construction line for the French railway system. The tracks eventually ran from the Gulf of Guinea to the Niger River. In letters home, Duggan told of the development of the Dahomeyan National League and jokingly challenged the pennant winners that year, the Brooklyn Bridegrooms and the Louisville Colonels, to a match.[150] He found a game similar to American baseball already existed in the region, a mix of batting, fielding, and running bases similar to backlot games played across the United States. The locals were agile, with wonderful skill, and with great aptitude when shown how to improve their play using American rules and techniques. The African game was played with three bases set in a triangle, a pitcher in the center, and as many outfielders as wanted to play. Baseballs were made of material from trees, covered with lion or monkey skin, and then soaked until they were hard. These were later improved by using antelope skin and rubber. Spectators sat on elevated ground to watch. Duggan wrote in a letter home, "Tell Ted Sullivan," a manager, player, promoter, and scout who authored books on barnstorming, "the expense of starting a league here would be small. I can get him franchises from the king."[151]

"You should have seen them when I pitched an old barrel hoop curve. It was big medicine; they came from all around to watch it," Duggan bragged. Those attending supposed he had put magic on the ball. In Duggan's view, "The women in this country are stronger and faster than the men, so I picked my team from a company of Amazons." He named his team the Browns after the color of the "near-uniform they wore." "In fighting, they wear short aprons of shell strung together, but when they play baseball, they discard all these." A second civil engineer, only referred to as Wilson from Elmira, New York, trained a team to play against Duggan's group. At the first Wilson-Duggan match, the Americans in the work party cheered for Duggan's team, not Wilson's, establishing an informal competition between the two men. Mafighbwebeke, whom Duggan called "Belle," was to be his pitcher. "Belle has speed, curves, and good command," observed Duggan, and she put "the kibosh on Wilson's team."

122 Women and War

Additional squads were organized in Savalous, Nikki, Parakou, Kllibo, Perere, Diguidirou, Dunkassa, and Carnotville. Moving on to work in Savalou, the enterprising ex-ball player continued to team up with locals to form additional ball clubs. There is no known ending to the story of Duggan in Africa, and the women are not believed to have ever come to America as barnstormers.

The fighting Dahomey Amazon from head to toe

A photograph from the London Exposition is the most replicated and cited source of how the Dahomey Amazons dressed for battle. The image in color is one of jaw-dropping beauty, and the group is disarmingly pageant-worthy. The photo is not, however, a realistic portrayal of war gear. An aura of theatricality, showiness, and entertainment is palpable in the extravagance of their wearable cowrie art and the choice of the rich carmine color of their clothing. Only royalty wore red in the kingdom of Whydah, at the base of what is now Benin on the Gulf of Guinea. The color choice can be read as a status symbol, and outsiders would probably have been clueless about its importance. All in the photo are youthful and poised. Their lovely faces, arms, and legs do not indicate the likelihood they had experienced the physical abuse of battle. It is also unknown if they are from the Fon culture or neighboring ethnic groups. Knowing that Xavier Pene or a similar huckster was the likely collector of the troupe gives credence to the thinking that the women were selected for the express purpose of showmanship, not as accredited assailants from the Franco-Dahomeyan Wars.

Each of the women, who look like they may range in age from six or seven to their late teens and early twenties, are dripping with valuable cowrie shells on their headbands, necklaces and earrings, armbands, and bracelets. Blue, white, and red striped silk sashes with fringe cinch their knee-length skirts at the waist. Hand-sewn, gold flower-like embroidery engulfs the cloth on the skirts. Most striking are the cowrie shell bodices. All are of unique design and created from hundreds of the kingdom's prized opaque gastropods. Due to the extravagance of what was worn, the women in the photo may have represented the wealthiest families in the kingdom or were benefactors of the highest-ranking members of their society. Some may have been chosen from the king's household because of their social status and physical virtues. The costumes represent Dahomeyan womanhood, fertility, noble or noble-associated birth lines, and wealth, but not war.

Dress of the Fon from the 18th century onward often incorporated textiles and aesthetics borrowed from outsiders. Before the slave trade increased the wealth and interface of the Fon people with other cultures from off the African continent, they wore few cloth items.[152] If these were part of their wardrobes, they used draping rather than stitching and cutting patterns in their designs. Royalty wore ornate items made from cotton and silk with many appliques, usually of two pieces comprised of a robe *Kansawu* and trousers. Royal caps were elaborate and made of imported silk with animal cutouts and fancy hand quilting embellishing the entire form. Jackets and surcoats with girdles could be made of hide, woolen, or flannel cloth. These were often decorated with fancy embroidery or bells.

Animalia symbols were specific to each king and often were sewn onto wearable fashions. For Gangnihessou 1600–1620, the King of Allada, the symbol was the bird and drum; for Dakodonou 1620–1625, the indigo jar and briquettes; for Houegbadja 1645–1685, the fish and wicker trap. Akabo, who reigned from 1685–1708, used the symbols of the wild boar, chameleon, and sword, Agadja 1708–1741, the boat signifying his contact with Europeans and the slave trade. King Tegbessou, 1741–1774, used the buffalo wearing a tunic dressed up, Kpeingla 1774–1789, symbols were the sparrow and the gun as a message about his ability to strengthen, arm, and conquer the coastal cities. Kpeingla was also known to have created a corps of Amazons. Angonglo, who reigned from 1789 to 1797 and was the only Dahomeyan king to marry a European woman, used the pineapple. Kings Ghezo and Glele's symbols were a buffalo without a dress and a lion. During the timeframe of the Exposition in London, King Gbehanzin was the ruler, and he used the royal symbols of a shark and an egg.[153] Using animal symbols to express lineage and incredible feats explains why Burton, Skertchly, Fobes, and Duncan often saw them.

Most European colonialists who lived among the Dahomey for short periods portray the Amazons as wearing two types of uniforms: those for fighting and those for parades and celebrations. Battle dress was somber, usually dark blue, wood color, or rusty. The colors red and blue were attained by soaking cloth in dyes made from seeds, flowers, and plants. The brown fabric was made using blood and bark as dying agents. Bystanders saw the Dahomey in blue and white striped shorts; others saw skirts of fresh-cut grasses.[154] Parade dress was often made of finer, brighter fabrics and more dazzling headgear. Tunics could be scarlet red, crimson, green, pale blue, half blue, red-blue, or multicolored and made of silk, velvet, chintz, and Indian cotton.

Duncan's description from 1845 told of the women wearing regimental caps. White skullcaps bearing the image of a crocodile in the center were visual reminders of the souls of ancestors and their roles as night hunters of meat. Five years later, Forbes saw regiments wearing a blue emblem with either a crocodile, cross, or crown on their caps. When Burton traveled to the area in 1863, he reported a variety of caps. Red caps with silver sharks on them or dark tortoises on gray or white caps signified an association with beaches, terrestrial turtles, and the blue sharks that stalked the Gulf of Guinea and Bight of Benin. Several Fon caps were blue, or a dingy white turned to a dreary gray due to their use in the bush. With the Fon, animalia appliques

124 Women and War

were the most common. Headwear also became pertinent as trade items. In 1847, Captain Willliam Winniett served as a military officer and later as the lieutenant governor of the Gold Coast (Ghana). He wrote a letter to Queen Victoria requesting 2000 war caps to be made for the female troops. The Queen eagerly obliged.

Cloth waist sashes, usually red, blue, or white, with or without a cartridge belt, were standard for most women.[155] Shoulder sashes were mentioned frequently, and Skertchly commented that he saw gray, brown, dark blue, and white sashes strung across the left shoulder. When Parisian M. Edmond Chaudoin, manager of the trading firm of Fabre and Company at Whydah, was captured by the King of Dahomey in the 1890s, he wrote of his time as a prisoner in the autobiography *Three Months of Captivity in Dahomey* of seeing little girls wearing a string of beads around their waists.[156] As they grew older and if a family was affluent, strings of up to ten rows, usually made of thick glass or coral, were added.

The illustrated Amazon

France's public remained fascinated with Dahomey for nearly one hundred years. Chronicles of their colonialist excursions began in the 18th century, and readers devoured each major event's details. Well before the French-Dahomey Wars had started and during the early years of the Republic's influence in Africa, French artist Jacques Grasset de Saint-Sauveur produced several glamorized prints and engravings of Amazons.[157] On their heads sat *turban et plumes*, popular during the Regency era; their poses were of seated or standing winsome coquettes. Some wore a type of Roman sandal, held arrows and bows, and sported quivers. Each of de Saint-sauveur's illustrations projected a sense of stage drama rather than replications of the warrior caste. This form of rosy fashion interpretation shifted toward greater realism during the timeframe of the Dahomey-Franco wars.

Some reasonable deductions can be made about what was actual battle gear and what was costume by looking at images of art and photography of the fighting women. Stories from French legionnaire Frederick Martyn and others experiencing direct contact with the Dahomeyans became helpful background material for creating true-to-life color illustrations in French news sources, travel periodicals, and popular journals like *Le Petit*.[158] *Le Petit* was a ten-page pulp sold to workers on the street at the same hour they left their offices in the evening, with stories of French colonialism, war, and political events. Its popularity was high due to its variety of content, which incorporated current events with printed horoscopes, opinion pieces, and a fictional series about a detective named Monsieur (the Rooster) Lecoq. Sir Arthur Conan Doyle referenced Lecoq as a "miserable bungler" in his introductory novel *A Study in Scarlet*, the first time

Uniforms as Artifacts   **125**

FIGURE 5.5   Picture postcard of the costumes and utensils of a Dahomey veteran tribe.

© Creative Commons CCO License File: The célébration at Abomey (1908). The veteran amazones (AHOSI) of the Fon king Béhanzin, Son of Roi Gélé.jpg – Wikipedia.

the British detective Sherlock Holmes and Dr. Watson appeared in print in *Beeton's Christmas Annual* in 1887.[159]

A colorized photo turned postcard from the 1863 travel journal *Le Tour du monde* depicted a line of veteran West Africa, Dahomey Abomey Amazons of Behanzin.

The women are in a straight line; all are tall, well beyond youth, muscular, and equal in projecting an austere, callused bearing that could only be derived from facing enemies in close quarters during their formative years. They wear multicolored clothes; cloth caps and underskirts are checkered with red motifs within each sizable square. Their bare arms and necks are adorned with woven, metal, ivory, and cowrie shell jewelry. All stand ramrod straight, holding staves with curved swords at their waists wrapped with many variegated patterned and plain silk and cotton sashes. This photographic portrayal is representative of the 50 original combatants known to still be alive in the 1890s. A warrior's disposition is clearly shown in the

126 Women and War

physical deportment and facial countenance of these women who had participated in the tortures and hell of war.

Uniform themes are evident across many of *Le Petit's* illustrations of the Amazons. Portrayals show bare upper torsos; others wear draped one-piece short-sleeved tunics that reach their knees. No footwear is worn, and arms are exposed with metal or gold armbands. Caps of red or bright-colored headbands are evident, with certain of these having feather attachments. Waist belts differ and are either cartridge clips with gunpowder bags or woven sashes used as sheaths to hold knives and spears. Usage of cowrie shells is minimal, and most often, if observed, they are shown strung as necklaces. In some instances, the women are crouching or standing waist-high in what appears to be elephant grass. The fighting looks intense, with a confused assortment of spears, long-barreled guns, and machetes being used to fight off the much heavier-outfitted, helmeted French artillery troops. In one setting, an Amazon clutches a rock, ready to crush an enemy's skull, which definitively aligns with oral histories left for generations of their first line of defense being the use of unarmed combat methods.

The death of Commander Faurax at the Battle of Dogba was recreated on the cover of *Le Monde Illustre* (The Illustrated World) news magazine, and several other interpretations of the event were broadcast in print. One shows four Dahomey warriors, two on the left and two on the right, at the front of the commotion, making them key in the layout of the illustration. Two Amazons on the lower left corner lay slain on the field; breasts bared with a striped cloth draped across their bodies, which imitated eyewitness accounts of cloth seen worn during community events. However, the fabric seems out of place since it is used artistically as a shroud. In the right front corner, central to a group of five Dahomey males, is an Amazon wearing a cowrie shell headband, several necklaces, and a short-sleeved bodice of sewn-together cowrie shells. She is fighting with bare hands and crouched in the bush grass, inches from her adversary. The male Dahomey surrounds her in varied fighting positions, one with a machete, one with a spear, one firing a long barrel gun, one deceased, and one dying. This drawing is unique. The women are highlighted at the forefront rather than the typical illustrated view from the vantage point of the colonialist troops. Commander Faurx is at the center-left, toppling from his horse. A mass of his ground troops is attempting to surround him.

Two additional French images, *Combat D'Atchoupa au Dahomey* and *Combat D'Atchoupa*, recreated the Amazons fighting in the last engagement of the First Franco-Dahomeyan War.[160] Three hundred and fifty French troops, assisted by King Toffa, a monarch who was open and cooperative with colonial expansionists, fought a force of 2000 Dahomey Amazons. The battle was bloody, and the Dahomey retreated across the Queme River and proceeded on a murderous rampage, burning down every village in their path until they reached Porto Novo. The two adversaries fought again, with King Behanzin sending 7000 of his troops comprised of 2000 Dahomey Amazons. The Amazon approach had a monstrous effect on the French forces. The onslaught was so severe that the colonialists were required to stop fighting in lines and regrouped using infantry squares, a close-order formation generally used in cavalry attacks. In the end, French firepower and discipline devastated the Dahomey. In the *Combat D'Atchoupa* drawings, the Amazons wear antler horns attached to iron bands, symbolizing power, strength, and flexibility. Their weapons are curved knives.

What is humorous about the *Combat D'Atchoupa* drawings is that the women's headdresses look more like Viking helmets than the field gear worn by the Amazons. Antlered and other horned headgear were only worn by the king's best and most lethal hunters and fighters, which is not seen later in artists' portrayals based on European first-hand accounts.

FIGURE 5.6 Two Dahomey Amazons wearing a band of iron crowned with two antelope horns symbolizing power, strength, and flexibility.

© Creative Commons CC0 1.0 Universal Public Domain Dedication ("CC0 1.0 Dedication") https://picryl.com/media/amazons-or-female-warriors-of-dahomey-4ce5f2.

128 Women and War

Since this was an earlier battle of the French Dahomeyan wars at Akba and Dogba, it may be surmised that as time passed, attrition from fighting resulted in the disappearance of the highly regarded intrepid, unconventional animal-hunting guerrilla warriors.[161] A circa 1890 sketched image of two female Dahomey soldiers in the New York Public Library collections clearly shows the uniform of the *gbeto* elephant hunters dressed in brown shirts and knee-length trousers with antelope horns attached to their forehead by an iron or gold ring. Other art in *Combat D'Atchoupa* are realistic depictions. The women are drawn as muscular and are clothed in red, yellow, blue, and green one-shoulder knee-length draped tunics. Their attire consists of cowrie shell necklaces, armbands, and ankle bands.

The Dahomey did not always lose to the more formidable French forces. On the cover of August 1892, *Let Petit Journal* is a color lithograph of a French gunboat with a group of mixed male and female combatants on the shore, in canoes and trees, shooting guns toward the river. The outcome of the fight was a French retreat, much to the astonishment of French officials who did not believe a force comprised mainly of women could beat them.[162] Amazons tower above the men, and nearly all carry guns. Each is outfitted in soft cloth knee-length tunics; a few are bareheaded, others wearing identifying caps of their units. Sometimes, the attribute of not giving up easily is sketched into drawings. Inside an 1890 *Illustrated Battles of the 19th Century*, published in Britain, is a fight between colonialist troops and the Dahomey at Cotopa.[163] An Amazon is portrayed fighting bare-fisted and being bayoneted and shot simultaneously by French troops at close quarters. She wears no bodice, has a metal arm ring on her bicep, and a waist belt with gun clips.

The iconography of Dahomey in the 21st century

Iconographic imaging identified as a realistic portrayal of the Dahomey Amazons, such as the photo from the London Exposition, did not end in the 19th century. In 2022, the film *The Woman King* screamed with blatant inaccuracies of the female body types and fighting garb of 19th-century fighters. Instead of the lean, tough, muscular women who fought in western Africa, the movie is full of prancing, large-bosomed, Playtex women, their hips jutting out in sexy poses, their guns tossed across the nape of their necks like the toughened U.S. Army youth who fought in the jungles of Vietnam in the 1960s. Instead of being historically accurate, the outfits were borrowed from costumes found in the *Le Petite* and photographs of expositions from the 1890s. Such sexualization of female warriors of the African Bush does little to promote the actualities of what it meant to be a female ground fighter. Instead, it marginalizes combatants by presenting them as spandex gym rats rather than as fierce, brutal, and avenging.

In the same year as the emergence of *The Woman King*, a statue of a Dahomeyan warrior was unveiled in Cotonou, Benin. Reports have surfaced that the figure was likely built at an art studio in North Korea, producing monolithic public renderings of the nation's dictators and tyrants. Julien Sinzogan, a Beninese artist and painter who studied architecture in Paris at the *Ecole Speciale des travaus Publics* designed the statue. The Benin government handed over Sinzogan's blueprint to the bronze casting specialists, the Chinese Blue Dragon International Development Company. The Blue Dragon is a front company for Mansuade, an art studio in North Korea. Utilizing such a company is a breach of United Nations sanctions against North Korea, and monies earned from the production of the statue likely contributed to the ongoing development of the weapons of mass destruction program under the dictatorial leader Kim Jong-un.[164]

Located in the *Esplanade des Amazones* public square in Cotonou, the deep bronze statue gleams in the African sunlight, towering over 90 feet in the air.[165] Grasping a rifle in her left hand and wielding a machete in her right, one of her bare feet strides toward the public audience that crowds around the flat open-level area to view the monolith. Her face is set in a forward, penetrating gaze. As with the American film rendering of the women, the statue is robed in a style unbefitting the true grit of their incredible legacy. Benin's statue placed prominently on African soil continues the insincere and objectified notion that the Dahomey women warriors are not presentable unless shrouded in sensual overtones.

Both artistic presentations in film and sculpture say much about the idea of enclothed cognition. The creative license used by the filmmaker and public sculptor shifted the original symbolic meaning attached to the women's uniforms away from reality and toward the current popularity of presenting females as nonsensical Barbie women ensconced in a Dacron costume. It seems that psychologically, the public is not ready to accept that women warriors do not operate in an environment of primping for sensual delight. The business of war is filthy, hostile, and unremitting, and the uniform of Dahomey was a bare-bones affair on purpose. Essential attributes of what they wore were tied first to their ability to sheath all their weapons for easy access. Second was the necessity to wear loose-fitting or no clothing to keep their appendages free for close quarters combat and to survive in what would have been the literal heat of battle. Third, as with all uniforms, applying a few differentiators in cap designs and cloth color was imperative in signifying their right to claim a fighting specialty or denote past heroics. The fighting Dahomey Amazons had a singular viewpoint about themselves.

War is our great friend; without it, there would be no cloth nor armlets; let us to war and conquer or die.

(Dahomey Oath)

130 Women and War

Notes

1 James C. Malin. "Carlyle's Philosophy of Clothes and Swedenborg's." *Scandinavian Studies* 33, no. 3 (1961): 155–68. http://www.jstor.org/stable/40916341.
   James C. Manlin. "Emanuel Swedenborg and His Clothes Philosophy." *Scandinavian Studies* 33, no. 2 (1961): 45–67. http://www.jstor.org/stable/40916327.
2 Ernst Harms. "The Psychology of Clothes." *American Journal of Sociology* 44, no. 2 (1938): 239–50. http://www.jstor.org/stable/2768730.
3 Alexandra H. Vinson. "Short White Coats: Knowledge, Identity, and Status Negotiations of First-Year Medical Students." *Symbolic Interaction* 42, no. 3 (2019): 395–411. https://www.jstor.org/stable/26760904.
4 Christian Jarrett. "Introduction 'Enclothed Cognition' How What We Wear Affects How We Think," The British Psychological Society Cognition and Perception, 01 March 2012. Introducing "enclothed cognition" – how what we wear affects how we think | BPS.
5 H. Adam, and A. D. Galinsky. "Enclothed Cognition." *Journal of Experimental Social Psychology* (2012). Doi: 10.1016/j.jesp.2012.02.008. Enclothed cognition (utoronto.ca).
6 Alexandra H. Vinson. "Short White Coats: Knowledge, Identity, and Status Negotiations of First-Year Medical Students." *Symbolic Interaction* 42, no. 3 (2019): 395–411. https://Www.Jstor.Org/Stable/26760904.
7 Ibid. p. 408.
8 Cornell Law School Legal Information Institute, 10 U.S. Code § 772 – When wearing by persons not on active duty authorized | U.S. Code | US Law | LII / Legal Information Institute (cornell.edu).
9 Sydney Johnson. "What Are the Rules for Wearing a US Military Uniform?" USO website, What Are the Rules for Wearing a U.S. Military Uniform? United Service Organizations (uso.org).
10 Nathan Joseph, and Nicholas Alex. "The Uniform: A Sociological Perspective." *American Journal of Sociology* 77, no. 4 (1972): 719–30. http://www.jstor.org/stable/2776756.
11 Paul Fussell. *Uniforms Why We Are What We Wear.* Boston: Houghton Mifflin, 2002.
12 Hilda Kuper. "Costume and Identity." *Comparative Studies in Society and History* 15, no. 3 (1973): 348–67. http://www.jstor.org/stable/178260.
13 Toni Pfanner. "Military Uniforms and the Law of War." *International Review of the Red Cross* 86, no. 853 (Mar 2004): 95.
14 Marie-Louise Nosch, and Henriette Koefoed. "Introduction and Acknowledgements." In *Wearing the Cloak: Dressing the Soldier in Roman Times*, edited by Marie-Louise Nosch, 10:v–viii. Oxbow Books, 2012. https://doi.org/10.2307/j.ctvh1ds7f.3.
   Michael Alexander Speidel. "Dressed for the Occasion: Clothes and Context in the Roman Army." In *Wearing the Cloak: Dressing the Soldier in Roman Times*, edited by Marie-Louise Nosch, 10:1–12. Oxbow Books, 2012. https://doi.org/10.2307/j.ctvh1ds7f.4.
15 Sidney Dean. "Ringing Out the Middle Ages: Landsknecht Mercenaries Lead Europe into the Renaissance." *Medieval Warfare* 1, no. 2 (2011): 12–17. https://www.jstor.org/stable/48577837.
16 "Landsknechte: Foot Soldiers of Fashion," Apr 30–Oct 30, 2016, Art Institute of Chicago Exhibition, Landsknechte: Foot Soldiers of Fashion | The Art Institute of Chicago (artic.edu).
17 Alfred P. Brainard. "Polish-Lithuanian Cavalry in the Late Seventeenth Century." *The Polish Review* 36, no. 1 (1991): 69–82. http://www.jstor.org/stable/25778547.

18 Ann Elias, Ross Harley, and Nicholas Tsoutas. "Introduction." In *Camouflage Cultures: Beyond the Art of Disappearance*, edited by Ann Elias, Ross Harley, and Nicholas Tsoutas, vii–x. Sydney University Press, 2015. http://www.jstor.org/stable/j.ctt1bh4b60.4.

Linda Tyler. "From Ghillie Suit to Glittering Kowhaiwhai – Contemporary New Zealand Artists Deploy the Camouflage Aesthetic." In *Camouflage Cultures: Beyond the Art of Disappearance*, edited by Ann Elias, Ross Harley, and Nicholas Tsoutas, 115–26. Sydney University Press, 2015. http://www.jstor.org/stable/j.ctt1bh4b60.13.

19 Robin Law. "The Slave-Trader as Historian: Robert Norris and the History of Dahomey." *History in Africa* 16 (1989): 219–35. https://doi.org/10.2307/3171786.

20 J. F. Ade Ajayi, and Robert Smith. *Yoruba Warfare in the Nineteenth Century.* Cambridge University Press, 1964.

I. A. Akinjogbin. "The Oyo Empire in the 18th Century – A Reassessment." *Journal of the Historical Society of Nigeria* 3, no. 3 (1966): 449–60. http://www.jstor.org/stable/41856706.

21 Edna G. Bay. "On the Trail of the Bush King: A Dahomean Lesson in the Use of Evidence." *History in Africa* 6 (1979): 1–15. https://doi.org/10.2307/3171738.

22 J. A. Skertchly. *Dahomey as it is: Being narrative of eight months' residence in that country, with a full account of the notorious annual customs and the social and religious institutions of the Ffons; also, an Appendix on Ashantee, and a Glossary of Dahoman Words and Titles*, 112. London: Chapman and Hall, 16 April 1874.

23 Robin Law. "Dahomey and the Slave Trade: Reflections on the Historiography of the Rise of Dahomey." *The Journal of African History* 27, no. 2 (1986): 237–67. http://www.jstor.org/stable/181135.

Robin Law. "Slave-Raiders and Middlemen, Monopolists and Free-Traders: The Supply of Slaves for the Atlantic Trade in Dahomey c. 1715–1850." *The Journal of African History* 30, no. 1 (1989): 45–68. http://www.jstor.org/stable/182694.

24 Patrick Manning. "The Slave Trade: The Formal Demography of a Global System." *Science History* 14 (1990): 2255–79.

25 Henry A. Gemery, and Jan S. Hogendorn, "The Uncommon Market Essay in the Economic History of the Atlantic Slave Trade, Studies in Social Discontinuity, 117. Academic Press, NY, 1979. SlaveryDahomey.pdf (pitt.edu).

26 Ibid.

27 Emilia Viotti da Costa. "The Portuguese African Slave Trade: A Lesson in Colonialism." *Latin American Perspectives* 12, no. 1 (1985): 41–61. http://www.jstor.org/stable/2633561.

28 "Dahomeyans Revel in Cruelty, the Savage African Tribe Which Delights to Kill and Torment," *Chicago Daily Tribune*, (1872–1922), Jun 13, 1892, ProQuest Historical Newspapers.

29 Ibid. Dahomeyans Revel.

30 Suzanne Preston Blier. "The Path of the Leopard: Motherhood and Majesty in Early Danhomè." *The Journal of African History* 36, no. 3 (1995): 391–417. http://www.jstor.org/stable/182468.

31 C. M. Peniston-Bird. *War in History* 8, no. 4 (2001): 483–85. http://www.jstor.org/stable/26013914.

32 R. A. Kea. "Firearms and Warfare on the Gold and Slave Coasts from the Sixteenth to the Nineteenth Centuries". *The Journal of African History* 12, no. 2 (1971): 185–213. Doi: 10.1017/S002185370001063X. ISSN 0021-8537. JSTOR 180879. S2CID 163027192.

33 Peter Morton-Williams. "A Yoruba Woman Remembers Servitude in a Palace of Dahomey, in the Reigns of Kings Glele and Behanzin." *Africa: Journal of the International African Institute* 63, no. 1 (1993): 102–17. https://doi.org/10.2307/1161300.

132 Women and War

34 "A mission to Gelele, king of Dahome. With notices of the so-called "Amazons," the grand customs, the yearly customs, the human sacrifices, the present state of the slave trade, and the Negro's place in nature," World Digital Library, General Collections, Library of Congress Online Catalog, Tinsley Brothers, 1864.

35 Agbenyega Adedze. "The Amazons of Dahomey," 29 May 2020. https://doi.org/10.1093/acrefore/9780190277734.013.274.

36 "Cowrie Shells, and Trade Power." National Museum of African American History and Culture, Cowrie Shells and Trade Power | National Museum of African American History and Culture (si.edu).

37 R. J. Bunche. *The Journal of Negro Education* 8, no. 2 (1939): 209–12. https://doi.org/10.2307/2292577. David Ross. "Mid-Nineteenth Century Dahomey: Recent Views vs. Contemporary Evidence." *History in Africa* 12 (1985): 307–23. https://doi.org/10.2307/3171725.

38 Robin Law. "Royal Monopoly and Private Enterprise in the Atlantic Trade: The Case of Dahomey." *The Journal of African History* 18, no. 4 (1977): 555–77. http://www.jstor.org/stable/180832.

39 Thomas Bierschenk. "The Creation of a Tradition: Fulani Chiefs in Dahomey/Bénin from the Late 19th Century." *Paideuma* 39 (1993): 217–44. http://www.jstor.org/stable/40341663.

Christopher Chamberlin. "Bulk Exports, Trade Tiers, Regulation, and Development: An Economic Approach to the Study of West Africa's 'Legitimate Trade.'" *The Journal of Economic History* 39, no. 2 (1979): 419–38. http://www.jstor.org/stable/2118946.

40 Simcha Lev-Yadun. "Does the whistling thorn acacia (Acacia drepanolobium) use auditory aposematism to deter mammalian herbivores?" *Plant Singal Behav* 11, no. 8 (2016): e 1307035. Doi: 10.1080/15592325.2016.1207035.

41 Margaret T. Shaw, Felicia Keesing, and Richard S. Ostfeld. "Herbivory on Acacia Seedlings in an East African Savanna." *Oikos* 98, no. 3 (2002): 385–92. http://www.jstor.org/stable/3547179.

42 Rory Pilossof. Review of *"Guns Don't Colonise People…": The Role and Use of Firearms in Pre-Colonial and Colonial Africa*, by John Lamphear, William K. Storey, Jeff Guy, and Joseph P. Smaldone. *Kronos*, no. 36 (2010): 266–77. http://www.jstor.org/stable/41056654.

43 "Woman as Warriors: Dahomey to Fight the French Invaders with Amazons. Severity of the Drill to Which Its Unique Army is Subjected–Kicked, Cuffed, Beaten and Starved, Its Members Develop Unnatural Ferocity – the Sacrifice of Human Victims is Another of the Little Peculiarities of the Country that France is about to Devour." *Chicago Daily Tribune (1872–1922)*, Aug 14, 1892. https://login.usnwc.idm.oclc.org/login?qurl=https%3A%2F%2Fwww.proquest.com%2Fhistorical-newspapers%2Fwoman-as-warriors%2Fdocview%2F174653846%2Fse-2%3Faccountid%3D322.

44 Ibid.

45 "The Dahoman Amazons: Their Reckless Daring and Bravery in Battle," *The Chicago Daily Tribune*, July 20, 1890, ProQuest Historical Newspapers: p. 27.

46 "Dahomeyans Revel in Cruelty, The Savage African Tribe which Delights to Kill and Torture," *Chicago Daily Tribune*, June 13, 1892, ProQuest Historical Newspapers, p. 10.

47 For additional opinion about the European travelers who went to Dahomey, themes, and viewpoints, see the chapter by Manning, "The Slave Trade in the Bight of Benin, 1640–1690, pp. 107–116. 1979. SlaveryDahomey.pdf (pitt.edu).

48 Op. cit. Skertchly Richard Francis Burton. *A Mission to Gelele, King of Dahome, In Two Volumes*. London: Tinsley Brothers, 1864. Frederick E. Forbes, *Dahomey, and the Dahomans being the journals of two missions to the king*

of Dahomey and residence in his capital in the years 1849 and 1850, London: Longman, Brown, Green, and Longmans, 1851. John Duncan. *Travels in Western Africa in 1845 and 1846 in two volumes comprising a journey from Whydah through the Kingdom of Dahome yto Adofoodia in the interior.* UK: Richard Bentley, 1847.

49 Tim Jeal. "Introduction: A Contradictory Hero." In *Livingstone: Revised and Expanded Edition*, 1–4. Yale University Press, 2013. http://www.jstor.org/stable/j.ctt32bm79.6.

Tim Jeal. "The Last Journey: 1872–1873." In *Livingstone: Revised and Expanded Edition*, 365–81. Yale University Press, 2013. http://www.jstor.org/stable/j.ctt32bm79.29.

50 Marion Johnson. "News from Nowhere: Duncan and 'Adofoodia.'" *History in Africa* 1 (1974): 55–66. https://doi.org/10.2307/3171760.

51 Op. cit. Duncan pp. iv, v.

52 Ibid. Footnote p. ix.

53 Kirkcudbright Parish. "John Duncan: Travels in Western Africa, 1845 and 1846," John Duncan: Travels in Western Africa, 1845 and 1846. (kirkcudbright.co).

54 Op. cit. Skertchley, p. 103 Image 125 of Volume 2 | Library of Congress (loc.gov).

55 R. F. Burton. "The Kong Mountains." *Proceedings of the Royal Geographical Society and Monthly Record of Geography* 4, no. 8 (1882): 484–86. https://doi.org/10.2307/1800716.

56 Derek O'Conner. "Joun Duncan African Explorer 1804–1849," John Duncan African Explorer, Clan Duncan Society – Scotland UK (clan-duncan.co.uk). Acknowledgement from the book *The Kings Stranger* by Derek O'Conner.

57 Ibid.

58 Robin Law. "Further Light on John Duncan's Account of the 'Fellatah Country' (1845)." *History in Africa* 28 (2001): 129–38. https://doi.org/10.2307/3172211.

59 Op. cit. Duncan, pp. 225–6.

60 Ibid. p. 228.

61 Ibid. p. 226.

62 Ibid. p 227.

63 Ibid.

64 Ibid.

65 Dahomey Skertchly as it is: Being a narrative of eight months' residence in that country ... : J. A. Skertchly (J. Alfred): Free Download, Borrow, and Streaming : Internet Archive, p. 145.

66 Ibid. p. 171.

67 Ibid. p. 168.

68 Ibid. p. 103. Library of Congress website.

69 Ibid. p. 166.

70 Ibid.

71 Ibid. p. 281.

72 Ibid. p. 344.

73 Ibid. p. 196.

74 Ibid. p. 189.

75 Roy Bridges. "The Visit of Frederick Forbes to the Somali Coast in 1833." *The International Journal of African Historical Studies* 19, no. 4 (1986): 679–91. https://doi.org/10.2307/219140.

"HMS Bonetta (1836) Royal Naval Vessels," HMS Bonetta (pdavis.nl).

76 Mary Wills. "Abolition at Sea." In *Envoys of Abolition: British Naval Officers and the Campaign Against the Slave Trade in West Africa*, 15–40. Liverpool University Press, 2019. https://doi.org/10.2307/j.ctvsn3p4h.7.

134 Women and War

Mary Wills. "Officers' Commitment to the Anti-Slavery Cause." In *Envoys of Abolition: British Naval Officers and the Campaign against the Slave Trade in West Africa*, 69–96. Liverpool University Press, 2019. https://doi.org/10.2307/j.ctvsn3p4h.9.

Mary Wills. "Officers' Contributions to Britain's Anti-Slavery Culture." In *Envoys of Abolition: British Naval Officers and the Campaign against the Slave Trade in West Africa*, 167–90. Liverpool University Press, 2019. https://doi.org/10.2307/j.ctvsn3p4h.12.

77 Jessica Brain. "The West Africa Squadron," Historic UK, 4 Mar 2023, The West Africa Squadron – Historic UK (historic-uk.com).

78 James C. Duram. "A Study of Frustration: Britain, the USA, and the African Slave Trade, 1815–1870." *Social Science* 40, no. 4 (1965): 220–25. http://www.jstor.org/stable/41885111.

79 Anita Rupprecht. "'All We Have Done, We Have Done for Freedom': The *Creole* Slave-Ship Revolt (1841) and the Revolutionary Atlantic." *International Review of Social History* 58 (2013): 253–77. https://www.jstor.org/stable/26394646.

80 Henry Highland Garnet. "An Address to the Slaves of the Corrupted United States," Blackpast, Jan 24, 2007 (1843). Henry Highland Garnet. "An Address to the Slaves of the United States" • (blackpast.org).

81 Karin Hoepker. "Frederick Douglass's 'The Heroic Slave' – Risk, Fiction, and Insurance in Antebellum America." *Amerikastudien / American Studies* 60, no. 4 (2015): 441–62. http://www.jstor.org/stable/44071920.

82 Naval History and Heritage Command, National Museum of the US Navy, "Anti-Slave Trade Patrols Bldg 76." Anti-Slave Trade Patrols (navy.mil).

83 Steven Mintz. "Facts about Slave Trade and Slavery," History Resources, The Gilder Lehrman Institute of American History, n.d. Historical Context: Facts about the Slave Trade and Slavery | Gilder Lehrman Institute of American History.

84 Robert Malcomson. "The Sad Case of Sir George." *Naval History Magazine* 24, no. 1 (Feb 2020), The Sad Case of Sir George | Naval History Magazine – February 2010 Volume 24, Number 1 (usni.org).

85 Op. cit. Brain.

86 Desmond Manderson. "Bodies in the Water: On Reading Images More Sensibly." *Law and Literature* 27, no. 2 (2015): 279–93. https://www.jstor.org/stable/26770753.

Andrew Walker. "From Private Sermon to Public Masterpiece: J. M. W. Turner's 'The Slave Ship' in Boston, 1876–1899." *Journal of the Museum of Fine Arts, Boston* 6 (1994): 4–13. http://www.jstor.org/stable/20519760.

87 "Joseph Mallord William Turner, The Deluge, Exhibited 1805," The Tate Museum, 'The Deluge', Joseph Mallord William Turner? Exhibited 1805 | Tate.

88 Op. cit. Forbes, p. 107.

89 Op. cit. Forbes, p. 107.

90 Ibid. p. 108.

91 Geoffrey Gorer. "Dahomey: The Women Fetishers," January 14, 2011. Dahomey: The Women Fetishers (thetravelclub.org). Taken from the book Geoffrey Gorer, *Africa Dances*, London: 1935.

92 Ibid. p. 109.

93 Ibid.

94 Ibid.

95 Ibid. p. 110.

96 Alfred Burdon B. Ellis, *The Land of the Fetish*, Chapman, and Hall Ltd., original publication date 1883. Martin Pettit and Online Distributed Proofreading team, Project Gutenberg, Aug 5, 2021 [ebook#65997], pp. 54–72. The Project Gutenberg eBook of The Land of Fetish, by A. B. Ellis.

Uniforms as Artifacts **135**

97 Op. cit. Gorer, p. 111.

98 Ibid. p. 114.

99 Megan Orr. "Ladylike in the Extreme: The Propogandism of Sarah Forbes Bonetta, Britians, 'African Princess.'" BYU Scholrs Archive Student Works, 12-2021. Ladylike in the Extreme: The Propogandism of Sarah Forbes Bonetta, Britain's "African Princess" (byu.edu).

100 "Sarah Forbes Bonetta, Queen Victoria's African Protegee," English Heritage History and Stories, Sarah Forbes Bonetta | English Heritage (English-heritage.org.uk).

101 Ibid. Sarah Forbes.

102 Ibid.

103 Ibid.

104 James R. Kincaid. "A Wild, Roving, Vagabond Life, that's what Isabel Burton wanted, and Sir Richard gave it to her," *The New York Times, Books,* January 17, 1999.

105 Richard F. Burton. *Falconry in the Valley of the Indus*, John Van Voorst 1852, p. 93.

106 Rebecca Romney. "The Story Behind Richard F Burton's Pilgrimage to Media and Mecca," Bauman Rare Books website, Aug 12, 2013.The Story Behind Richard F. Burton's Pilgrimage to Medina and Mecca – Bauman Rare Books.

107 Op. cit. Burton Library of Congress, p. 34.

108 Ibid. p. 112.

109 Ibid. p. 236.

110 Ibid. Burton, pp. 178–9.

111 Ibid. p. 179.

112 Ibid.

113 Op. cit. Henry A. Gemery, and Jan S. Hogendorn, p. 112.

114 UNESCO Digital Library. "The Women Soldiers of Dahomey pedagogical unit 2," The women soldiers of Dahomey pedagogical unit 2 | Women (unesco.org).

115 UNESCO Women in African History. The women soldiers of Dahomey pedagogical unit 2 | Women (unesco.org) and Jérôme C. Alladaye. 2010. *Le kpanlingan dans le Danxomè: historien de l'oralité.*

116 Danielle Paquette. "They were the world's only all-female army; their descendants are fighting to recapture their humanity. *The Washington Post*, August 26, 2021.

117 Op. cit. Rommney and Op. cit. Paquette.

118 T. Britannica. Editors of Encyclopaedia. "Alfred-Amédée Dodds." *Encyclopedia Britannica*, July 14, 2023. https://www.britannica.com/biography/Alfred-Amedee-Dodds.

   General Alfred Amedee Dodds (1842–1922) in Dahomey, from '*Le Petit Journal*', Illustrated Supplement, 3 December 1892 Image of General Alfred Amedee Dodds (1842–1922) in Dahomey, from 'Le Petit by Meyer, Henri (1841–99) (bridgemanimages.com).

119 Frederic Martyn, *Life in the Leg098: Amazon Warriors from Dahomey, 1893- Jeffrey Green Historian. ion: from a soldier's point of view*, NY: C Scribner's Sons, 1911. Life in the Legion: from a soldier's point of view: Martyn, Frederic: Free Download, Borrow, and Streaming: Internet Archive pp. 199–237.

120 "Women Fought in Battle Against Foreign Legion, More Deadly than the Male According to Frederick Martyn Who Served in the Famous French Command," *The New York Times*, January 7, 1912, p. SM9, ProQuest Historical Newspapers.

121 Ibid. Women Fought.

122 Ibid.

123 Ibid.

124 Ibid.

125 Ibid.

136 Women and War

126 Nori Katagiri. "Drawing Strategic Lessons from Dahomey's War, *ASPJ Africa & Francophonie*, 3rd Qt., 2012, pp. 59–78.

127 J. C. Monroe Building Power in Dahomey. In: *The Precolonial State in West Africa: Building Power in Dahomey*, 219–34. Cambridge University Press, 2014.

128 Raymond Corbey. "Ethnographic Showcases, 1870–1930." *Cultural Anthropology* 8, no. 3 (1993): 338–69. http://www.jstor.org/stable/656317.

129 G. Freville. "Dahomey-Expo Paris 1900," Worldfairs, 1900. Expo Paris 1900 | Dahomey | French Colonies (worldfairs.info).
Meg Armstrong. "'A Jumble of Foreignness': The Sublime Musayums of Nineteenth-Century Fairs and Expositions." *Cultural Critique* no. 23 (1992): 199–250. https://doi.org/10.2307/1354195.

130 Jeffrey Green. Historian. "098: Amazon Warriors from Dahomey, 1893," 098: Amazon Warriors from Dahomey, 1893 – Jeffrey Green. Historian.

131 Jann Pasler. *Composing the Citizen*, Chapter Title: The Dynamics of Identity and the Struggle for Distinction, University of California Press, 2009. http://222. jstor.org/stable/10.1525/.ett1ppfjp.17 music-web2.ucsd.edu/~jpasler/wp/wp-content/uploads/2023/02/012-Chapter-12-Composing-the-Citizen.pdf p.670.

132 Ibid. p. 670.

133 "Dahomey Amazons in London from the London Chronicle, *The Washington Post*, May 29, 1903, p. 6. Pro Quest Historical Newspapers.

134 Aaron Santesso. "The Literary Animal and the Narrativized Zoo." *Modern Fiction Studies* 60, no. 3 (2014): 444–63. https://www.jstor.org/stable/26421739.

135 Carmen Dexl. "Live Human Exhibits: The World Columbian Exposition as a Space of Empire," November 30, 2020, US Studies Online PGR and ECR Network for the British Association for American Studies. Live Human Exhibits: The World Columbian Exposition as a Space of Empire – U.S. Studies Online (usso. UK).

136 A. L. Kroeber. "Frederic Ward Putnam." *American Anthropologist* 17, no. 4 (1915): 712–18. http://www.jstor.org/stable/659986.

137 "World's Columbian Exposition May 1, 1893–October 30, 1893," Encyclopedia of Chicago, World's Columbian Exposition (chicagohistory.org).

138 Ibid. Notated as "Through the Looking Glass" *Chicago Tribune* 1 Nov 1893, 9, quoted in Robert Rydell, *All the World's a Fair: Visions of Empire at American International Expositions, 1876–1916*, 65. University of Chicago Press, 1984.

139 David Murphy, and Charles Forsdick. "Staging the Black Atlantic: From the Chicago World's Fair (1893 to the World Festival of Negro Arts) (Dakar 1966)," DM_StagingtheBlackAtlantic (strath.ac.uk). Accessed 2/4/2023.

140 The photograph may be accessed at Xavier Pene and his Dahomeyan Amazons, Cal Midwinter Exposi – Calisphere UC Berkeley Bancroft Library, California Midwinter International Exposition Souvenir.

141 Sarah Ruth Offhaus. "The Negro Exhibit at the Pan-Am," Buffalo Rising, "The Negro Exhibit" at the Pan-Am – Buffalo Rising.

142 "The Midway," Uncrowned Community Builders, Uncrowned Community Builders™: Articles n.d.

143 Kimberly Kutz Elliott. "The World's Columbian Exposition: The Midway," Smarthistory the Center for Public Art History, July 9, 2021. The World's Columbian Exposition: The Midway – Smarthistory. Accessed 2/4/2022.

144 Op. cit. Dexel.

145 The World's Columbian Exposition: The Midway Smarthistory.org. » The World's Columbian Exposition: The Midway (smarthistory.org).

146 "Dahomey Amazons to Visit Europe, from the *Pall Mall Gazette*, in the *New York Times*, Oct 23, 1890, ProQuest Historical Newspapers, p. 4.

147 "Fire in the Dahomey Village," *Chicago Daily Tribune*, Jun 8, 1893, ProQuest Historical Newspapers, p. 9.

148 Ibid. Fire.

149 Op. cit. Green.
150 "Base Ball Clubs Organized among Amazons Dahomey: No Expense for Uniforms, *Chicago Daily Tribune*, April 2, 1905, p. G4. ProQuest Historical Newspapers.
151 Ibid. Base Ball.
152 Christopher B. Steiner. "Another Image of Africa: Toward an Ethnohistory of European Cloth Marketed in West Africa, 1873–1960." *Ethnohistory* 32, no. 2 (1985): 91–110. https://doi.org/10.2307/482329.
153 Maryte Collard. "Kingdom of Dahomey, Quilts, Travel 9 Comments," Kingdom of Dahomey – Maryte Collard (marytequilts.eu) and "The Kingdom of Dahomey," Getty Museums, Palace Sculptures of Abomey (getty.edu), pp. 26–31.
   Suzanne Preston Blier. "Animalia: The Natural World, Art, and Theory," On the Human, n.d. Animalia: the Natural World, Art, and Theory « On the Human (nationalhumanitiescenter.org).
154 Louis Fagbohoun, and Cathy Vieillescazes. "Cultural Heritage Objects of Wourthern Benin: Plant Dyes and Exudates Used in Their Confection," Chapter from the edited volume, *Heritage*, Daniela turcanus-Carutiu (ed) Sept. 9, 2020, EBOOK 978-1-83881-926-2.
155 Patrick Manning. "The Technology of Production in Southern Dahomey, c. 1900." *African Economic History* no. 9 (1980): 49–67. https://doi.org/10.2307/3601387.
156 "Three Months of Captivity in Dahome." *Matura Ensign* 14, no. 1037 (5 December 1890): 10. "The King of Dahomey and his Captives." *The Town and Country Journal* (October 25, 1890): 40. Trove Newspapers and Gazettes, pp. 39–25, Oct. 1890 – Australian Town and Country Journal (Sydney, NSW: 1870 – 1919) – Trove (nla.gov.au).
157 Jacques Grasset de Saint-Sauveur "Tableau of the PrincipalPeoples of America (Tableau des principaux peoples de l'Ajmerique) 1798, The Met, Jacques Grasset de Saint-Sauveur | Tableau of the e Principal Peoples of America (Tableau des principaux peoples de l'Amérique) | French | The Metropolitan Museum of Art (metmuseum.org).
   "Grasset de Saint-Sauveur, Jacques, 1757–1810. National Library of New Zealand, (22 items) Grasset de Saint-Sauveur, Jacques, 17... | Items | National Library of New Zealand | National Library of New Zealand (natlib.govt.nz).
158 Raphael Levy. "The Daily Press in France." *The Modern Language Journal* 13, no. 4 (1929): 294–303. https://doi.org/10.2307/315897.
159 "M. Lecoq, the First Fictional Detective," The Pulp.Net, June 6, 2016, M. Lecoq, the first fictional detective – The Pulp Super-Fan.
160 Nori Katagiri. "Drawing Strategic Lessons from Dahomey's War. Air University, originally in *ASPJ Africa & Francophonie*, 3rd Quarter, 2012. katagiri_e.pdf (af.edu).
161 "Battles of Dogba and Akpa, Dahomey, Second Franco-Dahomean War, 1892," Look and Learn History Picture Archive, 2005–2024, Battles of Dogba and Akpa, Dahomey, Second Franco-Dahomean ... stock image | Look and Learn.
162 Op. cit. Getty.
163 Archibald Forbes, *Battles of the Nineteenth Century, Vol 2: With about 320 Illustrations and 80 Plans," reprint, 2018*. Forgotten Books, ISBN 0282511237.
164 "The Story Behind shy Benin Unveiled Gigantic Amazon Statue of an African Warrior Woman, 'YouTube, The Story Behind Why Benin Unveiled Gigantic Amazon Statue of an African Warrior Woman – YouTube. Accessed 2/4/2023. Henry Wilkins, "Woman King' Statue has Role in North Korea Sanctions Controversy," Voice of Africa, January 12, 2023, 'Woman King' Statue Has Role in North Korea Sanctions Controversy (voanews.com). Accessed 2/4/2023.
165 Patrick Nelle. Benin's 30m-tall "Amazon Statue Honors the Women Warriors of Dahomey," August 162022, Bella Naija, Benin's 30m-tall "Amazon" statue honors the women warriors of Dahomey | BellaNaija.

138 Women and War

Additional Resources

Alice Proctor. *The Whole Picture, the Colonial Story of the Art in Our Museums and Why We Need to Talk About It.* London: Octopus, 2020.

Colleen E. Kriger. *Cloth in West African History (African Archaeology Series).* Walnut Creek: Alta Mira Press, June 2, 2006.

Frederick Edwyn Forbes. *Dahomey, and the Dahomans: Being the Journals of Two Mission to the King of Dahomey, and Residence at His Capital in the Years 1849 and 1850.* Reprint Edition. Boston MA: Adamant Media Corporation, January 14, 2004.

J. A. Skertchly. *Dahomey as It Is: Being a Narrative of Eight Months' Residence in That Country, with a Full Account of the Notorious Annual Customs.* London, UK: Republished Legare Street Press, September 9, 2021.

Paul Fussell. *Uniforms Why We Are What We Wear.* Boston: Mariner Books, November 10, 2003.

Stanley B. Alpern. *Amazons of Black Sparta, (2nd Ed) The Women Warriors of Dahomey.* Anambra, Nigeria: NYU Press, April 11, 2011.

Anambra, Nigeria IAVN 13 979-8356113413.

Questions

How does enclothed cognition apply to the apparel of the Dahomey Amazons? What constitutes a uniform, and what constitutes a costume?

How does using the Dahomey as costumed marketable commodities at expositions and fairs make you feel? Do you believe those women in the productions understood why they were part of a European tour?

Are there any parallels between the story of the Dahomey Amazons and the stories from ancient Greek mythology? How is the portrayal of Amazons in Homer's epic poem The Iliad the same as or different from Dahomey's role in the West Africa colonial wars?

Why were the Dahomey so brutal? What was their role in exacerbating the slave trade?

What are the different values of oral and written histories? Are oral histories of the Dahomey Amazons likely more accurate than the Western interpretations of their culture?

Is the story of Sarah Forbes Bonetta one of saving a child's life or a window into racial beliefs expounded during the Victorian period? How have viewpoints of such actions changed today?

Modern take

Watch the film The Woman King, *Sony Pictures, September 9, 2022, United States (135 minutes). How are women portrayed in the movie? Is the storyline atypical for a Hollywood film? Why or Why not? Are there values, experiences, and representations of women in the movie you think are universal?*

The Dahomey Amazons have appeared in pop culture. Illustrations are as follows: (1) The 2015 UNESCO comic novel, The Women Soldiers of Dahomey. *(2) The play "The Last Amazon of Dahomey," from Bernardine Evaristo's Booker Prize-winning novel* Girl, Woman, Other. *(3) The Dora Milaje fictional characters in Marvel Comics are based on the Dahomey warriors. Similar characters appear in the 2022* Black Panther Wakanda Forever *superhero film (2022). Choose two items from this shortlist and compare and contrast the storylines and images to the nonfictional Dahomey.*

What forms of training are required of modern female combat troops? Is there any similarity to the training of the Dahomey Amazons?

How is the idea of colonialism now being presented in art museums?

How has the military addressed female race relations since Executive Order 998 was enacted in 1948?

Activities and discovery

Review short films with interviews of female combatants about their roles in 21st-century armed conflict. What are the hurdles these women face?

The Fon kings of Dahomey were patrons of the arts and had court artists create items that enhanced their status. Learn about the festival called the huetantu *and locate sculptures and textiles that would have been part of this gathering. What animals were represented and why? How was the warring culture represented?*

6
DECORATIVE ARTS MEDALS AS ARTIFACTS

Suffragism: The Women's Civil War 1840–1921

FIGURES 6.1 and 6.2   A suffragette valor medal for force-feeding and imprisonment with a portcullis on the top (Figure 6.1) and hunger strike medallion on the bottom (Figure 6.2).

© CC BY SA 3.0 Attribution share alike 3.0 unported Violet Ann Bland Medal (cropped).jpg – Wikimedia Commons.

DOI: 10.4324/9781003406372-7

FIGURES 6.1 and 6.2 *(Continued)*

Medals and honorary decorations

Medals or medallions commemorating a person or event were invented by Italian Antonio Pisano in the 15th century when he fashioned a face profile of Byzantine emperor John VIII Palaeologus, known for his oversight of the defense of Constantinople and consent to the union of the Greek and Roman churches.[1] The medal was presented during his visit to the Venetian-born pope Dugene IV of Italy in 1438. Medallions are generally large at four or more inches and too big to be worn easily. They were cast from wax, wood, or stone or using intaglio, *repousse*, or chasing. The intaglio technique required the medal image to be incised onto a surface; the sunken incisions then held the bronze or other metal to create an upraised area. Repousse required a medalist to hammer the intended motif from the final product's reverse side for a low-relief pattern. Chasing and embossing involved putting pressure on the front side of the metal, which caused the metal to sink. Most medals were drafted using two or more of these techniques.[2]

In France, the first known heraldic medals were struck in the mid-15th century to commemorate the eviction of the English from the Republic.[3] By the 16th century, several well-known medalists had arisen from the arts community in Germany and Austria. German Christoph Weiditz was employed

142 Women and War

by King Charles V as the court medalist and goldsmith.[4] Augsburg resident Hans Schwarz became famous for his mastery of capturing the personality of his sitters. Working in Cologne, Friedrich Hagenauer was a prolific creator of the 1600s, having produced more than 230 pieces.[5] He received several royal commissions from the court of Ferdinand I, Holy Roman Emperor and King of Bohemia, Hungary, and Croatia. In Nuremberg, Matthes Gebel produced silver and lead medals for upper-class individuals, among which were the Prince Bishop and civil ruler of Bamberg, the Elector of Saxony who was entitled to take part in the election of the Holy Roman Emperor, and the Dean of the Cathedral and head of the chapter of canons of Mainz.[6]

In the 17th century, the Netherlands, one of the first examples of producing large assemblages of propaganda medals, was undertaken to venerate important national political events, including the Thirty Years War and the Franco-Dutch wars.[7] France followed with their commemorative Louis XIV's Versailles medals.[8] Influenced by the German avant-garde expressionists, stylistic changes and materials for medals continued to shift to embracing more subjective qualities. These were supplanted by symmetrical and geometric Art Deco arrangements, which became popular just before the advent of World War I.[9] As the early 20th century gave way to the progressive era, medallions evolved into prizes or commendations for superiority in music, industry, communication, aviation, architecture, and the arts.[10]

Military-style medallions and medals

Ancient Egyptian and Greek societies were known to have given medals as awards for courage, merit, deeds, and heroism. However, it was only in the Roman period that the Legions paid tribute to their personnel with battle decorations for bravery and service.[11] Greek historian Polybius wrote in his diaries that if a soldier had distinguished himself, the legion commander would bring his troops together and call those forward to be decorated in front of their peers.

Polybius wrote,

A very excellent plan also is adopted for inducing young soldiers to brave danger. When an engagement has taken place and any of them have showed conspicuous gallantry, the Consul summons an assembly of the legion, puts forward those whom he considers to have distinguished themselves in any way, and first compliments each of them individually on his gallantry, and mentions any other distinction he may have earned in the course of his life, and then presents them with gifts: to the man who has wounded an enemy, a spear; to the man who has killed one and stripped his armor, a cup, if he be in the infantry, horse-trappings if in the cavalry: though originally the only present made was a spear.[12]

To receive a military decoration, the soldier had to have "without there being any positive necessity for them to expose themselves singly to danger, have done so voluntarily and deliberately."[13]

Necklaces, armbands, or disks were distributed for heroic feats, and the warrior could attach them to their armor. The Roman army's decoration for bravery was a golden circle necklet or Torque in the manner of the Celtic Warriors of Britain. Other valor awards were embossed or colored armbands known as *Armillae* and *Phalerae*, a disk that could be made of bronze, silver, or gold. A warrior's collection of these discs was often semi-permanently placed on a leather harness over their armor. Stamped on these were various crowns: Corona Aurea (Golden Crown), presented to Centurions for victories in combat, and *Corona Vallaris* (Fortification) for those who were the first legionnaires to climb enemy fortification walls. An exceptional accolade was to receive the *Corona Civia*, which allowed the recipient to serve as a Senator in the Roman State. Romans only awarded medals to living soldiers. There were no posthumous awards for the fallen.[14] Lighter cloth badges, medal ribbons, service ribbons, and ribbon bars replaced the impracticality of the large, heavy Roman decorations.

Medals symbolize a form of recognition and may or may not be limited to the precise roles of military accomplishments.[15] Medals are awarded and earned, not "won." The civilian sector has also developed decorations for having played a distinguished role of excellence within governmental, societal, communal, and humanitarian domains. The arts, cultural arenas, sports, academia, and media distinguish superior acts and talents of individuals with prizes, medals, trophies, and titles. Awarding pain, suffering, and bravery, the common basis behind many military honors, can also be found within the public sector. No matter the social neighborhood from which they arise, honorary recognitions are directly linked to reinforcing behavior, which can serve as intrinsic motivators for the individual to continue to perform at an elevated level. Observers of the celebration of an individual's estimable acts can also motivate those who are part of the same group to seek out situations and perform in a similarly elevated way. Venerating an individual's spirit, work, and vision also creates legacies for future generations to aspire to.

Women's suffragism: Long story of hard work and heartache (The women form camps: Antis, suffragists, suffragettes, and pacifists)

Not only have women fought in military environments, but they have also waged civil war to gain equitabilities under the law. The heftiest of these movements in sheer size was the international effort women organized to secure the right to vote beginning in the late 1700s and ending in the first quarter of the 20th century. The decades-long movement gained the name

144 Women and War

> **Anti-remonstrant** promoted domestic feminism and keeping the status quo. Believed women already had the right to complete freedom in their homes. Also known as female maternal reformers.
>
> **Suffragist** Use of peaceful, constitutional campaign methods to establish equality.
>
> **Suffragette** Beleaguered by the slow movement of the suffragists, this group proactively, through militant activities collected under the motto deeds not words.
>
> **Minority Suffragism** women of color who faced discrimination, yet organized political meetings and organized political societies to secure the right to vote.
>
> **Peace Activists** self-organizing social reformers and delegates not officially recognized by a government who supported non-aggression.

FIGURE 6.3 Primary groups in the suffrage movement.
© Author.

"suffragism," coined from the Latin *suffragium*, meaning a voting tablet, ballot, or vote. Its archetype may be connected to warriors and the clashing sound of weapons, which signified assent by an assemblage of fighters in battle.[16] Credit is given to journalist Charles Eustice Hands, who worked on the staff of the *London Daily Mail*, for creating an additional signifier for women's rights activists. The term "suffragette" was used in one of his 1906 articles covering women's activities in the United Kingdom. Hands' obituary from 1937 describes him as "one of the most famous reporters Fleet Street ever produced for his war correspondent activities in Africa, Cuba, and many other parts of the world."[17] He meant for the word's meaning to be derogatory and mocking, and its usage became associated with the militant arm of the women's cause. The group "reclaimed the word, hardening the "g" to pronounce the word 'suffra' and 'get', implying they would be successful."[18]

Three philosophical cliques arose around the women's civil rights fight: the anti-rights, antis or remonstrants, suffragists, and suffragettes. A fourth entity, the pacifists, emerged from all three circles of women's groups as France, the United Kingdom and its territories, Russia, Japan, Italy, and the

United States declared war on the central powers of Germany, Austria-Hungary, the Ottoman Empire, and Bulgaria.[19]

Antis did not want the vote – ever – and espoused numerous reasons why not.[20] In their arguments against suffragism, they asserted that "because the spheres of men and women, owing to natural causes, are essentially different, each's share in the public management of the State should be different."[21] Lyman Abbott, a Congregationalist theologian and author, wrote of the naturally occurring assignment of masculine and feminine roles in a 1903 article for *The Atlantic* entitled "Why Women do Not Wish the Suffrage." He prophesized that in the family, the role of the male was to go forth and fight the battle with Nature, "to compel the reluctant ground and to give *her* riches to use." "It is *not for woman* to hold the plough, or handle the hoe, or dig in the mine, or fell the forest. The war with Nature is not for her to wage."[22] Contentions also arose with this party that they were already taxed physically and emotionally enough at home; they did not need to worry further about municipal matters. Should women become involved in bothersome business and political concerns, two spheres beyond what natural law and selection had determined to be for them, domestic life would be in shambles. Such a movement within society would disrupt the social fabric of the church and hearth.[23] Many individuals in this assemblage could rely on a safety net through male family members' high social status and deep pockets. Under the nonvoting structure, the antis could continue to live as an unperturbed upper stratum within a system that privileged them.[24]

Remonstrant campaign posters and postcards reveal their sentiments about those rocking their proverbial social yachts.[25] To the anti-men and anti-women, suffragettes were ugly, self-centered spinsters who had destroyed families, placed their children in peril, were far too vocal for a female, and should never become a member of the professions. One postcard showed an unattractive row of shrew-like characters with the words, "suffragettes who have never been kissed," or in another instance, a card with a woman with a twisted puckered face, exclaiming, "Kiss me quick!" Both examples indicated that women's rights activists were revolting, unlovable, and not marriable. One of the most atrocious adverts shows a female Frankensteinish character's face with vampire teeth and black gums. "We want the vote" is written across the bottom. Another common theme and a prevalent attitude insinuated that suffragists were nags who should be stifled, showing their faces and lips chained with bizarre head harnesses to keep them quiet. The United States' anti-movement mirrored the sentiments expressed by their counterparts in the United Kingdom.

Josephine Jewell Dodge, the wealthy Vassar College dropout daughter of the Governor of Connecticut, founded the anti-suffragist National Association Against Women's Suffrage (NAAWS) in 1911.[26] Dodge's social status as the wife of the son of a Congressman gave her a network with enough clout

146 Women and War

FIGURES 6.4 and 6.5 A chromolithograph spoofing the differences between suffragettes (Figure 6.4) and remonstrants (Figure 6.5) entitled "Find the Group in Favor of Woman's Suffrage".

© Public domain media usage CC0.

to get her viewpoint on suffragism printed in a front-page article in Harrisburg, Pennsylvania's *Courier* on a Sunday in May of 1913.[27] Entitled "Low Cut Gowns and High Morals Suffrage and Sex," the article's subtitles proclaimed, "decent dress is more important than votes, woman's appeal to man (is in) back of movement, cut out the turkey trot, immodest gowns, and loose conversation." Josephine claimed suffragism was "a foolish fancy and unnecessary." She argued that suffragism was a "distortion of the sex question" and compared suffragism to a "sex disturbance." Dodge supposed the female outcasts were "straining after artificial happiness and unnatural enjoyment," resulting in an "unsatisfactory state of mind." In short, suffragists were mentally warped and the *grandes horizontales* of the 20th century. They were oversexed, foolish, and mentally deficient for their beliefs. According to the governor's daughter, it was a woman's role to bring up moral children for a better society, not waste time and resources being a protester or professing any ideas about government and governing.

In 1913, a lengthy full-page article was printed in the daily *National Times* in which the writer detailed an interview with the ardent anti-suffragist Helen Kendrick Johnson, who was the editor of the weekly *Women's Journal*, which published local, national, and international suffrage news, editorials, letters, short stories, and poetry. Helen was described by a close friend, Anna Brownell Jameson, in the front piece of Rossiter Kendrick's biography of his wife, "Besides the dignity, the sweetness, and the tenderness, which should distinguish her sex generally, she is individualized by qualities peculiar to herself, her high mental powers, her enthusiasm of temperament, her decision of purpose and her buoyancy of spirit."[28] Jameson was a prolific writer, one of her works being *Characteristics of Women Moral, Poetical, and Historical*, which analyzed William Shakespeare's heroines using three categories: intellect, passion, and imagination.[29]

Kendrick popularized her sentiments toward anti-suffragism in her 1897 book *Woman and the Republic, A Survey of the Woman-Suffrage Movement in the United States, and A Discussion of the Claims and Arguments of Its Foremost Advocates.*[30] Her closing chapter described her beliefs about suffragism,

> I have given it as my opinion that the movement to obtain the elective franchise for a woman is not in harmony with those through which woman and government have made progress,

and that her general conclusion as a participant in the era was

> that woman's relation to the Republic is as important as man's. A woman deals with the beginnings of life; man, with the product made from those beginnings; and this fact marks the difference in their spheres and reveals woman's immense advantage in moral opportunity.[31]

148 Women and War

What is remarkable about the *Times* piece is its size compared to the much smaller items that tended to appear about the pro-suffragist cause. Lengthy pro-suffragist pieces were uncommon, and some of the most written topics on suffragism were about media events such as their parades and street pageants.[32] Kendrick thought she had "absolute editorial eyes" from her experiences in magazine work. She claimed she endeavored to "find the false and see the true" within pro-suffragist arguments and that "most of the suffrage arguments were illogical and otherwise unworthy."[33] Helen maintained that "early on in the votes for women agitation, I predicted failure for the project should it ever have a trial" and that "woman suffrage has never succeeded anywhere (and) it never will succeed (because it) is founded on falsity."[34] "I cannot bring myself to think the extension of suffrage to women would mean any definite gain."[35] Dying in 1917 at 72, two and a half years before Congress passed the 19th Amendment, the remonstrant had lived through the entire history of the first wave of feminism in the United States. She was not alive to react to the passage of the Voting Rights Act, something to which she had a solid emotional, philosophical, and personal aversion.

Kendrick's anti-suffragist beliefs were based on a complex and often disjointed partisan set of claims. To make a case against suffragism, she borrowed ideas from Greek history. Helen had grown up under the guidance and educational tutoring of her father, Asahel Clarck Kendrick, a Greek professor at the University of Rochester and the son of a Baptist missionary. After her mother died, she moved between New York and Georgia, living with her aunts. She was forced to leave Atlanta on the last steamer as the Civil War erupted. Her advanced education included a year at Oread Institute; she then married a newspaper editor.

Asahel Clarck Kendrick's work on the New Testament, Greek grammar, and poetry likely influenced her thinking. But "she resisted all his efforts to make her a Greek scholar," and relative to her studies, "she went her own way, not caring much for any standard curriculum."[36] She supported the idea that in history, despotism and anarchy were "more friendly to woman's political aspirations than any form of constitutional government."[37] Quoting William H. Lecky's *History of European Morals from Augustus to Charlemagne*, she surmised, "one of the most perplexing facts in the moral history of Greece" was that it was only within "the ruder period that women achieved the highest place."[38] Added to Greek historicism was that the virginity of womanhood was imperative. Women and not men were birthers of life, and this meant women were responsible for the children's "legitimacy," which could be traced matrilineally "because the mother, though not always the father, could be known with certainty." A woman's responsibility was to keep female morality in check.

Kendrick peered into the realm of women and war by looking back at Sparta, a region that had raised female militarists and fighting queens. Still, she disallowed their activities and successes due to their polytheism and paganism.

In Sparta, women became soldiers as the democratic idea advanced. Princess Archidamia (Queen of Sparta 331-305 BC), marching at the head of her female troop to rebuke the senators for the decree that the women and children be removed from the city before the anticipated attack could come, is an example. The same was true in Etolia, Argos, and other states. Telesilla (a Peloponnesian lyric poet from Argos) led the women in battle and disciplined them in peace. But the world does not turn to Sparta for its ideal of a pre-Christian republic, and the Suffragists of our day do not propose to emulate the Spartan Amazon and hew their way to political power with the sword.[39]

Helen's interest in Greek history led her to an individualized interpretation of the tale by the Greek tragedian Aeschylus' play *Seven Against Thebes*. The Theban woman's job was to be prominent in the ceremonial and not governmental elements of life through maintaining and participating in citizens' clubs. Community activities were the only arena where women could deviate from a cloistered home life. Kendrick supported her arguments against suffragism from the idea that, in ancient Greece, "women's ritual participation... was energetically required" during the festivals of Thesmorphoira – reserved for citizen wives, or the Arrephoria, "a fest instituted in honor of Athena and a ritual for fertility as part of the agricultural cycle."[40] In Hellen's viewpoint, "In *Seven Against Thebes*, the woman plays the role of reconciler...(they bring peace to the city...and women's political activity stems (only) from their familial concerns."[41]

Theban women were forced into political activity, if at all, only due to the "delinquency of the Theban men" or to "fulfill obligations to male family members."[42] Women dared not speak openly; their actions and words regarding issues outside the home were kept personal and private.[43] In Kendrick's eyes, women were to be inconspicuous and generative and represent themselves only through community entertainment, social clubs, and ministering to the sick. There was also a sense that Kendrick was heavily attached to a strict adherence to unyielding marriage contracts. Just as in Greek society, women of Kendrick's era should adhere to the idea that "marriage did not require a young bride's consent," as she was to be passed from the protection of her father to that of her husband. A young woman in Classical Athens lacked citizenship rights and was to be *the wife of* an Athenian citizen, "not an equal citizen in the eyes of the law."[44]

Returning to the newspaper interview of 1913, now 69 years old, Helen declared that suffragism destroyed the sanctity, morality, and sacredness of marriage attained through religious law. The modern approach to marriage

150 Women and War

degraded the biblical essence of what constituted a proper family, and the free approach to coupling was a direct attack on the sacredness of the home. Scottish-born suffragist and Epicurean philosopher Frances Wright was submitted as the best example of what suffragism could do to the sanctity of homelife and marriage. Wright inherited wealth and was a free love advocate who maintained a relationship that could be consecrated as desired and did not require a civil or church registration. To Wright, pleasure was the highest good that could be attained on earth. She lobbied for universal education, legal rights for married women, and liberalizing divorce laws. Her free love notion, support for birth control, and attacks on churches as political influencers did not sit well with Kendrick. Wright was condemned for being "not only a communist but an avowed atheist, a propagandist of socialism, and irreligious."[45]

Helen showed distress during the newspaper interview, relaying that women being able to vote would lead to the demise of democracy and the rise of communism and socialism. American women supporting and applauding the lawlessness of the English suffragettes, a reference to the increase of Emmeline Pankhurst's freedom or death approach in leading the Woman's Social and Political Union, "Was a bad sign."[46] "War between the sexes can but mean first the wreckage of society and destruction of the human race."[47] A swerve was then made toward the faults of The Church of Jesus Christ of Latter-Day Saints, blaming them for the rise in suffragist ideals. Mormons had brought suffragism into the State of Utah, "and since then," she claimed, "no large body of thinkers has adopted the ideas save the socialists." It was the Mormons in Colorado who were to be rebuked for their establishing 1200 settlements, which in turn created a "suffragist power dynamic." "Mormonism is not really a church or religion," she declared, "but a strong political organization" that is utilizing women's votes to sustain its power.[48]

The antis in the United States were also the most racist of the suffragists, suffragettes, and pacifists. In the southern United States, at the Macon, Georgia headquarters of the Association Opposed to Women's Suffrage, an ephemeral card was printed in 1915 with a list of prejudicial proclamations.[49] If women attained the vote, they pronounced, it would wipe out Black disenfranchisement by state law, create a "danger to farmers," and incite a "danger to farmer's families." Further, if Black men voted in addition to the two million Black women who would benefit from the passage of an equal voting rights act, "farmlands would depreciate under universal suffrage." The card ended with black women not being given the vote because "White Supremacy must be maintained."[50]

Creation of the African American women's suffrage movement began around 1892 with the organization of the Colored Women's League (CWL) in Washington, D.C.[51] Under the direction of its president, Helen Appo Cook, the CWL consolidated over 113 women's clubs.

FIGURE 6.6 Mrs. Helen Appo Cook, Organizer and President of the Colored Women's League of Washington, D.C.

© Public domain. Published (or registered with the U.S. Copyright Office) before January 1, 1929. PD US expired. Helen Appo Cook from TheColoredAmerican DC 4 June1898, p. 2 – Helen Appo Cook – Wikipedia.

In 1896, the organization was reconsolidated to form the National Association of Colored Women (NACW) under President Mary Church Terrell, a graduate of Oberlin College in Ohio and daughter of a formerly enslaved father who had become a successful businessman.[52] First in the minds of the organizers was their desire to become unified on a national scale and collectively follow the motto, "Lifting as we Climb." The NACW expanded its mission to combat negative stereotypes of Black women, aid each other in becoming educated suffragists, practice community leadership, and promote voting rights.

Helen Appo Cook was well off with an estate valued at over five million dollars in present currency. She grew up with a prominent musician father and a mother who owned a top-line millinery business in New York City. Her financial and social fortune gave credence to the idea, "I was born to an inheritance of appreciation and sympathy for the cause of women's rights, my mother before me being so ardent a supporter of its doctrines that I felt,

152 Women and War

in a measure, identified with it."[53] Cook was a backer of Black voting rights, opposed racial segregation, and held night classes in German and English literature and hygiene, sewing, and mending. She called for training African American children to prepare them for occupations, morally educate her race, and encourage mental and physical development and training within the confines of the home. One of her primary ambitions was to target young people at the community level to prepare them for "the peculiar conditions in which they (would) find themselves" because of their race.[54]

In a mass of 5000 women at the Woman's Suffrage Parade in Washington, D.C., one day before President Woodrow Wilson's inauguration were 22 Howard University students who had founded the Delta Sigma Theta Sorority, and over 40 other Black women were in the procession.[55] Two carried the lead banners for their sections. All were required to attend with male chaperones. Mary Church Terrell and Ida B. Wells were in attendance. There were floats, golden chariots, and marching bands. African American Iris Calderhead, the daughter of the representative of the 5th district from the state of Kansas, participated. After meeting leading militant suffragette Lucy Burns in New York City, Iris joined the National Woman's Party and was assigned to help organize the Congressional Union's exhibit at the Panama-Pacific International Exposition and the Women's Voter Convention. Her work took her across Kansas, Arizona, and Oklahoma. Attempting to display a banner in 1917 in front of the Smithsonian Institution, where Woodrow Wilson was expected, she was arrested and jailed. She was incarcerated again as part of the Silent Sentinels at the White House and spent three days in the Occoquan Workhouse.[56]

The nonmilitant pro-voting rights contingent, referenced as suffragists, sat in the center between the anti and the suffragette positions. In the United Kingdom, the group was initially led by Dame Millicent Fawcett, who organized the National Union of Women's Suffrage Societies. Fawcett's sister, Elizabeth Garrett Anderson, became the first female doctor in the United Kingdom and opened one of the first women's medical colleges.[57] The NUWSS relied on nonconfrontational messaging using educational posters, leaflets, and staid public meetings to get the message of women's rights across to government officials and the general public. Before the British entity dispersed, it had grown to 449 societies united into 16 federations. An example of one of their peaceful protests occurring in 1913 was called "The Pilgrimage," which was comprised of several processions, lasting for weeks, which passed through towns and villages, with the women "wearing their badges and carrying banners, marching towards London splitting into groups on the eight great trunk roads."[58] "Until we win! We demand the vote!" was their motto.

Nonmilitant pro-suffrage in the United States is primarily described as emerging in Boston, Massachusetts, in 1869, when the National American

Women Suffrage Association (NAWSA) was organized.[59] The four women most associated with this effort were Elizabeth Cady Stanton, Susan B. Anthony, Carrie Chapman Catt, and Lucy Stone. Stanton was an active abolitionist and talented debater. In the late 1890s, she was ostracized for her radicalism in publishing *The Women's Bible*, in which she proposed that biblical teachings relegated women to an inferior status among men.[60] Anthony was also an abolitionist and had a lifelong friendship with Frederic Douglass of Maryland, who had escaped enslavement. Stone was the first woman from Massachusetts to earn a college degree. Chapman Catt was a protégé of Stanton's. Catt's strategy, called the society plan, relied upon recruiting wealthy members of women's civic improvement clubs to support voting and other rights through fundraising and personal connections. Dame Millicent Fawcett of the UK suffragist organization NUWSS, German feminist Marie Stritt, Carrie Chapman Catt, and Susan Anthony of NAWSA would later create the internationally based Women's Suffrage Alliance (WSA) in 1904.[61]

The rise of the militants

The argument of the broken pane of glass is the most valuable argument in modern politics. We have to free half of the human race, the women, so that they can help free the other half. Deeds, not words, was to be our permanent motto. Trust in God: She will provide.

(Emmeline Pankhurst)

The third denomination of suffragism was the suffragettes, spearheaded in the United Kingdom by Emmeline Pankhurst. Their motto was "Deeds, not Words." Rather than the pacifist approach of the NUWSS or the avoidance approach of the Anti-Suffrage League, the WSPU encouraged their members to march, heckle, conduct civil disobedience acts, and purposefully take direct action on their political adversaries. Alice Paul and Lucy Burns organized the militant arm of suffragettes in America. Paul was the instigator behind the first Woman Suffrage Procession, held in Washington, D.C., and was responsible for creating the Silent Sentinels protest effort.

Alice lived until the age of 93 and was a major influencer in later years during the second wave of feminism under US President Lyndon Johnson's Administration's fight for the 1964 Civil Rights Act. Lucy Burns was undertaking graduate studies in Germany when she met the Pankhurst women and quit her education to join the British suffragettes.[62] Paul moved to London to join Pankhurst's radical band. The two women first interfaced during their incarceration for disorderly conduct. In lockup together, they discovered their mutual passion for the fight for women's rights. Paul served three jail terms in the United Kingdom for her radical activities. Burns worked as a salaried organizer for Emmeline Pankhurst from 1909–1912 and was

154 Women and War

arrested six times in Britain and the United States for her extremist acts. One of her most aggressive plans was to break through the roof of St. Andrew's Roman Catholic Cathedral in Glasgow, Scotland, to disrupt an all-male political speech against women's rights.

Along with her English barrister and socialist husband, Richard, Emmeline Pankhurst helped organize the Women's Franchise League in 1889 and remained a part of its activities until its breakup in 1903. She then formed the Women's Social and Political Union (WSPU) with her three daughters, Christabel, Sylvia, and Adela. Richard, 24 years older than his wife, had long been a proponent of women's rights.[63] The spouses aided in the establishment of the Independent Labor Party, which supported the working classes, and he was a draftee of the first women's suffrage bill in England, the Women's Disabilities Removal Bill. He also authored the Married Women's Property Act of 1882, in which wives were given absolute control over their property and earnings. Richard died in 1898 but had set a solid foundation and left enough monetary resources for Emmeline to continue her women's rights campaigns.[64]

By 1905, interest began to wane in the media and political spheres regarding women's efforts to gain the vote in Britain. Until then, only nonconfrontational methods were utilized to change legislation. Pankhurst continued to lead, using a nonviolent path to equal voting rights for the next four years. But by 1909, she had come to accept that the moderate approach used by the other leading suffragist entity, the National Union of Women's Suffrage Societies, and their peaceful attempts at swaying Parliament was far less effective than it should have been.[65] Itching to incite greater and faster action in achieving national legal voting representation and fatigued by the yawning disinterest of the public and government in the movement, Pankhurst changed tactics and declared the WSPU conduct a series of staged militant activities.

Emmeline's passion for women was boundless, having arisen from her first-hand experiences as a volunteer among trade unions and single working mothers.[66] She observed that they had no legal recourse against the misfortunes they had to endure. They were forced to survive in dangerous work environments, accept low pay, take physical abuse, and were given no health care. There was a constant struggle to afford nourishment for themselves and their children. Pankhurst stated on October 17, 1912, in her first public address after being released from one of her early stints in prison for her activism, that,

> I shall never forget seeing a little girl of 13 lying in a bed playing with a doll - I was told she was on the eve of becoming a mother, and she was infected with a loathsome disease. Was not that enough to make me a Militant Suffragette? We women Suffragists have a mission - to free half the human race, and I incite this meeting to rebellion.[67]

Emmeline called for the WSPU to "Be militant each in your own way" by refusing to leave the House of Commons, face party mobs, and join anti-government bi-elections protests. Further, she declared, "Those of you who can break windows, do so," and "Those of you who can attack the secret idol of property...do so."[68] At one of her stump speeches in 1913, she justified the combative approach, "If men use explosives and bombs for their purpose, they call it war, and throwing a bomb that destroys other people is then described as a glorious and heroic deed. Why should a woman not make use of the same weapons as men? It is not only war we have declared. We are fighting for a revolution!"[69] Eldest daughter, Christabel Pankhurst, became her manager and idea guru for the imposed "reign of terror" and authored the weekly paper, *Suffragette*, which lauded the stories of the aggressive acts.[70]

Improvised explosive devices, fire, letter bombs, and physical attacks were the WSPU's choice of weapons.[71] By the campaign's conclusion two decades later, at least 24 people had been injured, and a few were killed, six of them suffragettes. Prime Minister Asquith, one of suffragism's biggest foes vehemently disapproving of women's votes since 1882, was singled out by one of Pankhurst's followers when she threw a hatchet at his head.[72] The weapon missed him and clipped Irish Nationalist Prime Minister John Redmond on the ear, who was also a determined opponent of the feminists. Asquith had led the suffragists to count on his backing the conciliation bills for voting rights.[73] Instead, he reversed his claim and supported a universal manhood suffrage bill. During his tenure, a conspiracy theory circulated and was placed in a report to the Cabinet that the suffragettes were planning to murder him because they were found practicing with a Browning pistol at a shooting range on Tottenham Court Road in Central London. An anonymous source known as "Mrs. Moore," a member of the offshoot WSPU, the Women's Freedom League, claimed she had seen two suffragettes practicing marksmanship at a local shooting range and was concerned for the Prime Minister's life.[74]

Three anti-suffragist cabinet ministers were attacked, a bomb was placed in the Home Secretaries Office, and the Dublin Theater was set on fire and bombed with an audience in attendance.[75] Four suffragettes conducted the theater attack using a canister of gunpowder and petrol lit by matches, which were thrown in among particularly combustible film reels in the projection booth. Letters were used to ignite post boxes. Railway signals were tampered with. Two hundred and forty women were jailed in 1912 to silence the women's increased use of physical pushback.[76]

In 1913, Pankhurst wrote her *Freedom or Death* speech that outlined her reasons for supporting insurrection. It was presented at Hartford, Connecticut, during a fund-raising tour at the invitation of future four-time Academy award-winning actress Katherine Hepburn's mother, who was president of the Woman Suffrage Association and a National Woman's Party member. Katherine would have been six years old at the time. *The Hartford Courant*

156 Women and War

reported that the seats at the event were perhaps one-third filled.[77] Several reasons for using an antagonistic approach to gaining equality were outlined in her two-hour talk. Calling herself a soldier having temporarily left the field of battle; she claimed that the idea of a revolution on behalf of a man as told by a man would need no explanation and that women were not allowed the same latitude because they were women. She exclaimed that the revolutionary had had to rely on physical grievance methods at certain points in time when there were no other avenues left. Her illustration was derived from the events ongoing in Ireland and the activities of the Irish Volunteers who organized to respond to the paramilitary Ulster Volunteer Force and fight against the home rule policy in support of Ireland's ability to frame their local government without interference. Emmeline cast the WSPU movement as a civil war, and the suffragettes were a women's regulated army with professional soldiers.[78]

Women's pacifism and the Hague

Emerging tangentially to the voting rights movement as World War I exploded in Europe was the pacifist approach to ending the conflict. Some women, though not a majority, exited the three suffragist camps and drifted toward the peace crusade. Europeans had participated in Nonaggression movements since the end of the Napoleonic Wars, when cross-national congresses were held to analyze and discuss foreign policies that resulted in conflict. Two Hague Peace Conferences were held in 1899 and 1907. Multilateral conventions for determining treaties relative to the conduct of warfare were derived during the Hague meetings based upon the Lieber Code, or "Instructions for the Government of the Armies of the US in the Field, to Unions Forces," which Abraham Lincoln had issued as General Orders Number 100 during the American Civil War. The Code outlined numerous instructions including directions for martial law, protection of public and private property during wartime, rules for prisoners of war, hostages, partisans, and booty on the battlefield. The 1863 missive attempted to codify appropriate military conduct of soldiers. In total, there were 157 provisions given which embraced principles of humanity, distinctions between a combatant and civilian, codifying forms of retaliation, and developing permissions for the methods and means of warfare.[79]

In the second Hague conference, initially proposed by Theodore Roosevelt but convened by Russian Tsar Nicholas II, the original convention regulations from 1899 were revised. There was an increased focus on naval warfare and discussions regarding disarmament, laws of war and war crimes, and creating a binding international court for compulsory arbitration to settle international disputes. Twelve treaties were ratified.[80] A recommendation was made to summon another conference in eight years. The 1915 conference was never assembled due to the outbreak of World War I. That same year, women pacifists organized an International Women's Peace Congress.

Initially, the women's peace conference participants had planned to host their gathering through the German Union for Woman Suffrage in Berlin. These plans were axed once Germany began their European invasion strategy. Dutch Jewess and medical doctor, Aleta Jacobs, one of the first women to graduate with a medical degree from the Netherlands, suggested in a letter written in *Jus Suffragii* that they meet in her neutral home country after the Germans cancelled the original meeting. Jacobs was known for her study of the use of diaphragms as a means of birth control. She and her husband joined the British Malthusian League, which advocated against penalties for supporting the use of contraception and worked to better conditions for the poor and working classes. An active suffragist, Aleta had lobbied the Dutch government to institute required breaks for workers in retail jobs.

A women's conference eventually materialized at the Hague and was billed as having more than 1500 anti-war representatives from 150 associations and 14 different countries.[81] American representatives came from numerous peace societies: the Daughters of the American Revolution, Boston Telephone Operators Union, Norwegian Salvation Army, University Club of Amsterdam, German suffrage associations from New York City, Belgian Society for Peace Through Education, and the Hungarian Agricultural Women's Laborers' Association.[82] The United States and British delegations were the largest at 50 and 24 women each.[83] Many nations curtailed women from attending due to problematic alliances forming on the Continent.

Because the women gathering at the Hague were not recognized as official state actors, they held the conference as an autonomous body. All clauses but one, which highlighted women's voting rights, had to do with multilateral disarmament, the right of nations to self-determination and peace, and the right of conquest not being recognized without the consent of the men and women in the overtaken territory.[84] Attendee Louis Lochner described the gathering. "They met their sisters from countries at war with their own in the spirit of sympathetic understanding and comradeship without once trying to assess upon the other's nation the responsibility for the world catastrophe."[85] American peace activist Jane Addams described the gathering as "inchoate and unorganized" but full of "the spirit of international goodwill...with a sense of comradeship."[86] The meeting had no direct influence on the war.[87] Its primary output was the development of a roadmap for permanent peace that could be used as a base for future international meetings.[88]

Suffragism and pacifism

Direct links between peace activism and suffragism are weak. Women, on an individual basis, who had been active in the voting rights movement, chose

158 Women and War

many different philosophical directions once conflict erupted and their support altered as each nation entered the fray. Some suffragettes and suffragists joined the Salvation Army, Red Cross, and the US Army and Navy Nurse Corps. The Medical Women's National Association raised money to send female doctors overseas to work near the front lines. Women's continuum of support and nonsupport for the war ranged from shifting away from voting rights to purely peace activism or continuing with voting rights and ignoring war-related work completely. Others placed their efforts toward supporting the war effort on the Homefront, signing up with nongovernment and non-profit organizations, or forming teams to go to the battle arena as medical or administrative professionals.

What was unique about the burgeoning 1915 peace movement was that "Never before had women organized for peace separately from men."[89] Opinion is divided on whether pacifism can be considered a "logically inevitable corollary of feminism."[90] "The picture is complex. Emmeline Pankhurst and her daughter Christabel identified their Women's Socialist Party movement with the war effort, stopping their voting rights work. Millicent Fawcett, the avowed nonmilitant suffragist heading the National Union of Women Suffrage Societies before the war, deduced that the verbal power of argument over revolutionary tactics was a better approach and supported the war effort and nationalism."[91] Suffragists surmised that by rendering all aid possible, the government and men would respect their efforts, aiding in the eventual passage of voting rights.

Women in the NUWSS and WSP became disheartened by the leadership of both organizations for their nationalistic approach to the war. Suffragists were bitterly divided in their moral view about warfare, and the fissures that existed during prewar years among the disparate approaches to women's rights grew wider.[92] One reason repeated often for women's support of pacifism was that females were supreme at valuing human life, and they, not men, "insisted on resolving conflicts without severing relations between individuals or nations."[93] Jane Addams believed that women had been the earliest custodians of fostering human life and protectors of the helpless. Due to their relations with children and childbearing, they gained insight into how conflicts developed and could be resolved.[94] "Women," she alleged, "were the moral watchdogs of society."[95]

Suffragists Sylvia Pankhurst, second daughter of Emmeline Pankhurst, Emily Hobhouse, Catherine Marshall, Helena Swanwick, Olive Schreiner, and Kate Courtney, were utterly opposed to the war. They saw militarism as another version of the strong oppressing the weak and classified war as a form of patriarchy. Sylvia completely broke away from her mother and sister and campaigned against fighting as a communist sympathizer and championed the Bolshevik Revolution. Hobhouse had received attention during the Boer War 12 years earlier for her efforts to emancipate the horrible conditions

Decorative Arts Medals as Artifacts **159**

in the British South African prisoner-of-war camps. She had seen firsthand some of the atrocities that war perpetrated on humankind. Kate Courtney and Catherine Marshall became part of the core dynamic of the NUWSS and had worked together closely for many years. Marshall quit the NUWSS to help organize the No-Conscription Fellowship (NCF) and was the romantic partner of Clifford Allan, one of the founders of the NCF, who was jailed three times for being a conscientious objector (CO). The No-Conscription Fellowship was able to place into law rights for COs, and they opposed the Non-Combatant Corps set up by the Army. Olive Schreiner was politically active in the fight for rights for Afrikaners, Indigenous people, Black people, Jews, and Indians in South Africa. Stanwick was an active member of the NUWSS and resigned when they refused to send delegates to the International Women's Congress at the Hague. She turned her efforts toward the Women's International League for Peace and Freedom (WICPP) along with Jane Addams.

Less fractious events that some suffragists participated in were peace parades. Notice was given in *The Times* in New York City about an upcoming gathering with the personal endorsement of state Senator and suffragist Helen Robinson of Colorado. Two key event organizers were the President General of the Daughters of the American Revolution and the National Woman Suffrage Association president, Carrie Chapman Catt, who oversaw a committee of 100 volunteers. To attract support for the event, the women used laundries throughout the boroughs of New York City to advertise a call for marchers. "Laundrymen consented to put a poster in each laundry package delivered to each woman in their homes."[96] Local government officials around the city supported the idea and the parade. President Woodrow Wilson "favored" the meaning behind the parade. No flags were allowed, except for one white banner held at the front of the procession with the word "PEACE" at the bottom and a dove carrying an olive branch in a circle above the lettering. No categorizations by nationality or any other denomination were endorsed.

One anti-suffragist writing to the editor of the *Times* on August 20, 1914, spoke that she "would never be willing to march for a personal or limited cause, such as suffrage, but welcomes the opportunity to express her deep feeling for a world monument which would better all mankind."[97] The benefit of such a parade declared the unknown writer, calling herself "A woman," saw the peace march as a means of "the exaltation of soul for the wider cause of human brotherhood" and that such a gathering "would be the spectacle of suffragist and anti, both erstwhile of narrow outlook and acid tongue, marching shoulder to shoulder for the greater vision."[98] "A woman" requested that the parade be held on a Sunday so that "many more working women would be free to participate because it is on them that the burdens of war fall most heavily."[99] The parade occurred

160 Women and War

on Saturday, August 29, 1914, with 1500 women robed in black, the four leaders dressed in white, and those observing and not participating wearing black armbands. Opponents of the idea suggested it was a waste of time and its costliness would have been better served by applying the outlay to mediation.[100] The parade was one of the first overt attempts rather than the prior behind-the-scenes approach to peace activism.

The women's peace party Jane Addams and Carrie Chapman Catt

Five months after the parade, the Woman's Peace Party was organized under the oversight of the social welfare and housing activist Jane Addams. Carrie Chapman Catt was contacted first to lead the organization of a permanent peace party. She dissented from the idea that attaining the vote lent itself to peace activism. Catt contacted Addams as a potential president, and she accepted. The organization's base became Chicago. A one-dollar annual membership fee was charged, and their first platform was to call for a "Program for Constructive Peace," which supported the limitation of armaments, opposing militarism and military intervention, and the removal of economic motivations of war. If the entity could not form a conference of neutral nations through their activism, they would call their own conference "of pacifists from the world over."[101] A merger brought together "women of different political views and philosophical and religious backgrounds determined to study and make known the causes of war and work for permanent peace."

War, according to Addams, debased women and forced them to become ensconced in a philosophy of tribal appeal. By extension to this mentality generated by men, women were made the standard of men's tribal conduct. To move in this direction was a loss to the achievements women had been able to secure and was placing them once again in the singular preeminent role of bearing children to feed the male population's thirst for war. She was appalled by the restoration of foundling boxes in France and Germany. The purpose of which, in her mind, was that women could secretly offer their unwelcome children to others and at the same time allow them to be kept for the nation to fight. Further, ideas like foundling boxes encouraged the dissolution of family ties, the bedrock of Christian society. It was appalling to Jane that the German Government's decision to send midwives and nurses to follow the armies to "care for women who have yielded to the temptation of the time or have fallen victims of the lust of soldiers."[102] The right to the woman's vote was tossed onto this spread-out menu of ideas in the belief that by becoming involved in peace activism, the electoral franchise for women could expand. The voting rights element of the peace cause was then linked to the misappropriated concept that women, not men, were natural peace activists because they bore and nurtured human life.

Addams' viewpoint was that the "denial of the sovereignty of reason and justice by which war and all that makes for war render impotent the idealism of the race" and "demanded that our (women's) right to be consulted in settlement of questions concerning not alone the life of individuals but of nations be recognized and respected, that women be given a share in deciding between war and peace."[103] The articles of the Women's Peace Party platform were a mind-numbing list of items that entailed the nationalization of the manufacture of arms, organized opposition to militarism in the United States, education of youth in the ideals of peace, democratic control of foreign policies, the further humanizing of government by the extension of the franchise to women, the concert of nations to supersede balance of power, substitute law for war, substitute international policy for rival armies and navies, removal of the economic causes of war, and the appointment of a government commission of men and women with adequate appropriations to promote international peace.[104] The staggering list of desires put forward showed an unsophisticated knowledge of the death and destruction inherent to trench warfare. These women lacked any firsthand experience of battle being fought in a matter of inches at a time in the trenches—the hellish environment of death, monotony, disease-ridden bodies, insanity, mud, gas, rats, and stench. Addams felt "The business of making public opinion for peace is surely women's work, if only because they feel the horrors of war more keenly than men do and respond less readily to the martial appeal."

Chapman Catt left the fold of pacifism and pledged the NAWSA organization would support the US entry into the war and organized the Woman's Committee of the Council of National Defense to give women a say in war initiatives.[105] In 1918, she wrote to President Wilson and requested his support for a constitutional amendment securing voting rights for all American women. "Our Country is asking its women to give their all, and upon their voluntary and free offering may depend on the outcome of the war. If the Amendment fails, it will take the heart out of thousands of women."[106] The National Woman's Party in the United States was one of the few suffrage movements that hardened their stance on voting rights rather than turning toward war work. Their war was not with an eye toward Europe; it was continuing the fight within the American legislative realm and pursuit of the passage of the 19th Amendment. They peacefully protested with placards at the gate of the White House with slogans: "The time has come to conquer or submit. For us, there is but one choice. We have made it." When men are denied justice, they go to war. "This is our war, only we are fighting it with banners."[107] The NAWSA and the National Woman's Party opined that after entering World War I US women had replaced men by bolstering its economy and taking on industrial and agricultural jobs. The nation owed them respect by securing for them, their voting rights.

The tide turns

By 1917, peace movement articles began to appear in newspapers across America, which were increasingly railing against the pacifist approach. Entry into the war, insisted one journalist, had the idealist pacifists with "their eyes on the stars being brought rudely back to earth by stumbling into reality."[108] "The movement has petered out. Its active membership has boiled down to the professional gasbag element." The Women's Peace Party, "the organization of which Jane Adams is president," has been sending propaganda throughout the country, "importuning women to oppose the draft and the government's war plans."[109] Public censure for pacifism was replacing prior commentary, which had labeled the pacifists as "doves of peace," and "earnest appealers for universal tranquility."[110] Former president and rough rider Teddy Roosevelt, who was publicly demanding speeding up the war by sending four million fighters to Europe "excoriated" all pacifists for not being "thorough-going one hundred percent." Roosevelt called the pacifists, "modycoddlers," "disloyal," "treacherous," and "hyphenated Americans." "In the last four years, the professed internationalists like the profound pacifists have played the game of brutal German autocracy, the game of the militaristic and capitalistic tyranny...American pacifism has been the tool and ally of German militarism and has represented, and always will represent, deep disloyalty to our beloved country,"[111]

Not all women aligned with the antiwar cadre and saw the timeframe to be ripe for pursuing their right to vote. In January 1918, a hearing was granted by the United States House of Representatives for the National American Woman Suffrage Association. Charges were made that the campaign for national woman suffrage was a pro-German, socialist movement. Dr. Anna Howard Shaw, who had been involved with suffragism since 1885 and knew Susan B. Anthony and served as the honorary president of the NAWSA and chaired the Woman's Committee of the Council for National Defense testified:

> The majority of women are opposed to an ill-advised peace...It is undoubtedly true that the majority of women are endowed by nature with great sympathy toward human suffering, but it is also true that they are endowed with intelligence and more or less knowledge, which combine to show them that in the present war, which is the only one in which we need to be concerned, greater suffering would result from an ill-advised peace than from such a termination of hostilities as would make it forever impossible that like suffering should visit the world again.[112]

In support of her argument, Shaw introduced data that for every male volunteer, there were ten women doing war work, and thousands of other women were standing in line to fill the vacancies left by fighting men in industry and agriculture. "The loyalty of American women demands that at this time the government shall recognize the services of its women" and grant them the right to enfranchisement. That same day, Theodore Roosevelt wrote a letter to the Chair of the Republican party to vote in favor of giving women suffrage. He advocated for a female member from every state to be placed on the committee.[113]

One letter to the press by a woman only referred to as MMe Grouitch called the pacifists "a handful of silly women trying to accomplish in the excitement of war what the wisest masculine brains failed to accomplish in the calm of peace with all the deliberately constructed machinery of the world placement."[114] The money being spent by the women headed to the Hague in the Netherlands for the peace conference would "have saved one million women and children in Serbia from typhus or possibly cholera."[115] Pacifism was denounced by speakers at the Navy League Dinner in 1916. This movement was a "miserable creed." "If George Washington had been a pacifist, we would now be a (British) colony." The resultant output of following a pacifist agenda would be "loss of loyalty owed to the country our forefathers died for."[116] Brooklyn Christian and Hebrew clergymen spoke out for righteous war in 1917 in a 100 signatory letter to President Wilson expressing admiration for the "clear and forceful way you have set for utterances the moral issues involved in the present war. We wish to record our condemnation of the doctrine for peace at any price, promulgated among us by a few mistaken individuals."[117]

What did peace suffragists accomplish?

Jane Addams wrote, "Our mission was simple. Foolish it may be, but it was not impossible." Despite their efforts to inaugurate a world without war, the pacifists in Great Britain and America could not halt the conflict or prevent other nations from entering the fray. Importantly, it was the non-concrete ideas that materialized from peace activities that would impact future generations. The Woman's Peace Party's notion of mediation as an imperative to foreign policy stuck as an instrumental negotiation tool. As did the creation of a foundation for pursuing a form of diplomacy based on international law and noncompulsory conciliation. Activities undertaken by the women pacifists also stimulated the use of citizen diplomacy during times of discord.[118] Participation by women in the peace process was eventually recognized at a high level when Jane Addams shared the Peace Prize in 1931 with Nicholas Murray Butler "for their assiduous effort to revive the ideal of peace and to rekindle the spirit of peace in their nation and the whole of mankind." A lasting organizational structure was built from the World War I Women's International Committee for Permanent Peace in the form of the WICPP, now

164 Women and War

headquartered in Geneva, Switzerland, with an office in the United Nations in New York City. National sections are spread across 37 countries. The modern version of the WICPP, the Women's International League for Peace and Freedom, organizes around the purpose of bringing together "women of different political views and philosophical and religious backgrounds to study and make known the causes of war, work for permanent peace, and unite women worldwide who oppose oppression and exploitation."[119]

Jewelry, pins, and clothing

Suffragist jewelry attached to the women's rights movement appeared during the rise of Revivalism, a romantic reaction to the impersonal nature of industrial society; Art Nouveau, a reaction to the cluttered designs of Victorian ear art; and the Arts and Crafts Movement, also a rebellion against the Industrial Revolution and Machine Age. Suffragist jewelry and pins mimicked these three artistic schools in their design. Items were given as presentational pieces for several reasons: to honor leadership, make a public statement of belongingness to a specific branch of the movement, and highlight admiration for participating in incidents that led to pioneering progress for equality. The wealthier of the movement purchased extravagant pieces using precious gems, usually of the colors of the specific suffragist unit to which the woman was attached.

Each suffragist, remonstrant, and suffragette movement contributed to sets of eclectic motifs to promote and represent their causes.[120] In each instance, decorative pieces were chosen carefully to reflect a mission and organizational personality.[121] In the United States, the remonstrants used the antisuffrage red rose or red and white pins, usually with the word "NO" or a floral composition at the center. There was even a song, with words and music by an obscure composer, Phil Hanna, called The Anti-Suffrage Rose, sung at meetings. Their adversaries, the suffragists and suffragettes were referred to as Jonquils a member of the narcissus family because the yellow blooms were considered lesser flowers in a self-imposed adaptation of a plant hierarchy.

Nonmilitants chose red, green, and white as their colors to distinguish themselves from the militants. Green, purple, and white were common choices of color with the militant movement in their crafts and jewelry. Gold or yellow were initially the only colors used by suffragist causes in the United States. White was employed purposefully to offset the press and anti-suffragists portrayals of them as hard, masculine, and ugly and represented purity of their cause. American Alice Paul brought the purple, white, and gold motif from Britain to the United States for the National Woman's Party, which adopted the colors in 1908. Most historical references state that purple signified loyalty, constancy, purpose, and unswerving steadfastness. Gold was the color of light and life, a torch guiding unswerving devotion to attain equality.[122]

Decorative clasps or pendants were informally issued and usually made individually by a jeweler or artist associated with a specific cadre of like thinkers.[123] Enameller Ernestine Mills and designer Jessie Marion King often made pieces on commission or to sell at fund-raising bazaars. King's exceptional talents were recognized when she was selected as a Tutor in Book Decoration and Design at Glasgow School of Art. After marrying, she chose to keep her maiden name and hired a nanny to continue her art career. She borrowed from styles popular in Germany and Italy and was influenced by and a devotee of the esteemed Italian Renaissance painter Sandro Botticelli. Mills' mother was an actress and classical musician, and she and her husband Thomas were both members of the Committee of the National Society for Women's Suffrage. Mills joined the Pankhurst militants in 1909 and became a member of the Fabian Art Society, which was a politically motivated enclave that had the desire to establish Great Britain as a democratic socialist state without having to resort to revolutionary tactics.

Big-name businesses also saw the value in making and selling suffragist products. Jewelry company Child & Child, which existed up through 1916 in Kensington, was known for its neo-Renaissance, Art Nouveau, and Edwardian-style jewelry. They made many suffragist pieces for their clientele. Mappin & Webb, an internationally recognized silversmith and jeweler, also sold suffragist pieces, and Selfridge's Department Store sold fine and costume necklaces and brooches. Jewelry and fashion consciousness went hand in hand. Christabel Pankhurst formally urged WSPU supporters not to be dowdy and asked them to outfit themselves appropriately.[124] During parades and civic addresses, there was an effort to be costumed in attractive tailored clothing. Middle-class suffragists tended to choose Derry and Thorn, Swan and Edgar, or Burberry for their outer and everyday wear. Here, they could acquire, at moderate prices, long-wearing, comfortable, and serviceable coats, skirts, and blouses. The militants tended to shop at the pricier Selfridges, where they could purchase more elegant clothing.[125]

Selfridge's ads appeared in the Pankhurst *Votes for Women* magazine and newspapers with large readerships pushing the notion of the well-dressed feminist. The store kept on hand dresses, coats, shoes, and blouses in combinations of green, purple, and white. One of their biggest sellers was white tea gowns. Derry & Toms placed an ad a few days before the London Great Procession: "Charming hats for the June 17 Demonstration...made in the colors of the various organizations in connection with the Woman-Suffrage movement."[126] Swan and Edgar advertised walking skirts, straw hats, and over cloaks known as Dumfries for the pilgrimage as "serviceable attire at modern prices," along with hats trimmed with ribbon in a selection of voting rights colors.[127] Women had their photographs taken or portraits painted wearing suffragist jewelry.

166 Women and War

Force-feedings, hunger strikes, and imprisonment

Many suffragette acts were considered illegal, and the women were imprisoned for their behavior. In protest of being denied political prisoner status and treated as felons, which was not done to men in similar situations, women began to employ the tactic of hunger strikes.[128] One of the first documented cases was written down in a smuggled letter by Charlotte Marsh to Selina Martin in 1909 at Winson Green Prison in Birmingham, United Kingdom. The two had been arrested with six other suffragettes for protesting during a meeting held by Prime Minister Herbert Asquith. Marsh's letter, written on a title page torn from a book, told of being fed by tube twice daily with the prison matron chasing her around her cell. As with many of the messages smuggled in and out of jail, she closed her note with the rallying cry, "No surrender!" A 92-hour hunger strike by Maron Wallace Dunlop after being incarcerated for one month at Holloway Prison on a vandalism charge the same year led authorities to release her due to fear she might die.[129]

Throughout 1909–1914, hunger strikes were punished using forcible feeding.[130] The abuse was meant to embarrass and turn the suffragettes into penitent, remorseful actors who would no longer desire to fight for equality. Instead of relenting, they held their ground. June Purvis, the founding editor of the international feminist journal *Women's History Review*, felt the visual and emotional impacts of the hunger strike had a particular cultural resonance with the women because it had been an effective measure of passive resistance used by men in their civil rights protests. It was an expedient agency of contesting an all-male government's refusal to allow them to enter the field of politics.[131] "Force-feeding was a subliminal form of oral rape, a way in which male protagonists could enter their bodies while they struggled under the weight of orderlies and with their legs and arms tied to chairs."[132]

Several women were blindfolded. Rubber tubes used were not sanitary, having been passed among the diseased and mentally ill internees first.

Mary Leigh, another prisoner at Winson Green jail in 1909, described the experience, "The drums of the ear seem to be bursting, a horrible pain in the throat and the breast. The tube is pushed down twenty inches…I resist and am overcome by weight in numbers."[133] By 1914, approximately 1000 suffragettes had been imprisoned. Leigh, along with Constance Lytton, Elsie Howey, Lucy Stone, Alice Paul, Flora Lion, Frances Parker, the Pankhurst women, and Ethel Moorehead, became part of more than 200 women who experienced this form of physical torture. Emmeline Pankhurst stood at the front of the pack, a willing exemplar, enduring ten hunger strikes and numerous force-feedings.

Lady Constance Lytton, who was imprisoned twice for demonstrating at the House of Commons and for throwing a stone wrapped in paper with the message "To Lloyd George, Rebellion against tyranny is obedience to God,

Decorative Arts Medals as Artifacts **167**

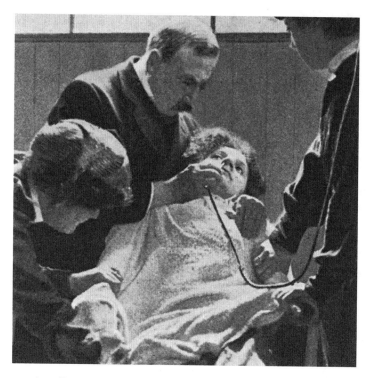

FIGURE 6.7 A suffragette being force-fed by two women and a man.
© Public domain. PDM 1.0 Deed | Public Domain Mark 1.0 Universal | Creative Commons.

Deeds, not Words," became angered when she was given special dispensations due to her social standing. Lytton's mother was the British aristocrat Edith Villiers, Vicereine of India, and was married to Robert Bulwer-Lytton, 1st Earl of Lytton. Their lineage could be traced to the 13th century, with a protracted line of peerages, several knights, and baronets. Villiers brought to the marriage a 6000-pound-a-year stipend, placing her and her husband in the upper strata of British society.

Lady Constance was not the only member of the Villiers family to participate in activism. Constance was the great-niece of radical and reformist politician Charles Pelham Villiers, who held parliamentary office for 54 years from 1835 to 1889 and supported the emerging women's campaign for women's suffrage. Considered an aristocratic Victorian radical, he aided in the creation and passage of the Metropolitan Poor Law Act of 1867. In conjunction with Florence Nightingale, he ensured legal oversight of professional requirements for women nurses serving in poor law districts and workhouses and funded the erection of public infirmaries. Charles's Public Works Act of 1863 was instrumental in creating jobs for public health projects, one of the

168 Women and War

employment arenas where women were allowed to participate without much pushback.[134]

Lytton was intensely devoted to suffragette philosophy. During one incarceration, she attempted to scar her chest with a needle to stencil "Votes for Women" on it permanently. After carving the letter "V" across her heart, the prison authorities stopped her. In 1910, she dressed as a working-class seamstress named Jane Warton and led a procession to the Prison Governor's house to protest the treatment of lower-class women in the prison system. Lytton was arrested in a rock-throwing incident that damaged the prison authority's car. She was sent to Walton Goal in Liverpool for two weeks for this act, sentenced to hard labor, and force-fed eight times.

Her accounts of imprisonment were printed in the suffragette paper *Votes for Women* and the daily national newspaper, *The Times*. In chapter eight of her autobiography, *Prisons and Prisoners*, Constance left for posterity a first-person account of the revulsive act of force-feeding pursued by prison officials on her and other suffragettes.

He said if I resisted so much with my teeth, he would have to feed me through the nose. The pain of it was intense, and at last, I must have given way, for he got the gag between my teeth when he proceeded to turn it much more than necessary until my jaws were fastened wide apart, far more than they could go naturally. Then he put down my throat a tube that seemed to me much too wide and was something like four feet in length. The irritation of the tube was excessive. I choked the moment it touched my throat until it had got down. Then the food was poured in quickly; it made me sick a few seconds after it was down, and the action of the sickness made my body and legs double up, but the wardresses instantly pressed back my head, and the doctor leaned on my knees. The horror of it was more than I can describe. I was sick over the doctor and wardresses, and it seemed a long time before they took the tube out. As the doctor left, he gave me a slap on the cheek, not violently, but, as it were, to express his contemptuous disapproval, and he seemed to take for granted that my distress was assumed... Before long, I heard the forced feeding in the next cell to mine. It was almost more than I could bear; it was Elsie Howey, I was sure. When the ghastly process was over and all quiet, I tapped on the wall and called out at the top of my voice, which wasn't much just then, "No surrender," there came the answer past any doubt in Elsie's voice, "No surrender."

The situation worsened for the hunger strikers with the passage of the Prisoners Temporary Discharge for Ill Health Act, passed under the direction of the militant's reviled politico, Prime Minister Herbert Asquith.[135] The act allowed prisoners to be released if they were weak due to hunger strikes. On discharge, the women would be sent out on a license that they would cease their political activities and be nursed back to health, then re-admitted once deemed well enough to complete a sentence. Many women on release evaded authorities and medical care to appear at public forums and legislative meetings. The catch-me-if-you-can attitude of the suffra-gettes combined with the in and out of jail sequence perpetrated by the ill-conceived legislation led the WSPU to brand the bill the cat and mouse act. Suffragettes printed a poster with a giant orange cat with bloodied teeth holding a limp suffragette in its mouth, a graphic rendering of the viciousness of the situation. Postcards with the same theme but different art were also circulated.

Apathy continued to reign in Parliament about the women's reports of poor treatment. Male news writers tended to agree that the plight of the women was of no concern due to the medical science behind the proce-dure. Parliamentarians used the misinformation as factual to allow the process to continue. One of the worst among the lot was Liberal Imperial-ist Reginald McKenna, who insisted the women experienced no pain nor were they in danger during the ordeal. Not all politicians were this sense-less, and in 1913, dismayed with what he was hearing, surgeon Charles Mansell-Moullin, the husband of the founder of the Suffrage Union in Wales, Edith Ruth Thomas, formed a committee of three experts to prove the statements false.[136] Charles had become incensed by what he heard from medical officers, prison officials, and House of Commons members who made asinine analogies about stuffing turkeys at Christmas, their exhibitions of ribald laughter, and telling of obscene jokes regarding the plight of the women.

Including Mansell-Moullin, the triad was filled out with accomplished sci-entist Sir Victor Horsley and Scottish pathologist Dr. Agnes Savill.[137] As a team, they investigated the cases of 102 suffragettes, of which 90 had been forcibly fed. The doctor, politician, and scientist produced a report of their findings and published them in the peer-reviewed medical journal *Lancet*. Charles also read the research findings before the government body. He pre-sented one particularly moving description of one suffragettes experience to the all-male room of peers:

From 4:30 until 8:30, I heard the most dreadful screams and yells com-ing from the cells...I had never heard of human beings being tortured before...I sat on my chair with my fingers in my ears for the greater part of that endless four hours. My heart was thumping against my ribs as I sat listening to the processions of the doctors and wardresses as they came to and frow, and passed from cell to cell, and the groans and cries of those who were being fed, until at last, the procession paused at my door. My turn had come.[138]

170 Women and War

Mansell confirmed that women entered a state of collapse, and that those inflicting the feeding continued even though the fluid was entering their lungs. Others had heart attacks or contracted pneumonia and pleurisy.

Men also supported the suffragette cause and were imprisoned for their activities. In his youth, William Ball had been a national-level track athlete. He later became a member of the National Transport Workers Federation, a body of journeymen comprised of dockworkers, seamen, tramwaymen, and road transport employees. He was jailed for two months at Pentonville Prison after breaking two windowpanes at the Home Office. His actions were in defense of Alan MacDougall, a civil engineer jailed for supporting suffragettes in their attempts to attend political meetings. Pentonville was a category B institution for inmates posing a risk to the public. He was denied the right to wear his clothing or see his wife and forbidden outside correspondence with his five children. The WSPU newspaper ran a front-page story on Ball, his photo at the center with the headline, "Torture in an English Prison." According to the report, Ball had been cruelly victimized by the government. He had daughters and sons and wanted as much protection for his girls as he did for his boys. On arriving at Pentonville, Ball demanded to be treated as a political offender, citing Winston Churchill's April 1910 regulation to view Suffrage prisoners convicted of offenses not involving dishonesty, cruelty, indecency, or serious violence, not as convicts.

Ball was refused an exit from incarceration on appeals even though he had five dependents at home and was the only wage earner in his family. This categorization usually would have meant leniency by the court. Jennie received a letter stating that her husband was certifiably insane and had been transferred to a pauper's asylum. He was force-fed twice daily for 37 days in a row. His spouse was finally allowed to visit him, found him very seriously ill and in an exceedingly emaciated condition with nose and throat swollen and inflamed from forcible feeding. He told her he had been locked in a punishment cell twice. His treatment was a testament to Constance Lytton's observation that if you were a suffragette from the working class, you would be treated far worse than those with upper-class status.[139] WSPU money and funds from the Men's League for Women's Suffrage (MLWS) paid for his case. MLWS distributed a pamphlet supporting Ball's experiences with the headline, "Official Brutality on the Increase."[140] *Votes for Women Weekly* ran a cover story on March 10, 1911, "Man Prisoner fed by Force."

For those who suffered the greatest atrocities of being imprisoned, bullied, and physically and mentally abused, the WSPU established an honorary medals program to recognize their gallantry. No record exists that male suffragettes received the medals.

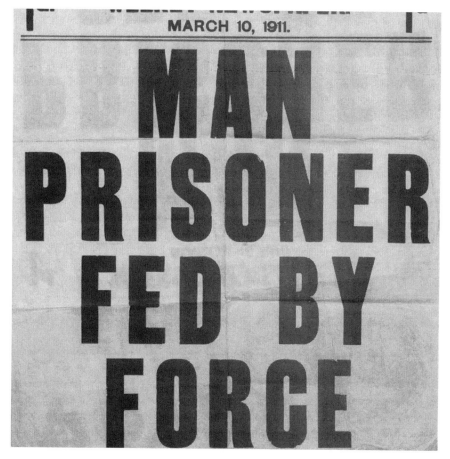

FIGURE 6.8 Votes for women poster advertising the story of William Ball.
© Public domain. Flickr by LSE Library at https://flickr.com/photos/35128489@N07/22896718036.

The American Night of Terror

In America, the women arrested for blocking foot traffic as they silently protested on November 14, 1917, in front of the White House were manhandled, placed in wagons, and sent to one of two facilities, either the jail in Washington, D.C. or one in Virginia.[141] Thirty-three picketers were incarcerated at the Occoquan Workhouse, a worm-ridden and filthy lockup.[142] On requesting they be treated as political prisoners in the strip-down room, the jail superintendent ordered a formal mandate to his guards to teach the women a lesson. He refused them counsel and called in the United States Marines to guard the building.[143] Even though they were sitting quietly, the workhouse sentries stormed the room, cudgels and fists at the ready, dragging them bodily and

172 Women and War

by the hair into the bowels of the jail, where they were thrown into cells without having been properly booked.[144]

Abusive behaviors at Occoquan involved clubbing, beatings, and torture, usually by male guards, but female guards also participated. Alice was placed in solitary confinement for two weeks and was given only bread and water. After being sent to the hospital ward, she immediately began a hunger strike, to which the jail administration replied by placing her in a psychiatric ward and threatening to put her in inpatient psychiatric care. She was repeatedly force-fed three times a day for three weeks. Lucy Burns was persecuted by manacling her hands above her head for talking in jail and forced to stand overnight and into part of the next day without reprieve.[145] Burns smuggled a note out of the jail that imparted information on the treatment of the women.

> Mrs. Nolan (the 73-year-old suffrage picket from Florida) flung in the cell. Mrs. Lewis dragged me past my door. I was handcuffed for calling to ask others how they were. I was threatened with a straight jacket and buckle gag...(Matron) Whittaker came, seized Julia Emory by the back of the neck, and threw her into the room brutally. She is a little girl. I asked (for information on my case), Told then to shut up, and threatened straight-jacket and gag again. They refused strenuously to put on prison clothes. Was thrown into a room where men with delirium tremens usually held.[146]

Tall, red-haired Lucy and the slighter, dark-haired Alice would end their early 20th-century suffragette careers as top contenders for jail time. Alice purposely strove to receive a maximum internment of seven months, the longest of all the suffragettes and was arrested seven times. Lucy's most prolonged single confinement was six months, and she was arrested six times. She recounted her experience with force-feeding:

> I had been fasting for six days and nights when they started in on me. It was a terrible experience, a horrible attempt to break my will. Five men and two women were employed in doing it. The men would pin me to the floor, several of them holding my arms by my sides. If I struggled, they would sit upon me. And while the men held me the women would insert a tube in my mouth through which a fluid of egg and milk would be forced into my stomach. I was weak from the fasting, but whenever I was strong enough, I would refuse to let them insert the tube into my stomach that way. Food so taken is not nourishing. It is not meant to be. It was done simply to break my will.[147]

Stories divulged by women like 73-year-old Mary Nolan from Jacksonville, Florida, who was placed in an Occoquan cell with 55-year-old Dora Lewis from Philadelphia and 48-year-old Alice Cosu from Louisiana, left no

Decorative Arts Medals as Artifacts **173**

doubt of the maniacal terror of that night perpetuated by law enforcement officials. Dora had her head slammed against an iron bedpost, knocking her out. Thinking she had been killed, Cosu had a heart attack but was denied medical treatment. Dora Lewis went on to amass a more extensive prison record for being the keynote speaker at an outdoor event in recognition of Inez Milholland, suffragette labor lawyer, war correspondent and the horse-riding Grand Marshal at the Woman Suffrage Procession in March of 1913 in Washington, D.C., and for participating during the watchfire demonstrations against President Wilson's speeches on democracy. It would not be until early 1918 that public pressure and outrage over the treatment of the women became so heightened that they were released. Washington, D.C.'s Court of Appeals found all the incarcerated women innocent and cited authorities for illegal arrest and imprisonment.[148]

The Occoquan experience did not deter the Women's Suffrage Association from continuing their pursuit of the right to vote. Twenty-six of its members began planning a cross-country train trip that took three weeks to complete. Mary Nolan, now 77, was aboard. Its primary purpose was to highlight the violent and anarchic measures of the federal government in its attempts to crush suffrage. The trip cost in 2023 currency would have equaled 380,000 dollars. Various benefactors assisted in funding, with wealthy mining engineer and financier William B. Thompson paying for the *Jailed for Freedom* pamphlet, copies of the NWP *Suffragist*, and other written materials to be distributed at each stop. The *Prison Special*, pulled by an engine they named *Democracy Limited*, began in Washington, D.C., and headed south.[149] A southern route was chosen first since the region had been notorious for opposing the amendment. Alabama rejected the amendment, as did South Carolina, Kentucky, Virginia, Maryland, Mississippi, and Louisiana. Stops were made in Jacksonville, Florida, and then the train turned west to Chattanooga, Tennessee; New Orleans, Louisiana; San Antonio, Texas; and Los Angeles and Sacramento, California. From the West Coast, the train turned back toward the East Coast, traveling through Denver, Colorado; Chicago, Illinois; Milwaukee, Wisconsin; Syracuse, New York; Boston, Massachusetts; and Hartford, Connecticut, stopping in New York City.

Along the route, speeches were given at rented halls, train stations, and standing from the back seats of rented automobiles. *The Women's Marseillaise*, an official anthem of the WSPU and composed by Britain's Florence MacAulay, was sung as were songs generated just for the trip.[150] Factual playlets of their real-life incarcerations were written and presented wearing replicas of prison uniforms. Large crowds sometimes formed to support them, booing and hissing at the treatments they had received, but this was not always the case. The mayor of Columbia warned them in South Carolina that "decidedly unnatural feminine sentiments" would not be allowed.[151] Three months after the tour finished, the US Congress voted to pass the

174 Women and War

19th Amendment. A year later, it was officially adopted. In the United Kingdom, The Representation of People Act was passed in 1918 but was limited in scope, enfranchising women only over the age of 30 who met property qualifications. It took ten more years to pass the Equal Franchise Act of 1928, which granted equal voting rights to men and women after reaching the age of 21. It passed on the second of July. Emmeline Pankhurst had died eighteen days earlier, on the fourteenth of June, aged 69, and there was a wireless article buried several pages deep within *The New York Times:* "Mrs. Pankhurst, suffragist, dead: famous leader of militant women a conservative at the end. Aspired to parliament. Death recalls her stormy career—vote won when government's foe supported the war."[152]

The Corona Aurea of the British and American suffragettes

There was no more prestigious honor in the British suffragette community than to receive a prison or force-feeding medal or brooch.[153] Presented only to those who had distinguished themselves in action against an enemy to the cause, the suffragette decoration was the pinnacle artifact representing self-sacrifice. Up until the first wave of feminism, decorations of the sort originating from the Pankhurst followers had only been dispensed for valorous military feats. The WSPU regarded their forces as valid and equal to a civil-military order for their voluntary and deliberate exposure to the dangers caused by following the deeds, not words' philosophy. It was essential to venerate the women for their bravery and stoicism with a medal of valor, and a brooch was introduced in 1909 after the first series of arrests and internments at Holloway Prison.[154]

The United States and United Kingdom suffragists memorialized arrests by formally presenting awards to those showing strength, determination, and resilience during incarceration. In December, following the Night of Terror in Virginia, the National Woman's Party awarded silver pins shaped like a cell door with a heart-shaped padlock to each woman jailed for freedom. The official cartoonist of the National Woman's Party, Nina Allender, who had studied painting at the Corcoran School of Art in Washington, D.C., and the Pennsylvania Academy of Fine Arts, styled the pin. By the close of the suffrage movement, she had contributed over 150 cartoons to the campaign.[155] Jewelry manufacturer Toye and Company minted the first Great Britain awards, and the WSPU treasurer paid one pound each for them from organizational funds. Of 50,000 WSPU members, only 135, or slightly less than three percent, received a medal. A silver bar engraved at the top, with the words "FOR VALOUR," was an overt imitation of the inscription on the Victoria Cross for intrepidness in the presence of a military enemy. On the reverse were the recipient's name and the words "HUNGER STRIKE." Silver bars on the face of the medal signified the number of hunger strikes a woman had endured and were stamped with the date of arrest. Enameled purple, white, and green bars for force-feeding were similarly engraved.[156]

Medals were presented in purple boxes with green velvet lining on the bottom and white silk on the inside lid printed with gold lettering, "presented by the WSPU" with the name of the recipient "in recognition of gallant action, whereby through endurance to the last extremity of hunger and hardship a great principle of political justice was vindicated." Medals were publicly presented at mass demonstrations or in less vigorous atmospheres of luncheons and meetings. Over the ensuing years, the importance of the medals was depleted, and many were thrown away by generations of families who did not know their significance. A 21st-century resurgence in interest in honoring the fight for women's rights has brought these rare objects back into the spotlight, with auction houses now giving them appropriate consideration regarding their sociological, political, and monetary value as important social artifacts.

World War I intervenes

In July 1914, Austria-Hungary declared war on Serbia, which began a conflict that drew European nations, North America, the Middle East, Africa, the Pacific, and Asia into contesting personal freedoms and geopolitical boundaries. The fighting lasted until November 1918.[157] At the direction of Carrie Chapman Catt, the nonmilitant NAWSA was formed into war effort departments for food conservation, protections for women replacing men in industrial jobs, wrapping bandages, and support for overseas hospitals.[158] Anna Howard Shaw, one of the mediators for bringing together the disparate personalities of the National Woman's Suffrage Association and American Women Suffrage Association into the fold of the NAWSA, stopped her voting rights work and placed her energy into foreign affairs and was the first woman to be recognized with the Distinguished Service Medal.[159] As chair of the Women's Committee on the United States Council for Defense, which worked with the Department of Interior on food waste and meatless and wheatless days, Shaw oversaw voluntary teams that raised money for the American Red Cross, supported liberty loans and savings stamp programs, and established standards for student nursing recruits. Forty-eight state divisions and 1800 women's organizations were tied to the Council.[160] The less militant offshoot of WSPU, the Women's Freedom League, agreed to continue their work on voting rights. The nonviolent NUWSS suspended their marches, and Millicent Fawcett turned to organizing women's hospital units in France.

The Women's Suffrage Association printed wartime flyers in Pennsylvania, purporting an ideological mingling between voting rights and wartime fervor. Ten questions were put forward on one of their posters. The answer to

176 Women and War

each query was the word, women. Who faces death to give life to men? Who rears the sons killed in battle? Who plants fields and crops when men are at war? Who nurses the wounded? Who suffers agony for soldiers killed? Who dares say that war is not their business? At the bottom were two lines. "In the name of justice and civilization, give women a voice in government and councils that make or prevent war. Vote for the Women Suffrage Amendment in November."[161] Militants in the United States used the events of the war to piggyback onto their voting rights quest, claiming that the President's belief in protecting freedom and democracy on the European continent made him a great equivocator. Political cartoons by Nina Allender were used to tie the war effort to the women's rights campaign.

In Britain, women's rights advocates began questioning their militant activities for the vote. Emmeline Pankhurst called for shelving suffrage in Britain and turning to war relief work.[162] Then started to discuss whether they should replace their suffragette energies with service roles for the war effort. Pankhurst's militants halted their rights campaigns entirely, believing the German threat was a far greater hindrance to humanity than securing the vote. A truce was made with the government, and negotiations resulted in the release of all women from jail. Pankhurst's daughter, Christabel, wrote in *Unshackled, The Story of How We Won the Vote,*

> War was the only course for our country to take. This was national militancy. As suffragettes, we could not be pacifists at any price. Mother and I declared support of our country. We declared an armistice with the government and suspended militancy for the duration of the war. Mother said, What would be the good of a vote without a country to vote in![163]

Not all women agreed with this defection; those who disagreed left England to join the US suffragist community. Others left the fold, never returning to the fight, and struck out to join the war effort closer to the front lines, learning first aid, serving in the ambulance corps, and raising war money for orphans, widows, and injured soldiers.

Whether the militant approach changed the course of the vote is still hotly contested. American suffragist, author, and columnist Ida Husted Harper, having lived through the entire suffrage experience in the United States, put down the history of the movement in a six-volume treatise, *The History of Women Suffrage.* In the last volume, she wrote,

> The earlier years of militant activity were, in my opinion, helpful to the whole movement, for up to 1908, the militants had only adopted sensational and unusual methods such as waving flags and making speeches in the lobby of the House and asking inconvenient questions at public meetings. They had suffered a great deal of violence but had used none... (does

it do) more harm or good to the suffrage cause? It certainly broke down the conspiracy of silence...when the militants after 1908 proceeded to acts of violence, every outrage against person or property were given the widest possible publicity not only in Great Britain but all over the world. There was soon not an intelligent human being in any country who was not discussing women's suffrage and arguing for or against it.

The suffragist cause had sown the seeds for the evolution of a company of women who were now ready to become part of the fighting forces of their nations.[164] They were asking, why shouldn't we be considered as equal members in our country's military fight to protect democratic ideals? Many volunteered for the ambulance corps and nursing duty. These jobs met the Victorian profile of a woman's fundamental role in society as a caregiver and devotee of health and well-being. Others began to fight for inclusion in military medicine. These women were on the precipice of participating in the subsequent greatest struggle of their lives, which was to be considered equally as viable as men in the arena of war.

Notes

1 J. B. "Renaissance Portrait Medals." *The Metropolitan Museum of Art Bulletin* 7, no. 3 (1912): 49–54. https://doi.org/10.2307/3252739.
  "Renaissance Portrait Medals from the Robert Lehman Collection," "Pisanello and the History of the Renaissance Medal." "Exhibition December 19, 2016–May 29, 2017," The Met, Portrait Medals: History and Production Processes | The Metropolitan Museum of Art (metmuseum.org).
2 Ibid. Renaissance "Portrait Medals: History and Production Processes."
3 Mark Jones. "The Medal as an Instrument of Propaganda in Late 17th and Early 18th Century Europe PART 2." *The Numismatic Chronicle (1966–)* 143 (1983): 202–13. http://www.jstor.org/stable/42665176.
4 Mieczysław Morka. "The Beginnings of Medallic Art in Poland during the Times of Zygmunt I and Bona Sforza." *Artibus et Historiae* 29, no. 58 (2008): 65–87. http://www.jstor.org/stable/40343650.
5 T. Whitcombe Greene. "German Medalists of the Sixteenth and Seventeenth Centuries." *The Numismatic Chronicle and Journal of the Numismatic Society* 8 (1888): 145–53. http://www.jstor.org/stable/42682590.
6 William M. Milliken. "Four Stone Models for German Medals." *The Bulletin of the Cleveland Museum of Art* 44, no. 6 (1957): 118–21. http://www.jstor.org/stable/25142217.
7 Jean Babelon. "The Medal in Art and Society." *Journal of the Royal Society of Arts* 103, no. 4961 (1955): 782–92. http://www.jstor.org/stable/41364760.
8 Alan M. Stahl. "The Classical Program of the Medallic Series of Louis XIV." *The Princeton University Library Chronicle* 76, no. 1–2 (2015): 267–87. https://doi.org/10.25290/prinunivlibrchro.76.1-2.0267.
9 D. Scarinci. "Medals are Sculpture For Everyone." *Sculpture Review* 69, no. 1 (2020): 24–26. https://doi.org/10.1177/0747528420926813.
10 Paul J. Bosco. Numismatic Website, "Art-Deco Medals: The Walter Glenn Collection." www.artdecomedals.com. Accessed 4/2/2022.

Anna Baranyi. "'Traditional' and Avant-Garde Bartók Medals in Hungarian Art." *Studia Musicologica Academiae Scientiarum Hungaricae* 40, no. 1/3 (1999): 85–93. https://doi.org/10.2307/902554.

11 J. M. C. Toynbee. "Roman Medallions: Their Scope and Purpose." *The Numismatic Chronicle and Journal of the Royal Numismatic Society* 4, no. 1/4 (1944): 27–44. http://www.jstor.org/stable/42663365.

12 Gregory R. Crane. Editor, Polybius, *Histories*, "Military Decorations," Plb6.39, Perseus Digital Library, Tufts University, Polybius, Histories, book 6, Military Decorations (tufts.edu).

13 Ibid.

14 Medals of America. "The Beginning of Military Awards," The Beginning of Military Awards | Medals of America Press. Accessed 4/1/2022.

15 Bruno S. Frey. "Giving and Receiving Awards." *Perspectives on Psychological Science* 1, no. 4 (2006): 377–88. http://www.jstor.org/stable/40212179.

16 Jyri Vaahtera. "The Origin of Latin Suffrāgium." *Glotta* 71, no. 1/2 (1993): 66–80. http://www.jstor.org/stable/40266951.

17 *The New York Times*, November 3, 1937, p. 23. Charles E. Hands, British Reporter; War Correspondent in Africa, Cuba and Many Other Parts of World Is Dead – The New York Times (nytimes.com).

18 "Taking up the Cause, How Women Won the Right to Vote," skyHistory, Taking Up The Cause: How Women Won the Vote | Sky HISTORY TV Channel, n.d.

19 Jo Vellacott Newberry. "Anti-War Suffragists." *History* 62, no. 206 (1977): 411–25. http://www.jstor.org/stable/24410789.

20 Gilbert E. Jones. "The Position of the Anti-Suffragists." *The Annals of the American Academy of Political and Social Science* 35 (1910): 16–22. http://www.jstor.org/stable/1011239.

   Hannah Dyson. "The 'Antis': Minnesota Women Opposed to Female Suffrage." *Minnesota History* 67, no. 3 (2020): 163–68. https://www.jstor.org/stable/26977824.

   Lisa Cochran Higgins. "Adulterous Individualism, Socialism, and Free Love in Nineteenth-Century Anti-Suffrage Writing." *Legacy* 21, no. 2 (2004): 193–209. http://www.jstor.org/stable/25679506.

21 Women's National Anti-Suffrage League Manifesto in Phelps, Edith M. (2013) Selected articles on woman suffrage London: Forgotten Books, pp. 257–59.

   The Ladies Battle, Molly Elliott Seawell.

   The Business of Being a Woman Ida M. Tarbell NY Macmillan 1912.

   Anti Suffrage, 10 Good reasons NY Duffield 1913, pp. 15–26, 43–50.

   The Eden Sphinx Annie Riley Hale, NY 1916.

22 Lymann Abbott. "Why Women Do Not Wish the Suffrage," September 1903 Issue, *The Atlantic*, Why Women Don't Want to Vote – The Atlantic. Accessed 4/4/2022.

23 Ibid. Abbott

24 Corrine McConnaughy. *The Woman Suffrage Movement in America: A Reassessment*. 2013.

25 Danny Lewis. "These Anti-Suffrage Postcards Warned against Giving Women the Vote," *Smithsonian Magazine*, July 19, 2016. These Anti-Suffrage Postcards Warned against Giving Women the Vote | Smart News | Smithsonian Magazine.

26 Susan Goodier. "Antis Win the New York State Campaign, 1912–1915." In *No Votes for Women: The New York State Anti-Suffrage Movement*, 67–92. University of Illinois Press, 2013. http://www.jstor.org/stable/10.5406/j.ctt2ttdcb.7.

   Karen Pastorello. *New York History* 99, no. 3/4 (2018): 484–87. https://www.jstor.org/stable/26908721.Book. Review of *Gilded Suffragists: The New York Socialites Who Fought for Women's Right to Vote*, by J. Neuman.

Decorative Arts Medals as Artifacts **179**

27 Freeview Newspaper articles. "Josephine Jewell Dodge on Immorality and Suffrage (1913)." Accessed 2/24/2021.

28 Rossiter Jounson. *Helen Kendrick Johnson (Mrs. Rossiter Johnson), The Story of Her Varied Activities*, NY, Publishers Printing, Co, 1917. Helen Kendrick Johnson (Mrs. Rossiter Johnson); the story of her varied activities – Women Working, 1800–1930 – CURIOSity Digital Collections (harvard.edu).

29 Mrs. Jameson (Anna Brownell Jameson). *Characteristics of Women: Moral, Poetical and Historical*. Boston: Houghton and Mifflin, 1887.

30 The Online Books Page Online Books by A. C. Kendrick (Kendrick, A. C. (Asahel Clark), 1809–1895) A. C. Kendrick (Kendrick, A. C. (Asahel Clark), 1809–1895) | The Online Books Page (upenn.edu).

31 Project Gutenberg's Woman and the Republic, by Helen Kendrick Johnson, January 1, 2005 [eBook #7300] produced by Olaf Voss, Tiffany Vergon, Charles Aldarondo, Charles Franks, and the Online Distributed Proofreading Team. The Project Gutenberg eBook of Woman and the Republic A Survey of the Woman-Suffrage Movement in the United States and a Discussion of the Claims and Arguments of Its Foremost Advocates, by Helen Kendrick Johnson.

32 Will Lead Pageant: Miss Inez Milholland to Be Dressed As Herald. Most Beautiful Suffragist New York Society Favorite Will Be Followed by Woman's Band and Petticoat Cavalry – Parade Will Consist of Forty Subdivisions and Thirty Floats – Many Professions in Line (1913, Jan 20). *The Washington Post (1877–1922)*. Retrieved from https://login.usnwc.idm.oclc.org/login?qurl=https%3A%2F%2Fwww.proquest.com%2Fhistorical-newspapers%2Fwill-lead-pageant%2Fdocview%2F145222624%2Fse-2%3Faccountid%3D322.

Woman's Beauty, Grace, and Art Bewilder the Capital: Miles of Fluttering Femininity Present Entrancing Suffrage Appeal. Pageant, Living Pictures, Oratory Richly Decorated Floats Tell The History and Point to the Future of Equal Eights Struggle – Entrancing Spectacle at Times Is Marred by Scenes of Disorder Along the Line of March – Procession, Blocked by Throngs, Moves Only Ten Blocks in an Hour – United States Troops From Fort Myer Come to Rescue. "General" Jones, Leading Her Pilgrims on Foot, Is Popular Heroine. Woman's Beauty, Grace, and Art Bewilder the Capital (1913, Mar 04). *The Washington Post (1877–1922)*. Retrieved from https://login.usnwc.idm.oclc.org/login?qurl=https%3A%2F%2Fwww.proquest.com%2Fhistorical-newspapers%2Fwomans-beauty-grace-art-bewilder-capital%2Fdocview%2F145222197%2Fse-2%3Faccountid%3D322.

Women Parade for Suffrage: Thousands in New York City Appeal for Votes; Fifth Avenue Given over to Largest Demonstration This Country Has Ever Seen – Many Mothers Push Baby Carriages – New Jersey Contingent is Represented (1915, Oct 24). *Los Angeles Times (1886–1922)*. Retrieved from https://login.usnwc.idm.oclc.org/login?qurl=https%3A%2F%2Fwww.proquest.com%2Fhistorical-newspapers%2Fwomen-parade-suffrage%2Fdocview%2F160224442%2Fse-2%3Faccountid%3D322.

New York Sees 33,000 March to Aid Women: Suffrage Parade Takes Four Hours to Pass in Fifth Avenue. Wind Is a Handicap (1915, Oct 24). *Chicago Daily Tribune (1872–1922)*. Retrieved from https://login.usnwc.idm.oclc.org/login?qurl=https%3A%2F%2Fwww.proquest.com%2Fhistorical-newspapers%2Fnew-york-sees-33-000-march-aid-women%2Fdocview%2F2F173955950%2Fse-2%3Faccountid%3D322.

33 Suffrage Appeals to Lawless and Hysterical Women: Mormonism Introduced the Idea into the United States, Says Mrs. Rossiter Johnson, and Since Then, No Large Body of Thinkers Has Adopted the Idea Except the Socialists (1913, Mar 30). *New York Times (1857–1922)*. Retrieved from https://login.usnwc.idm.oclc.org/login?qurl=https%3A%2F%2Fwww.

180 Women and War

proquest.com%2Fhistorical-newspapers%2Fsuffrage-appeals-lawless-hysterical-women%2Fdocview%2F97386379%2Fse-2%3Faccountid%3D322.
34 Ibid.
35 Ibid.
36 Op. cit. Rossiter Johnson. *Helen Kendrick Johnson (Mrs. Rossiter Johnson)*, p. 10.
37 Op. cit. Kendrick Project Gutenberg Chapter I, "Is Woman Suffrage Democratic?"
38 Ibid.
39 Ibid.
40 Ibid. p. 354.
41 Ibid. p. 356.
42 Ibid. p. 356. `
43 Ibid. p. 357.
44 Colette Hemmingway. "Women in Classical Greece." In *Heilbrunn Timeline of Art History*. New York: The Metropolitan Museum of Art, 2000. http://www.metmuseum.org/toah/hd/wmna/hd_wmna.htm (October 2004).
45 Op. cit. Suffrage appeals
46 Ibid.
47 Ibid.
48 Ibid.
49 Elizabeth Gillespie McRae. "Caretakers of Southern Civilization: Georgia Women and the Anti-Suffrage Campaign, 1914–1920." *The Georgia Historical Quarterly* 82, no. 4 (1998): 801–28. http://www.jstor.org/stable/40583906.
50 Vote Against Woman Suffrage – Georgia Association Opposed to Woman Suffrage, c. 1915 – National Association Opposed to Woman Suffrage – Wikipedia. Accessed 2/24/2021.
51 Carrie Williams Clifford, and Cathleen D. Cahill. "The Problem of the Color Line." In *Recasting the Vote: How Women of Color Transformed the Suffrage Movement*, 121–30. University of North Carolina Press, 2020.
Cathleen D. Cahill. "Epilogue: Remembering and Forgetting." In *Recasting the Vote: How Women of Color Transformed the Suffrage Movement*, 262–78. University of North Carolina Press, 2020. http://www.jstor.org/stable/10.5149/9781469659343_cahill.24.
http://www.jstor.org/stable/10.5149/9781469659343_cahill.11.
52 Ruby M. Kendrick. "They Also Serve: The National Association of Colored Women, Inc." *Negro History Bulletin* 17, no. 8 (1954): 171–75. http://www.jstor.org/stable/44214997.
53 Ann Gordon. *The Selected Papers of Elizabeth Cady Stanton, and Susan B. Anthony. An Awful Hush*, 1895–1906. Rutgers University Press, p. 204.
54 Stacy M. Brown. "Suffragist Helen Appo Cook: Wealthy Champion of the Poor," *The Washington Informer*, Jan 29, 2020.
55 Sydney Trent, "Battle for the Ballot, the Black Sorority that Faced Racism in the Suffrage Movement but Refused to Walk Away," *The Washington Post*, August 8, 2020. Deltas: Black sorority faced racism at suffrage parade in Washington in 1913 – Washington Post.
56 Belinda A. Stillion Southard. "Militancy, Power, and Identity: The Silent Sentinels as Women Fighting for Political Voice." *Rhetoric and Public Affairs* 10, no. 3 (2007): 399–417. http://www.jstor.org/stable/41940153.
57 Jihang Park. "The British Suffrage Activists of 1913: An Analysis." *Past & Present*, no. 120 (1988): 147–62. http://www.jstor.org/stable/650925.
58 Ida Husted Harper (Ed.). "*The History of Woman Suffrage*, illustrated with copperplate and photogravure engravings *in six volumes* volume vi 1900–1920," National American Woman Suffrage Association: 1922, pp. 729–38. http://www.gutenberg.org/files/30051/30051-h/30051-h.htm.

Jane Robinson. "Pilgrimage of Greats: Why the March of the Suffragists Should Be Commemorated." *TLS. Times Literary Supplement* no. 5993 (9 Feb. 2018): 16. *Gale Academic OneFile*, link.gale.com/apps/doc/A634971445/AONE?u=anon ~a4499de6&sid=googleScholar&xid=c0345b7d. Accessed 12/28/2023.

59 Holly J. McCammon. "Stirring up Suffrage Sentiment: The Formation of the State Woman Suffrage Organizations, 1866–1914." *Social Forces* 80, no. 2 (2001): 449–80. http://www.jstor.org/stable/2675586.

60 Kathi Kern. "Introduction." In *Mrs. Stanton's Bible*, 1–13. Cornell University Press, 2001. http://www.jstor.org/stable/10.7591/j.ctv5qdj6z.5.

Kathi Kern. "'A Great Feature of the General Uprising': The Revising Committee and the Woman's Bible." In *Mrs. Stanton's Bible*, 135–71. Cornell University Press, 2001. http://www.jstor.org/stable/10.7591/j.ctv5qdj6z.9.

Kathi Kern. "'The Bigots Promote the Sale': Responses to the Woman's Bible." In *Mrs. Stanton's Bible*, 172–222. Cornell University Press, 2001. http://www.jstor.org/stable/10.7591/j.ctv5qdj6z.10.

61 Ida Husted Harper. "Woman Suffrage throughout the World." *The North American Review* 186, no. 622 (1907): 55–71. http://www.jstor.org/stable/25105981.

62 Lauren Twomey. "The Story of Lucy Burns," Independent Research Study, Shippensburg University, Microsoft Word – LB Research Draft 12:15 Post Edit.docx (ship.edu).

Elizabeth Williamson. "Living Legacy of Suffrage," *NYT* 11 Aug 2020, p. A 19. ProQuest Historical Newspapers, Living Legacy of Suffrage – Historical Newspapers – ProQuest.

63 Carl Rollyson. "A Conservative Revolutionary: Emmeline Pankhurst (1857–1928)." *The Virginia Quarterly Review* 79, no. 2 (2003): 325–34. http://www.jstor.org/stable/26440996.

64 Laura E. Nym Mayhall. "Domesticating Emmeline: Representing the Suffragette, 1930–1993." *NWSA Journal* 11, no. 2 (1999): 1–24. http://www.jstor.org/stable/4316653.

65 The NUWSS eventually grew to 500 offices and 100,000 members.

66 Emmeline Pankhurst, *My Own Story*, Praeger, June 4, 1985, Reprint.

67 "History as a Weapon," I Incite This Meeting to Rebellion | Emmeline Pankhurst (October 17, 1912) (historyisaweapon.org). Accessed 2/22/2021.

68 "History Is a Weapon," I Incite this Meeting to Rebellion, Emmeline Pankhurst October 12, 2012. I Incite This Meeting to Rebellion | Emmeline Pankhurst (October 17, 1912) (historyisaweapon.com). Accessed 4/18/2022.

69 Fern Riddell. "Votes for Women, Suffragettes, Violence and Militancy." British Library, 6 Feb 2018 Suffragettes, violence and militancy – The British Library (bl.uk).

70 Timothy Larsen. "Epilogue: Forgetting and Remembering." In *Christabel Pankhurst: Fundamentalism and Feminism in Coalition*, NED-New edition, 139–42. Boydell & Brewer, 2002. http://www.jstor.org/stable/10.7722/j.ctt14brvj4.11.

71 Keith Curry Lance. "Strategy Choices of the British Women's Social and Political Union, 1903–18." *Social Science Quarterly* 60, no. 1 (1979): 51–61. http://www.jstor.org/stable/42860512.

72 Roland Quinault. "Asquith's Liberalism." *History* 77, no. 249 (1992): 33–49. http://www.jstor.org/stable/24420531.

73 Cameron Hazlehurst. "Asquith as Prime Minister, 1908–1916." *The English Historical Review* 85, no. 336 (1970): 502–31. http://www.jstor.org/stable/563193.

74 "Government Feared Suffragette Plot to Kill Asquith, *The Guardian*, Government feared suffragette plot to kill Asquith | UK news | The Guardian. Accessed 3/1/2021.

182 Women and War

75 Evans Clark. "Woman Suffrage in Parliament. A Test for Cabinet Autocracy." *The American Political Science Review* 11, no. 2 (1917): 284–309. https://doi.org/10.2307/1943988.

76 Mary Winsor. "The Militant Suffrage Movement." *The Annals of the American Academy of Political and Social Science* 56 (1914): 134–42. http://www.jstor.org/stable/1011988.

77 *Hartford Courant*, 14 Nov 1913, p. 12.

78 Emmeline Pankhurst. Freedom, or Death, reproduced, "Great Speeches of the 21st Century, Emmeline Pankhurst's Freedom, or Death," The Guardian 27 April 2007.
   https://www.theguardian.com/theguardian/2007/apr/27/greatspeeches. Accessed 12/2018.

79 Jenny Gesley. "The Lieber Code the First Modern Codification of the Laws of War," Library of Congress Blogs, April 24, 2018. The "Lieber Code" – the First Modern Codification of the Laws of War | In Custodia Legis (loc.gov).

80 Pacific Settlement of International Disputes, Limitation of the Employment of Force for Recovery of Contract Debts, Opening of Hostilities respecting the Laws and Customs of War on Land, Rights, and Duties of Neutral Powers and Persons in case of War on Land Legal Position of Enemy Merchant Ships at the Start of Hostilities, Conversion of Merchant Ships into War-ships, Laying of Automatic Submarine Contact Mines, Bombardment by Naval Forces in Time of War, Adaptation to Maritime Warfare of the Principles of the Geneva Convention (of 6 July 1906), Certain Restrictions about the Exercise of the Right of Capture in Naval War, Establishment of an International Prize Court, Rights and Duties of Neutral Powers in Naval War, and Prohibiting the Discharge of Projectiles and Explosives from Balloons.

81 "International Women's Day 8 March," United Nations, Background | International Women's Day | United Nations.

82 Ibid., p. 174.

83 Ibid., the number fifty comes from Lochner's conference review.

84 Ibid., p. 173.

85 Ibid., p. 173.

86 Ibid., p. 175.

87 For specifics on the 20 resolutions passed and the number of nations and groups in attendance, see John Paull (2018). The Women Who Tried to Stop the Great War: The International Congress of Women at The Hague 1915. 10.4018/978-1-5225-4993-2.ch012.

88 Ibid., Paull

89 Op. cit. Vellacott

90 Ibid., p. 382.

91 Melissa Terras and Elizabeth Crawford, Millicent Garrett Fawcett Selected Writings," UCL Press, 2022, London, UK.

92 Op. cit. Byles

93 Ibid.

94 Ibid.

95 Harriet Hyman Alonso. "Peace and Women's Issues in U.S. History." *OAH Magazine of History* 8, no. 3 (1994): 20–25. http://www.jstor.org/stable/25162961.

96 "Peace Parade Indorsed: New York Women's Idea May Be Adopted Elsewhere," *New York Times* 1857–1922: New York, NY 24 Aug 1914:14.

97 The women's peace parade (1914, Aug 20). *New York Times (1857–1922)*. Retrieved from https://login.usnwc.idm.oclc.org/login?qurl=https%3A%2F%2Fwww.proquest.com%2Fhistorical-newspapers%2Fwomens-peace-parade%2Fdocview%2F97642807%2Fse-2%3Faccountid%3D322.

Decorative Arts Medals as Artifacts **183**

98 Ibid.
99 Ibid. President Favors Peace Parade Plan: No National Flags Will Be Carried by Women. Speaking Also Barred in Order to Preserve Strict Neutrality. (1914, Aug 21). *Boston Daily Globe (1872–1922)*. Retrieved from https://login.usnwc.idm.oclc.org/login?qurl=https%3A%2F%2Fwww.proquest.com%2Fhistorical-newspapers%2Fpresident-favors-peace-parade-plan%2Fdocview%2F502635129%2Fse-2%3Faccountid%3D322.
100 Op. cit. The Women's Peace Parade.
101 Quoted from Wikipedia. "A Woman's Peace Party Full Fledged for Action." *The Survey* 33, no. 17 (Jan 23, 1915): 433–34. Discussion available in Doris Groshen Daniels. "Theodore Roosevelt and Gender Roles." *Presidential Studies Quarterly* 26, no. 3 (1996): 648–65. http://www.jstor.org/stable/27551623.
102 Edward Marshall (E. M.) (1915, May 02). War's Debasement of Women: Jane Addams Calls It the Greatest Threat against Family, Reducing Woman to Tribal Stage of Childbearing to Fill Ranks. *New York Times (1857–1922)*. Retrieved from https://login.usnwc.idm.oclc.org/login?qurl=https%3A%2F%2Fwww.proquest.com%2Fhistorical-newspapers%2Fwars-debasement-women%2Fdocview%2F97726028%2Fse-2%3Faccountid%3D322.
103 End This war, Addams Party Plea to Women: Brand Draft Slavery and Condemn American Resort to Arms, *Chicago Daily Tribune (1872–1922)*, Chicago, IL, 13 Aug 1917:2.
104 Ibid., E.M.
105 Claire Marsden. "The Woman's Huor Has Struck: How the National American Woman Suffrage Association Secured the Nineteenth Amendment through War Activism in World War I," Historical Perspectives: Santa Clara University Undergraduate *Journal of History, Series II*, Vol. 26, Article 8 2021. https://scholarcommons.scu.edu/cgi/viewcontent.cgi?article=1267&context=historical-perspectives.
106 "Carrie Chapman Catt to Woodrow Wilson, September 29, 1918." Woodrow Wilson Papers, Manuscript Division, A Position Changed, A Changing America Echoes of the Great War, Library of Congress. A Position Changed | A Changing America | Over Here | Explore | Echoes of the Great War: American Experiences of World War I | Exhibitions at the Library of Congress | Library of Congress (loc.gov).
107 "National Woman's Party Protests during World War I." National Park Service, National Woman's Party Protests during World War I (U.S. National Park Service) (nps.gov).
108 George MacAdam Underwood and Underwood, *New York Times (1857–1922)*, New York, NY, 23 Dec 1917: 56.
109 Ibid., MacAdam
110 Doves of Peace Flutter Here: Parade and Mass Meeting Mark Celebration; President Sends Greetings to Women's Million Club – Homing Pigeon Brings Message from San Francisco Mayor – Speakers Pray for Tranquility in Europe (1914, Sep 25). *Los Angeles Times (1886–1922)*. Retrieved from https://login.usnwc.idm.oclc.org/login?qurl=https%3A%2F%2Fwww.proquest.com%2Fhistorical-newspapers%2Fdoves-peace-flutter-here%2Fdocview%2F160002993%2Fse-2%3Faccountid%3D322.
111 Roosevelt Demands Speed-Up of War: Would Send 4,000,000 Fighters, Thousands of Guns, and a Vast Air Fleet by April. Excoriates All Pacifists Says We Must Make Ready to Solve Industrial Problems that Will Come with Peace. American Pacifism Disloyal. An Army of the People (1918, Aug 27). *New York Times (1857–1922)*. Retrieved from https://login.usnwc.idm.oclc.org/login?qurl=https%3A%2F%2Fwww.proquest.com%2Fhistorical-

184 Women and War

newspapers%2Froosevelt-demands-speed-up-war%2Fdocview%2F100205971%2Fse-2%3Faccountid%3D322.

112 A Staff Correspondent. "Dr Shaw Shows Solons Women are Patriotic Stamps an Untrue Claim That Pacifists Back Suffrage Law," *Chicago Daily Tribune* (1872–1922), ProQuest Historical Newspapers, *Chicago Tribune* p. 4.

113 "Roosevelt Urges Suffrage, Oyster Bay, NY. Jan 3, [Special] *The Chicago Tribune*, Jan 4, 1918.p. 4.

114 Some Pacifists Uphold Colonel on Peace Stand: Margaret Dobyne and Mrs. Severin Call Roosevelt Letter "Wise And Sane." Others see it differently (1915, Apr 17). *Chicago Daily Tribune (1872–1922)*. Retrieved from https://login.usnwc.idm.oclc.org/login?qurl=https%3A%2F%2Fwww.proquest.com%2Fhistorical-newspapers%2Fsome-pacifists-uphold-colonel-on-peace-stand%2Fdocview%2F173891471%2Fse-2%3Faccountid%3D322.

115 Ibid.

116 Menace to the Nation: Pacifism Denounced by Speakers at Navy League Dinner. Breckinridge Praises Army Former Assistant Secretary of War, David Jayne Hill, and Others Make Earnest Appeals for National Pre-Paredness – Henry Ford's Cash to Aid the Cause (1916, Apr 13). *The Washington Post (1877–1922)*. Retrieved from https://login.usnwc.idm.oclc.org/login?qurl=https%3A%2F%2Fwww.proquest.com%2Fhistorical-newspapers%2Fmenace-nation%2Fdocview%2F145455985%2Fse-2%3Faccountid%3D322.

117 William Sheafe Chase, J. C. J. (1917, Jul 08). A Rebuke to Pacifism: Brooklyn Clergymen Speak for Righteous War. *New York Times (1857–1922)*. Retrieved from https://login.usnwc.idm.oclc.org/login?qurl=https%3A%2F%2Fwww.proquest.com%2Fhistorical-newspapers%2Frebuke-pacifism%2Fdocview%2F99905878%2Fse-2%3Faccountid%3D322.

118 Harriet Hyman Alonso. "One Woman's Journey into the World of Women's Peace History." *Women's Studies Quarterly* 23, no. 3/4 (1995): 170–82. http://www.jstor.org/stable/40003514. Harriet Hyman Alonso. "Gender and Peace Politics in the First World War United States: The People's Council of America." *The International History Review* 19, no. 1 (1997): 83–102. http://www.jstor.org/stable/40108085.

119 Home – WILPF.

120 Annette Atkins. "Dressing for Success, Suffrage Style." *Minnesota History* 67, no. 3 (2020): 140–45. https://www.jstor.org/stable/26977819.
Lynn Yaeger. "Inside the Suffragists' Jewelry Box: How Women of the Movement Wore Their Pride on Their Sleeves," *Vogue*, Oct. 26, 2015. Suffrage Jewelry, a Brief History | Vogue.

121 Amy Helene Forss. "Introduction." In *Borrowing from Our Foremothers: Reexamining the Women's Movement through Material Culture, 1848–2017*, 1–12. University of Nebraska Press, 2021. https://doi.org/10.2307/j.ctv21fqjp5.5.
Amy Helene Forss. "Parading Their Colors." In *Borrowing from Our Foremothers: Reexamining the Women's Movement through Material Culture, 1848–2017*, 33–48. University of Nebraska Press, 2021. https://doi.org/10.2307/j.ctv21fqjp5.7.
Amy Helene Forss. "Silently Disobedient." In *Borrowing from Our Foremothers: Reexamining the Women's Movement through Material Culture, 1848–2017*, 49–62. University of Nebraska Press, 2021. https://doi.org/10.2307/j.ctv21fqjp5.8.

122 Becky Stone. "Jewels for Votes for Women: Let's Talk Suffragette Jewelry," Diamonds in the Library, October 24, 2016 Jewels for votes for women: Let's talk suffragette jewelry (diamondsinthelibrary.com).

Decorative Arts Medals as Artifacts **185**

123 Lynn Yaeger. "Inside the Suffragists' Jewelry Box: How Women of the Movement Wore Their Pride on Their Sleeves." Oct. 26, 2015. *Vogue*.
124 Art and Architecture, mainly. "Selfridge's Suffragettes and Fashion," April 22, 2009. Art and Architecture, mainly: Selfridge's Suffragettes and Fashion (melbourneblogger.blogspot.com). Accessed 4/7/2022.
125 Ibid., Art and Architecture.
126 Ibid.
127 Ibid.
128 Ian Miller, "Forcible Feeding and the Cat and Mouse Act: One Hundred Years On, June 19 2013 OUPblog Oxford University Press Forcible feeding and the Cat and Mouse Act: one hundred years on | OUPblog.
   Kevin Grant. "British Suffragettes and the Russian Method of Hunger Strike." *Comparative Studies in Society and History* 53, no. 1 (2011): 113–43. http://www.jstor.org/stable/41241735.
   'A Prostitution of the Profession'?: The Ethical Dilemma of Suffragette Force-Feeding, 1909–14 – A History of Force Feeding – NCBI Bookshelf (nih.gov).
129 For an interesting aside, see "Women Soldiers on Duth with Men: Both Sexes Working on Equal Terms," Cable to the *Chicago Tribune, Chicago Daily Tribune (1872–1922)* Apr. 8, 1912; ProQuest Historical Newspapers: p. 1.
130 Howard Finn. "Modernism and the Suffragette Prison Narratives." *Key Words: A Journal of Cultural Materialism*, no. 3 (2000): 94–108. https://www.jstor.org/stable/26920224.
131 June Purvis. "Cat and Mouse: Force Feeding the Suffragettes," *History Extra*, Cat and Mouse: Suffragette Force Feeding | History Extra. Accessed 4/18/2022.
132 Ibid.
133 Ibid.
134 Roger Swift, Charles Pellham Villiers Aristocratic Victorian Rebel.
135 "1913 Cat and Mouse Act, UK Parliamentary Archives # HL/PO/PU/1/1913/3&4G5c4 Cat and Mouse Act first page – UK Parliament.
136 Op. cit. Miller
137 Ibid. Miller
138 John Simkin. "Men's League for Women's Suffrage, Men's League for Women's Suffrage (spartacus-educational.com) Sept 1997 updated 2020. Accessed 2/23/2021.
139 Diane Atkinson. *Rise up, Women, the Remarkable Lives of the Suffragettes*. London: Bloomsbury, 2018. pp. 289–90 and 293, 294.
140 Museum of London, collections.museumoflondon.org.uk. Retrieved 4/18/2022.
141 Janice Law Trecker. "The Suffrage Prisoners." *The American Scholar* 41, no. 3 (1972): 409–23. http://www.jstor.org/stable/41208790.
142 C. S. Carter Olson (2021). "To Ask Freedom for Women": The Night of Terror and Public Memory. *Journalism & Mass Communication Quarterly* 98, no. 1 (2021): 179–99. https://doi.org/10.1177/1077699020927118.
143 Ibid. Olson
144 Gallery of Suffrage Prisoners, Women of Protest: Photographs from the Records of the National Woman's Party, Library of Congress, Gallery of Suffrage Prisoners | Articles and Essays | Women of Protest: Photographs from the Records of the National Woman's Party | Digital Collections | Library of Congress (loc.gov).
145 "Use Iron Hands on Militants, Smuggled Note Discloses Workhouse Methods, Mrs Lucy Burns Handcuffed for Talking in Jail; Virgina Judge Grants Write of *habeus corpus*," *Los Angeles Times (1886–1922)* Nov 18, 1917; ProQuest Historical Newspapers: *Los Angeles Times*, p. 18.
146 Ibid. Use Iron Hands

186 Women and War

147 David M. Dismore. "Today in Feminist History: A Post-Prison Suffragette Nationwide Tour (March 5, 1919, *Ms.* March 5, 2020). Today in Feminist History: A Post-Prison Suffragette Nationwide Tour (March 5, 1919) – Ms. Magazine (msmagazine.com).

148 "Move Militants from Workhouse: Confinement There Illegal, Judge Waddill Holds Sends 25 Back to Washington Jail," Special to the *New York Times. NYT* (1857–1922; Nov 25, 1917; ProQuest Historical Newspapers: *The New York Times* p. 6. MOVE MILITANTS FROM WORKHOUSE: Confinement There Illegal, Judge Waddill Holds – Sends 25 Back to Washington Jail. THREE RELEASED ON PAROLE So Weak Their Deaths Were Feared – Dr. Brannan's Graphic Account of Workhouse "Brutality." Accuses Whittaker of Brutality. Outrageously Handled. – Historical Newspapers – ProQuest.

Sarah Pruitt. "The Night of Terror: When Suffragists Were Imprisoned and Tortured in 1917," April 17, 2019. 19th Amendment, 1920, History.com. The Night of Terror: When Suffragists Were Imprisoned and Tortured – HISTORY.

149 Brianna Nunez-Franklin. "Democracy Limited: The Prison Special Tour of 1919," National Park Service, Democracy Limited: The Prison Special (U.S. National Park Service) (nps.gov).

150 David M. Dinsmore. "Today in Feminist History: A Post Prison Suffragette Nationwide Tour (March 5, 1919) reprinted March 5, 2020. *Ms.* Today in Feminist History: A Post-Prison Suffragette Nationwide Tour (March 5, 1919) – Ms. Magazine (msmagazine.com). Accessed 4/19/2022.

"For International Women's Day: "Shout, Shout, Up with Your Song," Woman and her Sphere, for International Women's Day: 'Shout, Shout, Up with your Song' | Woman and her Sphere.

151 Quoted from an endnote. Cassondra St. Cyr, Anne Peterson, Taylor Franks, National Woman's Party Project, Chapter 4, (2015) *Mapping American Social Movements Through the 20th century.*

152 "Mrs. Pankhurst, Suffragist, Dead; Famous Leader of Militant Women a Conservative at the End, Aspired to Parliament Death Recalls Her Stormy career – Vote Won When government's Foe Supported War," *The New York Times,* June 15, 1928, MRS. PANKHURST, SUFFRAGIST, DEAD; Famous Leader of Militant Women a Conservative at the End. ASPIRED TO PARLIAMENT Death Recalls Her Stormy Career – Vote Won When Government's Foe Supported War – The New York Times (nytimes.com).

153 Kim Cassidy. "Jewels of Denial: A Look at British Suffrage Jewelry, April 16, 2020, The Frick Museum, Jewels of Denial | The Frick Pittsburgh.

154 Barbara Green. "From Visible Flâneuse to Spectacular Suffragette? The Prison, the Street, and the Sites of Suffrage." *Discourse* 17, no. 2 (1994): 67–97. http:// www.jstor.org/stable/41389369.

155 National Park Service. "Nina Allender Political Cartoons, Belmont-Paul Women's Equality National Monument," Photo Gallery (U.S. National Park Service) (nps.gov). Accessed 4/19/2022.

156 Kim Cady. "Jewels of Denial: A Look at British Suffrage Jewelry," April 16, 2020.

157 Joan Montgomery Byles. "Women's Experience of World War One: Suffragists, Pacifists and Poets." *Women's Studies International Forum* 8, no. 5 (1985): 473–87. https://doi.org/10.1016/0277-5395(85)90078-0.

Harriet Hyman Alonso. "Peace and Women's Issues in U.S. History." *OAH Magazine of History* 8, no. 3 (1994): 20–25. http://www.jstor.org/ stable/25162961. Pp. 20–22.

158 "Turning Point Suffrage Memorial," Turning Point Suffragist Memorial Association, Turning Point Suffragist Memorial 2024.

159 Lynn Dumenil. "Women's Reform Organizations and Wartime Mobilization in World War I-Era Los Angeles." *The Journal of the Gilded Age and Progressive Era* 10, no. 2 (2011): 213–45. http://www.jstor.org/stable/23045158.
160 Elizabeth Boyd. "Woman's Committee of the Council of National Defense," Hankey Center & C. Elizabeth Boyd '33 Archives, Wilson College, n.d. Woman's Committee of the Council of National Defense Hannah J. Patterson: Feminist Trailblazer Hankey Center for the History of Women's Education (wilson. edu).
161 Lindseth Collection of American Woman Suffrage, (ca. 1820). http://rmc.library. corenell.edu. Accessed 9/2/2019.
162 "Shelve Suffrage in Britain: Militants Have Turned to War Relief Work, Says Mrs. Pankhurst," *The Washington Post (1877–1922)* Feb 20, 1916; ProQuest Historical Newspapers: *The Washington Post*, p. 13. SHELVE SUFFRAGE IN BRITAIN: Militants Have Turned to War Relief Work, Says Mrs. Pankhurst. – Historical Newspapers – ProQuest "War Supplants Suffrage with Mrs. Pankhurst: English Leader No Longer on the Stump for Women's rights," *Chicago Daily Tribune (1872–1922)*; Mar 22, 1916; ProQuest Historical Newspapers: *Chicago Tribune*, p. 7. WAR SUPPLANTS SUFFRAGE WITH MRS. PANKHURST: English Leader No Longer on the Stump for Women's Rights. – Historical Newspapers – ProQuest.
163 Christabel Pankhurst. *Unshackled the Story of How We Won the Vote*, Hutchinson (1959).
164 Sharon Hartman Strom. "Leadership and Tactics in the American Woman Suffrage Movement: A New Perspective from Massachusetts." *The Journal of American History* 62, no. 2 (1975): 296–315. https://doi.org/10.2307/1903256.

Additional Resources

Christabel Pankhurst. *Unshackled: The Story of How We Won the Vote*. Century London: Hutchinson, 1987.
Emmeline Pankhurst. *Freedom or Death*. Glasgow: Good Press, 2020.
J. D. Zahniser, and Amelia R. Fry. *Alice Paul: Claiming Power*. Oxford: Oxford University Press, 2014.
Jason Nord. *The Silent Sentinels*. Lincoln: Equality Press, 2015.
Jo Vellacott. *Pacifists, Patriots and the Vote: The Erosion of Democratic Suffragism in Britain during the First World War*. London, UK: Palgrave, 2007.
Miranda Garrett, and Zoe Thomas. *Suffrage, and the Arts: Visual Culture, Politics and Enterprise*. Camden: Bloomsbury Visual Arts, 2020.
Paulette Beete. *Creativity and Persistence the Art that Fueled the Fight for Women's Suffrage*. Washington, D.C.: National Endowment for the Arts, 2020
Rosalyn Terborg-Penn. *African American Women in the Struggle for the Vote, 1850– 1920*. Bloomington: Indiana University Press, 1998.

Questions

How does fighting for a women's civil cause differ from fighting for one's country in the military?

Why was the suffragist movement important to the future of women being able to serve in the military?

188 Women and War

Why were art and jewelry important to the suffragist movement?

Did the suffragette idea of militancy help or hinder the women's rights movement?

How did the pacifists help or hinder the voting rights movement?

Nursing was considered an arena where women were "allowed" to participate during the war. What were the reasons for this acceptance?

Consider whether you would have been a suffragist, remonstrant, or militant. What might have led you to support your chosen group? Would you have been able to keep the militant cause by going to jail, going on hunger strike, and being force-fed?

Modern take

How has the idea of feminism changed since voting rights legislation was passed?

What are some differences between the 20th-century Women's International Committee for Permanent Peace and the 21st-century United Nations Women Peace and Security Initiative?

Who is Gloria Steinem, Malala Yousafzai, Chimamanda Ngozi Adichie, and Angela Davis? What are some of the feminist platforms they have built?

Feminist theory extends feminism into theoretical, fictional, or philosophical discourse. What is the difference between theory and the "Deeds not Words" approach to suffragism?

Did you or anyone you know join the 21st-century Women's March in Washington, D.C.? Why was this worldwide protest started? What was the meaning of the pussy-hat?

Materials highlighting the role of minorities in the suffragist movement are now available. Examples are the Jewish League for Woman Suffrage, Asians, Pacific Islanders, and the Native women of the Six Nations Haudenosaunee

Confederacy. Who were some of these women? What were their primary thoughts and feelings about equality under the law? How were their experiences the same or different than those of their fellow suffragists? What rights do these women continue to address in the 21st century?

What are some challenges of pacifism and nonviolence in the 21st century? What women's groups exist today that propose peace through pacifism?

Activities and discovery

There are numerous banks of materials about the women's suffrage movement in museums. Visit websites and discover artifacts and artwork from the first feminist period. What positive and negative stories do the artifacts and art tell?

Search your family history. Were there any suffragists in your family? What was their story?

Watch a film related to suffragism. Are the film's portrayal of events and people representative of the first wave of feminism, or have they been modernized? Iron Jawed Angels (2004) Suffragette Mothers. Daughters Rebels (2015) PBS American Experience: The Vote (2020) Black Sorority Project You Tube (2013).

There is a category of art known as "Pacifist War Art." Discover some artists who worked in this genre and become acquainted with their narratives in posters, photographs, pamphlets, and art installations.

7
PORTRAITURE AS A HISTORICAL RECORD

Mable Annie St. Clair Stobart and the Serbian Women's Sick and Wounded Convoy Corps

FIGURE 7.1 George James Rankin's painting, Lady of the Black Horse, showing Mable Stobart Leading Serbian Troops through the Montenegrin Mountains during The Great Retreat.

© Public domain. Evidence reported by judyjordan for item flamingswordinse00stobrich on November 6, 2007.

DOI: 10.4324/9781003406372-8

A short art history lesson 1870s–1920s

The Gilded Age of rapid economic growth and the Progressive Era, a period of political reform and social activism, overlapped but generally can be placed historically between 1879 and 1929.[1] In Europe, Austria-Hungary had undergone a political realignment, and from 1890 through the 1920s, three movements of Pan-Germanism, Christian Socialism, and Democratic Socialism buffeted the region.[2] Antagonistic monarchist and liberal French journalist, historian, and Left Center leader Adolphe Thiers became the first elected president of the French Third Republic, dying in 1877. His replacement was the French General Marshal of France, Patrice de MacMahon, who served for six years. MacMahon was replaced by moderate Republican Jules Grevy, who remained president until 1887. In the next two decades, the Boulanger crisis rocked France, the Panama scandal broke out in the French Third Republic, and the Dreyfus affair ended in the sentencing to life imprisonment for Captain Alred Dreyfus for communicating French military secrets to the German Embassy.[3] The nation would be racked by collapsing governing coalitions that rarely lasted more than a few months, swinging between radicalism, socialism, liberalism, conservativism, republicanism, and monarchism.

Smaller nations like Serbia were in tumult as well. In the timeframe of the late 19th century into the 1920s, the country experienced the Ottoman uprising, war with Bulgaria, a coup d'état, a battle between themselves and Austria-Hungary, the annexation of Bosnia and Herzegovina, the Balkan Wars, and the declaration of war by the German Empire on their homeland.[4] The more extensive German Empire had been forged in 1871. It was governed under a constitution created by upperclassman Otto von Bismarck, a highly adept balance-of-power diplomat who provoked three wars against the nations of Denmark, Austria, and France. Later, he warned against any military involvement in the Balkan disputes.[5] He had risen to power on his blood and iron ideology, which proposed power and strength as critical determinants of unification over sociological and political means.[6] His efforts were placed on offsetting Catholic political power by imposing exile on many clerics, abandoning free trade, and implementing protectionist tariffs during the Long Depression. Bismarck also attempted to nationalize minorities along the borders of Germany and forbade socialist organizations and meetings yet promoted socialism through his working-class policies in a Sickness Insurance Law, benefits for accidents under the Accident Insurance Law, and old age insurance under the Old Age and Disability Insurance Law. Bismarck's predecessors quickly abandoned his treaties and ideals.[7] In 1895, there was a surge in interest in Max Weber's claims of German global dominance, eventually turning the country toward the ideology of a conservative plutocracy and declaring war on Russia in 1914, tromping through Belgium to capture Paris, France.

192 Women and War

The art world was buffeted by these cataclysmic events, resulting in the emergence of just as many protracted schools of thought as emerging political upheavals.[8] Art ideologies arose dizzily, careening from one style to the next alongside the emerging philosophical and newly formed geographic boundaries rising and falling on the Continent.[9] Two primary sectors of artists appeared in France: the Impressionists and Postimpressionists.[10] The Impressionist gathering lasted from about 1867 through 1886 and included renowned artists Claude Monet, Edouard Manet, Camille Pissarro, Edgar Degas, and Mary Cassatt.[11] Common within their painting technique was the conspicuous use of small brush strokes and unblended colors. New thinking about how and what to paint meant a complete ditching of romanticized mannerisms employed by their academically trained predecessors. Turning away from Greco-Roman, religious, and mythological subjects, their depictions were of middle and lower-class men, women, and children found in the trades, bars, brothels, on city and country streets, or at leisure. The concentrated practice of presenting outdoor lighting was found in their paintings of parks, fields, and gardens. Called out by art critics as being too realistic and degenerative to be shown at prestigious art academies, the group rebelled against academic polling bodies that determined whether their compositions could be exhibited in the highly regarded salons.[12] Walking away from the formalized equations shown in what was fast appearing to be outdated thinking, the artists began to organize their displays and fill their soirees with increasingly more abstract artwork.

Fauvism, an avant-garde, experimental art style, also arose in the early 1900s, lasting five years from 1905 through 1910.[13] Art critic Louis Vauxcelles, upon viewing their unique paintings at a salon in Paris, attached the moniker "les fauves" to their collective of pieces. The term was a mocking criticism of "the small clan of youngsters," which translated from the French as "the wild beasts."[14] Fauvists developed interesting, experimental, and unorthodox ways to use colors. All of them were blatant and unrelenting in their fierce brushwork and application of pure oranges, reds, turquoises, mauves, and heavy blues. Compositions were made by squirting paint directly from tubes onto a canvas.

Exaggerated use of color and line and mentally subjective dissonant distortions of people and scenes continued to expand. Cubism, the name coming from artists attempting to geometrically show all possible viewpoints of a person or object at once, appeared around 1907.[15] Importance was placed on monochromatic and neutral color palettes and the volume of a line's, mass, and weight.[16] During World War I and afterward, German artists had so many protest movements aligned with war and technological and cultural change that it was difficult to sort through them all. A group of artists in Munich joined under the banner of The Blue Rider Movement in 1911, formed after young artists became incensed by an art academy's rejection of

Wassily Kandinsky's 1912 painting, *The Last Judgment*.[17] With its emotion and force using primary colors, red, blue, and yellow, free-flowing black shapes, and lines, the piece was non-representational and abstract. A notable feature is a non-concrete angel on the upper right side, representing the Last Judgment, the Second Coming of Christ, and the resurrection of souls. Kandinsky, a synesthete who saw colors on hearing music, believed color to be the keyboard; the artist's eyes were the harmonies, and the artist's soul was the piano with many strings.[18]

Two vital influencers in the evolution of cubist art were the Spaniard Pablo Picasso, who spent most of his career on French soil, and Frenchman Georges Braque. The men became inseparable, constantly entering each other's studios, sharing techniques, and critiquing each other's skills.[19] The concept of collage art arose from Picasso's and Braque's experimental applications in this period. After Braque's conscription in 1914 into the French Army and his subsequent head wound from fighting in the trenches, which caused temporary blindness, he and Picasso, whose home country had remained neutral and did not serve in any military role, moved onward into separate creative directions.[20] In 1917, now having recuperated from war wounds, Braque began a collegial relationship with Spanish cubist painter Juan Gris, who had moved to France during World War I and was spending time in the company of Picasso and Henri Matisse. Gris relied on precise measurements in his distinctive cubist portraits and still lifes and incorporated the golden mean as a guidepost.[21] Braque's style shifted to become less constrained and less diagrammatic.[22] Picasso continued his trajectory upward, achieving stratospheric fame.

Wartime Art: A review of the Serbian Art Scene and the Balkan Wars

During wartime, many artists, no matter how they employ color and composition, produce images guided by their observations of political, military, and social events unfolding around them.[23] Such art might express disagreement or support for a government's policies and decision-making. Scenes might concentrate on the lines behind the battle, after the battle, or on the Homefront. Common subject matter was portraying the horrors of war from the viewpoint of the trenches. Terror, pain, grief, desolation, exhilaration, and a sense of purpose were all emotions elicited by war art created near or on the front lines of battle. Trench and battle art did two things.[24] It inflamed public sentiments to support the military and seek peace and created a record for future generations as reminders of the miseries and pathos of war. Art could also serve as an accurate record of military technology, uniforms, and fighting units. Homefront scenes took the viewer into the perspective of those waiting for the return of family members and logged damage to cities, towns, and land.[25]

194 Women and War

The first and second Balkan Wars occurred between 1912 and 1913, telegraphing the continental uprisings that would explode into World War I in 1914.[26] Balkan League members Serbia, Bulgaria, and Montenegro joined a loosely organized alliance to eliminate the Ottoman Empire from Europe. Serbian troops broke the western Ottoman army and successfully stifled resistance in Macedonia, Kosovo, and Albania, ending their onslaught at the Adriatic Sea.[27] A quarter of a million people from the Serbian population fought in the First Balkan War, comprised of the First, Second, and Third Armies with ten infantry divisions, two brigades, and a cavalry division.

Fighting frequently occurred in the region's rugged, low, and medium-high mountain terrain, with the highest altitude at Velika Rudoka, soaring to 8730 feet. The Serbs and Greeks gained substantial geographic territory, provoking their former ally Bulgaria, who had sided with them during the extrication of the Ottoman Empire. Bulgaria counter attacked. The continuation of hostilities among the nations led to the Second Balkan or Interallied War. Romania reentered the fight by intervening against Bulgaria, gaining ground to the south, easily overtaking the territory, and moving quickly toward the capital of Sofia. The Bulgarians sought an armistice, not wanting to engage in more bloodshed. Hostilities abated with the signing of the Treaty of Bucharest, which required the release of territory gained from the First Balkan War back to their enemies. At the end of the Second Balkan War, Serbia had become the most militarily powerful government south of the Danube River.[28]

The beginnings of Serbian art are traced to the ancient Lepinski Vir located on the right bank of the Danube River, where whirlpools and abundant fish attracted settlement and satellite villages.[29] From 7000 BC, several geometric and humanoid sculptures of the region played a role in the stylizations found in expressionist art. Mid-19th-century British sculptor Henry Spencer Moore's semi-abstract public bronzes and carvings borrowed from the characteristics of the ancient Danube designs. During the 1800s, the Serbs popularized nationalist art using the newly created graphic design of lithography. The medium helped speed the production of political messages and popular folklife motifs. Much effort was put into producing historicist art, the regeneration of subject matter, and artistic techniques from past ages. The result was a nationalist treatment which incorporated civil, social, and cultural philosophies supporting the nation's newly emerging identity.[30]

In the last decade of the 19th century, painter and illustrator Cyril Kutlik fostered the national Serbian Drawing and Painting School as impressionism gave way to fauvism in the West.[31] The institutional hierarchy encouraged students to travel to other European art centers, and many students went on personal pilgrimages to the avant-garde German Academy of Fine Art. Another fashionable destination for students was to attend classes at the Vienna Academy. Here, they could practice and learn their craft among the many talented historical painters and orientalists on the teaching faculty.

Symbolist styles, which reflected emotions and ideas over more objective features, were brought back to Serbia from Germany and Austria.[32] This new generation of Serbian artists began using indirect and suggestive compositional painterly techniques borrowed from their fauvist, cubist, and avant-garde teachers. They replaced the nationally acceptable genres of church and religious themes with sociological art cants.[33]

Serbian War Artists Natalija, Babette, and Nadezda

Natalija Cvetkovic was one of the art students who stopped her career and training in Kutlik's school to volunteer as a nurse during the Balkan Wars.[34] Before entering the conflict, she composed numerous *plenaries*, which were outdoor compositions of landscapes, and switched her style toward Munich impressionism. Her artistic tone became an apex of Serbian modernism.[35] Natalija studied theory and technique under wealthy Austrian-born Serbian transplant Babette Bachmayer (Beta Vukanovic), an originator of Serbian caricature art.[36] Learning under the Slovene realist painter Anton Azbe in Belgrade and learning design and painting techniques at the School of Arts and Crafts in Munich, Germany, she eventually settled upon realism as her most prolific methodology.[37] A lifetime collection contains 500 images of commonplace social and cultural scenes she compiled, tramping among the eclectic population of Belgrade.[38] Bachmayer survived four wars and spent the Balkan campaigns as a volunteer nurse in field operating rooms. She was awarded the Order and Medal for Services of the Red Cross of Serbia.

During World War I, stationed at a military hospital at Nis, she cared for typhus patients, including her husband, Rista Vukanovic, also a painter.[39] The couple received legal permission from the Ministry of Education in 1899 to inherit folklife artist Kiril Kutlik's Serbian painting and drawing school from the family of its deceased founder.[40] Later, she traveled with an army medical unit to Thessaloniki and Marseilles, France. Two of her pictures from this period include a caricature of French soldiers in a canteen and a watercolor of a tent camp at Marseilles. Both are now housed in the Military Museum in Belgrade. She stayed near the frontlines for the duration of the war, refusing to return to native soil until the final transport of refugees was sent home, even though she had been granted an early exit. She died in Belgrade in 1972 at the age of 100.[41]

Nadezda Petrovic not only painted war scenes but was a leading proponent of the growing field of war photography.[42] Studying art in Munich during the fauvist onslaught resulted in her taking on a continuum of styles using a mix of symbolism, impressionism, and secessionist decorative floral ornamentation and repetition of shapes.[43] While at the Academy of Fine Arts in Munich for over four years, she came into contact with and was heavily influenced by Wassily Kandinsky. Moving on to Paris, she crossed paths

196 Women and War

with Picasso and Rodin, the sculptor who composed the widely recognized *The Thinker.* As an organizer of numerous art exhibitions, Petrovic brought creators together under the frameworks of several art societies and pioneered art criticism. Her nationalist volunteerism spanned three conflicts, and she was politically aligned in support of the unification of the Yugoslav nations and protested the Austro-Hungarian annexation of Bosnia and Herzegovina. Even when entrenched in nursing field activities, she continued to paint.

A devoted patriot and volunteer nurse, Nadezda was one of three noteworthy cofounders of the humanitarian aid organization Circle of Serbian Sisters, or *Kolo Srpskih Sestara,* which was organized to assist Serbs trapped in Kosovo and Macedonia when the region was under the control of the Turkish Empire.[44] Circle members were known for their ability to provide material, financial, and moral support in all areas of occupied Serbian lands. Petrovic and others of the 3000-strong organization visited monasteries, trained medical staff, recruited women volunteer nurses, and provided shelter and hiding places in the mountains for soldiers and civilians. They organized and ran the IV Reserve Hospital and developed 42 aid stations and field hospitals along rail lines.[45] Many nurses were part of the Great Retreat of 1915, when Albania's civilian populations and the Serbian Army escaped the synchronized offensive planned by Germany, Austria-Hungary, and Bulgaria. Their columns became part of the intense skirmishes that occurred between enemy forces.

When the Austria-Hungary war was declared in 1914, the Supreme Command offered her the role of a representative to the Rome Conference or to serve in hospitals to the rear in Belgrade and Nis.[46] Petrovic flatly declined the safer pacifist course and returned to the frontline hospital units. The following year, she died during an outbreak of typhoid fever in a 2210-bed naval hospital serving wounded military, refugees, prisoners, and civilians in Vallejo.[47] She was awarded the Medal of Bravery Order of Sat Sava and an Order of the Red Cross. A bronze monument of the artistic missionary, nurse, and patriot resides in Novi Sad, and a white stone monument memorializing her stands under the trees in Belgrade's Pioneers Park. Another bronze bust of her rests atop a red marble podium alongside an artist pallet in a garden of monuments in Chisinau, Moldova, and a bronze bust is dedicated to her in the Serbian Cultural Garden in Cleveland, Ohio.

The Women's Sick and Wounded Convoy Corps, FANY, and the Red Cross

The Boer War found the British courtier, diplomat, and liberal MP Reginald Brett, 2nd Viscount Escher, acting as a private fixer, preferring the latitude of working in de facto roles between His Royal Highness King George V and Parliament. Escher was a consummate insider in politics and war, holding

many formal and informal seats in the government from the time of the Somaliland Campaign on the Horn of Africa through the armed Kurdish uprisings of the Second Barzanji Revolt.[48] In 1904, he set up a subcommittee
for the Committee of Imperial Defense to assist the King in redesigning the
Royal Army.[49] The Viscount was integral to all behind-the-scenes and secre-
tive activities of pre-World War I military reforms and became the informal
head of British military intelligence in France.[50] He believed that outside one's
responsibilities, every person could and should do something for their country.[51] His early academic connections and subsequent posts with parliamentarians and barristers assisted him in developing a far-reaching network of
those at the top of British society.[52]

Brett circulated among the cliques of socialite suffragists. One such association was with militant suffragette Lady Ada Cecile Granville-Wright,
who served numerous prison terms for rushing the House of Commons,
throwing stones through a government office at Whitehall, taking part in
the suffragette demonstration at Parliament Square, the window smashing
campaign of 1911, and helping the leader of the suffragettes in Britain, Emmeline Pankhurst escape from Mouse Castle in Kensington which was the
home of suffragette Marie Brackenbury that had been turned into a recovery
center during the timeframe of the passage of the Cat and Mouse Act. Lady
Granville-Wright's numerous incarcerations lasted for two weeks, two terms
of one month, two of 14 days, and one of six months. Ada was force-fed
twice daily for ten days and, in one instance, was left unconscious on the
floor. For her bravery, Granville-Wright was awarded the suffragette Hunger
Strike Medal for valor. As national sentiments against the Kaiser began to fo-
ment because of the country's efforts to break up the French-Russian alliance,
Ada and Lady Constance Lytton worked closely together in a fund-raising
campaign for the emigration of an anonymous British-German suffragette
to the United States. During World War I, she volunteered as an ambulance
driver, horse groomer, and mess hall helper.

The FANY and Red Cross

It was not by chance that Escher became acquainted with Mabel Annie St.
Clair Stobart.[53] Stobart was raised the daughter of a baronet and Knight of
Grace whose wealth had accrued into a substantial financial empire from
his business successes with the Dominion Tar and Chemical Company and
the British Australian Timber Company.[54] During her first marriage to St.
Clair Kilburn Mulholland, an Irish barrister and granite merchant, Stobart
moved to the Transvaal with him after his finances began to fail to build a
farm and trading store. This, too, failed, and Mable returned to Britain to
wait for his return. He died at sea on his journey home in 1908. Mabel denounced the non-physical roles most Victorian females had an aversion to

and pursued horseback riding, golf, fishing, and tennis and was trilingual in German, French, and English. Once widowed, she kept her maiden name after marrying her second husband, barrister John Herbert Greenhalgh, who used the cojoined moniker of Stobart-Greenlaugh. A productive writer, her first published books were on fishing and women's golf. Later, she turned to composing her beliefs about women's roles in post-Victorian society and became a keen supporter of suffrage before World War I.[55] She also dabbled in politics, running on a platform supporting public housing and emergency medical services for laborers. She placed third in a field of four candidates standing for a county election.

Observing the Balkan instabilities ongoing in Europe, Stobart believed in the inevitability of total war on the continent and felt it essential to be prepared for such an eventuality. This thinking led to her desire to join the female horseback riders of the Princess Royal's British First Aid Nursing Yeomanry Corps (FANY) in 1907.[56] The group wore a military-style uniform with a cap badge with the words CIVIL, RESPONSE, and MILITARY arching under a red cross. Organizers approached the British War Office to become members of the regular and reserve armies as paramedics and were soundly obstructed by male military officials. This was absurd since the group had been organized by a male veteran of the Soudan Campaign, Warrant Officer Edward Baker of the 21st Lancers, who was wounded in battle in 1898. He proclaimed that the women's role as nurses should be appealing to the Army, not offensive, as they would be a valuable addition to the fieldwork of the Army medical corps.

Baker's experience as a wounded soldier led him to place a high value on emergency medical care near firing lines before being transported by ambulance closer to safety behind the front for long-term care.[57] Excerpts from his writings showed his passion for changing the abysmal situation in how the battle wounded were cared for.

> During my period of service with Lord Kitchener in the Soudan Campaign, where I had the misfortune to be wounded, it occurred to me that there was a missing link somewhere in the Ambulance Department which, despite the changes in warfare, had not altered very materially since the days of Crimea when Florence Nightingale and her courageous band of helpers went out to succor and saved the wounded. On my return from active service, I thought out a plan that I anticipated would meet the want, but it was not until September 1907 that I founded a troop of young women to see how my ideas on the subject would work.[58]

He set up a plan of action whereby each member of this nursing corps would receive thorough training in first aid, drilling in cavalry movements, signaling, and camp construction. These women were prepared to ride onto the battlefield to deal with the wounded, who might otherwise have been left to a slow death.[59]

Serving near the front lines and having trained in signaling and drilling as cavalry, the women of the FANY rightly perceived themselves as combat medics. Undeterred by the rebuff in the UK, women left to operate with the Belgians, opened a casualty clearing station near the Front, and established an ambulance corps and transportation system for the wounded. FANY women were highly decorated for their heroics and bravery. One received the Medaille de la Reine Elisabeth, 32 the Croix de Guerre, ten, the Silver Star, and 17 the Bronze Star, of which one was awarded the Palm Leaf. One woman received the Legion d'Honneur, 20 the *Medaille de Societe aux Blesses Militaires*, and one the Serbian Order of St. Sava.[60]

Mabel volunteered for the FANY and the Red Cross but quickly became disenchanted with how both were being run.[61] The longer she stayed in the two spheres, the larger her dislike of the attitudes of the leadership and their blockage of skill sets women were bringing to the war. Stobart verbalized that the cliques amused themselves with women rather than assigning them responsibilities and giving them the recognition they deserved for their efforts.[62] The introduction to her autobiographical, *War and Women, From Experience in the Balkans and Elsewhere*, leaves no doubt of her animosity toward both groups.

> If women are to give their very best to the national service, they must be trained and adopted wholeheartedly by the Territorial Army, (the) Red Cross is directed to a past rather than the future, so I have resigned...the organization is not the appropriate way to get women trained.

Then Mabel added,

> Women, in general, refuse to see the need to give a practical demonstration of running a program rather than in the burlesque fashion in which they (the Red Cross) approached the situation...setting them up to be trashed by the anti-suffragists.[63]

In a public tandem effort with Viscount Escher, both resigned their memberships with the Red Cross.[64] From 1907 onward, Mable relied on her innate entrepreneurial and leadership talents to maneuver around the formal British military structure.

Escher agreed to write the Preface to Stobart's 1913 *War and Women*, highlighting her experiences in field medical unit oversight in the Balkans with the Women's Sick and Wounded Convoy Corps (WSWCC). Membership of the group was made up entirely of females, many having joined due

200 Women and War

to their disenchantment with the FANYs. The Viscount submitted that Mrs. Stobart "has proved by experience and example what women can achieve in war" and then added a well-worn caveat for the times that "nursing the sick and wounded in war is woman's work."[65] He reproached the Army Reserve Medical Corps for their tendency to think they "know it all" about field medical assistance and that "women know nothing." Then explained, "Stobart's book is important because it goes against this fallacy." Then Escher backed women's medical assistance near the front lines by stating Stobart's experience was a "practical example of women taking a share in national defense."[66]

Escher's writing in support of Stobart was a coup for women who wanted to be participants in their nation's conflicts. His knowledge of wartime organization and politics and his expansive network and informal power among the heads of the British government and monarchy gave him the authority Mable desired to promote her programs. Along with Escher's support and that of the Liberal Party, there would be no turning back from the example Stobart's successful excursions into frontline field medicine left on the population of Great Britain. It would, however, take two more wars before women in Western democracies were formally accepted into the 20th-century military with appropriate ranks and received equitable pay and a semblance of formal authority to conduct jobs beyond the medical corps.

Mable's Corps becomes a Reality

The WSWCC began in the mind of St. Clair Stobart around 1905, two years after the Circle of Sisters was founded in Belgrade, Serbia. At its inception, 50 volunteers signed on, including seven women doctors.[67] Their names are recounted here to show the makeup of the entire group: Mrs. King-May Atkinson, M.B., Ch.B., Miss Beatrice Coxon, D.R.C.P.S.R., Miss Helen B. Hanson, M.D., B.S., D.P.H., Miss Mabel Eliza King-May, M.B., Ch.B., Miss Edith Maude Marsden, M.B., Ch.B., Miss Catherine Payne, M.B., and Miss Isobel Tate, M.D., N.U.I.[68] Credentials held by the women's unit was remarkable for the period, given that most women were shut out of quantitative programs in schools in Europe and America, each having earned multiple degrees in the sciences, medicine, and public health. Along with the doctors were 18 trained nurses and several cooks, orderlies, chauffeurs, and interpreters. Many of the women possessed outstanding equestrian skills. Uniforms consisted of a blue-gray divided skirt, Norfolk jacket, helmet, and haversack. Mabel held her first exercise living in tents at an encampment in Studland, a civil parish on the Isle of Purbeck in Dorset, England. Training began with first aid classes and practicing the evacuation of wounded soldiers from the front lines. The Corps marched and learned the techniques of wagon loading and hauling. *The New York*

Times carried a short story highlighting their daily ritual. Days began at 6 a.m. with a bugle call, followed by bandaging and stretcher drills. Everyone was required to take a swim, which was Mabel's daily practice until her death. Midday meals included physiology, hygiene, signaling, and ambulance lectures.[69]

A second Studland campout was held in the fall of 1912 at the outbreak of the Balkan wars. Stobart visited the British Red Cross chairman, offering her team as a medical aid service for the Bulgarian wounded just behind the fighting lines. She was rebuffed and told that treating war casualties was not a woman's place and that her sex had no business near battlefields. Now practiced in ignoring dismissals, she traveled to Serbia and Bulgaria on her own, bankrolling herself and acquiring funds from affluent friends. Once Britain took up arms against Germany in the late summer of 1914, Stobart sailed to the Balkans with her medical team and established a tent field hospital at the then-national capital, Kragujevatz.[70] The Serbian military appointed her to run the First Serbian Field Hospital close to the front.

FIGURE 7.2 Mable Stobart with the commander of the Schumadia Division repitiching a tent.

© Public domain under the terms of the Project Gutenberg License.

202 Women and War

For her excellent governance across all aspects of moving and stationary medical camps, the Serbian Army promoted her to Major. With this came the formal authority to lead enlisted and officer personnel and civilians. Her column comprised infantry, mounted personnel, and ox-led medical wagons. Besides Stobart's team, 600 British women contributed to the war effort in Serbia during World War I. Most were doctors, nurses, and ambulance drivers. Mabel left a history in her autobiographical accounts of the many instances of going before obstructive bureaucracies and bureaucrats to state her case for women's inclusion in war-ravaged Europe. Her exasperation was keenly expressed regarding the pushback she knew she would receive after she decided to go with her traveling medical team to the international ferry terminal at Cherbourg in France to connect with the Serbian military. "I dreaded going to London, facing the endless red tape, snubs, opposition, collecting money, and creating a unit, difficulties of all sorts with which I was now familiar."[71] She wrote,

> I had one day the privilege of a conversation with an official of the British Red Cross Society, and, to my surprise, he repeated the stale old story that women surgeons were not strong enough to operate in hospitals of war and that women could not endure the hardships and privations incidental to campaigns. I then reminded him of the women at Kirk Kilisse. Ah! he replied, but that was exceptional.[72]

His pushback rung hollow with the well-traveled infighter. Kirk Kilisse was a reference to the defeat of the Turks by mixed national forces from Serbia and Bulgaria in October of 1912 during the First Balkan War.[73] Stobart's example was highly appropriate, pointing to the all-female *Kolo srpskih sestara* organized by Nadezda Petrovic. Women joined in organizing the group at the outset of the war by collecting over 1000 signatures of female medical service volunteers. The thousand-name petition found its way into the Serbian Ministry of the Military, and the government approved 25 female doctors to be engaged in the medical corps immediately after mobilization to replace Army medics who had been moved forward to the battlefields. The Serbs had far fewer reservations about their nation's women serving at the front.[74]

A leading founding member of the Serbian nurses' cooperative along with artist Nadezda Petrovic was Serbian suffragist Savka Subotic.[75] Savka advocated the need for women's education and employment to increase their power and influence. She also organized the First Women's Cooperative in her hometown, Novi Sad, a 17th-century merchant colony located on the Danube River, which supported training for poor girls to be employed as teachers. She died in 1918 as the Serbian Army liberated her birthplace. Staunch followers continued her legacy by not stopping their emancipation

FIGURE 7.3 Cover of War Illustrated highlighting Mable Stobart's volunteer work in Serbia.

© Public Domain All issues of the British WW1-era magazine The War Illustrated Jul–Dec 1915 Internet Archive HTML5 Uploader 1.6.4 Scanned and cropped by self from original document.

fight. The right to vote was achieved later in the same year upon annexing the Kingdom of Serbia into the Kingdom of Serbs, Croats, and Slovenes.[76]

Media reported positively on many of Mabel's exploits in 1914 and 1915. The *Daily Record* headlined with "British Lady's Adventure," *The Evening News*, "Stirring Story of Mrs. Stobart; Commanded Hospital in Serbian Retreat, A Fleeing Nation," and *The Times* wrote, "In the Footsteps of Florence Nightingale." The suffragette paper, *Votes for Women*, ran an expose on "Women Doctors at the Front." In America, the *New York Evening Sun* published, "Militarism is Maleness Run Riot: And it can only be Destroyed with Woman's Aid, Declares Pioneer Field Hospital Worker,"[77] On a Serbian fund-raising visit to Omaha, Nebraska, a state still four years away from ratifying the vote, Mabel's story was written up on the front page of the local American newspaper, the *Omaha Bee*.

Adjacent to the article was a short piece extolling what was considered an odd experiment of placing two women in a mail carrier position. Time was spent discussing the difficulty of what to call these women: mail women, carrierettes, or post women. Also included was the caveat that the occupation was one to which the all-male hierarchy of postal officials had deemed to be as well suited to women as it was to men.[78] Two words stood out in the article about mail carriers: "experiment" and "suitability." It seems remarkable that posting a woman as a mail carrier received this sort of attention, but it is a telling anecdote about what women were facing who had begun to break the barrier of the walls found against them by the all-male military medical structure in Europe.

Mabel's headliner in the *Bee* appeared in large and bold letters exclaiming, "First Woman Major Raps Silly Knitting Needles." In smaller type were the words, "Mrs. St. Clair Stobart, first woman major in the world, in Omaha to speak on Serbian relief work, believes able-bodied women should put aside their silly knitting needles and train to take the places of men who will go in the draft."[79] "She is a slight little woman," begins the discussion, "with iron-gray hair, and distinctly feminine in manner, until she speaks of the great world tragedy." Her face suggests firmness, said the author, which "entitled her to leadership in the Serbian Army." Mention is made of her having been the head of a hospital unit during the Balkan War and her ten years of medical line experiences and training women in national defense.[80]

A whirlwind life

During the war years, Mable lived in a bubble of high-speed adventure.[81] Rebuffed in 1912 by Sir Frederick Treves, Chair of the British Red Cross, she formed her hospital behind the front at Adrianpole, where her team extracted bullets, stitched wounds, amputated limbs, and conducted battlefield nursing duties.[82] At the beginning of World War I in 1914, an attempt was made to form the Women's National Service League, but higher authorities spurned the idea. Traveling with her husband, she headed to Brussels to start a war wound hospital and was captured by the Germans, arrested as a spy, and told she would face a firing squad. Her ability to talk her way out of sticky situations allowed her and her husband to return to Britain alive.

In a matter of days, she headed to Antwerp to set up a hospital at the Summer Concert Hall never halting with her mission throughout the harassing artillery bombardments. After being forced to evacuate to Chateau Tourlaville outside Cherbourg, another hospital was set up in conjunction with the French Red Cross. Shortly afterward, the Austro-Hungarian forces crossed the Serbian Border, and the typhus epidemic broke out.[83] It was 1915, and her efforts at Cherbourg were running smoothly. Mable became bored with the repetitiveness that had set in and left on the *SS Saidich* with a new team in conjunction with the Serbian Relief Fund Organization. On this excursion, equipment included 60 tents, 200 beds, an operating theater, an x-ray machine, six Ford ambulances, and an ox wagon.

Traveling through the Greek port at Salonika to eastern Siberia and Kragujevatz south of Belgrade, she oversaw six roadside dispensaries. She managed the constant influx of civilians and military personnel during a raging typhus outbreak. She then set up a separate military hospital for surgical cases at a local racetrack, and her efforts came to the attention of Serbian Crown Prince Alexander, who visited her facilities. The army asked that her mobile hospital be moved to the front lines to serve as a flying field hospital formally named The First Serbian-English Field Hospital (Front) in cooperation with the Serbian Army Schumadia Division.[84] This time, the group moved to Pirot in southeast Serbia, near the Bulgarian front.

FIGURE 7.4 Mable Stobart's flying field hospital train leaving for the front.

© Public domain under the terms of the Project Gutenberg.

206 Women and War

Upon moving to Pirot, Mabel was promoted to Army Major at the Bulgarian Front to command the entire unit. Enemy lines punctured the area, forcing her corps to retreat from the Austrian and German onslaught.[85]

Shepherding her soldiers to Nis and then north to Smederevska, the group rested at Azanj, then decamped again to Bacinac. The retreat became hazardous as the teams came closer to the Montenegrin mountains. Heavy rains, increased winds, and falling temperatures made the journey miserable as everyone slogged onward through Lapovo at Brazan, Via Blace, Kursumlija, and Dumnice e Posthme. By mid-November, her medical corps reached Pprishtina and turned westward, with high winds and heavy snows slowing their progress. Arriving at the foot of the Montenegrin mountains, she ordered the soldiers to abandon more oversized items in their supply train, including the wagons, which she ordered cut into two-wheeled carts. Oxen and pack ponies were loaded with the remaining materials. Now, Mable dodged enemy gunfire and spent an unremitting 18 hours a day on her horse.

The retreat

Kragujevatz fell eight months after Mable's unit arrived, and the Serbian military was forced to flee alongside a mass exodus of civilians toward the Albanian border.[86] Under her steely and steadfast direction, her medical team continued to treat their wounded on the move through the Montenegrin mountains. The winter trip was hazardous, and the ranges they crossed were composed of 30 peaks at over 6500 feet. Temperatures dropped to between minus 15 and 20 Fahrenheit, and the medical unit was pummeled by snow and rain as they moved through enemy gunfire. At one point in the trek, she consecutively remained on horseback for 75 hours. In late December, her command arrived at the border between Montenegro and Albania and arrived in Scutaria near Christmas day. It was the only unit that suffered no losses in a melee that cost 100,000 people their lives.[87]

Major Stobart described the retreat in *The Flaming Sword in Serbia and Elsewhere,*

> The difficulty of getting to the line was great because convoys and fugitives converged from all directions on this one road of escape...Bulgarian guns were dinning louder and louder every minute...the Bulgars captured some thousands of people left on the plains...the Germans, the Austrians...the Bulgars, the Arnauts, and Albanians kept making sporadic and murderous raids upon the convoys...the sad cortege was winding its way like a writhing snake without end...horses fell. Their riders were thrown into the slush, wagons overturned, and were then with their contents destroyed as the quickest remedy...The cold was horrible all day...that first night at

Petch, it was intense...we guessed that it might not be possible that even the two-wheeled (ox) carts could continue to Scutari...There was no time for sentiment; we were obliged to harden our hearts and burn or otherwise destroy the carts...(this) meant abandoning our beautiful hospital material and camp equipment...but I determined to save the instruments and to carry them with us at whatever trouble they might cost us...Into the land of Montenegro, the Black Mountains...our first path, about two feet wide, ran through a thick wood; I went first and led my horse...We were now in a narrow valley with steep mountains on either side of us... prevented ourselves (during sleep) from slipping down the mountainside by logs of wood placed at our feet...As the physical difficulties of the route increased, the problem for all the columns of securing bread for men and hay for oxen and horses increased...The track became more thickly lined with the dead bodies of oxen, horses, and, worse still, men. Men by the hundred lay dead."[88]

Pankhurst, Stobart, and Pacifism

Newsreels and articles in Allied countries cried out about Serbia's last stand and the harrowing 81-day retreat. Emmeline Pankhurst traveled to the United States in February 1916 to speak at the Belasco Theatre on West 44th Street in New York City. She stood on the stage in the intimacy of the purposefully designed gathering place with its living room feel to raise money for "women, children, and old men" impacted by displacement brought on by the invasion of Austro-Germany. The Labor Department and Immigration authorities barred her from attempting to enter the country due to her UK suffragette militancy prison record. A special board of inquiry was convened to review her case. The final decision by the board was that since her offenses were political and not because of moral turpitude, she should be allowed unconditional entry.[89]

Along with her that day was Chaddomil Miyatovitch, the former Secretary of State of Serbia who was the head of the Serbian Mission in the city. Having no first-hand knowledge of the retreat, Pankhurst urged the creation of a Serbian mission in the United States, using vivid imagery describing those who had fled through the snow-covered Montenegrin Mountains. The talk raised 1400 dollars, mostly from pledged IOUs. In 1916, posters designed by Swiss-born French political Art Nouveau painter and printmaker Théophile Alexandre Steinlen went up around the city with the plea, "Save Serbia Our Ally." Using austere colors to set the tone of an overcast day, a mass exodus is evident in the background over white snow fields, and a close-up of fatigued fleeing women and men and military personnel takes up the front space of the scene. Illustrator and painter Boardman Robinson created another poster for the same purpose. Six dejected and weary people

208 Women and War

of three generations of a family are gathered in a tight group. A woman holding a baby stands while two older women crouch at her feet, a small boy sits on the ground in front of her, and a beleaguered man in a fur cap and heavy outerwear, also on the ground, sits next to his son.[90] Both posters requested funds and contributions be sent to the Serbian Relief Committee of America at number 70, 5th Avenue, NYC.[91]

Pankhurst told her audience that the "sterling worth of the Serbian women" and their "fortitude" had been shown in their voluntary engagement in agriculture and industry and assistance in military campaign work while the men were at war. She felt such activism clearly made them worthy of US support in general and warranted their acceptance as equals in "the (global women's voting) franchise." Applause was given for her proposal to create a fleet of ships to go to Serbia to collect escaping refugees and take them to the Aegean Islands, Italy, and Corsica. Where Emmeline acquired her information to make such a speech is unknown. It may have been that she procured first-hand knowledge of the Serbian retreat through WSPU suffragette Evilena Scarlett, who had been an active, entrenched member of the Deeds, not Words cadre, and was arrested several times for breaking windows on government buildings and once for assaulting a police officer after hitting him in the mouth. Scarlett left the WSPU to create the Women's Emergency Corps to train women doctors, nurses, and motorcycle messengers. As a nurse, she was stationed at the Scottish Women's Hospital run by Elsie Inglis, the Chief Medical Officer of a medical unit that supported the country through the typhus epidemic at a field unit in Kragujevac in central Serbia. Evilena was part of the chaotic retreat as part of the Scottish Women's Hospital and gave press interviews in England on her return in early 1916.

Fresh from the killing fields in Serbia, Mable wrote a letter to the editor of the *New York Times* on November 14, 1917, in objection to the pacifist movement, warning the American public of the defective drawbacks of such thinking.[92] Suffrage women, she alleged, who want to lay down arms show either ignorance or brutality "for if they knew one-tenth of the sufferings," they would not pursue their anti-militaristic actions. A peace "at this moment would mean German peace only and world dominance, leading to subjugation, militarism, barbarism, and slavery across the European continent." Stobart told of her captivity as a German spy as proof of the cruel German mind. She knew from her experiences during the German occupation that war was "literally hell on earth." Participating in the retreat with millions of the Serbian population and having a frontline view of a massive number of Serbian deaths had made her aware of the brutality of the German infiltration.

She had seen many children under two years of age perishing and 30,000 young boys dying during the mountain retreat. Each was proof that Germany should be fought and not allowed to walk away in a peace agreement that would only assist them in keeping up their appalling approach to global dominance. Other firsthand experiences described involved the German atrocities she observed toward women and children. These innocents were driven into buildings that were set ablaze. Another one hundred people were pinioned, wrapped in a wire coil, placed on the edge of a pit, and shot, and then buried alive if they had managed to survive the cowardly show of force. "At this crisis of human history," it is perplexing that "there can exist women who seem chiefly concerned with personal politics rather than the outrages perpetrated by the enemy." "They are like Nero," argued Stobart, the cruel, debauched, and eccentric Roman ruler. "German victory and German peace would mean the enslavement of the world." "I have been an ardent suffragist, but since 1907, a reference to her organizing the Woman's Sick and Wounded Convoy Corps, I have contended that women should prove they are capable of taking a share of national defense before agitating for a share of political responsibility." "Look after the national defense, and the vote will look after itself." "Before the outbreak of this war, I was a member of peace societies. On the evening when war was declared, I was speaking at a meeting that had been convened by Mrs. Fawcett and other women in the hope that peace might be maintained." Now, "those women are using their own enfranchisement to further the disfranchisement of all mankind."

Lady of the Black Horse

The painting, *Lady of the Black Horse*, spotlights Mable, the suffragist, aid worker, military officer, and medical field organizer, descending the Montenegrin Mountains as her Serbian military company retreated through Albania in the winter of 1915.[93] Such images were a rarity because this one highlighted a female protagonist leading military personnel out of danger. Its completion date was 1916, and it is not widely known if the artist, George James Rankin, was commissioned to complete the painting or who was the originator of the idea to document the event.

Rankin was considered a talented wildlife watercolorist and was particularly sought out for his images of farm animals, mainly horses and fowl. His genre paintings were realistic and far removed from the Impressionist, Cubist, and Fauvist currents buffeting the world of art. Prints of his wildlife were sold as postcards and appeared on the backs of playing cards as collectible sets inside Gallaher's Cigarette packages.[94] He was more widely known for being the illustrator of children's books, one of which, *How to Have Bird Neighbors*, was advertised as a delightful season gift book for girls. His illustrations were also found in *Britain's Birds and Their Nests, Pheasants and Covert Shooting, Partridges, and Partridge Manors*.

Mable Stobart's portrait shows the artist's elevated skill level in natural atmospherics and sunlight. A brown wash was used to reflect light and dimension, and the sky and mountains in the distance have an almost surreal feeling, skillfully represented using blue, pink, purple, and orange hues. She is painted clearly of and not on her black steed, ascending along a precarious mud and rock trail as she leads the Serbian military, who are mounted, on foot or attending to oxcart trains. The medical red cross can be seen on several flags and the canvas cart coverings, signifying their status as a hospital team. Two soldiers have died from cold, illness, and hunger and lie on the side of the precipitous cliffs in a cavernous ditch. Mabel's first-hand account of her crossing the mountains in the Serbian retreat through Albania to Scutari had this passage which so well encapsulates the ambiance Rankin has instilled in his painting, "moist clouds, and mist, came down from heaven to try and veil the harshness of the mountains, in gossamers of mauve and purple, dragged from the setting sun, but they could not veil the memory of the suffering they enclosed."[95] The painting resides in the Red Cross Museum in Britain, where she would not likely have wanted it to be housed, knowing her distaste for the organization.

While media claims were mostly positive about Stobart's efforts, the reality was that it was nearly impossible for women to enroll in science, technology, or medical academic programs. Only the wealthy and well-placed could build an exemplary medical team, put them to the test, and prove their viability. Mable had never completed formal college study in the medical arena, where she excelled. Her talents were in the natural discriminating ability to assemble talented lineups and organize and lead others in the face of severely uncommon and dangerous circumstances. The physically accurate historical painting of her by Raskin is a testament to her as a physically adept cavalrywoman and army leader. It is an essential truthful portrayal and record of a first in the line of women who successfully fought for and prevailed as a military professional.

Mabel was decorated with the Serbian orders of the White Eagle and St. Sava and honored with a badge and ribbon, Order of the Red Cross, Serbia. She was revered as a Dame of Grace of the Order of the Hospital of St. John of Jerusalem in England. After Serbia, she traveled widely, giving guest lectures to the public about the value of frontline hospitals and female military medical corps.[96] In the late 1920s, she was one of the founding members of a social services society that assisted with housing for the unemployed. Her attention turned to mysticism and spiritualism, and she went on to write *Torchbearers of Spiritualism*, in which she devoted chapters to a wide range of people and writings from Völuspá Viking Age Poetry to France's divinely guided Joan of Arc, English dissenter George Fox, the Greek philosopher Socrates, and Athenian philosopher Plato.[97] She died well into the 20th century in 1954 at 92 in Bournemouth, England.

Stobart's negative experiences in convincing the military of the value of women's frontline medical teams were a customary part of being a female in search of equal rights. Finally, a slight shift in viewpoint by English authorities occurred in 1915–1916, when numerous reports began surfacing, extolling the virtues of women's contribution to the war in national and provincial newspapers, women's and girl's magazines, and the medical press.[98] In an October 1916 edition of the *Daily Telegraph Report* was the laudatory comment, "To the women doctors, the war has brought triumph."[99] In tandem with the newspaper onslaught was Queen Mary's decision to open the doors of the London School of Medicine to female students.

The suffragist community Stobart belonged to was tight, and other medical professionals with formal degrees and training watched and learned from her efforts to stand firm against the thrashing they received from the government and military bureaucracy.[100] British doctors Flora Murray and Louisa Garrett Anderson, two avowed suffragettes, would become key examples of how professionalism could lead to success in creating a formal women's medical corps. Their story is equally captivating but for distinct reasons beyond Mabel's. The two doctors did not have the same geopolitical war experiences as Mable. Instead, their talents lay in being effective political infighters and possessing the heft for breaking down barriers: their medical and academic credentials, scientific brains, and surgical skills.

Notes

1 Ballard Campbell. "Comparative Perspectives on the Gilded Age and Progressive Era." *The Journal of the Gilded Age and Progressive Era* 1, no. 2 (2002): 154–78. http://www.jstor.org/stable/25144294.
2 David Starr Jordan. "The Ways of Pangermany." *The Scientific Monthly* 4, no. 1 (1917): 27–40. http://www.jstor.org/stable/22612.
3 Mike Hawkins. "What's in a Name? Republicanism and Conservatism in France 1871–1879." *History of Political Thought* 26, no. 1 (2005): 120–41. http://www.jstor.org/stable/26221728.
4 Alex N. Dragnich. "Leadership and Politics: Nineteenth Century Serbia." *The Journal of Politics* 37, no. 2 (1975): 344–61. https://doi.org/10.2307/2128998.
5 Henry A. Kissinger. "The White Revolutionary: Reflections on Bismarck." *Daedalus* 97, no. 3 (1968): 888–924. http://www.jstor.org/stable/20023844.
6 Lecture 2:5: "National Unification: Europe's Dominant Powers" Source 10 Bismarck's Blood and Iron Speech. Centre for Comparative and Public History Chinese University of Hong Kong, Bismarck's "Blood and Iron" Speech (edb.gov.hk).
7 Sidney B. Fay. "Bismarck's Welfare State." *Current History* 18, no. 101 (1950): 1–7. http://www.jstor.org/stable/45307677.
8 Richard Schiff. "Art History and the Nineteenth Century: Realism and Resistance." *The Art Bulletin* 70, no. 1 (1988): 25–48. https://doi.org/10.2307/3051152.
9 Nicholas Green. "Dealing in Temperaments: Economic Transformation of the Artistic Field in France during the Second Half of the Nineteenth Century." In *Critical Readings in Impressionism and Post-Impressionism: An Anthology*, edited by Mary Tompkins Lewis, 1st ed., 31–47. University of California Press, 2007. https://doi.org/10.2307/jj.8501295.6.

212 Women and War

10 Mary Tompkins Lewis. "Introduction: The Critical History of Impressionism: An Overview." In *Critical Readings in Impressionism and Post-Impressionism: An Anthology*, edited by Mary Tompkins Lewis, 1st ed., 1–20. University of California Press, 2007. https://doi.org/10.2307/jj.8501295.4.

Stephen F. Eisenman. "The Intransigent Artist or How the Impressionists Got Their Name." In *Critical Readings in Impressionism and Post-Impressionism: An Anthology*, edited by Mary Tompkins Lewis, 1st ed., 149–61. University of California Press, 2007. https://doi.org/10.2307/jj.8501295.10.

11 Paul Tucker. "Monet and the Challenges to Impressionism in the 1880s." In *Critical Readings in Impressionism and Post-Impressionism: An Anthology*, edited by Mary Tompkins Lewis, 1st ed., 227–50. University of California Press, 2007. https://doi.org/10.2307/jj.8501295.15.

12 I. L. Zupnick. "The Social Conflict of the Impressionists. Zola's Opinions versus Evidence in Portraits." *College Art Journal* 19, no. 2 (1959): 146–53. https://doi.org/10.2307/774121.

13 Charles W. Millard. "Fauvism." *The Hudson Review* 29, no. 4 (1976): 576–80. https://doi.org/10.2307/3850497.

14 Russel T. Clement. *Les Fauves: A Sourcebook*, Greenwood Press, 1994.

John Turpin. "Art History and Art Criticism: Incompatible Partners?" *The Maynooth Review / Revieú Mhá Nuad* 5, no. 2 (1979): 15–24. http://www.jstor.org/stable/20556934.

15 Charles W. Millard. "Varieties of Cubism." *The Hudson Review* 24, no. 3 (1971): 476–81. https://doi.org/10.2307/3849472.

16 "Pablo Picasso, 1881–1973 Biography," Guggenheim Internet Archive. Collection Online | Pablo Picasso. Carafe, Jug, and Fruit Bowl. Horta de Ebro, summer 1909 (archive.org). Accessed 4/20/2022.

17 Dorothy Price, and Christopher Short. "Introduction: Why Does Der Blaue Reiter Still Matter?" In *German Expressionism: Der Blaue Reiter and Its Legacies*, edited by Dorothy Price, 1st ed., 1–14. Manchester University Press, 2020. http://www.jstor.org/stable/j.ctv1384308.6.

"8 Wasily Kandinsky *Zum Theme Jungstes Gericht* (On the theme of the Last Judgment," southeby's Impresionist and Modern Art Evening Sale Lot 8, (#8) Wassily Kandinsky | Zum Thema Jüngstes Gericht (On the Theme of the Last Judgement) (sothebys.com).

Franz Marc, and Wassily Kandinsky. *The Blaue Reiter Almanac*, Da Capo Press, March 1989 (reprint). ISBN: 0306803461.

18 Wassily Kandinsky. *Concerning the Spiritual in Art*, Dover Publications, June 1977. ISBN: 0486234118.

19 William Rubin. *Picasso, and Braque: Pioneering Cubism*, Museum of Modern Art (1st ed), Sept. 1, 1989.

20 Jeanne Willette. "French Artists During the Great War: Braque, Part One, arthistoryunstuffed, French Artists During the Great War: Braque, Part One | Art History Unstuffed.

21 Nicole Myers (ed), Katherine Rothkopf (ed), Anna Katherine Brodbeck, et al. *Cubism in Color: The Still Lifes of Juan Gris*, Dallas Museum of Art, Arpil 20, 2021.

22 "Collection online, Georges Braque," Guggenheim, Georges Braque | The Guggenheim Museums and Foundation. Accessed 4/20/2022.

23 Patricia Leighten. "Response: Artists in Times of War." *The Art Bulletin* 91, no. 1 (2009): 35–44. http://www.jstor.org/stable/20619654.

24 Sarah Forgey. "Art in the Trenches: The World War I Paintings of Samuel Johnson Woolf." *Army History*, no. 95 (2015): 26–31. http://www.jstor.org/stable/26300397.

Jeffrey T. Sammons, and John H. Morrow Jr. "Horace Pippin: World War I Soldier, Narrator, and Artist." *Pennsylvania Legacies* 17, no. 1 (2017): 12–19. https://doi.org/10.5215/pennlega.17.1.0012.

25 Nancy Minty. "Painting for Peace: Art Exposes the Cruelty of War," JSTOR.org, Oct 13, 2022, Painting for peace: Art exposes the cruelty of war – About JSTOR. Patricia Leighten. "Response: Artists in Times of War." *The Art Bulletin* 91, no. 1 (2009): 35–44. http://www.jstor.org/stable/20619654.

26 E. R. Hooton. *Prelude to the First World War: The Balkan Wars 1912–1913*, Fonthill Media, Oct 19, 2014.

27 H. Charles Woods. "The Balkans, Macedonia, and the War." *Geographical Review* 6, no. 1 (1918): 19–36. https://doi.org/10.2307/207447.

28 Richard C. Hall. *The Balkan Wars, 1912–1913 prelude to the First World War*, 2000. ISBN 0-415-22946-4 Routledge, p. 125.

29 John Robb. "Prehistoric Art in Europe: A Deep-Time Social History." *American Antiquity* 80, no. 4 (2015): 635–54. http://www.jstor.org/stable/24712796.

30 Bratislav Pantelić. "Nationalism and Architecture: The Creation of a National Style in Serbian Architecture and Its Political Implications." *Journal of the Society of Architectural Historians* 56, no. 1 (1997): 16–41. https://doi.org/10.2307/991214.

31 Jasana M. Jovanov. "Cyril Kutlik and Early Modernism in Serbia," Translated to English, Academia.edu. (99+) Kiril Kutlik i počeci moderne umetnosti u Srbiji/ Cyril Kutlík and Early Modernism in Serbia | Jasna M Jovanov – Academia.edu.

32 Ljubisa Nikolic. "Serbian Painters in the Army Medical Corps 1914–1918," *Vojnosanitetski Pregled*, Strana 622, Vol 68, Number 7. (99+) Serbian Painters in the Great War, by Ljubiša Nikolić | Danja Beba – Academia.edu.

33 Unknown Author, *Serbian Religious Art in Hungary*, ASIN 8683603601.

34 Ljubisa Nikolic. "Serbian Painters in the Army Medical Corps 1914–1918." *History of Medicine* 68, no. 7:621–25. Microsoft Word – 001_Korice_Internet.doc (ceon.rs). Accessed 4/9/2022.

35 S. A. Mansback. *Modern Art in Eastern Europe, From the Baltic to the Balkans, ca. 1890–1939*, Pratt Institute, NY 2001.
Robin Lenman. "A Community in Transition: Painters in Munich, 1886–1924." *Central European History* 15, no. 1 (1982): 3–33. http://www.jstor.org/stable/4545947.

36 Dragon Cvetkovic. "Beta Vukanovic Babette Bachmayer 1872–1972," Beta Vukanović Babette Bachmayer 1872–1972 – YouTube.

37 Yu S. Meretskaya. "Roman Circle: German Formalism Influence on the Anton Azbe's Pedagogical Method, Russian State University for the Humanities. https://doi.org/10.28995/2073-6401-2019-1-66-75.

38 A video of her work can be located at Beta Vukanović Babette Bachmayer 1872–1972 – YouTube. Accessed 4/22/2022.

39 Simona Cupic. "THeInterpretation of Female Bodies as a Projection of Identity: The Orient, the Balkans or Something Else?" 20, no. 1 (2022): 91. Indiana University Scholar Works. 390-Article Text-1695-1-10-20100412.pdf.

40 Alison Hilton. "From Abramtsevo to Zakopane: Folk Art and National Ideals in Russia and Eastern Europe." *Russian History* 46, no. 4 (2019): 241–61. https://www.jstor.org/stable/26870021.

41 Information from "With Golden Hands, Beta Cared for the Serbian Wounded," *Leutar*, September 8, 2017. Original in Serbian, translated using Google translate. "Golden" hands of Beta cared for Serbian wounded – Leutar.net (leutar-net. translate.goog).

42 Jasna M. Jovanov. "Photography as an (E)Vocation of the Painter. Forgotten Hobby of Nadežda Petrović" archived from the original on 1/31/2021; Retrieved 9/25/2019.

214 Women and War

43 "Nadezda Petrovic Oct 12 1873–Apr. 3, 1915," Nadežda Petrović – Google Arts & Culture.
44 M. Jovanović (2010). The Heroic Circle of Serbian Sisters: A History. *Serbian Studies: Journal of the North American Society for Serbian Studies* 24(1), 125–39. https://doi.org/10.1353/ser.2012.0011.
45 Francisca de Haan, Daskalova, Krasimira; Loutfi, Anna (January 2006). *Biographical Dictionary of Women's Movements and Feminisms in Central, Eastern, and Southeastern Europe: 19th and 20th Centuries.* ISBN: 9789637326394.
46 Snezana Milikic Nikolic. "Nadezda Petrovic (12 October 1872–3 April 1915) IV," Virily Culture.2018. Nadezda Petrovic (12 October 1873–3 April 1915) IV – Virily Translated for Serbian. Accessed 4/9/2022.
47 R. Babić Rade. (2008). "Nadežda Petrović – a female painter and a nurse" (PDF). *Istorija Medicine.* 10: 1. Archived (PDF) from the original on 7/5/2019; Retrieved 7/5/2019.
48 Maurice V. Brett. *Journals and Letters of Reginald Viscount Escher,* Ivor Nicolson & Watson, Ltd: London: 1934.
49 "Records of the Committee of Imperial Defense," The National Archives, UK, Records of the Committee of Imperial Defence | The National Archives.
50 J. O. Baylen. "Politics and the 'New Journalism': Lord Esher's Use of the 'Pall Mall Gazette.'" *Victorian Periodicals Review* 20, no. 4 (1987): 126–41. http://www.jstor.org/stable/20082281.
51 Michael Humphries. "'Perfectly Secret and Perfectly Democratic': Lord Esher and the Society of Islanders, 1909–14." *The English Historical Review* 127, no. 528 (2012): 1156–79. http://www.jstor.org/stable/23272742.
52 "Artware fine art Gallery, Reginald Baliol Brett," Portrait of Reginald Brett, 2nd Viscount Esher 1852–1930, GCVO, KCB, PC, DL, in Diplomatic Dress & the Order of the Bath | Artware Fine Art. Accessed 4/21/2022.
53 War and Women, From Experience in the Balkans and elsewhere the story of Mrs. St. Clair Stobart and her experiences during her time serving as a British nurse during the Balkan Wars Create Space Independent Publishing Platform, Jan 21, 2018, Original publication date 1862 ISBN: 1983913006. *Stobart, Mabel Annie Boulton (1913). War and Women, from Experience in the Balkans and Elsewhere.* London: G. Bell & Sons, Ltd.
54 "Domtar, History," Dominion Tar and Chemical Company History – Domtar.
55 A. K. Smith. 'The Woman Who Dared': Major Mabel St. Clair Stobart. In: Fell, A.S., and Sharp, I. (eds). The Women's Movement in Wartime. London: Palgrave Macmillan, 2007. https://doi.org/10.1057/9780230210790_10 r.
56 For an excellent history of the FANY, see "FANY at the Western Front, an Overview of the Role of the First Aid Nursing Yeomanry Corps in WW1: 1914–1919." http://fany.org.uk/public/FANY_WW1_Overview_Pdf.pdf | WWI | FANY (PRVC) – Princess Royal's Volunteer Corps. Accessed 4/22/2022.
57 "The History of the Corps," First Aid Yeomanry Emergency Response, First Aid Nursing Yeomanry > History (fany.org.uk).
58 Hugh Popham. *The FANY in Peace and War: The Story of the First Aid Nursing Yeomanry 1907–2003.* p. 2. Leo Cooper, Barnsley, 2003.
59 Ibid. Popham
60 WWI Medals | WWI | FANY (PRVC) – Princess Royal's Volunteer Corps. Accessed 4/22/2022.
61 Opcit Smith
62 Monica Krippner. *The Quality of Mercy: Women at War, Serbia 1915–1918,* David, and Charles:London, 1980.
63 War and Women a free librivox audio book. https://archive.org/details/warand-women_1802_librivox. War and Women by Mabel Annie Stobart Publication

date 2018-02-19 Usage Public Domain Mark 1.0 LibriVox recording of War and Women by Mabel Annie Stobart. Read in English by Celine Major. Accessed 02/05/2019.

64 Mrs. St. Clair Stobart. *The Flaming Sword in Serbia and Elsewhere*. London: Hodder and Stoughton, 1916. By the end of 1914, 40,018 women members of the Red Cross detachments and 17,696 men.
   Mabel Stobart. *Miracles and Adventures*. London: Rider & Co., 1935.

65 Mabel Annie Boulton Stobart. *War and Women, from Experience in the Balkans and Elsewhere*. London: G. Bell & Sons, Ltd., Preface 2013.

66 Ibid. Preface

67 Pete London. "Dorset's Wartime Heroine-Mabel St. Clair Stobart," *Dorset Life*, 2015. Dorset's wartime heroine – Mabel St. Clair Stobart | Dorset Life – The Dorset Magazine.

68 "The Women of Mrs. Stobart's Unit of the Serbian Relief Fund," Lives of the First World War, Imperial War Museums, Community: The Women of Mrs Stobart's Unit of the Serbian Relief Fund | Lives of the First World War (iwm.org.uk).

69 "English Sick and Wounded Convoy Corps, First Aid and Stretcher Drill at the Camp Near Swanage," Special Correspondence, *The New York Times* (1857–1922); Sep. 18, 1910; ProQuest Historical Newspapers, p. C4. Article 12 – No Title – Historical Newspapers – ProQuest.

70 For a photo of a typical field hospital, see: "A Serbian field hospital on the Serb0-Bulgarian frontier, 1915, Library of Congress A Serbian field hospital on the Serbo-Bulgarian frontier, 1915 Hôpital de campagne Serbe à la frontière Serbo-Bulgare, 1915. | Library of Congress (loc.gov). Also, see photos of Kragujevatz flying field hospital and oxcart dispensary. Pp. 50–51 op. cit. eBook Guttenburt.

71 Op. cit. Stobart: The Flaming Sword, p. 13.

72 Kirk Kilisse, or the Battle of Lozengrad, was part of the 1st Balkan War between the armies of Bulgaria and the Ottoman Empire on 24 Oct. 1912, when the Bulgarian army defeated an Ottoman army in Eastern Thrace.

73 "Bulgarian Capture of Kirk Kilisse was First Big Victory: By Means of this Success the Allies Were Placed in Possession of Good Road to Adrianople. *The Christian Science Monitor (1908-)* Nov. 6, 1912; ProQUest Historical Newspapers: *The Christian Science Monitor*, p. 6.

74 H. B. Hanson. "Serbia as Seen By a Red Cross Worker." *Journal of the Royal Society of Arts* 64, no. 3301 (1916): 291–307. http://www.jstor.org/stable/41346856.

75 Redakcija. "Benefactors of Novi Sad and Their Significance," 20 October 2016. J News, 2024. Benefactors of Novi Sad and their significance – I love Novi Sad.

76 Ivana Spasović. "Seven Women Members of Parliament on the Grand National Assembly in Novi Sad on 25th November 1918." *Komunikacije, Mediji, Kultura* 10. no. 10: 37–52, 30 December 2018, from the original on 30 December 2021. doi: 10.5937/gfkm1810037S. Archived.

77 A. K. Smith. 'The Woman Who Dared': Major Mabel St. Clair Stobart. In: Fell A. S., and Sharp I (eds). *The Women's Movement in Wartime*. London: Palgrave Macmillan, 2007. https://doi.org/10.1057/9780230210790_10. 'The Woman Who Dared': Major Mabel St. Clair Stobart | SpringerLink.

78 "First Nebraska Mail Women to Begin Carrying their routes," *Omaha Daily Bee*. March 14, 1918, ISSN: 2169-7264., p. 1. Accessed 2/5/2019.

79 Ibid. *Omaha Daily Bee*.

80 Ibid. First Woman Major, p. 1.

81 This chronology comes from *The Flaming Sword in Serbia and Elsewhere*, London: Hodder and Stoughton, 1916.

82 "Mable St. Clair Stobart," *Britannica*, Mabel St. Clair Stobart | Britannica "Unsung Heroine," Keymilitary.com. 28 Nov 2019. An English Heroine (keymilitary.com).

216 Women and War

83 "Heroines of the Great War: Mabel Stobart & the Retreat from Serbia in 1915," 11 Feb. 2015. The Serbian House Exhibition, Dorset County Museum, Heroines of the Great War: Mabel Stobart & The Retreat from Serbia in 1915 (spclondon.org.uk).

84 Catherine Payne. Oldham Doctor in Serbia: A Lady's Thrilling Experience," GM 1914 The First World War in Greater Manchester, Oldham Doctor in Serbia: A Lady's Thrilling Experience – GM 1914 (wordpress.com).

85 Richard C. Hall. "Bulgaria in the First World War." *The Historian* 73, no. 2 (2011): 300–15. http://www.jstor.org/stable/24455092.

86 G. Gordon-Smith. "The Retreat of the Serbian Army." *Current History (1916–1940)* 11, no. 2 (1920): 329–37. http://www.jstor.org/stable/45328963.

87 Mabel's 1916 book opened by telling her readers its content dealt with two subjects: women and war, and that it is time for "beauty and the beast to make their alliance." She warned that militarists and anti-feminists would be offended by what she had to say. Over eleven chapters are related to her ten weeks of experience administering an all-female field hospital. Punctuating her descriptions with private opinions and thoughts, she asked, "Ought women to take a share in national defense?" Then answers this question: "Ought to be misleading as it assumes something right and wrong." Stobart cited the success of Florence Nightingale as an example of the argument that a woman needs to show through involvement, not just verbalization, that women can do war work. Several programmatic and philosophical weaknesses regarding medical practice, as they existed in a time of war, were brought to light. Philosophically, she noted there was the mental requirement that women must share in the belief that they are part of the defense of a nation. Pragmatically, she stated there is a gap in the flow of military medical operations between field and base hospitals, causing war wounded to die due to not receiving aid near the battle. She applied her vision of recruiting women for medical detachment assistance within this gaping organizational and administrative hole.

88 M. A. Stobart., *The flaming sword in Serbia and elsewhere*, 123–307. London, New York: Hodder and Stoughton, 1916.

89 "To Let Mrs. Pankhurst in: Labor Department Orders Her Admitted to Country Unconditionally," *New York Times, (1857–1922)*, Jan. 19, 1916; ProQuest Historical Newspapers, The New York Times.

90 "Left Behind in Serbia Send Money for the Women and Children to the Serbian Relief," National Museum of American History, Left Behind in Serbia Send Money for the Women and Children to the Serbian Relief | Smithsonian Institution (si.edu).

91 "Save Serbia Our Ally," Photo, print, drawing, Library of Congress, Save Serbia our ally. Send contributions to Serbian Relief Committee of America – digital file from original print | Library of Congress (loc.gov).

92 All quotes in this section which is comprised of two paragraphs, are from "The Answer to the Peace Suffragists: A Woman Who Has Seen the Germans at War Tells What Their Peace Would Mean," *New York Times (1857–1922)*, Nov. 14, 1917; ProQuest Historical Newspapers The New York Times.

93 The war was not going well for Serbia in the autumn of 1915. Bulgaria had joined the fight against Serbia. After fierce fighting, the army and civilians retreated through Albania. The retreat was a complete shambles with terrible freezing weather, mud-bound roads, constant enemy attacks, and a lack of food and other supplies. Estimates put the costs at well over 250,000 soldiers dying or missing. There is no estimate of the number of civilians that died. Stobart arrived at the front with her unit right before the start of the retreat. Her crew was one of the last units to start the dangerous crossing of the mountains but could stick together with little loss. Taken from Angela K. Smith, *British Women of the Eastern Front War, Writing and Experience in Serbia and Russia*. Oxford University Press, 2016.

94 Ephemera art refers to items of collectible memorabilia, typically written or printed, that were initially expected to have only short-term usefulness or popularity.
95 Mable St. Clair Stobart. *The Flaming Sword in Serbia and Elsewhere*, "Part III Diary of the Serbian Retreat," July 7, 2013, eBook #43124 ISO 8859-1. The Project Gutenberg eBook of The Flaming Sword in Serbia and Elsewhere, by Mabel Annie Boulton Stobart. This eBook also has the original photographs of the first edition, which were not found in more recent renderings.
96 Mabel St. Clair Stobart. *Miracles and Adventures: An Autobiography*, London: rider and Co., 1935.
97 "The mists which shroud these questions: Mable St. Clair Stobart, the First World War and Faith," *St. Jude on the Hill Parish Paper*, 5 Dec. 1924 (1). "The mists which shroud these questions": Mabel St. Clair Stobart, the First World War and faith. – Free Online Library (thefreelibrary.com).
98 Ibid. Medical Women, p. 162.
99 Ibid.
100 "Mable St. Clair Stobart," video (3:04) *Encyclopedia Britannica*, Article media library. Mabel St. Clair Stobart | Britannica n.d.

Additional Resources

A. K Smith. 'The Woman Who Dared': Major Mabel St Clair Stobart. In Fell A. S., Sharp I. (eds). *The Women's Movement in Wartime*. London: Palgrave Macmillan, 2007. https://doi.org/10.1057/9780230210790_10.

Alfred Emile Cornebise. *Art from the Trenches: America's Uniformed Artists in World War I*. College Station: Texas A&M Press, 1991.

I. Hutton. *With a Woman's Unit in Serbia, Salonika, and Sevastopol*. London: Williams and Norgate, 1928.

Mable St. Clair Stobart (Mabel Annie Boulton). *War and Women. From Experiences in the Balkans and Elsewhere. With a Preface by Viscount Esher*. London: G Bell and Sons, 1913.

Mable St. Clair Stobart. *The Flaming Sword in Serbia and Elsewhere*. London: Hodder and Stoughton, 1916.

Monica M. Stanley. *The Stobart Nurses: Accounts of British Volunteer Nurses during the First World War – My Diary in Serbia April 1, 1915–Nov. 1, 1915*. Driffield: Leonaur Ltd., September 2014.

Paul Wood, David Batchelor, and Briony Fer. *Realism, Rationalism, Surrealism, Art Between the Wars*. New Haven: Yale University Press, June 1993.

Yvonne Fitzroy. *Scottish Nurses in the First World War with the Scottish Nurses in Roumania and a History of the Scottish Women's Hospitals*. Driffield: Leonaur Ltd., December 2015.

Questions

Why is the story of Mabel St. Clair Stobart central to the history of women in war and combat?

What elements distinguish the art periods of fauvism, cubism, impressionism, and art-nouveau?

218 Women and War

Why is the historically accurate painting of Mable Stobart an artifact of importance in recording the history of women in war?

How did wealth impact the avenues that Mable Stobart could pursue?

Under what artistic style would you place Woman of the Black Horse? *Describe Rankin's technique and color palette.*

Modern take

Fourteen percent of the US military enlisted personnel are female, and 16 percent serve as officers. However, these increases have only been two to four percent since 1973. Why has there yet to be a higher number of women serving in the armed forces?

Most women, 14.79 percent of those on active duty, serve in the medical field. Of this percentage, one quarter holds administrative positions, with only slightly more than two percent serving in a technical capacity, such as medical equipment or field specialists. Why are so few women serving as physicians, surgeons, or radiologists and instead, filling roles as physical therapists, dietitians, nurses, and physician assistants?

Does gender disparity in military medicine mimic the medical professions in the civilian sector?

Activities and discovery

Study the Artvirtual Gallery of paintings by Serbian war artist Natalija Cvetkovic and her teacher, Beta Vukanovic. Describe their styles relative to your newfound art vocabulary located in this chapter.

Search the Gallery I Muzeji website for a virtual exhibition on "Painters/ Warriors/Witnesses," which highlights painters and photographers in the Serbian Army in the first decades of the 20th century; pausing the virtual tour to study paintings or enlarge the placards for information. Painters/Warriors/ Witnesses – Galerije i muzeji.

Discover the art of Serbian war artist Miodrag Petrović. What styles and techniques does he use? What was his role in the military? What did he do after 1915? Choose a favorite work and create a poem about what you see. Begin with this website: "Stories of a Serbian War Artist: A Remarkable Story from World War One." Stories of a Serbian War Artist | Europeana.

Study the paintings of the Fauvists, Henri Matisse, Vincent van Gough, and Paul Gaugin. Photocopy an image from each artist showing similar subject matter and compare their styles and the emotions they elicit. How do their paintings communicate joy for life, art, and artwork?

Compare photographs of the Great Retreat and photographs of Mable St. Clair Stobart with the painting Woman of the Black Horse. *What are the strengths of photography and painting? What are their weaknesses?*

Uncover photographs of Mabel St. Clair Stobart and describe the effects of lighting and the ways the palette of black and white photography presents a mood. Look at her portrait photos and write a description of her. Copy the pictures and make a computerized storyboard of her life and exploits. Create a small art exhibit about Mabel.

Learn about other women in the medical field who served during the Serbian campaigns and World War I. What are their backgrounds, and why did they volunteer their services? What challenges did they face?

8
PAINTING AS SOCIAL COMMENTARY
Drs. Flora Murray and Louisa Garrett Anderson and the Endell Street Hospital

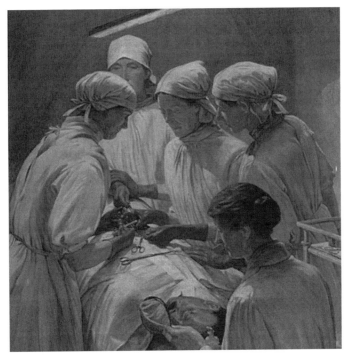

FIGURE 8.1 The Francis Dodd painting of an operation at the Endell Hospital showing Drs. Lousia Garrett, Flora Murray, and W. Buckley.

© Public domain File: An Operation at the Military Hospital, Endell Street – Dr. L Garrett, Dr. Flora Murray, Dr. W Buckley Art.IWMART4084.jpg – Wikipedia.

DOI: 10.4324/9781003406372-9

More about the art of this period

The early 20th-century artist was bored. They looked back at what had come before them. They saw only obedience and submission toward academic regulations that had guided artisans since the first Academy of Design appeared in the 16th century in Florence, Italy. These non-conformists believed a new society was emerging that would break apart the ages-old social structure of the European haves and have-nots. A driving movement in all the artists' backyards from the United Kingdom on the Atlantic Ocean to the western Russian steppes was pummeling the values formally placed upon ancient monarchal rule. Cross-border kinships that had existed for centuries were about to be blown to bits. Artistic youths born into this broadening chasm and a few of their older compatriots would become the directors and perpetrators of a one-of-a-kind creative explosion that would forever change the countenance of the meaning and definition of art.[1]

Artists imbued with the new zeal for change lived and worked in Europe's most populated cities, expanded and bloated by immigration and industry. Noise, traffic jams, slums, air pollution, sanitation, and health problems transformed the demeanor of all the artist meccas – Paris, Moscow, Munich, Zurich, Berlin, Cologne, London, Weimar, and Dessau. This novel culture needed contemporary art to match societal vehemence, filth, and decapitation of open spaces. The renegades were insulted by the bourgeois tendencies allied with the old-time regulated atmospheres with their canonical ideas about how art should be created. Perpetrators of the old school philosophies of art like the *Accademia di San Luca* in Rome, the *Ecole des Beaux-Arts*, The Salon Julian and Salon of Paris, and the Royal Academy of Arts and Slade School of Fine Art in London were in for a bludgeoning. Academies had been vital because they represented the apex of the best artistic talent up to this new generation. They adhered to strict ideological conventions based upon a formula of aesthetics. To be a part of an academy meant you had been recognized as a naturally endowed superior talent. But at the beginning of the 20th century, these scholarly houses represented a high-mindedness not appreciated by cutting-edge artists who no longer wanted to adhere to such blatant cultural control of their innovative endeavors.[2] Defectors of the academy system were jammed into the classification of modernist. They were caught up in the feelings elicited by industrialization and the philosophical and emotional influence political upheavals had on society. Values permeating the cast-off psyche of these creative minds included social Darwinism, global imperialism, populism, Marxism, communism, and socialism. A 1917 publication by a professor of art at Columbia University, Arthur Wesley Dow, who had become a foremost commercial designer noted for his colorful East Asian composition style and his quest for synthesizing the virtues of

222 Women and War

Eastern and Western artistic qualities related to the art world's feelings about modernism in this way,

> Modernism is an inclusive name applied to the many forms of rebellion against the accepted and traditional...When modernist art is shown, old man know-it-all denounces these "fakirs," "freaks," and "queerists" with their "crazy quilt" art. He calls this the cult of "crudity and ugliness" and their canvases "color puddles" of "delirious dyers."[3]

Rebels took their cues from four late 19th-century geniuses who had unprecedentedly advanced the art world. At first, they became enamored with Vicent van Gogh's Japanese stylizations, Paul Gauguin's technique of broad, flat spaces and excessively bright colors, Paul Cezanne's experimentations with repetitive, exploratory brushstrokes, and Georges Seurat's chromoluminarism and pointillism.[4] Deserters eventually obliterated any direct ties with what they considered these aging approaches. Painting turned toward pure and near quasi- or pseudo-abstractions and then to complete abstraction. It was a vigorous time, with 12 prominent philosophic collectives rapidly emerging from 1900 through the end of World War I, with none of the groups lasting for more than seven years.[5] The newborn movements had names to match the intellectual and geographical churn of the time: Fauvists, Cubists, Expressionists, Futurists, Orphists, Suprematists, Constructivists, Dadaists, Purists, Neoplasticists, Abstractionists, and Surrealists.[6]

The art manifesto and artists' participation in war

Excited by their newfound approach to art, these purveyors of innovation and novelty began writing personal and group manifestos to replace scholastic training diatribes. Each believed they warranted a separate genre for their work.[7] The new artists did not like what the critics said about their technique, so they became their own personal self-censors and publicists. Artists' declarations were printed in newspapers, in self-generated booklets, or as flyers handed out at art shows. The missives were used to espouse subjective opinions and visions for art and to change the track of art's seven common elements: line, shape, texture, form, space, color, and value. Revelations in the declarations aligned with prevalent ideological and social crusades of reform, revolution, reaction, and religiosity.[8]

1909 marked the appearance of Italian Filippo Thomas Marinetti's Founding Manifesto of Futurism in the French newspaper *La Figaro*. Once an empire, Italy was deteriorating, and Marinetti and other young upstarts did not like what they were seeing. Their nation was lagging in cultural and technological development; for a country to regain its supremacy, it was believed a social revival was essential. Writing the manifesto and placing it in print

Painting as Social Commentary **223**

media was a phenomenal publicity stunt, was proto-fascist, and shocked the public. The piece represented the embryo of what would become a full-blown shift in the philosophy of what constituted art.[9] Marinetti's written ideology was instrumental in jump-starting artmaking of Pablo Picasso's and Georges Braque's Cubism, Hugo Ball's Dadaism, Wassily Kandinsky and Franz Marc's non-figurative art and forms of Surrealism and the occult emanating from artists like Josephine Peledan and Austin Osman Spare. Cubism took objects from life, carved them into distinct planes, and reassembled them in abstract forms. Dadaism was an illogical, irrational, and absurd form of art with seemingly no formulaic. Non-figurative art used color and shape to present an idea rather than realistic forms or figures. Surrealist and occult art endeavored to use the flow of the unconscious mind to create.

Marinetti alleged it was time for action, not sentiment, in the creative process. His declaration proposed to infuse modern art with the machine age's vitality, energy, violence, and motion.[10] It also proclaimed war as an ally to rebirth and regeneration. Philippo pronounced, "We want to sing the love of danger, the habit of energy and rashness...essential elements will be courage, audacity, and revolt."[11] It wasn't just painting that the manifesto was describing. The declaration was meant to apply to the other six forms of art: performance, architecture, sculpture, literature, music, and cinema. Sentiment poured from the charter; artists were to sing the love of danger and imbue a habit of energy and fearlessness. They were to "show courage, boldness, and rebellion, glorify aggressive action, and live in restful wakefulness with the slap and punching of fists."[12] He wanted a clean slate from the bondages of past art through the outward application of speed, youthful vigor, mechanization, and violence.

Marinetti's externally driven art theory was of an entirely different aesthetic vein than that of Russian painter and art theorist Wassily Kandinsky, who believed that art was an abstract manifestation of the internal creative psyche and proposed a psychology of color existed.[13] He wrote of the importance of the ability to express an artist's inner life on canvas in his 1912 book, *On the Spiritual in Art*. He, like Marinetti, though in an entirely different vein, claimed to be moving forward away from prior generations of artistic philosophies. "The impressions of impressionists, the emotions of expressionists, the experiments of cubists-all these stages have long been passed, and now the task of the art viewer is to see the beauty of pure color and shapes."[14] Kandinsky's colors moved beyond the application of mere pigment. Each shade was chosen based on an innermost etherial choice.

Just before the outbreak of World War I, Wassily, who had been living as a Russian national in Germany, cofounded the *Der Blaue Reiter* group with Franz Marc. *Blaue Reiter* artists explored the spiritual values of art as a counter to "what they saw as the corruption and materialism of their age."[15] The two began organizing their exhibitions and published a 1912 almanac

224 Women and War

of the same name, which they hoped would become a yearly publication. World War I would stop their trajectory. Today, the almanac is considered the first modern *gesamtkunstwerk*, meaning the art covered globally and historically many art forms in one space: visual, written, and musical. Both artists believed art knew "no borders or nations, only humanity." "We are standing at the threshold of one of the greatest epochs that mankind has ever experienced, the epoch of Great Spirituality."[16] Where Marinetti's approach to changing the world of art was harsh and externally driven, Kandinsky and Marc's approach emphasized a form of utopian socialism inwardly devised.

The native Russian was forced to extricate himself from German soil and return to his homeland in Moscow as the fumes of hatred for Russia began to make his life in Germany unsafe. Kandinsky became involved in Russian cultural politics and was assigned by the government to establish the Museum of the Culture of Painting. He left Russia again in 1922 and returned to Germany as a member of the Bauhaus school, founded by German architect Walter Gropius, whose art vision was to form a global utopian craft guild combining architecture, sculpture, and painting into a single creative expression.[17] Kandinsky eventually moved to Paris, where he remained.[18]

As World War I unfolded, Franz Marc's style became tenser, as if he anticipated his fate and the tumult that would rock Europe.[19] For Franz, the color blue played a significant role in his paintings, believing it had exceptional psychological and spiritual value.[20] Before 1914, his reputation was built upon his production of brightly colored animals, especially horses, to convey profound messages about the fate of humanity and the natural world. "Art has always been in its very essence the boldest departure from nature," wrote Marc in 1912. "It is the bridge into the spirit world."[21] Marc wanted to paint images that "quivered and flowed" with the use of brilliant semi-cubist images. His versions of animals seemed to "melt into form and color like a hallucinogenic, ultra-modern Garden of Eden."[22]

Franz was drafted into the Imperial German Army and served as a cavalryman in a military camouflage unit that hid artillery from aerial observation using tarps painted in a pointillist style. Marc wrote to Kandinsky of the war, "This is the only way of cleaning out the Augean stables," an equine reference to a condition marked by a great accumulation of filth and corruption, and continued with the sentiment, "Is there a single person who does not wish this war might happen?"[23] Franz was killed at the Battle of Verdun in France by shrapnel from a shell blast. Nearly half a million soldiers were lost during the staggering nine-month-long fight. Marc's good friend and colleague from *Der Blaue Rider*, August Macke, also enlisted in 1914 and died in the second month of the war at the Western Front near Champagne, France. Marc wrote of his friend, saying that with his death, one of the most beautiful and wild curves of German artist development abruptly dropped, which none of us can continue.[24] On Marc's death in

Painting as Social Commentary **225**

1916, Kandinsky wrote, "It is sad that, beyond the Rhine, so little importance has been attached to commemorating one of Germany's finest artistic hopes."[25] The triad that had brought spiritualism into the realm of color, Marc, Macke, and Kandinsky, ended with Kandinsky, the lone survivor of the trio. Like the Picasso-Braque dyad, only one within the original core was left and moved on to attain inordinate fame.

In 1914, many European modernist art community participants signed up to go to war. Others who objected to the fighting fled their respective nations.[26] Pablo Picasso saw his two friends, Georges Braque and Andre Derain, the cofounder of Fauvism with artist Henri Matisse, off to the battlefields at the train station on mobilization day. Obsessed with the conflicts unfolding around him, the Spaniard was living in Paris as an expatriate whose country of birth remained nonaligned with the fighting.[27] It would mark the end of the yoke that had connected the friendship and professional exchange between the two men for many years and annihilate any semblance of Cubism's former dynamism.[28] Derain mobilized in 1914 as an artillery truck driver and did not serve as close to combat as Braque. His age, maturity, and the fact that Derain was not on the war's losing side may have had a bearing on his post-war art, not showing intense emotional scarring.[29] Once away from battle and the war ended, Georges art was often filled with agony and mental misery.

It was not uncommon for artists to experience emotional trauma from what they faced on the front. German expressionist painter Max Beckman entered the war in 1914 and served as an orderly for the medical corps in Belgium. He had hoped to become a history painter as a younger man. Max suffered emotional exhaustion one year later and was discharged. From that point forward until he died in 1950, he painted destructive, haunting, distorted, angular images of torturers, amputees, and clowns.

Two of his dry points, *Happy New Year* from 1917 and *Madhouse* from 1918, reflect war's mental and physical impact on him. Beckman's *The Night*, painted in 1919, shows a family being tortured, a scene soldiers witnessed in areas of German occupation.[30] In peacetime, he turned toward the New Objectivity movement, which popularized unsentimental reality and focused his effort on images of disfigurement and brutality.

Braque became critical of artists like French avant-garde painter Francis Picabia and cubist Albert Gleizes, French orphist chromatic scale painter Robert Delaunay, and sculptor and futurist Marcel Duchamp because they circumvented the war.[31] During the Second Battle of Artois near Vimy Ridge in 1915, as part of the German offensive of the Second Battle of Ypres, Braque lost consciousness on the battlefield outside the trenches when he sustained a shrapnel wound to the head. It took a year of intense rehabilitation before he could return to painting. Medical treatments involved trepanation, the drilling of a hole into the skull causing a coma and temporary blindness.[32]

Picabia evaded duty through his well-connected father-in-law, claimed a mental disorder, sought exile in New York, Barcelona, and Switzerland, and, after the war ceased, he immediately returned to Paris. Serving on the front lines, the painter became succinct about his view of the anti-militarist Gleizes when he commented his former associate had avoided the fight with a convenient medical condition. Records show Gleizes enlisted in the French infantry in the 1880s. In World War I, he was attached to a group that served in entertainment and, through accommodation by a regimental surgeon, was allowed to paint while being militarily obligated.[33] He was discharged in 1915, left for America with his spouse, and became part of the same circle of artists and patrons as dadaist Marcel Duchamp.

So confident was Matisse that he was going to fight that he purchased his uniform and boots before enlisting. During the medical exam, it was discovered that Henri had a weak heart and was rejected. He was also 44 years old. Unable to accept his plight, he wrote to a government official to rescind the medical order and was told that what you can do for the country is to paint well.[34] This kindly directive was a hint to continue his course in the French painting mode because German expressionism, with its sharp, raw, powerful, dark, angular, stark soul, seemed to be overtaking what he had established in his fauvist and impressionistic style.[35] In the German expressionist collective manifesto, the *Bridge*, written on a woodcut print, the group stated they were "calling together all youth" to evolve "in opposition to older, well-established powers continually."[36] Unlike other artists who either sat out the war or fled to North America or other parts of the world and continued their lucrative occupations, Matisse stayed in southern France, where he "sold prints to buy food to send to his compatriots and refused to do solo shows while they were fighting."[37]

In 1916, the Zurich-based artist Hugo Ball composed the politically caustic statement entitled the *Dada Manifesto*. Ball's idea was to express nonsense, irrationality, and anti-bourgeois protest in artwork.[38] Dada, Ball proclaimed in the fashion of nonsensical prose, "comes from the dictionary. It is simple. In French, it means hobby horse. In German, it means Goodbye, Get off my back, Be seeing you sometime. In Romanian: Yes, indeed, you are right, that's it. But of course, yes, definitely, right. And so forth."[39] His apostles created simultaneous and sound poems read before groups at coffee houses. Simultaneous poetry had three or more participants concurrently speaking, singing, whistling, or bellowing different nonsensical words.[40] Sound poems were illogical syllables uttered in patterns that created rhythm and emotion with no resemblance to any known language.[41] Another method of creating poetry was to cut single words out of a newspaper, toss them in a bag, shake the contents, and let the words flutter onto a table. The pieces of paper, in order of where they lay, were pasted into a chance poem. The atmospherics of Dada were a suggestion of the inability of European diplomats to resolve

Painting as Social Commentary **227**

political issues.[42] The noise and bizarreness of Dada seemed parallel to the din and confusion of a battlefield and industrial plants.

One of the most representative items from the Dada art period was Marcel Duchamp's *Fountain*. An example of readymade art, which is made from humanly manufactured objects, is a urinal presented on its back and signed with the nonsensical "R. Mutt, 1917" on its lower right side.

> When asked whether 'R. Mutt' was a pun on the German word *Armut*, meaning poverty; Duchamp was quoted as explaining Mutt comes from Mott Works, the name of a large sanitary equipment manufacturer. But Mott was too close, so I altered it to Mutt, after the daily cartoon strip "Mutt and Jeff," which appeared at the time and with which everyone was familiar. Thus, from the start, there was an interplay between Mutt, a fat little funny man, and Jeff, a tall, thin man. I wanted any old name. And I added Richard [French slang for money bags]. That's not a bad name for a *pissotière* (meaning public urinal). Get it? The opposite of poverty. But not even that much, just R. MUTT.[43]

The piece was submitted to the Society of Independent Artists in New York for their 1917 exhibit. The Society's written constitution required them to accept all submissions and followed the policy of no juries or prizes. But *Fountain* was even too much for this ultramodern philosophy. They rejected it because a piece of sanitary ware associated with bodily waste could not be considered a work of art.[44] It was an indecency for any woman who would be at the exhibit. A board voted narrowly to exclude the piece. Duchamp immediately resigned, angry that a seemingly academic approach had been used to exclude him when this was exactly what the new breed of artists sought to annihilate. On the show's first day in New York City, Duchamp and two friends submitted the first Dada periodical in the city entitled *Blindman*, a direct hit at the board's decision.[45] He had tested the commitment of the new American Society and their supposed belief in the tolerance of freedom of expression and lost. "The board issued a statement defending its position: 'The *Fountain* may be a very useful object in its place, but its place is not in an art exhibition, and it is, by no definition, a work of art.'"[46]

Followers of Ball supported far-left politics. Ball attempted to enlist three times in the German Army but was turned away from the war for medical reasons.[47] He turned conscientious objector after witnessing the 18-day invasion of Belgium, claiming "the war is founded on a glaring mistake; men have been confused with machines."[48] Ball and his renouncers were drawn together under an umbrella of distaste for the logic and reasoning that they saw as being inherent to the values of capitalist democracies. One of his key influences was Kandinsky's abstractionism.[49] "Hugo Ball and the Zurich Dadaists revered Kandinsky, included his paintings in their exhibitions, and read his poetry at their soirees."[50] Regarding industrialization and war, Ball declared society, on the one hand, a tottering world in flight, bethroed to the glockenspiel of hell...(the world) was rough, bouncing, and riding on hiccups...behind which was a crippled world and literary quacks with a mania for improvement.[51] He alluded to the bourgeois class and the Big Four: Prime Minister of Great Britain, David Lloyd George, Italian statesman Vittorio Orlando, Prime Minister of France, Georges Clemenceau, and United States President Woodrow Wilson. One summary of Dadaism states that

> Dada strategies included mockery and parody and sarcasm. The artists mocked and rejected the naïve ideas of the old men who led the young men off to a certain death. For the Dada artist, "art" is a metaphor for all the Western civilization has built so proudly. But a civilization that planted Flanders Fields and that ordered Gallipoli must be rejected. Art was a part of the natural order that had to be destroyed and replaced with actual nature, which acts for itself, is senseless, indifferent to the plans of humans, and is direct and relentless. A genuine force...If they could re-set society, then perhaps the next world would be better.[52]

After the shocking experience in Belgium, the Dada leader channeled his emotions against war by staging several anti-war protests in Berlin, speaking out against the hypocrisy of war and how humankind had been confused by the power of machine guns, artillery, submarines, poison gas, warplanes, and tanks.[53] This observation marked him a traitor, and he slipped across the frontier to Switzerland with his future wife, a cabaret performer.[54] They lived in relative obscurity in a Swiss borough opening the Cabaret Voltaire, and he began writing propaganda and morality pieces for radical newspapers.[55] Styles of artists Wassily Kandinsky, Fillipo Marinetti, and Hugo Ball show the vast spectrum of ideologies emerging in art as the European continent exploded with strife. Kandinsky's abstract symphonies of colors based upon egoistic choice and the harsh noise and antiwar, anti-bourgeois, Marinetti's futurist doctrine and anti-art antics of Hugo Ball show just how complicated the art world had become. In a fourth arena sat the occultists.

In the early 1890s in Paris, Josephin Peladan, a societal reformist, novelist, and student of alchemy and occultism, believed man's salvation in the turbulent times in which he lived could be resolved through the use of spiritualism and the seeking of absolute truths through language and metaphorical imaging. His book *Art as a Religion* outlines his manifesto, which claims artists were selected individuals comparable to priests who could bring a small part of the divine into the sphere of every masterpiece. In composing a piece, a ray of divinity would descend upon an altar. He established a salon, Mystic Order of the Rose +Croix, for painters, writers, and musicians, which

Painting as Social Commentary **229**

organized an annual exhibition in Paris.[56] Objects chosen for display were to be representative of Peladan's Rosicrucian religious order. An essential element of Rosicrucianism was theosophy, a belief that humans can establish direct contact with spiritual elements "through their intuition, meditation, or other transcending normal human consciousness."[57] The order defines itself today as "A community of philosophers who study Natural Laws to live in harmony with them" and provides for the study of the mysteries of birth and death, the illusory nature of time and space, awakening of the psychic consciousness, cosmic consciousness, vowel sounds and mantras, creative visualization, intuition, metaphysical healing, and spiritual alchemy.[58] "Symbolist art shifted the emphasis from direct representation of nature to the world of imagination. These individuals wanted to replace pragmatic reality with visions, dreams, imagined commotions, and spiritual awakenings on canvas."[59] Peleadan believed he could see and hear "at the greatest distances," a talent which could be "useful in controlling enemy councils and suppressing espionage."[60] Critics labeled their pieces "creepy."[61]

In Great Britain, Austin Osman Spare arose as a preeminent occult artist.[62] Occultism was allied with but not the same as Peleadan's symbolist view. In Occultism, boundaries were not as broad or religiously oriented as those found in Peleadan's teachings. There is also no known direct tie between Peleadan and Spare. Instead, creativity was directly linked to the mysterious supernatural veiled, eerie psychic unknown. The shock factor of his heavily symbolic and grotesque art afforded him a short time as a celebrity. An *Art Journal* piece from 1907 said about Spare, "Few people in London interested in art had not heard the name."[63] Due to the stylistic intricacies of his draughts and paintings, he was imprecisely likened to German printmaker Albrecht Durer, the High Renaissance youthful successes of Michelangelo, and Golden Age Dutch painter Rembrandt's printmaking.[64]

Typical with most occultists, Spare told stories of his otherworldly life, which he said began as a young man. One pivotal message he claimed to be true was that as a High Anglican schoolboy, he had been seduced by an elderly woman known as Witch Patterson, "who claimed descent from the 17th century Salem, Massachusetts, witches and taught him magic."[65] It is unknown if Patterson existed with enough inconsistencies in the tale, leading to the belief that Spare may have made her up.[66] In many ways, his story of Patterson resembles that of the theosophist and spiritual medium Madame Blavatsky. Pinpointing her true background has not been successful. Some reports she claimed were that she had visited Tibetan Spiritualists and visited Egypt and the Middle East. Other claims associate her with an illegitimate child and a hawker with a circus. Witch Patterson was to have been an accurate fortune teller, was old and unattractive, had a limited vocabulary, and was uneducated. Spare said the witch could externalize her thoughts and transform herself into a youthful beauty. She took him to nocturnal

230 Women and War

gatherings of witches, not in real-time but in metaphysical space. On initiating him into a cult, she bestowed on Spare the name "Zos," Osman referred to her as his witch mother.[67] Blatsky died when Spare was five, and her Theosophical Society in London was active during his lifetime. He likely knew of the group. Spare developed his belief system around the Witch Patterson tale eventually rejecting conventional occultism in favor of the grotesque and semi-human spiritual world.[68] Witchcraft, magic, and trances became primary influencers in his artwork.

Spare's manifesto can be found combined in his numerous books, which included *The Book of Pleasure, The Book of Automatic Drawing, The Focus of Life, Automatic Drawing, The Book of Satyrs, The Valley of Fear, The Book of Ugly Ecstasy,* and *Ethos.* Among the most consistent ideology in his written materials was the concept of Zos which was "a basic theory that all dreams or desires, all wishes or beliefs, anything in fact which a person nurtures in their innermost being may be called forth in the flesh as a living truth by a particular method of magical evocation."[69] This he named atavistic resurgence or the primal urges toward the union with witchcraft, sorcery, and magic. "Any wish may be given symbolic form, but the form should bear no pictorial approximation to the particular desire in question."[70] The occultist went on to become an official war artist and was conscripted in 1917 as a medical orderly into the Royal Army Medical Corps but would not see action as his service played out in London.[71] In this capacity, he would come face to face with two powerful suffragist women running the Endell Street Army Hospital, Drs. Flora Murray and Louisa Garrett Anderson.

Occultist Austin Osman Spare, Realist Francis Dodd, and the War Propaganda Bureau

Austin Osman Spare was born in 1886, attended the Lambeth School of Art and the Royal College of Art (RAC), and was talented enough as a young teenager when his exhibit "Black and White Drawings" appeared at the Royal Academy of Art (RA), and he received a scholarship to study drafting there. A portrait of Spare as a young man shows a head of dark prolific hair atop a pleasant face, arms casually crossed over a woolen coat with an unbuttoned cotton shirt poking out of the top of a tightly cinched vest. In later photos, as an older man, he seems a completely changed person with his wild, Einsteinesque intensity, paintbrush at the ready, and not an individual living a relaxed or happy life. He drifted in and out of poverty for much of his career. Early in his art education, his technique combined art nouveau and esoteric symbolism to create sexual imagery and monster-like beings. In a local media interview with the protégé about his future, Osman stated that his primary purpose was to create his own religion.[72] *The Daily Chronicle* review of his art was not flattering, citing his "conceptions of men and things were weird in the extreme; his figures have faces that suggest nightmares, and all the terrors of Dante's *Inferno*."[73] One critic called his art too strong a medicine for the average man.[74] Others saw his heavily symbolic and grotesque art as extraordinary and the product of a genius.

Osman, and artistically talented suffragette, Sylvia Pankhurst found themselves in the same circles, and they became strong acquaintances, which was not surprising, as she and Spare had distinctive world views about the state of society and their placement within it.[75] Pankhurst attended the Manchester School of Art, leaving in 1902 and moving on to the RAC in London from 1904 to 1906. After marrying in 1911, Spare and his wife, a vaguely known actress and prostitute with one child, Eily Gertrude Shaw, became neighbors to Sylvia in the London suburb of Golders Green, which was becoming a growing settlement for Jewish families and businesses. He would construct several drawings and paintings of Eily. As with her likeness, nearly all females he depicted had an air of languishing, listlessness, droopiness, and melancholy. Spare though, could produce a chameleonic range of output. This is shown in the draftsman-like detail of his exquisite stylizations of film stars, pastel portraits of locals in his neighborhood, satirized or surrealist images of his sitters, and imagined bizarre renderings of angels and demons from the netherworld. The marriage would not remain intact; Eily did not like any of his male friends and she was too materialistic for him. They did not divorce, with Eily moving on to another partner.[76]

At 18, Osman published his first book of spells and incantations – a grimoire of black magic entitled *Earth Inferno*, one of many he wrote up until the beginning of World War II. *Earth Inferno* reacted to the negative publicity he received regarding submitting his two occult drawings at the Royal Academy during the summer show of 1904. Spare printed 265 numbered and signed copies. Sylvia Pankhurst was asked by the younger female student body to serve as a go-between to purchase the book since the content was not acceptable in gentile society, and many young women were uncomfortable with creating an open social relationship with Spare.[77]

The book was a mix of poems, commentary on decorative paintings, and his first statements on orphic principles. The prose exhibited is that of an automatic writer, allowing language, drawings, and images to be produced by a spiritual, occult, or subconscious agency rather than a prescribed conscious intention.[78] Stories, language, and illustrations unfolded clairvoyantly in alignment with the absurdity of the Dadaist's sound poems and nonsensical words. Pankhurst was also a language activist who joined the craze to create a single global linguistic formula. The idea, known as interlingua, held that an artificial language could be made that, once implanted into a machine, could be converted in such a way as to draw out distinctions among all dialects so that they could be transformed into an understandable format by everyone.[79]

232 Women and War

These activists believed that language lexicon should originate from the same family of words to avoid confusion and that the only alphabet tolerated would be Latin. Further, every word in the world should be placed in a standard dictionary; all languages would be systematized and simplified into one global typology, and the grammatical gender of inanimate objects would be eliminated. The difference between Pankhurst and Spare was that the former saw language as a formula of global socialist expression for the masses, and the latter saw language as emerging as needed from an abstruse realm. Sylvia, the socialist, valued the concept of a Marxist-centered linguistic community, and Spare valued the anarchist approach, placing the individualization of each person's syntax above the larger community.[80]

Spare's occultist practices would eventually override what society and critics expected of him, that he had the potential to become the next Michelangelo. By 1921, he had cast off the West End London Gallery scene due to his distaste for its poseurs and the financial favoritisms by galleries of certain socially positioned artists over others. He swapped any semblance of normalcy in his professional relationships by creating an eclectic inner circle of patrons, authors, and professionals. His self-selected peers were as confused and complex as his art.[81] There were Kenneth and Steffi Grant, art connoisseurs and friends; Frank Letchford, an occultist, his biographer; BBC executive Dennis Bardens; art nouveau designer Pickford Waller; journalist, and drama critic Hannen Swaffer; author and editor Frederic Carter; and New Zealand Rhodes scholar Dr. James Bertram.[82] Spare's art sold only occasionally as he began to refuse to use the gallery middlemen to hawk his work, cutting off any third-party intervention required of the professional artists if they wanted to live off their talent. In the later part of his life, well after his role in World War I in the War Arts Program of Britain, anyone interested in his creations had to come to his flat to make a purchase where he would ask only for nominal cash amounts.

War art programs

Early in the war, France and Germany opened official programs authorizing artists to visit the front. In Germany, those selected were allowed to connect with press units.[83] In France, a purchasing scheme was established for paintings and drawings completed by unofficial artists who could ally themselves with military troop movements. At first, serving soldiers were not given the latitude to be released from their duty to make art. This cadre of painters was mainly comprised of older men not associated with the modern styles of the Cubists, Fauvists, and other offshoot groups from Europe.[84] One exception was when French Les Nabis abstract and symbolist artists and Cubists from Western Europe were allowed to visit the German front with official permits and support from private or semi-private funds to paint and draw.[85] At the outbreak of the war in Britain, radical politician Charles Masterman was tasked to oversee Wellington House, where the British Propaganda Bureau was located. Under the program, 40-year-old lithographer Muirhead Bone, known for his etchings and dry points, was enlisted as the first official war artist in the United Kingdom with a salary of 500 pounds and an honorary military commission of second lieutenant.[86]

Bone had no experience as a combatant and wilted emotionally at his first exposure to battle. From then on, he could not return to the Western Front to paint and draw. His were generational-style war paintings. As with older artists of the period, he focused on realistic scenes of after-battle ruins, encampments, troops resting or performing everyday tasks, landscapes, and buildings. At one point, Bone was requested to turn his attention to making a pictorial record of military commanders in portraiture. Since this was not where his talents were strongest, he withdrew and recommended his 42-year-old brother-in-law, Francis Edgar Dodd, a draftsman, painter, and printmaker trained at the Glasgow School of Art, to complete the task. During his time as a war artist, Dodd completed thirty portraits of generals of the British Army and admirals of the British Navy and was positively reviewed for his ability to present truthful impressions of military leadership.

One of the more popular themes of World War I paintings was the replication of the lives and experiences of orderlies and doctors in the British Medical Corps. A characteristic illustration of this type is found in *A Royal Army Medical Corps Bearer Supplying Water to the Front Line* by Haydan Reynolds Mackey.[87] Haydan was officially assigned as an artist with the Royal Army Medical Corps on the Western Front and had trained at the Slade School of Art in London. The painting's color is simple: red, brown, and flesh tones, with the water bearer at a three-quarter turn toward the viewer painted from just below the shoulders. He wears a metal helmet, khaki uniform, and red cross armband and holds a tin water container. Mackey's repertoire of paintings included the women's voluntary aid detachment service, the British Red Cross, dressing stations, and soldier's canteens. Other subjects from his World War I compositions embodied the aftermath of the battle at Epehy, Ypres, and Nurlu, and more figurative pieces representing the impact and pathos of war on civilians and prisoners and domestic scenes from the Homefront. Artists like Mackey and Dodd were acclaimed for their ability to depict life during the conflict in a faithful manner. Their art world was staid, old-school realism, not that of the younger generation's angry industrialism, color spiritualism, and occultist flavor.

Trench fighting and military action as subjects of war art would appear more readily after the British propaganda unit was reorganized in early 1917 into the Department of Information. Baron Beaverbrook became its minister and immediately established a commemorative artwork commissioning program.[88] Artists were compensated for making a single canvas or were

234 Women and War

employed full-time for 10 out of 12 months of the year. Recruitment swelled with the entrance of young avant-garde, allegorical, pacifist-leaning artists, and salaries were paid through the civil service system, with a few receiving military ranks.[89] All the material became the foundation for the collection housed at the Tate Gallery, where Francis Dodd became its trustee in 1929. The more youthful war art matched the modern war's desolation caused by the contemporary killing machines, its ghastliness of massive death, and the desire to produce graphic scenes from the front. Back home, the public reveled in these artists' innovative efforts.

In 1917, Britain passed the Military Service Act III, conscripting all men previously rejected for service on medical grounds. Osman Spare, now 27, was obligated to join the Royal Army Medical Corps. His first assignment was to create images of the depot at the large seaside town on the Irish Sea coast, where he was ordered to serve as a medical orderly in the tetanus vaccine clinic. His uncleanliness resulted in numerous verbal reprimands, and he began complaining about part of his pay being set aside for a morale-driven sports fund. The Army, fatigued by his lackadaisical attitude, reassigned him to King George's Hospital Barracks at Stamford Street in London with the rank of Acting Staff Sergeant. Spare was told to illustrate the war with a group of artists physically situated in a studio built for them between South Kensington and Fulham. At the workspace, the artists, doubling as models, added military accouterments to their clothing and bandaged themselves.[90] His scenes of medical care on the front suggest a closer affinity to war than what his behind-the-lines experiences would seem to have offered. They are lifelike and poignant. Spare was ordered to move on to become the artistic record maker at the all-suffragette military hospital in London.

The Edinburgh Seven

If a female wished to practice medicine and serve as a medical doctor and not a nurse in alliance with a role in the military, they first had to overcome the idea that women were not suited to the medical sciences. Those who desired to study medicine were met with hatred and hostility by most male doctors. In many countries, they were barred legislatively from attending medical school. With these types of logjams and disenfranchisement facing women, it is unsurprising that the first military doctors to integrate into the services had been ardent suffragists and suffragettes.

To understand what it was like for a woman to try to earn a medical degree, the story of the Edinburgh Seven is enlightening.[91] After the University Court rejected applicant Sophia Jex-Blake's application to study medicine with the excuse that they could not make the necessary physical arrangements in the interest of only one lady, she advertised in national newspapers to have other women join her in her fight to seek a medical degree.

Six stepped forward; Isabel Thorne, Edith Pechey, Matilda Chaplin, Helen Evans, Mary Anderson Marshall, and Emily Bovell became the first women to matriculate in medicine in the UK when they enrolled together in 1869.

Jex Blake's sense of sarcasm can be seen in naming the group after the 476 BC Greek play *Seven Against Thebes*. It is easy to see the linkages related to the women's plight and the trilogy by the ancient dramatist Aeschylus. The play contains rich dialogues between the citizens of Thebes and their king, Eteocles, who is threatened by a hostile army divided among seven captains who stand at his city gates. Thematic discussions in the play included an inability among competitors to settle disputes, retaliation against each other, and a failure to share power. Aeschylus' messages mirrored the women's endurance of the vehemence of academics against them in grading their projects and blocking their classroom participation. They were charged exorbitant prices for attendance, and those with administrative powers obstructed them from receiving academic prizes when they earned them. All were denied the correct certificates for their completed academic efforts. They were given bogus credits through the made-up category of "ladies matriculation" rather than receiving regular grades. The term was preposterous and a blatant attempt to relegate them to a category below the male students which was laughable since they had taken the same classes as the men. Jex-Blake realized the credits were useless and called them strawberry jam labels. This episode, demeaning women's academic prowess, gained national attention, with some writers publicly supporting them.

There were numerous derogatory and defaming declarations about female students. One of their detractors noted that women seeking medical careers might be basely inclined because of their interface with nude male bodies. Another claimed they were better off as midwives, not doctors. Several professors turned entirely away from teaching them. Male students were offensive and insolent, slamming doors in their faces, taking up their seats, and horse-laughing when they approached classroom doors, attempted to participate in lecture halls, or added their ideas to discussions. One of the women's doorbells was wrenched from her entry, smoke was blown into their faces, and they were followed in the streets with foul epithets such as "whore" shouted at them. As they came to take their anatomy exam on a late afternoon in the fall of 1870, all seven were blocked by several hundred men who pelted them with rubbish, mud, and verbal insults. Declared in newspapers as the Surgeon's Hall Riot, the event elicited a turning point toward greater acceptance of their desire to become doctors when a small group of male student escorts arose from the fray and physically protected them for the remainder of their time on campus. Former Edinburgh student Charles Darwin also wrote in support of their study for a medical degree.

Once they completed their educations, the seven were prevented from graduating or qualifying as doctors, and all were refused the required clinical

236 Women and War

instruction within the school's infirmary. Matilda Chaplain was barred from teaching in higher branches of medicine, but a legal intervention on her behalf resulted in her gaining high honors in anatomy and surgery in 1871. In 1872, the courts upheld the university's right to deny women their degrees noting they should not have been admitted in the first place. Five of the seven women, Bovell, Chaplin, Jex-Blake, Marshall, and Pechy, left Britain and earned their MDs in Bern and Paris.

Drs. Flora Murray and Louisa Garrett Anderson

Flora Murray completed her medical training in Durham, Scotland, receiving an MD in 1905, and Anderson qualified at the London School of Medicine in 1900. Louisa was the daughter of medical pioneer Elizabeth Garrett Anderson and the niece of Millicent Fawcett, the head of the non-militant equal rights movement organization NUWSS. Flora was the daughter of a Royal Navy Captain; Louisa's father was a co-owner of the Orient Steamship Company. Her mother, Elizabeth, was the first woman to gain medical credentials and practice in Britain and opened a medical school for women. Both Louisa and Flora were avowed suffragettes and became lifelong companions. Murray joined the NUWWS as a suffragist, and 1908 shifted her allegiance as 1 of 140 women who became long-term participants in the militant Women's Social and Political Union organized by Emmeline Pankhurst.

After joining Pankhurst's WSPU campaign, Anderson participated in the large-scale smashing of shop windows, for which she was charged with a six-week stay in Holloway prison. Authorities, believing Louisa would attempt a hunger strike and fearful of her aunt's and mother's political connections, released her from jail at the four-week mark. Writing to her mother from prison, Anderson stated she was glad and proud of her actions, which she believed were necessary to win the women's rights cause.[92] Flora was selected to oversee Emmeline's recovery after she became ill from hunger strikes and was force-fed by jail guards and doctors. Anderson also became embroiled in a libel suit after taking to task prison doctors who had sedated women before force-feeding them. The pair were involved in the recovery of WSPU antagonists at Notting Hill Nursing Home who had suffered wounds during their militant activities.

Knowing the British Army would reject their idea to serve as medical doctors when the war started, Murray and Anderson approached the French Red Cross to submit their credentials. The French were empathetic, but they did not support them at first. With 2500 dollars of funding from wealthy suffragettes and eventual sponsorship from the French Army, the doctors set up a women's hospital corps at the Claridge Hotel in Paris on the Champs Elysée.[93] Louisa's mother, Elizabeth, then 80 years old, saw the corps off at the docks. Turning to her daughter, she pronounced, "If you go, and if you succeed, you will put your cause forward a hundred years." Wistfully watching as her daughter led the packing on the ship, she lamented, "Twenty

Painting as Social Commentary **237**

years younger, and I would have taken them myself."[94] Louisa wrote to her mother on the train trip to Paris, "This is just what you would have done at my age. I hope I can do it half as well as you would." As their mission started in France, Elizabeth received a letter from Louisa.

> After years of unpopularity over the suffrage, it is very exhilarating to be on top of the wave, helped and approved by everyone, except perhaps the English War Office, while all the time we are doing suffrage work—or woman's work—in another form...I wish the whole organization for the care of the wounded...could be put into the hand of women...It is merely a matter of organization, common sense, attention to detail, and a determination to avoid unnecessary suffering and loss of life.[95]

The British and French press questioned the women as the unit's vocation became known. Murray described one interview in her autobiography when a reporter asked her in disbelief if the women were operating and not the men. When she replied in the affirmative, the press was unconvinced and demanded to see them in action in the operating theater as proof of their abilities. Success in France meant the doctors came to the attention of the Surgeon General of the British Army, who asked that they transfer to British soil and establish a 500-bed military hospital for the war wounded near Covent Garden in central London.

Endell Hospital was conspicuously and intentionally run under the suffragette banner of "Deeds, not Words." Every person in the unit was either a suffragist or a suffragette. They all wore the suffragettes' purple, white, and green pins on their uniform lapels.[96] Among the hospital's prominent visitors was WPSU president Emmeline Pankhurst. Flora related a story about Pankhurst. During the suffragette leader's stopover at Christmas, a patient declared to her, "I would rather have seen that lady (Pankhurst) than the Queen who came to visit the other day. I do declare to you, lady, that this war has shown me that the 'spear' of women is something different to which I thought it had been."[97] Murray and Anderson left no ambiguity about their aims in creating the Endell program. They explicitly linked their production with their equal rights, aspirations, and values. It was expected that the women under their charge not only be high-caliber medical professionals but also contemplate their role in broader society as future citizens. One hospital employee revealed that Murray and Anderson were

> not willing to be identified as a women's operation or confused with other hospitals run by non-professional women. Indeed, the staff was expected to excel at their work. We had this drilled into us: you have not only got to do a good job, but you must do a superior job. What would be accepted by a man will not be accepted by a woman. You must do better.[98]

In a stunning reversal of the Army's belief system, the Endell Street Corps received the pay and benefits of military grades. Murray and Anderson were promoted to Lieutenant and Lieutenant Colonel. However, these ranks were deemed unofficial, and no woman was allowed to command a man. Anderson served as the doctor in charge and chief surgeon, and Murray as the chief of medicine. Many philosophies guiding the hospital were ahead of their time. Staff believed that the psychological techniques for the wounded mind had direct links to the wounded body. Rooms were decorated with fresh flowers and bright quilts. There was an extensive library and lectures for the patients. Visitations, fresh air, reading hours, and writing letters for the convalescents were encouraged as part of a formula for healing. Flora Anderson described the atmosphere they were attempting to perpetuate, "I like still more the opportunity of being a little good to these bruised men. Their minds are full of horrors, and it is a help to them to come into a soothing atmosphere with decent food and soft beds and our gentle, merry young, orderly girls who feed them with cigarettes and write to their mothers and read to them."[99]

The hospital team pioneered an antiseptic ointment for wounds that aided in preventing amputations. Its doctors were among the first women to publish important medical findings in peer-reviewed British medical journals. Studies were conducted on clinical trials of anaerobic infection, antiserums, and gas gangrene. Twenty-six thousand troops passed through Endell over five years, and over 7000 operations were performed. The hospital closed in 1919, and unbelievably, medical schools returned to barring female students again shortly after that. Murray died of cancer at the age of 54. Anderson joined the conservative party and became a justice of the peace and mayor of Aldeburgh, Suffolk. During World War II, she was employed on the surgical staff of Elizabeth Garrett Anderson Hospital and died of a malignant disease in 1943. The families of the two women ensured they were buried next to each other in the Holy Trinity Churchyard at Buckinghamshire, England.

The painting: Austin Osman Spare and Francis Dodd

Osman Spare was hired by the Women's Work Committee and Women's Hospital Corps to create a record of women's war efforts. The items were to be shown at The Nations War Paintings and Other Records exhibition in 1919 at the Royal Academy of Arts. He began the job by painting portraits of socially prominent women such as Dame Crowdy, the Principal Commandant of Voluntary Aid Detachments (VAD) in Belgium and France. Dame Crowdy was stunned and horrified at the final product Spare offered her and refused to accept the piece. Compared to photographs of Dame Crowdy, Spare's pastel drawing is reasonably accurate regarding facial structure. Crowley disliked the piece because she was made to look like a pouty, slightly ethereal adolescent instead of the educated and politically astute Principal Commandant of the VAD.

Painting as Social Commentary **239**

FIGURE 8.2   Dame Rachel Crowdy, Principal Commander of the VAD by Austin Osman Spare.

© Public domain. File: Dame Rachel Crowdy, the Principal Commander of the VADs (Art. IWM ART 3205).jpg – Wikimedia Commons.

Spare was given a follow-up assignment to construct a tribute to the efforts carried out by the women at Endell Street Hospital. Several pastel sketches were made of the nursing staff. The artist was also ordered to create an active portrait scene depicting the doctors in the operating sphere. Upon seeing his rendition of their profession, Flora Murray notified medical officer Army Lieutenant Colonel Frederick Brereton, a war hero and later commissioned author of children's books about heroic war deeds, that the image needed to be destroyed. Spare's choice of pastels over paint, the setting he portrayed, and the concentration on the draping of the women's hospital garb gave it a "Pre-Raphaelite doominess."[100] Murray was disgusted by the homogonous

FIGURE 8.3   Pastel image of a nurse in indoor uniform at Endell Hospital drawn by Austin Osman Spare. A nurse in a white lab coat.

© Public domain. HMSO has declared that the expiry of Crown Copyrights applies worldwide. File: A Nursing Orderly (indoor) – Endell Street Military Hospital, London Art.IWMART2853.jpg – Wikimedia Commons.

ethereal qualities and the youthful slimness of the women and believed her staff looked like schoolgirls playacting in a drama.[101]

The doctor was aghast at what was portrayed in the scene's background in the operation room. There was a haphazard scattering of a couch, a kneeling nurse, a discarded splint, and a set of unkempt metal drums for holding sterilized bandages and instruments. There was no sense of a wartime operating theater's high-tech equipment, rigid cleanliness, solemnness, concentration, or teamwork.[102]

Lieutenant Colonel Brereton disregarded Murray's request to delete the material from the exhibition. Dr. Murray, in turn, contacted the head of the

Painting as Social Commentary 241

FIGURE 8.4 Pastel drawing of a nurse at Endell Street in outdoor uniform drawn by Austin Osman Spare.

© Public domain. HMSO. File: A Nursing Orderly (Outdoors), Endell Street Military Hospital, London (Art. IWM ART 2854).jpg – Wikimedia Commons.

women's section of the Imperial War Museum, who was the British activist and suffragist Lady Florence Priscilla Norman, and expressed her concerns. Lady Norman was married to Sir Henry Norman, 1st Baronet, a liberal politician who was an active member of the Liberal Women's Suffrage Union and the Women's Liberal Federation. In her letter to Dame Norman, Flora wrote that Spare's art was "a misrepresentation of the work of professional women. It is full of errors that, though they may not strike the layperson, make it an object of ridicule to all those with some professional knowledge…We would rather have no record of our work than a false record, and Dr. Garrett Anderson and I must earnestly ask you to do all you can to have this picture destroyed…the credit of women surgeons is at stake."[103]

Lady Norman took up the cause and wrote to Spare, telling him the doctors would rather not have the object than present it at the upcoming *Great Victory Exhibition* at Crystal Palace. She voiced her concern in writing that what he had composed "Looks ludicrous to the technical mind" and requested he at least remove the out-of-place items strewn in the background as

242 Women and War

a middle-of-the-road resolution. To do this would have meant Spare would have had to delete the entire bottom half of the piece and leave only the heads of the women. Angry, Spare retorted, "I *cannot* consent to the mutilation of my picture...I actually saw at Endell Street *everything* I have put into my picture." Then, he placed a stake in the ground regarding the occultist and avant-garde artist community of which he was a part when he pronounced,

> Doubtless many soldiers will feel that their work in the Great War has been made to appear "ludicrous" by certain *modern* artists, but that is no reason for banning such works from the honorable positions they will receive in the Imperial War Museum.[104]

One of Spare's friends recalled that the attack disillusioned the occultist so much that the women's forces and The Red Cross had broken his artistic voice.[105]

Dr. Murray's request eventually won out in the confrontation, and portraitist Francis Dodd stepped in under a separate commission to complete the piece. Dodd was the antithesis of Spare. He was a realistic old-school etcher and landscapist, described as having the ability to represent portraits in a manner of "telling exactly what everyone wishes to know about such figures," with each rendering "soliciting the dignity of the frame."[106] The freshly appointed artist was given access to the Elizabeth Garrett War Hospital, and he sat, making drawings of the surgical theater to take back to his studio. He used photography of women to compose their faces and other scenes of women from World War I, laboring in field hospitals to create his final scene. Much effort was spent projecting professionalism, leaving the viewer no doubt that this surgical team knew what it was doing.[107] Dodd said one critic "had captured the quintessential spirit of Endell Street."[108] Drs. Anderson and Murray were pleased with the outcome, believing Dodd had created a scene for posterity that future generations of female medical doctors would appreciate. At the war's end, Murray and Anderson continued in private practice and were awarded the Order of the British Empire at a ceremony in Buckingham Palace. The next global conflict would not arise until the early 1940s with the outbreak of World War II. Women's resilience would be tested mightily again. Female medical corps personnel were captured and served as prisoners of war in the Pacific Theater, and one US Air Force nurse was interned by the German Luftwaffe in Europe.

Notes

1 James M. Thompson (ed). "Introduction." In *Twentieth Century Theories of Art*, xi–xii. McGill-Queen's University Press, 1990. http://www.jstor.org/stable/j.ctt1cd0kz3.4.

2 G. Julian Moore. "Meissonier and the Salon Julian." *Fortnightly Review, May 1865–June 1934* 48, no. 283 (1890). ProQuest.

Painting as Social Commentary **243**

"Paris Salons (1673-Present)" Art Institute of Chicago Paris Salons (1673–present) | The Art Institute of Chicago (artic.edu).

The History of the Academia de San Luca, c. 1590–1635: Documents from the *Archivio di Stato di Roma*, National Gallery of Art, Intro (nga.gov).

Alisa Luxenberg, "Originality and Freedom: The 1863 Reforms to the École des Beaux-Arts and the Involvement of Léon Bonnat." *Nineteenth-Century Art Worldwide* 16, no. 2 (Autumn 2017), https://doi.org/10.29411/ncaw.2017.16.2.3.

"A Brief History of the RA," Royal Academy of Arts, A brief history of the RA | Royal Academy of Arts.

"History, Slade School of Fine Art," History • Slade School of Fine Art (ucl. ac.uk).

3 Arthur Wesley Dow. "Modernism in Art." *The American Magazine of Art* 8, no. 3 (1917): 113–16. http://www.jstor.org/stable/23934265.

4 A. Clutton-Brock. "The Post-Impressionists." *The Burlington Magazine for Connoisseurs* 18, no. 94 (1911): 216–19. http://www.jstor.org/stable/858608.

Vincent van Gogh, Wassily Kandinsky, Juan Gris, Paul Klee, Fernand Léger, Piet Mondrian, Joan Miró, et al. "Statements and Documents: Artists on Art and Reality, on Their Work, and on Values." *Daedalus* 89, no. 1 (1960): 79–126. http://www.jstor.org/stable/20026551.

5 Edward M. Levine. "Abstract Expressionism: The Mystical Experience." *Art Journal* 31, no. 1 (1971): 22–25. https://doi.org/10.2307/775629.

6 Op. cit. Dow.

See Alfred H. Barr, Jr. *Cubism and Abstract Art, Painting, Sculpture, Constructions, Photography, Architecture, Industrial Art, Theater, Films, Posters, Typography*. The Museum of Modern Art, NY Graphic Society, Boston. 1936.

"Past Exhibition from Fauvism to Surrealism. Masterpieces from the *Musee d'Art Moderne de Paris* 2-11-2022-05-22-2022," Guggenheim Bilboa, from Fauvism to Surrealism. Masterpieces from the Musée d'Art Moderne de Paris | Guggenheim Museum Bilbao (guggenheim-bilbao.eus).

Helene LeRoy (Contributor). Geaninne Gutierrez-Guimaraes (Contributor), La Fabrica, Madrid, Oct. 18, 2022.

7 Johanna E. Vondeling. "The Manifest Professional: Manifestos and Modernist Legitimation." *College Literature* 27, no. 2 (2000): 127–45. http://www.jstor.org/stable/25112518.

Marjorie Perloff. "'Violence and Precision': The Manifesto as Art Form." *Chicago Review* 34, no. 2 (1984): 65–101. https://doi.org/10.2307/25305249.

8 Luca Somigli. "Strategies of Legitimation: The Manifesto from Politics to Aesthetics." In *Legitimizing the Artist: Manifesto Writing and European Modernism 1885-1915*, 29–92. University of Toronto Press, 2003. http://www.jstor.org/stable/10.3138/j.ctt130jvhd.5.

9 Filippo Tommaso Marinetti. "The Futurist Manifesto," Microsoft Word – manifesto_futurista.doc (societyforasianart.org).

10 Shira Wolfe. "Art Movement: Futurism-Celebration of Movement," *Artland Magazine*, n.d. Art Movement: Futurism – Celebration of Movement (artland. com).

11 Ibid. Maifesto Marinetti.

12 Words of F. T. Marinetti, 1909, as quoted from Harriet Baker.

13 John H. Hanson. "The Aesthetics of Futurism." *The Comparatist* 7 (1983): 19–28. http://www.jstor.org/stable/44366696.

14 Wassily Kandinsky. *On the Spiritual in Art (Uber das Geisteg in der Kunst)*. Munich: R Piper & Company Verlag, 1912.

15 "Der Blaue Reiter (The Blue Rider)," MOMA, NY. Der Blaue Reiter (The Blue Rider) | MoMA.
16 Op. cit. Kandinsky and Marc.
17 Alexander Griffith Winton. "The Bauhaus, 1919-1933," Helbrunn Timeline of Art History Essays, The Met, The Bauhaus, 1919–1933 | Essay | The Metropolitan Museum of Art | Heilbrunn Timeline of Art History (metmuseum.org).
18 Jack Pritchard. "Gropius, The Bauhaus And The Future." *Journal of the Royal Society of Arts* 117, no. 5150 (1969): 75–94. http://www.jstor.org/stable/41370286.
19 The Art Story Franz Marc Paintings, Bio, Ideas | TheArtStory.
20 John F. Moffitt. "'Fighting Forms: The Fate of the Animals.' The Occultist Origins of Franz Marc's 'Farbentheorie.'" *Artibus et Historiae* 6, no. 12 (1985): 107–26. https://doi.org/10.2307/1483239.
21 "The Mystical modernism of Franz Marc, whose art was a 'bridge into the spirit world," Christie's 3-feb 2022, The mystical Modernism of Franz Marc, whose art was a 'bridge into the spirit world' | Christie's (christies.com).
22 Ibid. Mystical Modernism.
23 Ibid. The Art Story.
24 Mark Dober. "Franz Marc: Utopia Hopes for Art and the Great War," *Overland*, 23 April 2013.
25 Op. cit. Mystical Modernism.
26 For a concise summary of artistic exchanges during World War I, see Sue Malvern, "Art, The Nature of the First World War put an end to traditions for battle painting," 10 November 2016. Art | International Encyclopedia of the First World War (WW1) (1914-1918-online.net).
27 "William and Judith Cousins Ruben, *Picasso and Braque Pioneering Cubism*, New York: The Museum of Modern Art, 1ˢᵗ ed. Jan. 1, 1989.
28 Michael Brenson. "Picasso and Braque, Brothers in Cubism." *The New York Times*, Sept. 22, 1989, Picasso and Braque, Brothers in Cubism – The New York Times (nytimes.com).
  Patricia Leighten. "Revising Cubism." *Art Journal* 47, no. 4 (1988): 269–76. https://doi.org/10.2307/776977.
29 SUSTL Digital Gateway Image Collections and Exhibitions Andre Derain. World War I and its Effects on Expressionist Aesthetic Direction WUSTL Digital Gateway Image Collections & Exhibitions.
30 Ginny A. Roth. "National Library of Medicine bog, Max Beckman: The Faces of World War I," April 12, 2018, Max Beckmann: The Faces of World War I – Circulating Now from the NLM Historical Collections (nih.gov).
31 Pierre Cabanne, and Marcel Duchamp. "INTERVIEW: Marcel Duchamp." *The American Scholar* 40, no. 2 (1971): 273–83. http://www.jstor.org/stable/41209846.
  Gordon Hughes. "Envisioning Abstraction: The Simultaneity of Robert Delaunay's 'First Disk.'" *The Art Bulletin* 89, no. 2 (2007): 306–32. http://www.jstor.org/stable/25067319.
  Mark Antliff. "Cubism, Futurism, Anarchism: The 'Aestheticism' of the 'Action d'art' Group, 1906–1920." *Oxford Art Journal* 21, no. 2 (1998): 99–120. http://www.jstor.org/stable/1360616.
  Yve-Alain Bois, and Thomas Repensek. "Francis Picabia: From Dada to Pétain." *October* 30 (1984): 121–27. https://doi.org/10.2307/778301.
32 D. W. Zaidel. "Braque and Kokoschka: Brain Tissue Injury and Preservation of Artistic Skill." *Behav Sci* (Basel) 7, no. 3 (2017 Aug. 19): 56. https://doi.org/10.3390/bs7030056.
33 J. Fiona Ragheb. "Albert Gleizes Portrait of a Military Doctor," Guggenheim, Albert Gleizes | Portrait of a Military Doctor | The Guggenheim Museums and

Foundation Albert Gleizes | Portrait of a Military Doctor | The Guggenheim Museums and Foundation.

34 Liane Hansen. "A Wartime Matisse Full of Pain and Beauty," NPR 88.5 nepm, June 13, 2010, A Wartime Matisse Full of Pain and Beauty: NPR.

35 Effie Rentzou. "Messy Internationalism: Dada, Anarchism, and Picabia's Group Portraits." In *Concepts of the World: The French Avant-Garde and the Idea of the International, 1910–1940*, 97–152. Northwestern University Press, 2022. https://doi.org/10.2307/j.ctv2rcnqh7.7.

36 "Die Brucke (The Bridge). Story of Expressionism, Leicester's German Expressionist Collection," Die Brücke (The Bridge) – Leicester's German Expressionist Collection (germanexpressionismleicester.org).

37 Edward Lifson. "A Wartiem Matisse Full of Pain and Beauty," June 13, 2010. NPR Weekend Edition Sunday, A Wartime Matisse Full of Pain and Beauty: NPR.

38 Eli Anapur. "Dada Manifesto Explained – Hugo Ball versus Tristan Tzara, Art History," Widewalls, Dec. 17, 2016. DADA Manifesto Explained – Hugo Ball versus Tristan Tzara | Widewalls.

39 Hugo Ball. "The Dada Manifesto, Read at the first public by Dada soiree, Zurich, July 14, 1916," The Anarchist Library, Dada Manifesto (theanarchistlibrary.org). p. 1. Accessed 3/22/2021.

40 Elena Martinique. "Stumbling Across Dada Poetry," December 23, 2016, Widewalls, Stumbling Across DADA Poetry | Widewalls. Accessed 3/19/2021.

41 There are several YouTube items available showing Hugo Ball reciting Dada poetry. Of these, the most complete is Hugo Ball-Six Sound Poems (1916) – YouTube. Accessed 12/27/2023.
    Matthew Wills. "Dada at 100, or I Zimbra! The anti-art movement Dada was born in 1916 in Zurich's Cabaret Voltaire," Nov 11, 2016, JSTOR Daily Art and Art History, DADA at 100, or, I Zimbra! – JSTOR Daily.

42 J. C. Middleton. "'Bolshevism in Art': Dada and Politics." *Texas Studies in Literature and Language* 4, no. 3 (1962): 408–30. http://www.jstor.org/stable/40753524.

43 Quoted from Tate website, 'Fountain', Marcel Duchamp, 1917, replica 1964 | Tate referenced from William Camfield, *Marcel Duchamp: Fountain*, Houston 1989.

44 "Marcel Duchamp Fountain, 1917, Replica 1974," 'Fountain', Marcel Duchamp, 1917, replica 1964 | Tate.

45 Henri-Pierre Roché, 'The Blind Man', *Blindman*, no. 1, 10 Apr. 1917, p. 3.

46 Quoted from Tate website, referencing Francis M. Naumann, *The Recurrent, Haunting Ghost: Essays on the Art, Life and Legacy of Marcel Duchamp*, New York, 2012, pp. 70–81.

47 Jeanne Willett. "Dada and the Great War," arthistoryunstuffed, May 27, 2011. Dada and the Great War | Art History Unstuffed.

48 Jacqueline Lewis. "Hugo Ball: Founder of the Dada Moveent," Mar. 1, 2020, The Collector, Hugo Ball: Founder of The Dada Movement (thecollector.com).

49 Peter Selz. "The Aesthetic Theories of Wassily Kandinsky and Their Relationship to the Origin of Non-Objective Painting." *The Art Bulletin* 39, no. 2 (1957): 127–36. https://doi.org/10.2307/3047696.

50 Roberta Smith. "Kandinsky The Angel in the Architecture." *The New York Times*, Art Review Sept. 17, 2009, The Angel in the Architecture – The New York Times (nytimes.com).
    Debbie Lewer. "Hugo Ball, Iconoclasm and the Origins of Dada in Zurich." *Oxford Art Journal* 32, no. 1 (2009): 17–35. http://www.jstor.org/stable/25650841.

51 Tristan Tzara. *Dada Manifesto 1918*, OCR0001.rtf (upenn.edu).

52 Ibid. Willett.

246 Women and War

53 Sherwin Simmons. "Advertising Seizes Control of Life: Berlin Dada and the Power of Advertising." *Oxford Art Journal* 22, no. 1 (1999): 119–46. http://www.jstor.org/stable/1360686.

54 Information taken from "Bibliography Ball, Hugo 1886–1927." *Encyuclopedia. com* Ball, Hugo (1886–1927) | Encyclopedia.com.

55 Hugo Ball, and Gerhardt Edward Steinke. *THe Life and Work of Hugo Ball (Founder of Dadaism)*, Mouton The Hague paris, 1967.

56 "Mystic Symbolism: The Salon de la Rose + Croix in Paris, 1892–1897," The Guggenheim, Mystical Symbolism: The Salon de la Rose+Croix in Paris, 1892–1897 | The Guggenheim Museums and Foundation.

57 Matthew Wills. "Spiritualism, Science and the Mysterious Madame Blavatsky," JSTOR Daily, Oct. 26, 2016.

58 "Introduction to the Rosicrucian Order," The Rosicrucian Order, AMORC.

59 "Symbolism, Glossary Terms" National Galleries of Scotland, Symbolism | National Galleries of Scotland.

60 Alex Ross, The Occult Roots of Modernism Joséphin Péladan's mystical art exhibitions, in Paris, set the stage for everything from Kandinsky's abstractions to Eliot's "The Waste Land," *The New Yorker*, June 19, 2017. The Occult Roots of Modernism | The New Yorker.

61 Ibid. Ross.

62 See "The Influence of Spiritualism and the Occult on the Modern Art Movement," Phillipsmuseum, The Influence of Spiritualism and the Occult on the Modern Art Movement – YouTube 1:07:29, 2021.

63 Phil Baker. "Austin Osman Spare: Cockney Visionary," Art Review *The Guardian*, Austin Osman Spare: Cockney visionary | Art | The Guardian.

64 Ibid. Baker.

65 "My Favorite Painting: Viktor Wynd," *Country Life* Feb. 17, 2020, My Favourite Painting: Viktor Wynd – Country Life.

66 Ibid. My favorite.

67 "Seductive New England Witches: Part I Mrs. Patterson," New England Folklore, August 16, 2016. NEW ENGLAND FOLKLORE: Seductive New England Witches, Part One: Mrs. Paterson. Accessed 3/18/2021.

68 Austin Osman Spare. A Preliminary Inventory of His Art Collection at the Harry Ransom Center, Art Collection AR-00260 (32 items). Various Accession Numbers. University of Texas.

69 Kenneth Grant. "Austin Osman Spare: AN Introduction to his Psycho-magical Philosophy," Vol. 4 Carfax Mongraphs, Reprinted from essays by Kenneth and Steffi Grant. Austin Osman Spare: An introduction to his psycho-magical philosophy | Pastelegram.

70 Ibid. Grant.

71 "Austin Osman Spare, War Artist, World War Pictures Posters, Photos, Poets and Artists," Austin Osman Spare, Official War Artist (world-war-pictures.com).

72 The complete quote by Spare at 17 years of age was, "I have practically none… All faiths are to me the same. I go to the Church in which I was born – the Established – but without the slightest faith. I am devising a religion that embodies my conception of what we were, are, and shall be in the future." Phil Baker. *Austin Osman Spare: The Occult Life of London's Legendary Artist*. Berkeley: North Atlantic Books, 2014. p. 28.

73 Ibid. Baker, p. 28.

74 *The Book of Ugly Ecstasy|The Fire Lizard* Chapter four details the early life of Austin Osman Spare, Dark Spirits, Part Two: Austin Soman Spare posted by Salamander and Sons in A. O. Spare, Magic Books, Nov. 15, 2012. The Book of Ugly Ecstasy | The Fire Lizard (wordpress.com). Accessed 3/19/2021.

75 "The Artists, Austin Osman Spare," arthistoryproject, Austin Osman Spare – I Obelisk Art History (arthistoryproject.com) 2022.
76 Robert Ansell. "Austin Osman Spare, Biography," Fulgur, 2007. Austin Osman Spare – Fulgur Press.
77 Phil Baker, *Austin Osman Spare, Revised Edition, The Life and Legend of London's Lost Artist*, Strange Attractor Press, Nov. 21, 2023.
78 Austin Osman Spare. *Earth Inferno*, Independently published, March 8, 2019. TASCHEN books.
79 Başak Array. "Sylvia Pankhurst and the International Auxiliary Language," Język. Komunikacja. Informacja. 103–12. 10.14746/jki.2017.12.7.
80 Basaj Aray. "Sylvia Pankhurst and the International Auxiliary Language," academia.edu, (99+) Sylvia Pankhurst and the international auxiliary language I Başak Aray – Academia.edu.
81 Phil Baker. *Austin Osman Spare: The Life and Legend of London's Lost Artist*, Strange Attractor, London: Jan 1, 2010.
82 Gary Sargeant. *Friends and Influences: The Memoirs of an Artist*. London: Jersalem Press, Ltd, n.d.
83 William Cloonan. "Expressing the Inexpressible: World War I and the Challenge to Art." *The French Review* 87, no. 4 (2014): 15–23. http://www.jstor.org/stable/24549273.
   "The Study of Art in War Time." *College Art Journal* 2, no. 1 (1942): 13–19. https://doi.org/10.2307/772507.
   Charles Ffoulkes. "War and Its Influence on the Arts." *Journal of the Royal Society of Arts* 77, no. 3996 (1929): 784–96. http://www.jstor.org/stable/41358250.
84 "How the British Government Sponsored the Arts in the First World War," Imperial War Museums, 2024, How The Arts Were Sponsored In WW1 I Imperial War Museums (iwm.org.uk).
85 Some of these artists were Les Nabis, Pierre Bonnard (1867–1947), Édouard Vuillard (1868–1940), Felix Valloton (1865–1925), and Maurice Denis (1870–1943), and two Cubist artists: André Lhote (1885–1962) and Jean Marchand (1883–1941).
86 Sylvester Bone. "Muirhead Bone and the Society of XII." *The British Art Journal* 4, no. 2 (2003): 66–73. http://www.jstor.org/stable/41614462.
87 For examples, see: Haydn Reynolds Mackey, "First World War: A Royal Army Medical Corps Bearer Supplying Water to the Front Line," Wellcome Collection, First World War: A Royal Army Medical Corps Bearer Supplying Water to the Front Line I Art UK Haydn Reynolds Mackey, "First World War: The Royal Army Medical Corps on Active Service, Wellcome Collection," First World War: The Royal Army Medical Corps on Active Service I Art UK.
88 Graham Seal. "'We're Here Because We're Here': Trench Culture of the Great War." *Folklore* 124, no. 2 (2013): 178–99. http://www.jstor.org/stable/43297688.
89 Art I International Encyclopedia of the First World War (WW1) (1914–1918-online.net). Gilbert Rogers, Welcome Collection, "First World War: Stretcher Beaarers of the Royal Army Medical Corps (RAMC) Lifting a Wounded Man out of a Trench," First World War: Stretcher Bearers of the Royal Army Medical Corps (RAMC) Lifting a Wounded Man out of a Trench I Art UK.
90 This section is derived from Phil Baker, *Austin Osman Spare, The Occult Life of London's Legendary Artist*, pp. 125–28.
91 James C. Albisetti. "American Women's Colleges through European Eyes, 1865–1914." *History of Education Quarterly* 32, no. 4 (1992): 439–58. https://doi.org/10.2307/368958.
   Eleanor Cornelius Knight. "Women in Medicine." *Bios* 18, no. 4 (1947): 220–24. http://www.jstor.org/stable/4605053.

92 Wendy Moore. "The Medical Suffragettes," *The Lancet, Perspectives The Art of Medicine* 391 (February 3, 2018): 422–23.
93 For details of the medical program, see "Chapter 14 France," In Anne Powell's *Women in the War Zone, Hospital Service in the First World War*, The History Press, Gloucestershire, 2009.
94 Flora Murray. *Women as Army Surgeons: Being the History of the Women's Hospital Corps in Paris, Wimereux and Endell Street, September 1914-October 1919.* London: Hodder & Stoughton, 1920.
95 Elizabeth Crawford. "Women, and the First World War, the work of women doctors," Woman and her Sphere Website, originally published July 2006 *Ancestors* The National Archives London. https://womanandhersphere.com/2014/05/06/women-and-the-first-world-war-the-work-of-women-doctors/. Accessed 02/2019.
96 The meaning of the pins has existed since 1908, when the WPSU's newspaper *Votes for Women* co-editor Emmeline Pethick-Lawrence developed the color scheme.
97 Op. cit. Murray.
98 Ibid.
99 Anne Cooper, "The Endell Street Military Hospital," *Heoketen International: A Journal of Medical Humanities* Winter, 2015. https://hekint.org/2017/02/22/the-endell-street-military-hospital/. Accessed 4/28/2020.
100 Op. cit. Baker p. 127.
101 Wendy Moore, *Endell Street: The Trailblazing Women Who Ran World War One's Most Remarkable Military Hospital.* (Chapter 11) London: Atlantic Books, 2 Apr. 2020.
102 Ibid. Moore.
103 Op. cit. Baker, p. 127.
104 Ibid. p. 128.
105 Jason Louve, The Strange Life of Austin Osman Spare, Chaos Magician, *Ultraculture*, The Strange Life of Austin Osman Spare, Chaos Magician (ultraculture.org). Accessed 4/2/52022.
106 The Publishers Trade List Annual, Part 1. RR Bowker and Company, 1918, p. 32.
107 Op. cit. Moore, Chapter 11.
108 Ibid. Chapter 11.

Additional Sources

Austin Osman Spare, and Jake Dirnberger. *The Pocket Austin Osman Spare.* Norwell: Trident Business Partners, Jan. 22, 2020.
David M. Lubin. *Grand Illusions: American Art and the First World War.* Oxford: Oxford University Press, 2016.
Flora Murray. *Women as Army Surgeons: Being the History of the Women's Hospital Corps in Paris, Wimereux and Endell Street, September 1914–October 1919.* Cambridge: Cambridge Library Collection-History of Medicine (April 2014) original publication date, 1920.
Janice P. Nimura. *The Doctors Blackwell: How Two Pioneering Sisters Brought Medicine to Women and Women to Medicine,* 1st edition. New York: W.W. Norton & Company, Jan. 19, 2021.
Jason Weems, and Alexander Nemerov. *The Art of World War I.* Philadelphia: Pennsylvania Academy of Fine Arts, Nov. 6, 2016.

Louisa Garrett Anderson. "The Papers of Louisa Garrett Anderson 1879–1943," London: Women's Library Archives, Joint Information Systems Committee, United Kingdom. Papers of Louisa Garrett Anderson – Archives Hub (jisc.ac.uk)

Wendy Moore. *No Man's Land: The Trailblazing Women Who Ran Britain's Most Extraordinary Military Hospital during World War I.* New York: Basic Books, Apr. 2020.

Questions

What differences existed between the old-school painters and younger painters during World War I?

What were the stakes involved for women's equality in medicine? Should Spare's painting have been allowed to proceed? What is the importance of the early accurate portrayal of trailblazing women in their professional environments?

Why was the artistic freedom of Osman Spare important?

Artists express their ideas through various mediums, such as collages, pastels, paints, pencils, and chalk. What varied expressions may be achieved through the use of different mediums?

How is art an important record of social history? Should social history paintings be accurate? Why or why not?

What are the differences between a doctor and a nurse? Why was it more difficult for women to be war doctors than nurses?

Modern take

Challenges faced by women physicians in the military and private sector have not disappeared. There is still less tolerance for family issues, pregnancy, and maternity leave. Where might these issues have their roots, and why are the attitudes hard to change?

Currently, women in the healthcare sector hold 25 percent of senior decision-making roles and, at the same time, earn 24 percent less than their male counterparts. How do you believe Drs. Murray and Anderson would react to this information over one hundred years after their fight for the right to serve their country during war?

250 Women and War

Activities and discovery

Discover other paintings of females in the medical profession during World War I. What roles are most often presented? What artistic styles and mediums tell their stories?

In the March 1917 edition of the London (Royal Free Hospital) School of Medicine for Women Magazine, *an anonymous poem, the author expressed frustration at being confined to the home front during wartime. What meanings does the poem convey about the roles women had to endure? Where does the poet wish they were, and why? Try writing a few lines of a poem that relate to the war stories from this chapter.*

9
PULP ART
Prisoner of War, Chief Navy Nurse, Marion Olds

FIGURE 9.1 Cover of *Sensation* magazine in which Marion Olds story appeared. A blonde nurse and a pilot holding a gun in a crouched position.

© Roger Mansell, Palo Alto, CA. Public domain. File: News From the Past – JAP ATROCITIES AROUSE NATION (mansell.com).

DOI: 10.4324/9781003406372-10

252 Women and War

The rise of modern art and more manifestos

Modern art refers to a century of change in styles that began in the mid-1800s with the exhibition of Edouard Manet's painting *Luncheon on the Grass* and continues to exist in various forms into the 21st century. Manet's painting depicts a nude female seated on the ground at a picnic in an outdoor glen with two fully clothed men. In the center, behind the men and uncovered, is a woman dressed in what could pass for a nightgown or slip, bending over at the bank of a stream near a rowboat. A turned-over picnic basket and the unclothed woman's blue dress and summer hat are crumpled at her hip. The landscape surrounding the entourage resembles a painted scene that could pass for the backdrop of a stage play instead of being composed as true to life. How the scene was organized and the modernity of the protagonists in the painting separated this artwork from all the others. Manet broke the scholastic rules for the presentation of a woman's nakedness. Nudity had always been acceptable by art critics at the highest echelons if those without clothes were painted as allegorical or mythical, not realistically. Live models were often used in old-style art, but thematically they were unrecognizable as themselves, subsumed by biblical and mythic narratives, and placed within historical scenery. Manet had shown a contemporary orgy. Its size was also disconcerting at seven feet by eight-and-one-half feet, the unmissable carousing shouting at its audience from within a massive frame.[1]

Manet's painting incited a scandal in the world of art. The jury of the official 1863 Paris Salon sponsored by the French government and the Academy of Fine Arts rejected *Luncheon in the Grass* as an exhibition piece.[2] In their eyes, the scene was offensive; a modern naked woman in the company of two fully clothed young men in street attire was seen as vulgar and threatening to the frameworks espoused by academies based on Renaissance ideals. Critics of the impressionist style claimed the artists could not draw, their compositions strange, their colors vulgar, and the painting technique made their work ineligible. The canvases seemed unfinished.[3] One spectator was heard muttering about the painting. It resembled "a bunch of lunatics and a woman."[4] Manet was not the only artist the academy hierarchy rejected; other young artists had discovered a refreshing icon to be copied in Manet. That year, the judges scorned almost two-thirds of the work submitted by the new wave of artists.

Numerous protests against the Academy's rulings reached Emperor Napoleon III, and he had his public relations office issue an official declaration. "His Majesty, wishing to let the public judge the legitimacy of these complaints, has decided that the works of art which were refused should be displayed in another part of the Palace of Industry."[5] Creators of the rejected art set up the *Salon des Refusés*, which translates to an exhibition of rejects. Audiences mocked ostracized work. Laughter and joking filled the rooms where the paintings were hung.[6] No matter, Manet had forever changed the dynamism of the art world with his *Luncheon in the Grass*, opening the door for those who followed to make their own decisions about their subject matter, pallet, and technique.[7] This new art form led to an acceptance of artistic versions of women in a more contemporary, exploitative, and sensationalized manner.

Art and the world at war, again

Many of the modern art activities from the late 19th century through the end of World War II were impacted by a series of global social and political disturbances, just as had occurred across Europe in the period of World War I. By the 1930s, artists were once again linking their creative endeavors to the ongoing tumult. Art stimulated noise and protest about economic disasters, psychological instability, military conflict, technological advances, and non-democratic political philosophies.[8] Partisan extremism was rising, and the totalitarian far-right racist National Socialist German Worker's Party was gaining popularity. Support for Adolph Hitler, an Austrian-born, brutal, and violent originator of the Sturmabteilung paramilitary or brownshirts, was on the upsurge. In 1933, Germany left the post-World War I League of Nations, organized to avoid future death and destruction by pursuing disarmament, collective security, negotiation, and diplomacy. Hitler took control of and instigated a series of planned terrorist acts, genocidal killings, and crimes against humanity until May 7, 1945, when the Instrument of Surrender ending World War II in Europe was signed.

Fascist Italian politician and journalist Benito Mussolini was forming a far-right, authoritarian political cadre to regiment the lives of those within his geopolitical control.[9] The self-selected Duce was anti-intellectual and proud that he had never set foot in a museum more than twice. And, while he did not publicly and directly oppose unofficial art styles, he had an unwritten channel for art based on the proposal that art's certification and not its ideal were necessary. He required all exhibitions to have government authorization and be placed in a journal of record.

To the southeast in Spain, the Civil War sparked by a failed military revolt against the Republican government divided the country among nationalists, republicans, the Falange, and militant anarchists. The unrest did not cease until dictator Francisco Franco Bahamonde came to power, holding his grip on the nation for 40 years. The same year Franco took control, Germany attempted to annex Austria and seized the Czech Republic. Italy followed by invading Ethiopia, with Germany and Russia signing a non-aggression pact. In the fall of 1939, Great Britain and France declared war on Germany, and 14 days later, Germany invaded Poland. On December 7, 1941, Japan

254 Women and War

staged a surprise attack on the US territory of Hawaii when they bombed Pearl Harbor, situated 2000 miles away from the US mainland in the Pacific Ocean. Immediately after the bombing of Pearl Harbor, President Franklin Delano Roosevelt declared war on Japan, with Germany and Italy countering by declaring war on the United States. Four days after the declaration of war on Japan, in a joint congressional resolution, the United States declared war on Germany.

As internal instabilities around the globe arose, additional manifestos appeared. Two of significance were the *Concrete Art Manifesto*, composed by Dutch painter Theo van Doesburg, and the 1938 *Manifesto for Independent Revolutionary Art*.[10] Doesburg's writings attracted followers, including Swedish avant-garde painter and art critic Otto G. Carlsund, Armenian painter and surrealist artist Leon Arthur Tutundijian, French artist Jean Helion, and non-artist, French teenager Marcel Wantz, who was employed as a typographer for the group. Marcel and Jean lodged together. Less political than their predecessors who touted futurism, these artists preached about technique and were proponents of theoretical and geometrical art derived from mathematics.[11] Their self-imposed rule was that art must be conceived entirely in the mind before execution, and its constructs are limited to planes and colors without any pictorial sense. Arithmetical abstract shapes and formulaic design were to replace scenery, still life, and history painting with art that elicited mechanical appeal.[12]

Helion joined the Free French Forces in 1940, sailing from his residence in America to fight the Nazis. Six months after his arrival, the Vichy he was attached to was captured and marched almost 200 miles without food for five days. His profoundly moving autobiographical account of his internment, *They Shall Not Have Me*, described the sights and sounds within the camps.[13] Helion and the other captives were put on trains in Orleans under the German guise that they were headed home. Instead, they were taken to a baronial estate in Pomerania. Here, they were sent to German-run farms as slave labor. Helion was moved to a camp at Stettin in eastern Germany, where he was made a prison interpreter, allowing him to pick up geographical data of the region as a German translator in prison camp offices. Many internees were placed as forced labor on German assembly lines and, through sluggishness and trickery, decelerated the work as much as possible. Captives who desired to escape rather than remain in confinement throughout the war spent time creating forged official documents, altering clothes, and rehearsing potential interfaces with an enemy. Using a Shell Oil, road map, Helion studied the area's geography, plotting a route of escape to Switzerland. He then purchased a complete outfit from the black market and secured a leave card and passport of a Belgian factory worker. There would be five false starts before the sixth attempt got him beyond the confines of the prison gates. On the day of his escape, he faked a toothache to stay away from the assembly line for several hours and exchanged his prison garb for civilian garments he had hidden under a latrine floor. During a well-rehearsed outdoor volleyball game, the gates opened, and in the confusion of admitting prisoners returning from work, Helion walked out of the facility.

Delayed in a restricted area, a Nazi policeman queried the escapee about why he was there. Claiming to be a worker from Antwerp and looking for a bar, the officer gave directions to his favorite tavern. With secreted travel money, the next leg of the journey led to Berlin, where Helion spent all day hiding in a large department store. Now posing as a Flemish worker on vacation and after boarding a train for Cologne, he crossed the Belgian border. By stealing a series of rides on trucks, the flight to the French frontier ended successfully. Friends from the quasi-Free French military housed Helion and assisted him in crossing into Vichy, France, where he was welcomed into a demobilization camp. Payment was given for his 21 months of captivity and safe expediting out of Europe to America. On reuniting with his daughter and wife in Virginia and walking into his art studio, the now safe fugitive found his unfinished paintings on the easels exactly where he had left them.[14]

In 1938, the *Manifesto Towards a Free Revolutionary Art* was dually created by French writer, poet, Dadaist, and author of the *Surrealist Manifesto* of 1924, Andre Robert Breton and Marxist co-leader of the October Revolution of 1917 and founder of the Red Army, Leon Trotsky.[15] Primarily the work of Trotsky, the *Revolutionary Manifesto* was conceived when the two men met in secret near a hidden community of exiled intellectuals who had congregated at the foot of the Popocatepetl and Ixtacciuatl volcanoes in central Mexico. Feminist daughter of a German father and Mexican mother, Frida Kahlo, and her husband, mixed-race fresco and mural painter Diego Rivera, were among the artistic luminaries encamped in the region. Banishment from Russia by the Politburo after Vladimir Lenin's death and Joseph Stalin's rise led Trotsky to seek refuge on the island of Prinkipo in Turkey and then travel through France and Norway.

Trotsky's and Breton's proclamation "sought to establish an International Federation of Independent Revolutionary Art as a bridge between anti-fascist and anti-Stalinist cultural workers."[16] Trotsky supported the classical high art of the Greeks, Romans, and Italian Renaissance.[17] An "Art and Politics in Our Epoch" letter supporting the manifesto was published in June of 1938 for the New York City-based *Partisan Review* under the direction of editors who were deeply critical of Stalin's USSR. Verbiage within the piece was dense, typical for Trotsky's written communication style. Expounded upon was a personal viewpoint that art was essential for establishing societal harmony. Veering next into a discussion of art history, the Marxist stated that every new tendency in art was born out of a cycle of a fight and

256 Women and War

misalignment between the latest and the old, eventually leading to bourgeois acceptance of the new.[18] This rhythm was evidenced in the timeline of art and the shifts in movements dating to classicism and emerging during the art periods of romanticism, realism, naturalism, symbolism, impressionism, cubism, and futurism. A great many disjointed ideas flow from the rant. References are made to the decadence of capitalist society, the October Revolution, and the writing of Nobel Prize-nominated writer Leo Tolstoy. Following these were mentions of the Soviet papers *Izvestia* and *Pravda*, the newly formed official rules for Soviet painting, the revolutionary art of Diego Rivera, and the Thermidorian coup of 1794 in France, under which the leftist movement was brutally suppressed. Overall, the manifesto was a statement about art being a vital expression of creativity imperative to a harmonious and complete life. In this case, the best life was achievable only under the guiding principles found in the socioeconomic philosophy of Marxism.[19]

Trotsky's art principles were never realized. Having survived a machine gun attack conducted by Stalin's thugs, he was murdered in Mexico City in the summer of 1940 by Spanish communist Ramon Mercader, an agent of the Soviet NKVD secret police employed under cover of being a household assistant. Andre Breton's approach to art was more scientifically based and far less philosophical than Trotsky's. Their manifesto combined the sociological and cerebral elements that would become focal points for surrealist art. His studies in psychiatry and neurology at the Sorbonne Medical School, where he became a devotee of Sigmund Freud's work, and the evolution of a fascination with mental illnesses were instrumental in his pure psychic automatism style which methods involved spontaneously recording images, free brushstrokes, and chance drippings of paint. During World War I, because of his education in brain-induced diseases, the Army placed Breton in the medical corps at a neurological ward in Nantes, France. He served again during World War II in the medical corps but sought exile to the United States after one tour of duty. For the next 50 years, the artist's efforts were focused on expanding the theory of surrealism, which became the critical foundation for the next generation of post-modern art of the 1960s and 1970s.[20]

Pulp art

During the most significant period of momentum in Manet's career and the growth of modern art, popular pulp literature sales were exploding in Victorian England. Called penny dreadfuls for their one penny price, they were filled with sensationalized anecdotes, carnal or brutally charged artwork, and exposes like "Black Bess, the Knight of the Road," or "Varney the Vampire." This new form of media was surrounded by controversy as not being a suitable influence on children.[21] Adults raged that the books were subverting the nature of what they believed to be a primarily male working-class readership toward indecent behavior. *The Review of Reviews* produced a piece in 1895 about how to counteract the penny dreadful, and in 1896, the *Dundee Courier* wrote of the impact such literature had on society.[22]

Other outlets publicly denounced the stupidity of such thinking. Media sources came out in support of pulps.[23] In 1895, *Punch* and *The Speaker* broadcast a retractor to critics. Readership was on the rise, and all levels of society and age groups were enthusiastic about this new form of fiction and its artistically blatant sideshows. Many women and the educated and business classes enjoyed the short eight pages of content.[24] Easily carried and thrown away, reading the narratives was a way of taking a brief hiatus from the Depression and war news during a ride in the back of a taxi, on a bus, or when commuting on a train or subway. Everyone liked at least one pulp. The President of the United States, Harry Truman, and gangster and crime boss, Al "Scarface" Capone, were mentioned as subscribers.[25]

With the penny dreadful came a new form of art and illustration known as the pulp style.[26] It was maligned for its extravagant novelty, cheesiness, bright colors, and titillating subject matter. Dramatic perspective, compressed composition, and vibrant contrasting colors were essential to good pulp art.[27] Half-clad buxom women were shown draped across murderers, rapists, sadists, gangsters, and space aliens. Female forms swooned, slumped, fainted, and cried, their bright crimson lips quivering, makeup streaming down their faces. Women on pulp covers were always erotic and presented as objects of male desire, as the weaker person, in peril, half-collapsed, and emotionally overcome by vigilantes. Women were presented as strong characters only in the role of villainesses. Racy art was the perfect muse for action-adventure and love stories between the covers of fiction magazines. Themes varied, but larger-than-life romance, war, crime, science fiction, horror, fantasy, and adventure stories were the most popular. Fabricated characters like Captain Future, The Shadow, and G-Men rated individual serials. The purpose of the artist hired to illustrate the content within the pulps was to transform an author's mostly fictional and part-factual tale into a dynamic visual representation that would grab a reader's attention, enticing them into buying the weekly or monthly publication.

As competition within the magazine industry increased, cover art became more salacious. Potential buyers were met with choices at newsstands of up to ten rows high of reading materials packed together like sardines, on-street vendor tables, storefront street turntables, and wire metal racks in drug and grocery stores. Pulps competed with buyers of the slicks, magazines like *Vanity Fair, Saturday Evening Post, and Better Homes and Gardens* that catered to a more elite audience with their high-quality glossy paper and photography.[28] A Brooklyn Museum summary of a pulp art collection

258 Women and War

discussed how the format changed over time, "During the heyday of the pulp magazines from the 1920s through the 1940s, Americans lived through an era of unprecedented scientific, industrial, technological, cultural, and social change...Pulp art offered a glimpse of how Americans responded to the changes...Many of these had been set in motion during World War I, such as increased immigration and urbanization and the growth of a giant consumer industry."[29]

Female pulp artists

Women worked as pulp illustrators during World War II, taking on replacement jobs for men who had enlisted.[30] Each had a distinct and easily recognizable style. Illustrator and painter Margaret Brundage, the wife of leftist revolutionary Slim Brundage, whom she met at the "wildly bohemian *Dil Pickle Club* during the Chicago Renaissance, was a prolific cover artist."[31] One of her classmates at McKinley High School in Chicago was Walt Disney. She created most of the cover art for *Weird Tales* for five years between 1933 and 1938. She amassed an astounding 66 artwork covers with lush, smoldering young women bearing whips.[32] Being paid ninety dollars per cover, equivalent to over 1000 dollars in the 21st century, allowed her to support herself, her son, and her ailing mother without assistance from a male family member. Complaints about her work and the company's move to New York City at the same time when Mayor LaGuardia's decency standards for cover art on magazines were raging, her talents for pulp art plummeted. Unable to make a living in the field, Brundage died in relative poverty in 1976.[33]

At 18, Dorothy Flack had already become a fashion designer for a New York import company. In 1926, her first illustrations appeared in the pulp magazine *Love Story*, and she did freelance work for *All-Story Love* and designs for fiction sections of the *Saturday Free Press Magazine*. A secret marriage was arranged with World War I veteran Walter Robert Gillette Flack, who had served overseas as a lieutenant in an army engineering division.[34] Three months later, Walter was shot in his bedroom by veteran Herman Borgstede, who had been gassed and suffered dementia and shell shock. Her husband died less than two weeks later from wounds sustained during the attack. Flack's talent in fashion design was ideal for the women's section of newspapers with drawings of curly-haired "Mary Pickford beauties in a pen and ink style."[35] *The New York Evening Journal* employed her for over a decade. A male colleague described her artistic abilities as a genius in portraying women, with a gift of imagining an author's ideas in an art form that emotionally connected with readers.[36]

Tereska Torres received extensive notoriety compared to most females earning a living in the pulp fiction and art industries.[37] Her Jewish father was a practicing sculptor who served in the Polish Armed Forces in the

West, fighting alongside allies against the Nazis. Able to secure visas through diplomatic connections in Spain and with the Portuguese vice-consul as a signatory, the Szwarc family emigrated to Western Europe. In 1939, at 19, Tereska enlisted in Charles de Gaulle's Free French forces with the *Corps des Volontaires Francsies*. Her first assignment was as a rank-and-file soldier in London, after which the administration moved her to the press and information unit and then to President de Gaulle's central intelligence and operations program. In London, Tereska fell in love with Georges Torres, a Free French soldier. Three weeks after their marriage in 1944, he was shipped to France and was killed in action on the Alsace front. Their daughter, Gabriel, was born four months after his death. Now a mother and widow at 21, her husband's step-father-in-law, Leon Blum, and his wife Jeanne took the saddened woman into their care. Leon and Jenne had survived most of the war as internees at Buchenwald with other Jews, Poles, Slavs, the mentally ill, and the physically disabled. Bleakness overtook the eventual novelist, and she nearly lost her life in an unsuccessful suicide attempt.

Now living with her deceased husband's family, Tereska met American novelist and filmmaker Meyer Levin, whom she married in 1948. Her remarkable life story is retold in her 1970 autobiography, *Convert*. *New York Times* book reviewer Sara Blackburn described the chronicle as a distinct super drama by a woman who lived through it all as a kind of history's rag doll, at times mentally limping through the world but also able to tell intimate, engrossing, and unusual stories.[38] In 1950, Meyer encouraged his wife to turn her London wartime diaries into novels. The result was the completion of the pulp novel *Women's Barracks*. Torres was a productive writer, completing 20 books during her lifetime, with *Women's Barracks* becoming the most known. Gold Medal Books hired Illustrator Bayre Phillips, who was given the moniker the king of paperbacks, to complete the cover art. Before being drafted in World War II, Bayre worked as a bullpen artist for Columbia Pictures. He illustrated propaganda materials for the US Army Corps of Engineers and became one of the most popular cover artists for fiction writing in the United States during the 1950s and 1960s.

Art on the cover of Tereska's *Women's Barracks* is typical for pulp drama of the World War II era and not nearly as sensual as the cheaper serials. In a locker room, four half-clad young women and one uniformed female soldier look like they are conversing with one another. Two of the women are smoking cigarettes. On the flyleaf is a drawing of a young woman in brazier and underpants, a military cap on her head with her back turned away from the reader, ready to don her military tunic. Next to the black and white line drawing are the words,

This is the story of what happens when scores of young girls live intimately together in a French military barracks. Many of these innocent

260 Women and War

and inexperienced girls met other women who had lived every type of experience. Their problems, temptations, fights, and failures are faced by all women who are forced to live together without normal emotional outlets.[39]

Torres mentioned her time in London, "What can you expect? We were young people thrown together. We became adults very quickly. We had a sense of constant danger but also a sense of constant excitement. That's how I best remember London in wartime. The constant feeling of excitement."[40]

Two years after the book was put out, the US House Select Committee on Current Pornographic Materials was formed, and Arkansas congressman Ezekiel C. Gathings was appointed as Chairman. Gathings had stood against all civil rights legislation during his four years in office and was a signatory for the *Southern Manifesto*, which opposed racial integration in public spaces. The Committee was tasked to investigate "the kind of filthy sex books," likened to the writing of Torres that sold at the corner store and the "lurid and daring illustrations of voluptuous young women on the covers of books."[41] Investigations were undertaken concerning the "extraordinary tangle of fugitive love affairs between men and women and women and women in uniform."[42] The relationships described in the political proclamation resulted in Torres being labeled as the paragon of lesbian writing.

Of the categorization placed upon her by others, Torres remarked in a 2007 interview that it was exasperating that the novel had a steamy reputation and such iconic status. "Do you know, I now hate to look up Google and type in my name...the first thing that comes up is *Women's Barracks*...of which there were five main characters, only one and a half of them can be considered lesbian...I find it maddening. I don't see why it is considered a lesbian classic."[43] Several states went on to ban the novel from being sold, and it was prohibited from publication and distribution by a Court in Ottawa, Canada. Adverse publicity for *Women's Barracks* incited a bloated public curiosity about its contents, and sales skyrocketed with another one million copies being sold. Globally, sales reached four million copies with translations into 12 languages.

Other lighter versions of pulp novels were written for the teen market using military nurses as lead characters. *Cherry Ames, Chief Nurse*, and *Cherry Ames, Senior Nurse*, and other books about Army, Flight, and Veteran's Administration nurses were created by Helen Wells. *Ginger Lee, War Nurse*, was Dorothy Deming's inspiration. Both writers placed their fictitious young women in situations relatable to the US entry into the war. Wells was a social worker from Illinois and a graduate of New York University. She served with the State Department Office of the Coordinator of Inter-American Affairs. Her primary duty was to escort Latin American dignitaries around the US. Deming was a practicing public health nurse and general director of the

National Organization for Public Health Nursing. After completing a degree at Yale and graduating as a registered nurse from the Presbyterian Hospital School of Nursing, Deming completed a final training series during the 1918 flu epidemic.

Ginger Lee War Nurse was written in 1942 as a combined novelette and training book. Red-haired Ginger is a practicing public health nurse interested in becoming an industrial nurse and is questioning whether to enter the Army Nurse Corps. The fact that the protagonist uses the divisive term prig in describing another character makes her a controversial modern woman. A married best friend and former nursing school study mate, Penny, lives comfortably in suburbia, raising her twins. Miles Nash, the boyfriend, is attending medical school at the University of California, Berkeley. He is denied entry into the Naval Flight Medical Corps due to a heart condition.

References are made to The Red Cross, military pay and benefits, and relative military ranks, and there is a line diagram of a fictional barracks at Ginger's boot camp. Deciding to enter the Army Nursing Corps training program, the chapters switch in topic to a year of unfolding experiences as a trainee in the Army. Much time is spent with Ginger debating whether to get married or continue her service overseas. The life described is far removed from the typical American youth of the time. Ginger has ample money for extravagances, purchasing several evening gowns, traveling to the suburbs to see her friends, attending parties, and flying locally and across the country in commercial carriers. Class consciousness rears its head when she mulls over the difficulty of telling the banker's son from the bootblack in the man's world of military training. Cliches abound: it is all right for a man to enter the military but not a woman, no, indeed! There was also the don't hate me because I am a beautiful angle. Ginger couldn't help that she was pretty; boys were always interested in her. After Miles warns her not to volunteer for service, she sends him a Western Union telegram with the cryptic message, I'm joining Florence Nightingale in the Crimea. Fly over some time. The story ends with Ginger, headed for marital bliss, in Miles' arms. Deming was so popular that students in intermediate and high schools organized clubs where devotees could discuss her books.

In *Cherry Ames, Chief Nurse*, Cherry is whisked off to an island in the Pacific near enemy lines and is criticized by a commanding officer, saying that her youth and looks are detractors to supervising other nurses and corpsmen. Under constant attack by the Japanese, Cherry and her brother, who is stationed nearby, solve a mystery surrounding a taciturn hospitalized pilot. Brother and sister discover the pilot's malaise is due to his inadvertently knowing an enemy's secret weapon and being unsure what to do with the information. *Cherry Ames, Senior Nurse*, follows the adventures of a young woman as she gains emotional maturity as her career expands into taking on greater responsibilities in a pediatric ward. A tale of the secret drug penicillin

262 Women and War

is intertwined with the mysterious thievery of the drug's creator's notes and formulas. Subject matter in both novels is based on factual events pulled from media sources. Penicillin was used to successfully treat the first patient for septicemia in March of 1942. Media printed full-page advertisements extolling the value of antibiotics to the war effort. One advertisement read, "Thanks to penicillin, he will come home!" Artwork of a medical corpsman on the battlefield jabbing a syringe into the arm of a wounded soldier appears below the script.

Pulps and prisoner of war, US Chief Navy Nurse Marion Olds

Far away from the pulp fiction school clubs in suburban America; in the Pacific, the Japanese were overtaking numerous islands in the Pacific. A small group of US Navy nurses were captured by the Japanese on Guam in 1941. An iconographic brightly colored pulp rendering of the leader of this group of nurses was created for the 1943 cover of *Sensation* magazine. In the lower left-hand corner is a yellow box with the words, "Navy Nurse: The Story of the Capture of Guam by Marion Olds, Chief Navy Nurse." Marion Olds is artistically represented as a 20-something woman with reddish-blonde hair wearing a pristine, starched, white uniform with a nurse's cap sitting atop her beauty parlor coiffure. Scarlet-pink lipstick and painted eyebrows round out the vision. The blonde's topaz eyes stare at an unseen enemy, with a body poised as if in shock and fearful of what lurks in front of her. In a tense heroic pose, a pilot seems ready to avenge the limp female. He wears a leather aviator cover with large earflaps, a chin strap, and no bill. Flying goggles are perched on his forehead, and he is tightly grasping the nurse's shoulder with one hand. In the other, he clamps a handgun. His features are grave, lips pursed, and his physical demeanor of aggressiveness promotes a masculine readiness to avenge the angelic nurse in his charge. A potential reader may have contemplated what will become of this beautiful young nurse. Can the pilot save her from the unidentified enemy? In the vocabulary of the time: What's a dame doing in this predicament?

Marion Olds did not resemble the young woman depicted. She was in her fifties when she was captured.

If assigned to field hospitals, nurses wore their hair clipped tightly at their necks or cut short for hygienic and safety reasons. A youthful photo of Olds believed to be from a high school or early college publication, appeared in the press after her disappearance. The face is one of serious concentration, with a feeling projected that any enemy or problem would be met head-on in Guam. This person would not shirk from impending danger. The hero protecting the nurse would not have been part of a contingent on Guam just after the Japanese captured the island. Pilots did not crouch around or near the nurses in barnstorming garb. Those still alive after Pearl Harbor would have been

Pulp Art **263**

FIGURE 9.2   Left to right Doris Yetter, Leona Jackson, Lorraine Christansen, and Marion Olds near Zensuji Prison Camp, Japan.

© Sponsored by the Roger Mansell group, Palo Alto, CA. Public domain. File: The Research Center (mansell.com).

flying over the Pacific, avenging thousands of personnel killed after over 300 aircraft successfully conducted Hirohito's Hawaii operation. Military nurses were usually far enough behind the battle line to remain safe. Olds found herself in the middle of seven hours of coordinated attacks by the Japanese as air bombings co-occurred in the Philippines, Wake Island, Malaysia, Singapore, and Hong Kong. The Navy medical corps became entangled in the direct line of fire of the enemy as McArthur pulled out, unraveling the allied forces across the region. Including nurses captured on Corregidor four months later, the service women became the largest contingent of female military prisoners of war captured in Modern Warfare.

264 Women and War

Sensation magazine

Sensation magazine was written and distributed under Alex Hillman's Rarity Press, which also dispensed books and paper copies and the titles *Indecent, Crime Detective, Rocket Comics, Air Fighters,* and *Real Adventure.* All pulps mixed partial truths with fallacious and faulty themes and commentary. Hillman's empire was attached to many dubious people and schemers. David Saunders, who compiled a website on the history of American pulp fiction, noted that many of the magazines owned by Alex Hillman would operate a second division to extort money from subjects who wished to stop the publication of damaging half-truths or lies that were innate to the culture of this form of press.

Men behind the gossipy pulp empires were as crafty as the titles that sold their publications. Owners and writers were imprisoned for the frauds they perpetrated.[44] In civil case number 4720, filed on September 25, 1945, a plaintiff, shown only as J. Morgan, charged Hillman Periodicals, Hillman Brothers, and *Sensation* magazine with making libelous statements and using his photograph without his consent. These acts "had injured his reputation and good name." It was discovered during the trial that the publishing houses and owners were shills made up of mobile and foreign non-entities and had never qualified to transact business in the state in which Mr. Morgan resided. The representative name given to Morgan from the Hillman group to oversee the case was proven deceased. In the final brief submitted, Morgan was protected by his "garb of legal innocence" and was deemed unfortunate to have been "underlaid by such a shield of legal thorns."[45] Another plaintiff in the State of Arizona, Charles Reed, a Phoenix grocery clerk and meat cutter, filed a $50,000 lawsuit against Alex Hillman's Real Detective Company for a libelous tale printed about him in May of 1942.[46] *The Arizona Republic* gossip section made fun of the sensationalism of hawking stories for-profit and joked, "What has-been *dead* it or just peddled a vile piece about a has-been hero to *Sensation,* the magazine? Sayin' in his note to the magazine editor: "I know this is low—but I need the dough."[47]

Alex L. Hillman, the son of Russian immigrants, grew up in Chicago and graduated from high school and then the University of Chicago. Less than half a year after earning his degree, he worked as a lawyer for an organized group of investors, including yellow journalist, politician, and businessman William Randolph Hearst, Sr., and Arthur Brisbane, a well-known newspaper editor, writer, and orator. Also among his inner circle was newspaper empire builder Moe L. Annenberg, who, during the Roosevelt administration, was indicted for tax evasion for five consecutive years from 1932–1937. Ultimately, he owed over 56 million dollars to the IRS. Annenberg was also involved in a Chicago-based news and publication circulation war that included firebombings, murders, and violent intimidations.

In 1926, these entrepreneurial risk-takers and tacticians backed a new product division that developed radio receivers and transmitters to put their pulp on the airwaves. They sent Alex Hillman to China to supervise the creation of an innovative sales model for radio and newspaper advertising with *The Chinese Free Press*. On his return to the United States, Hillman relocated to New York City and became affiliated with national crime syndicate developer Lucky Luciano, who ran the Five Points Gang. Others within Hillmans' business circle were Theodore Epstein, publisher of tattle stories, adventure, combat, and men's magazines and books; Warren A. Angel, who ran several pulps and was charged with second-degree forgery; Paul H. Sampliner, who formed the Eastern Distributing Corporation with Warren Angel who handled many digest-sized fan magazines; divorcee and businessman Irving S. Manhemer, whom his wife accused of "staying away at nights" and spending money "on young women whose acquaintance he made on trips to the Jewish resorts of the Catskills." Manhemer was caught posing as a single man under the false name of the wealthy Guggenheim family. Rounding out the circle of actors was Harry Donefeld, one of the original owners of the Marlin Printing Company and later Irwin Printing Company, which produced leftist materials.[48]

Epstein, Angel, Sampliner, Manhemer, and Donefeld all shared office space at four West 45th Street in New York City.[49] Co-owned businesses constantly changed their addresses and company names to avoid prosecution. Money was made hawking versions of classic erotic novels and other pornographic works under shill groups, Erotica Books, Rarity Press Incorporated, Panurge Press, Falstaff Books, William Faro Books, and Eugenics Publishing Company. Two years after World War II ended, Hillman Periodicals was one of six publication distributors named in a conspiracy to monopolize the dispensing of magazines. His name was interwoven with the 1950 testimony of William Molasky, an ex-convict with ties to mafia gambling and racing, and Pioneer News, which distributed publications for Hillman Periodicals.

Even though Hillman's career was rife with tainted transactions, he became a wealthy New York icon. He and his wife Rita were enthusiastic art collectors. "(I) spent most of (my) time trying to make enough money to buy pictures," noted Hillman.[50] His art collection included Impressionist Matisse, Manet, Renoir, Degas, and Post-Impressionist Toulouse-Lautrec paintings. The couple often lent their holdings to small and nationally recognized museums. In 1966, after a lingering illness, his wife, in appreciation of the care she received, sold the Picasso painting *Mother and Child* and used the proceeds to establish a Hillman Scholarship Program for Nursing at the University of Pennsylvania. After receiving their degrees, the students who earned grants were required to work for two years in New York City's hospitals. Rita, says one foundation website, "was a devoted presence at

266 Women and War

scholar events and delighted in meeting young Hillmans, whom she considered as part of her extended family."[51] Fifteen hundred nurses have benefited from Rita Hillman's philanthropy. Alex Hillman's obituary in the New York Times left out his unsavory history. It lauded his life as a 67-year-old ex-publisher and noted art collector who led a successful investment firm.

Sensation carried two types of war-related stories from 1941 to 1946: those that placed female protagonists in carnal, erotic encounters with leaders of the Axis powers of Germany, Italy, and Japan, or more generically presented yarns of women and their loss of virginal maidenhood to evil enemy Asian or German soldiers. Front covers shouted, "Love Cult a la Hitler," "I was a Victim of Goebbels' Lust," "My Hell in the Nazi Coffin on Rails," and "I was a Japanese Love Dope Slave." Each narrative was presented under the pretense that they were the true unknown stories behind official news headlines. A second formula used was exaggerating partial information from interviews with political and armed service leaders or creating accounts of military heroism in the face of an enemy. The "Wings over Malta" saga shared a headline with "My Sub Sank 6 Ships." Heroic acts were narrated in "I Fought the Japanese on the Java Sea, Coxswain Claude Becker's Own Story," and "I Manned a Tank Killer in Africa." Salacious politically based accounts were promoted with headlines like "Sex Kreig Over Germany" or "What Makes Gromyko Tick?"[52] With these sorts of characters on the front page and understanding the one-lane portrayal of women in the pulps as wilting, dangerous, passionate objects, how Marion Olds' experience was portrayed in art would not have been much of an oddity. Her narration fit the heroic acts genre of the day, and her story was probably lifted directly from *Navy Nurse* magazine word for word. It is doubtful Marion was given any monetary stipend, and no information can be located as to whether the Hillman editors approached Olds about printing the story. Since Department of Defense materials are usually not controlled by tight copyright restrictions, it would have been simple to plagiarize her narrative and then add a pulp art cover of a woman in peril, wearing a vestal white uniform, waiting to be saved by a ready and able hero.

The bona fide account

From 1939 through 1945, over 50,000 American nurses served in the Army Nurse Corps, and 14,000 served in the Navy. There was no formal training for army nurses until 1943, when Fort Meade, Maryland's first essential training center, opened. To be accepted into the program, a woman had to be 21–40 years of age, a high school graduate, have completed a three-year nursing training program, be licensed in one state, and be a citizen of the United States or one of its allied nations. The American Red Cross served as the traditional reserve for the Army Nurse Corps and a recruiting entity for both the Army and Navy. Nurses served in the Pacific from 1941 until the war ended in 1945, most stationed in Hawaii, Australia, New Zealand, Fiji, New Caledonia, and the New Hebrides. US Chief Army Nurse Maude Davison began a slimming down process of her nurse corps to 66 women, sending those who tended toward spending excessive time on beautification, flirting, and dating in lieu of stepping up for challenging work back to the states in the event her team became prisoners of the Japanese. The prediction came true when, on May 6, 1942, the largest group of American military women in history were captured. Their liberation did not occur until February 1945.

Nursing duty stations were placed behind the front lines per military regulations. Five hundred Army nurses were assigned to medical air evacuation squadrons. US military flight nurses assisted in vacating over one million patients. Seventeen of the Army air nurses lost their lives. Seventy-seven American Army and Navy nurses were captured by the Japanese. One European Campaign nurse, Second Lieutenant Reba Zitella Whittle, was captured on September 27, 1944, when the Advanced Landing Ground A-92 she was assigned to was hit by German flak near St. Trond, Belgium, and crashed. The German Luftwaffe interned her in quarters at or near Stalag IX-C northeast of Frankfurt, Germany.

Events in order of occurrence that placed the Pacific nurses front and center in a headlong Japanese advance from December of 1941 to 1942 began when Canaco Naval Hospital in Manila was hit, Guam was attacked, Singapore fell, and Bataan was overrun. US and allied nurses from Australia, the United Kingdom, and New Guinea were also interned in and around the nation of Japan and the outlying Pacific Islands for four years until a truce was called on VJ day, September 2, 1945. Nuns and civilian nurses were also captured. Fifty-nine Australian Army nursing sisters were incarcerated, and 22 Australian Army nurses were murdered off Bangka Island. When the Japanese overtook Rabaul, New Britain, in January 1942, six Australian Army Nursing Service sisters were taken prisoner. They were interned at a mission hospital at Vunapope and then moved to various internment camps around Japan until the war ended. Due to their small contingent and being caught in a less critical strategic area, they became a forgotten footnote compared to other highly publicized events.

The American nurses were given nicknames. Army nurses were called The Battling Belles of Bataan, and the Navy, The Twelve Anchors. Allied nations issued government posters as a reminder of the nurse's plights. The United States issued Work to Set 'em Free, and Work, Save, Fight and Avenge the Nurses! was printed in Australia. On the American propaganda poster, as with Olds' pulp cover, the nurses look like a modeling advertisement for new uniforms rather than their actual condition of being near starvation at the time of their release. Six nurses look plaintively out at the viewer as they

268 Women and War

stand behind a barbed wire fence dressed in navy and crimson capes, white stockings, and pristine starched hats in front of a Japanese guard with a bayonet. Camp life was filthy and closed, and tempers could run high due to the stressors of vindictive guards and the mix of personalities and nationalities. The Australian poster style was more in touch with reality. A hospital ship is ablaze in the background, victims are jumping into the sea, and two women are waterlogged in the forefront with a tight grip on flotsam lit by the fire glow permeating the night sky.

Fifty-year-old Lieutenant Commander Laura Mae Cobb had served at the Cañacao Naval Hospital at the end of World War I. She volunteered for international fieldwork as World War II approached because "Someone had to go."[53] In the spring of 1940, Cobb was sent to Guam, transferred to the Philippines, and then returned to Cañacao Naval Hospital in Manilla. Her deep nursing experience and quiet and professional demeanor made her an esteemed member of the camps among the Japanese guards, those serving under her, the prisoner-of-war camp supervisors, and allied nation government officials who were interned with the Navy POWs. Cobb did not hesitate to go before the Japanese Army officials to cite infractions of rules or make requests.

Later at Corregidor, 66 army nurses arrived in the civilian internment center at Santo Tomas after the Navy nurses under the leadership of Captain Maude Davison. Sensing a rise in the competitive nature between the Army and Navy personnel, Cobb requested a transfer to the newly formed Los Banos internment camp to set up a new medical program. In both camps, the women were subjected to a Japanese edict of purposeful starvation near the war's end with a food allowance of fewer than 300 grams of rice, equal to one-half cup per day. Davison's and Cobb's leadership talents, tenacity, perseverance, and intellect under pressure were the reasons they brought all their women out alive. The day the Japanese entered the rock cave on Corregidor where Davison's team slept, enemy soldiers headed directly to female quarters for who knows what form of maltreatment, as they had been bayoneting bedridden soldiers who were physically unable to react to the onslaught. Maude, small in stature at under five feet, placed herself physically between the nurse's quarters curtain and the Imperial Japanese Army, told them to halt, and that they had no permission to go beyond her. The armed aggressors retreated. After her release, she had no interest in staying connected with any of the Battling Belles. Davison was posthumously awarded the Distinguished Service Medal in 2001 due to the dogged pursuit of those who had served under her, believing she deserved the decoration.

Cobb's experience is notable in many ways, but two instances show her ability to lead under stress. Nurses' records were hidden from guards by pinning them to the underside of her uniform and kept there for the duration of the internment. When the Japanese uprooted the group, Cobb would place a lei over her collar to ensure the papers did not peek out from her uniform. Any slip that the documents had been saved would have been met with brutality and confiscation of the identifications. As the Japanese closed in on the Cañacao hospital, Cobb instructed personnel to mislabel as many quinine bottles with unessential pharmacological names as possible. This quick thinking meant the Japanese were kept from confiscating the valuable medicine needed to treat malarial and other parasitic diseases. Cobb has yet to receive the appropriate honors for her leadership.

Lieutenant Junior, Grade Marion Olds, grew up in Chicago and graduated from George Washington Hospital. By the time she was on duty in Guam, she had served in the Navy for 15 years. The Oceana posting was the first in the role of superintendent. A usual term of duty in Guam lasted a year, after which a transfer was ordered to the Naval Hospital at Cañacao Bay, located within Manila Bay in Luzon, the Philippines. Her two orders on arrival were to train the Chamorros, the island's Indigenous peoples, in nursing skills and to administer to the needs of the island garrison personnel. The American Navy nurses under Olds's direction were Lieutenants Junior Grade, Leona Jackson, Lorraine Christiansen, Virginia Fogerty, and Doris Yetter.

Leona Jackson entered the Navy in 1936 and, during her career, was promoted to the rank of captain and became the third Director of the United States Navy Nurse Corps. Lorraine Christiansen, a native of Utah, received her nursing training at Holy Cross Hospital and married eight years after the war ended. Then, she moved to California, where she was employed as the senior nurse for the San Francisco Post Office.[54] Her primary assignment in Guam was in the operating room. Virginia Fogarty worked in the diet kitchen. Doris Margaret Yetter's Navy enlistment began in March of 1938, with continuous service after her captivity until October 1961, when she retired as a commander. She came to Guam with a background in teaching student nurses at Temple University Hospital in Philadelphia. Yetter received the Prisoner of War Medal, American Defense Service Medal, Asiatic Pacific Campaign Medal, American Campaign Medal, and World War II Victory Medal.[55]

Leona Jackson wrote a highly sanitized version of their imprisonment in *The American Nursing Journal* dated November 1942. "I Was on Gaum" spoke of how pleasant the island was during off-duty time with the numerous recreations available, including tennis, golf, badminton, swimming, sailing, and deep-sea fishing. A native staff, usually around 30, was also mentioned as being pleasant and courteous in their mannerisms with nursing experience in surgery, obstetrics, pediatrics, orthopedics, infectious diseases, clinics, operating rooms, delivery room techniques, and dietary science. Jackson's story began by referencing the round-the-clock rotations of the nurses for the first two days after the bombings. She

270 Women and War

reacted to the situation: "This was the time for which we had trained all these years, the Final Examination in the School of Professional Experience."[56] All the women automatically reacted to what had been thrown at them, with "quiet voices, making rounds, checking treatments, administering medications, and overseeing the native nursing staff." Jackson prayed for the young Guamanians to be safe until the Americans could return since the US nurses "would be powerless to aid them in their dark hours ahead."

With few details, no emotion, and reading more like a memorandum than a harrowing experience, the sequence of events of the capture is repeated. The team was forced to leave the island on January tenth, arriving in Japan five days later, where they were in Zentsuji, housed in "an old Army barracks, long unused, cold, and dreary." Straw mats over straw became hospital beds for the patients shipped with them from Guam. In a few weeks, all prisoners were reassigned to larger spaces, and repairs were made to the buildings. Stoves were issued for a semblance of warmth. Their only food was "weed and water soup," rice mixed with wheat, and 12 ounces of bread per person. Every two weeks, a piece of fruit might be added.

Men in the camp created study groups, and Jackson was asked to teach a dietetics class since many corpsmen often failed the subject. One month after capture, on March 12, the nurses were shipped to Kobe, Japan, where they arrived after one day of travel and were met by an English-speaking official, then were placed in a detention house. Other internees at Kobe were allied powers' nationals, ten American civilian missionaries, a teacher, and several businesspeople. In May, it was rumored that the prisoners would be exchanged, and in June, the women were sent home to America, arriving in New York Harbor on August 25. In one repatriation discussion among the navy nurses, Jackson recalled that Doris Yetter had "skeptically remarked that she would eat her words if she saw New York before the end of the war." "A few days out from New York," remembered Jackson, "one of the priests who had been in on the original conversation laughed heartily to see at Miss Yetter's table placement a cake inscribed, eat your words, this is New York."[57]

Doris Yetter's explanation of events adds missing details from Jackson's account. Her description of captivity begins with the third day of the war, when the American flag came down on Guam. With this event, she knew they were prisoners of war. Stoically, all continued their duties, with the Japanese constantly wandering through their hospital, taking anything, they wanted. Her memory of the internment building in Kobe was that it was a "fifth-rate westernized hotel" that had been converted to house prisoners of war. Japanese soldiers tried to convince the nurses that the US military had been wiped out. To their enjoyment, this lie was disproved in April as they observed overhead a five-person crew in a US Army B-25 bomber headed inland. Recognizing the US markings, Yetter and the other women became even more determined to return to the United States to "continue the job they had been sent to do."

Marion Olds' delivery of her experience of capture and imprisonment remains the most dynamic and animated.[58] Because Olds was a leader in a situation of such magnitude, she would have had to quickly gather details of all the goings-on and make split-second decisions. A considerable effort was expended to keep her women focused and safe. Conducting a mission for the Navy and patriotism are two recurring themes in the reminiscence. "I had faith in the aggressive daring of our Navy. You see, I am Navy. I'm steeped in Navy tradition. That tradition calls for more than dauntless courage and sacrifice. It calls for offense. The Navy's record tells us that any Navy man can take a temporary setback indomitably. So, too, can Navy nurses. Defeat isn't written in the logbook."[59]

Looking skyward and seeing nine Japanese planes coming in at high altitudes, Olds wondered if these aircraft were on reconnaissance. In the distance, dull, flat echoes told her otherwise. According to her account, Marines and sailors numbering 500 "were up against it" as they had no artillery to return fire. The officers in charge gave the nurses orders to pack and remove the gold braid from their caps to keep the Japanese from knowing they were in the military. She watched enemy planes fill the sky and observed, "At moments like that, you are without fear; reactions to our plight could be saved for later. I know that I was unafraid." Bombers and fighters came in waves, strafing anything that moved. The nurses fell in and began a round-the-clock rotation, managing the scores of wounded from the attack. No reports were made of the unfolding defeat of the allies until three-thirty in the afternoon when they learned that hostilities were raging in the southern hills near Agana, the capital of Guam. News traveled to the hospital that civilians were being machine-gunned in the streets. Native hospital wards were invaded, and patients were shot or stabbed.

On December 10th, 5000 Japanese troops landed. Olds' restraint as a participant in the scene surrounding her was remarkable. "Some persons will tell you they thrill to battle. A Navy nurse or an Army nurse, for that matter, doesn't. Care of the wounded with their torn and bleeding bodies isn't a thing that brings you thrills."[60] She thought about the medical revulsions caused by men and weapons on humanity. "One grows accustomed quickly to the horrors of war, and it makes for a general informality. Someone once wrote it was Quentin Reynolds, I think" a reference to American journalist and World War II war correspondent, "that the wounded don't cry. Ours didn't. With characteristic American grit," the injured enlisted and officers "grinned at us and wisecracked a bit. I know it made my task a lot easier."[61] Dropping automatically to the floor as the hospital roof was pelted with machine-gun bullets became customary practice. Staring out the window as the mayhem

272 Women and War

continued and the enemy swarmed the grounds, "I saw them rush in, shouting and gesticulating wildly. They scrambled for the shade of trees, dropping their packs and guns as they flopped to the ground. And then they did an amazing thing. They produced bamboo fans and started fanning themselves. It was almost laughable."[62] What Olds detested most about being invaded was how the American flag was treated. A scene she never wanted to see again, comparing the incident as being worse than seeing the dead, the dying, and the wounded.

Information began to filter in about more barbarism and brutality ongoing around the island. Women were raped, men and children were bayonetted, and houses and businesses were ransacked. Back at the Navy hospital, the Japanese summoned the nurses and ordered them to stand and watch as they made a parade of captured allied equipment. An American flag was placed on a hillock. Machine guns opened fire and shredded it to a pulp. Next, the nurses were forced to watch soldiers dramatically perform practice drills with their flamethrowers, a fear tactic and deterrent met with dispassionate feelings about the display: "I was not impressed."

One nurse was slapped when she failed to understand an order, and immediate punches and slaps were given for not bowing low enough at the waist in the presence of their captors. On the 15th of January, the women were moved through Todatsu, located in southern Japan in the Nakatado District of the Kagawa Prefecture on the northeastern coast. Forced to ride on a truck on top of their baggage for about six miles, they were let off at a small port where a large ship laid off the reef. Whether they were headed to the mainland or one of the mandated islands was unknown. Small launches appeared and were boarded and pulled alongside an anchored steamer. Their headcount had increased by two. One of the group's new members was Mrs. Ruby Hellmers, the wife of a petty officer. With Ruby was her six-week-old daughter, Charlene.

Olds organized the group swiftly. With four bunks for six women and a baby, the decision was made to rotate sleeping in twos on the floor. Helmers gave the career Navy officer courage when her feelings were at their lowest. The mother's infectious smile reduced the tension and doldrums of the chief nurse and made her reflect that "this was possibly the bravest of us all." One thing that disturbed Olds about being transported by sea was that being placed in the hold of a Japanese ship meant the potential for death by friendly fire by the US Navy. The vessel slowed down on day five of the water journey, and its inhabitants were told to gather their things. Marching everyone onto the deck, the prisoners were told to sit there for hours until dark. It was bitter cold, and the small boats moving about in the harbor were covered with thick snow and ice. Olds gave her navy blue nurse's cape with crimson lining to Mrs. Hellmers and her baby. A scow arrived, and they were motored ashore, placed in an ambulance, and deposited at an enormous soldier's barracks. They had reached Zentsuji Prison Camp, Hiroshima POW Camp #1B, located 96 miles north and east of Hiroshima.

An incomplete interim camp roster for American POWs who spent time at Zentsuji shows no American women. It is estimated that over 500 United States military men who were attached to the Marine Corps, Air Force, Navy, Army Air Corps, Naval Reserve, Marine Corps Reserve, and Merchant Marine passed through the camp. There were both enlisted and officers from the ranks of private first-class to major. They came from assignments to the coast artillery, tanks, infantry, supply, medical, engineering, materiel, warfare, ordinance, and the signal corps. Represented were the All-American Airborne, Wake Signal Detachment, Guam Insular Patrol, Army Quartermaster Corps, the 60th Air Defense Artillery, 59th Air Defense Artillery, 192nd Tanks Regiment, 1st Filipino Infantry Regiment, 24th Field Artillery Philippine Scouts, and Harbor Defense. Specialties and rates differed, and the fields of Finance, Dental, Warrant Officer, Pay Clerk, Coxswain, and Chief Electricians Mate were represented. Naval personnel included those captured from *USS Houston, USS Penguin, USS Yorktown, USS Wright, USS RL Barnes, USS President Harrison, USS Perch*, and the *USS Pope*.[63]

Zentsuji was considered a Japanese show camp for housing officers and government professional internees. It sat on a flat, fertile plain bounded on one side by a Shinto Shrine and lay approximately five miles inland.[64] The same ground housed captives during the Russo-Japanese War in 1904. During Olds' interment, buildings were utilized as a control center for dolling prisoners to various work camps. A large fence enclosed the property. Buildings were constructed of pointed bamboo staves, and in front was an obstruction of an eight-strand barbwire enclosure. Two two-story-high barracks had served as warehouses before the war, of which Japanese camp officials occupied one-half. The building was built poorly of green wood, with little heat and running water. Bed bugs, lice, and fleas made sleeping impossibly uncomfortable. Prisoners slept on decks raised 16 inches above the floor on grass mats. Each room held 32 men.

Compared to other camps, the fact that there were crude latrines about 50 feet away from the barracks with 12 stalls and wash racks for the men made it slightly more endurable. There was an awful stench to be contended with. Hot baths were supposed to be available on a semi-monthly basis during wintry weather, and there were two tables and four benches in each of the 32 rooms. One officer recalled, "Although we were uncomfortable, we had adequate clothing."[65] Lack of food was a monumental problem, and no hospital or medical aid was provided. On rare occasions, the prisoners received American Red Cross parcels with foodstuffs, tobacco, shoes, clothing, and games. A small library was established when US Ambassador Joseph Grew was repatriated early in the war and forwarded 200 books to the camp, which the men were allowed to unpack and distribute. Because of the space given to the men and the less horrific conditions compared to other prisoner-of-war sites, Zentsuji was used for propaganda photos, and allowances were occasionally made for tours of visiting officials.

Harassment and cruelty by those with power over the internees were constant.[66] Olds could hear the horrendous shrieks and sounds from the men's area at night. Guards often heckled and slapped the prisoners. Nicknames were doled out to the four worst of the lot, "Saki Pete," "Leatherwrist," "Buttons," and "Club Fist." Camp Commander Tame Kondo, who arrived in December of 1944, was sentenced to five years of hard labor at the Yokohama War Crimes Trials and convicted of mistreating allied prisoners. Ten men out of an estimated total of up to 950 died in the camp from January 1942 to June 1945. Seven were Americans, two were British, and one was an Australian soldier. Low mortality occurred, wrote one unnamed internee, because of the skill of the American medical officer.[67] In a show of compassion for the deaths of the ten prisoners, A Japanese man living near the camp, Mr. Fumio Okita, began to hold memorial services for the deceased souls of the prisoners. His son continued his eulogy by building an enshrined Buddhist memorial table on a handmade altar, which included a paper list of the ten men's names written in Japanese.[68]

The nurses were isolated during their time at Zentsuji.[69] On her first night as a prisoner, Olds had reached a feeling of utter desolation for the first time in the ordeal. Each of the women was fatigued and suffering from nervous exhaustion. The barracks were miserably frigid, and all five slept completely clothed, including layering up with their coats and gloves. One of the more irritating occurrences was that Japanese soldiers constantly entered the women's rooms unannounced. Olds affirmed that there was no meat or salt, and during the "fifty-odd days that we were at Zentsuji, we received eggs twice and fruit three times. I think the women fared far better than the men." "I know for certain that our quarters, bad as they were, were luxurious compared to those of the male prisoners."[70] Communication with the male population was forbidden, and the Japanese guards took delight in tormenting them. With their vitality ebbing fast and their weight teetering toward being a primary concern, the women were transferred once again – this time to the northeast to Kobe.

Arriving on March 12, they were interned in better quarters, and soldier sentries were replaced with police guards. Olds believed and was correct in her assumption that this change in treatment was because they were in line to be exchanged, and the enemy did not want them to tell stories of deprivation, brutality, or barbarism. The women were fattened with a steady edible diet and used for propaganda photos as they walked escorted through the city streets in Japanese robes. They were also photographed shopping for clothing and household items, which was a complete ruse as they had been given no money, their captors lurking off-camera so they would not attempt to escape. The police officer in charge, only referenced by his first name as Isumida, had been an immigration officer before the war. He spoke perfect English and told Olds he had lived in the United States for two and a half decades. Three months later, the Navy nurses were told they would be released as prisoners of war. A train took them to Yokohama, where they boarded the late 1920s ocean liner *Asama Maru*. As the war progressed, *Asama Maru* became one of the infamous hell ships used for transporting thousands of Allied prisoners to their fates in prison camps. After a brief stop in Hong Kong, they were transferred to the *Gripsholm*, sailed to Mozambique, and onward to New York Harbor. Their repatriation occurred in August 1942 to no fanfare. Newspapers carrying their stories refused to identify them as US Navy military nurses.

Notes

1 My Modern Met, The Significance of 'The Luncheon on the Grass' by Edouard Manet (mymodernmet.com). Accessed 2/16/2022.
2 "No Longer Scandalous: Manet in America," JSTOR blog, May 1, 2015, No longer scandalous: Manet in America – About JSTOR. Petronius Arbiter, "A Degenerate Work of Art: 'Lunch on the Grass' by Manet." *The Art World* 1, no. 4 (1917): 273–75, 272. https://doi.org/10.2307/25587747.
3 "About Impressionism Radicalism of Impressionism: Trees are not violent; the sky is not butter," What is Impressionism, History of Impressionism and Impressionists, start of impressionism movement. Accessed 4/26/2022.
4 Ibid. About Impressionism.
5 Published in *Le Moniteur* on 24 April 1863. Cited in Maneglier, Hervé, *Paris Impérial – La vie quotidienne sous le Second Empire*, p. 173.
6 Benedetta Ricci. The Shows that made contemporary art history: the *Salon des refuses*, Artland Magazine, n.d. Lincoln, NE. https://magazine.artland.com/the-shows-that-made-contemporary-art-history-the-salon-des-refuses/
7 Ibid. p. 253.
8 While certainly not a complete list, nor are the types of art always easily separated into distinct time frames, several movements prominent around the period of the 1930s leading up to World War II were Pulp Art (1890s–late 1950s), Futurism (1909–1914), De Stijl (1917–1931), The Bauhaus Movement (1919–1933), The Harlem Renaissance (1920s–early 1940s), Czech Devetsil Avant-Garde (1920–1935), The Group of Seven Algonquin School (1920–1933), The School of American Regionalism (1928–1943), The Northwest School Art Movement (1930s–1940s), The Allianz Art Movement or Concrete Art Theory (1930–1959), Leningrad Social Realism (1932–1988), Abstract Expressionism (1943–mid 1950s), and Lyrical Informel (1943–1950s). Of these, the two more manganous in terms of overall influence and change were Futurism, primarily in Europe, and Abstract Expressionism, which had its roots in New York City.
9 Mark Antliff, "Fascism, Modernism, and Modernity." *The Art Bulletin* 84, no. 1 (2002): 148–69. https://doi.org/10.2307/3177257.
10 "Manifesto for an Independent Revolutionary Art Signed by Andre Breton and Diego Rivera," Diego Rivera (marxists.org). Accessed 4/26/2022. "Concrete

Art Manifesto," bbm:978-1-4614-7052-6/1.pdf (springer.com). Accessed 4/26/2022.

11 Carlsund, von Doesburg, Helion, Wantz, Tutundijan. Base de la peinture concrete (1930) Base de la peinture concrète (1930) – Otto G. Carlsund, Theo van Doesburg, Jean Hélion, Marcel Wantz, Léon Arthur Tutundjian – 391.org. Accessed 4/22/2021.

12 David Pimm. "Some Notes on Theo van Doesburg (1883–1931) and His 'Arithmetic Composition 1.'" *For the Learning of Mathematics* 21, no. 2 (2001): 31–36. http://www.jstor.org/stable/40248360.

13 Jean Helion. *They shall not have me: The capture, forced labor and escape of a French prisoner in World War II.* Arcade reprint, 2014.

14 "Art Self Abstraction from the Nazis," *Time* archives, November 23, 1942 Art: Self-Abstraction from the Nazis – TIME. Accessed 4/26/2022. "Books: Escape," *Time* archives, Aug. 30, 1943, Books: Escape – TIME. Accessed 4/26/2022.

15 Manifesto of Surrealism by Andre Breton, 1924, Manifesto of Surrealism (hawaii.edu).

16 Pierre Taminiaux. "Breton and Trotsky: The Revolutionary Memory of Surrealism." *Yale French Studies*, no. 109 (2006): 52–66. http://www.jstor.org/stable/4149285.

17 For details on defining high and low art, see John A. Fisher. *The Routledge Companion to Aesthetics*, Apr. 2013. Or pdf file 9780415782869 1.681 (colorado.edu). Chapter 46, pp. 473–84. Accessed 4/21/2021. Also see "Trotsky on revolutionary art," Trotsky's theory of art and revolution reconsidered (by L. Proyect) (columbia.edu). Accessed 4/21/2021.

18 Michael Lowy. "Leon Trotsky and Revolutionary Art, For the 80th Anniversary of His Death," International Viewpoint, Aug. 24, 2020, Leon Trotsky and revolutionary art – International Viewpoint – online socialist magazine.

19 Leon Trotsky. "Art and Politics in Our Epic." first published *Partisan Review,* 18 June 1938. Source: Fourth International, March–April 1950, Vol. 11 No. 2, pp. 61–64.

20 Alan Woods. "Marxism and Art: Introduction to Trotsky's Writings on Art and Culture." In Defense of Marxism, Dec. 14, 2000.

21 Troy Boon. *Youth of Darkest England: Working-Class Children at the Heart of Victorian Empire.* New York: Routledge, 2005.
   Mimi Matthews. "Penny Dreadfuls, Juvenile Crime, and Late-Victorian Moral Panic," The Victorian Web, Penny dreadfuls, juvenile crime, and late-Victorian moral panic (victorianweb.org).

22 "The Effects of Reading Penny Dreadfuls." *Dundee Courier.* June 17, 1896. "How to Counteract the Penny Dreadful." *The Review of Reviews Annual.* Vol. XII. London: Mowbray House, 1895.

23 "That Poor Penny Dreadful," Punch. Vol. CVIII. London Fleet Street, 1895. "The Poor Little Penny Dreadful." The Speaker. Vol XII. London: Fleet Street, 1895.

24 Mimi Matthews. Penny dreadfuls, juvenile crime, and late-Victorian moral panic, The Victorian Web, Literature, History and Culture in the Age of Victoria, Penny dreadfuls, juvenile crime, and late-Victorian moral panic (victorianweb.org). Accessed 2/24/2022.

25 According to "Pulp Magazines," Encyclopedia.com, this comment is attributed to Henry Steeger, cofounder with Harold S. Goldsmith of Popular Publications.

26 For examples, see "Pulp Fiction Covers," Fleet Library RISD, and JSTOR Pulp Fiction Covers on JSTOR.

27 Press Release. Pulp Art: Vamps, Villains, and Victors from the Robert Lesser Collection, May 16, 2003, through October 19, 2003. Special Exhibition, Contemporary Art. Brooklyn Museum. Accessed 2/23/2022.

Pulp Art **277**

28 R. D. Mullen. "R. D. Mullen's From Standard Magazines to Pulps and Big Slicks," *The Pulp Magazines Project An Archive of All Fiction Pulpwood Magazines from 1896–1946*, Pulps & Big Slicks (pulpmags.org). Accessed 3/16/2022.
29 "Pulp Art: Vamps, Villains, and Victors from the Robert Lesser Collection." Brooklyn Museum, May 16, 2003, Brooklyn Museum.
30 Cori Urban. "Female 'Pulp' Illustrators Get Their Due at Museum Talk," Mass Live Entertainment, May 23, 2018, Female 'pulp' illustrators get their due at museum talk – masslive.com.
31 David Spurlock, and Stephen D. Korshak. *Alluring Art of Margaret Brundage: Queen of Pulp Pin-Up Art*, Vanguard, May 13, 2013.
32 Ibid. Spurlock
33 David Saunders. "Margaret Brundage, 1900–1976," *Field Guide to Wild American Pulp Artists*. Catalog (pulpartists.com). Accessed 3/14/2022.
34 Ibid. "Dorothy Flack"
35 Ibid. "Dorothy Flack" ("Catalog")
36 Ibid. "Dorothy Flack"
37 For an excellent summary of the highlights of her life, see Jewish Paris Goldenberg, "A Journey With the Schwarz's" "a Jewish Family of All Arts," June 6, 2020, le marais jewish stories Archives – Jewish Tours Paris (jewish-paris-tours. com). Accessed 4/26/2021.
38 Sara Blackburn. "The Converts," *The New York Times*, The Converts – The New York Times (nytimes.com). Accessed 4/26/2021. Tereska Torres, The *Converts*, New York: Alfred A Knopf, 1970.
39 Digital Collections, Yale University Library, Women's barracks – Yale University Library. Accessed 4/16/2021.
40 Interview *The London Independent*, Jun 16, 2007.
41 Ezekial Candler Gathings. World Cat, Report of the Select Committee on Current Pornographic Materials, House of Representatives, Eighty-second Congress: Pursuant to H. res. 596, a resolution creating a select committee to conduct a study and investigation of current pornographic materials. (Book, 1952) [WorldCat. org]. Accessed 4/16/2021.
42 John Lichfield. "O! What a Steamy War," *The London Independent*, June 16, 2007, Internet Archive Wayback Machine. http://findarticles.com/p/articles/mi_qn4158/is_20070616ai_n19310147. Accessed 4/12/2021.
43 Ibid. Lichfield
   "Tereska Torres: The Reluctant Queen of Lesbian Literature," *Independent*, Feb. 5, 2010, Tereska Torres: The reluctant queen of lesbian literature | The Independent | The Independent.
44 David Saunders. Re "Sensation (magazine?)" Message to Mary Raum. April 16, 2021. E-mail.
45 Casetext. Reed v Real Detective PUbl Co. Summary. Reed v. Real Detective Pub. Co., 63 Ariz. 294 | Casetext Search + Citator. Accessed 4/19/2021.
46 Op. cit. Saunders, "Defendants Added in Libel Action," *Arizona Republic*, n.d.
47 Ibid.
48 Irving S. Manhemer. Catalog (pulpartists.com). Accessed 4/19/2021.
49 Ibid. Alex Hillman. Accessed 4/19/2021.
50 "Rita and Alex Hillman Foundation," History | The Rita & Alex Hillman Foundation (rahf.org). Accessed 4/19/2021.
51 Ibid. ("About – The Rita and Alex Hillman Foundation").
52 During World War II, Andrei Andreyevich Gromyko became the Head of the Department of the America's eventually becoming the top decider for much of Soviet Policy as Chairman of the Minister of Foreign Affairs throughout the Cold War.

278 Women and War

53 Laura Mae Cobb File. Department of the Navy, Bureau of Medicine and Surgery, 2300 E Street, NW Washington, D.C.
54 "Obituary, Lorraine Christiansen Halliday." The *Desert News*, Feb. 20, 2006. Obituary: Lorraine Christiansen Halliday – Deseret News. Accessed 4/20/2021.
55 Sources for this section: YETTER-DORIS | The United States Navy Memorial; Newspapers.com archive Daily News from New York, New York on August 30, 1942, 116 (newspapers.com); "Hiroshima POW Camp #1B" Hiroshima #1 POW Camp – Zentsuji, Japan (mansell.com); "News From the Past," News From the Past – JAP ATROCITIES AROUSE NATION (mansell.com); "Navy Nurse of Guam Wed," NAVY NURSE OF GUAM WED; Virginia Fogarty and Frederick Mann Met on Exchange Ship – The New York Times (nytimes.com); "Obituary Lorraine Christiansen Halliday, Obituary: Lorraine Christiansen Halliday – Deseret News"; "Hall of Valor Project," Doris Yetter – Recipient – (militarytimes.com).
56 Leona Jackson. "I Was on Guam." *The American Journal of Nursing* 42, no. 11 (Nov. 1942): 1245 of pp. 1244–46.
57 Leona Jackson. "I Was on Guam." *The American Journal of Nursing* 42, no. 11 (1942): 1244–46. https://doi.org/10.2307/3415546.
58 What follows is paraphrasing directly from Olds' "The Story of the Capture of Guam," printed in *Navy Nurse* and republished in *Sensation* magazine.
59 "News from the past – JAP atrocities arouse nation," The Sheboygan Press. News From the Past – JAP Atrocities Arouse Nation (mansell.com). Accessed 4/26/2023
60 Ibid. News
61 Ibid. News
62 Ibid. News
63 Retired Brigadier General Charles S. Todd. United States Marine Corps, compiled this list. American POWs at Zentsuji POW Camp, Shikoku, Japan (mansell.com). Accessed 4/28/2021. The site links to an interesting newspaper article, "Prisoners OF War Wrote Recipes to While Away Time in Jap Prison," Cowart_article.pdf (mansell.com). There is no date or publisher shown. The site also links to *Guest of the Emperor*, written by Captain Kary Cadmus, United States Army Quartermaster Corps, 1977. Microsoft Word – KCE77_01.doc (okstate.edu). Accessed 4/28/2021. Guam Insular Patrol and the Army Quartermaster Corps. There is also a book that relates some of the history of John F. Kinney, who escaped from a prisoner of war camp, written by himself and James McCaffrey called *Wake Island Pilot: A World War II Memoir*, Brassey's US January 1, 2004.
64 The information contained here is summarized from John M. Gibbs, "Prisoners of War Camps in Japan and Japanese Controlled Areas as Taken From Reports of Interned American Prisoners Liaison and Research Branch American Prisoner of War Information Bureau," July 31, 1946. Microsoft Word – PAC-ZENTSUJI (axpow.org).
65 Ibid. Gibbs, p. 3.
66 War Crimes records RG 389.
67 Ibid. p. 1. Accessed 4/28/2021.
68 http://home.comcast.net/~winjerd/Supply/splymssn.htm#ANNEX_A. Accessed 2/28/2009.
69 Op. cit. Olds. paraphrasing directly from Olds' "The Story of the Capture of Guam," printed in the military publication *Navy Nurse* and republished in *Sensation* magazine. Also, Center for Research Allied POWs under the Japanese, News From the Past – JAP Atrocities Arouse Nation (mansell.com). Accessed 4/28/2021.
70 Op. cit. News from the past.

Additional Resources

Ed Hulse. *The Art of Pulp Fiction: An Illustrated History of Vintage Paperbacks.* San Diego, CA: IDW Publishing, illustrated edition, Sept. 7, 2021.

Elizabeth Norman. *We Band of Angels, The Untold Story of American Nurses Trapped on Bataan by the Japanese.* New York, NY: Pocket Books, Oct. 29, 2013.

Emilie Le Beau Lucchesi. *This Is Really War: The Incredible True Story of a Navy Nurse POW in the Occupied Philippines.* Chicago, IL: Chicago Review Press, 1st edition. May 7, 2019.

Joanna Bourke. *War and Art: A Visual History of Modern Conflict.* London: Reaktion Books, 2017.

Mary Ann Caws. *Manifesto: A Century of Isms.* Stamford, CT: Griffin Books, Dec. 1, 2000.

Monica Bohm-Duchen. *Art and the Second World War.* Princeton, TX: Princeton University Press, 2014.

Tereska Torres. *Women's Barracks (Femmes Fatales)* reprint. Manhattan, NY: The Feminist Press at CUNY May 1, 2005.

Questions

What social and political events and wartime hostilities drove the creation of so many art movements between the 1930s and 1940s?

How were manifestos related to modern art, and how and why did they arise during World War II?

What are the characteristics of pulp art, and why might the creators of these images have wanted their work to be anonymous?

How do propaganda and pulp differ?

Why were imprisoned women not given the appropriate accolades on returning home, and why did it take decades to be recognized as heroines with appropriate medals and honors?

What type of leadership traits did the nurses exhibit? Why was their demeanor extraordinary considering their lack of training to manage the wounded under battle conditions? Would you have been as calm and courageous in the same circumstances? Why or why not?

Modern take

Discover the biographies of four prisoners of war captured in the late 20th and early 21st centuries from the United States: Brigadier General Rhonda

280 Women and War

Cornum, United States Army (1991 Gulf War), Specialist Shoshana Johnson, United States Army (Invasion of Iraq 2003), Private First-Class Jessica Lunch, United States Army (Invasion of Iraq 2003), Specialist Lori Piestewa, United States Army, posthumous (Invasion of Iraq 2003). How were their captivities different from the experiences of military women in the Pacific during World War II? What do their racial makeup, backgrounds, and service roles say about changes that have occurred for women in the military over time? How did the media treat their capture of African American Shoshana Johnson and the death of Native and Mexican American Specialist Lori Piestewa?

Unearth the history behind creating the United States prisoner of war and missing-in-action flag. What is depicted on the banner? Should an updated version be designed to cover all genders who have become military prisoners of war?

How are women and men presented contrarily in pulp art covers? How have their characteristics been modified in media representations today?

Activities and discovery

Numerous artistic styles and artists were involved in the Modern Art Movement. Select a piece of modern art and describe the artist's vision for creating it.

Locate prisoner-of-war posters of male internees from World War II and compare them to those of female captives.

Research the female military prisoners of war during World War II. Locate their reminisces and diaries and read their first-hand accounts of their experiences. What were the numerous psychological and physical ways they approached their internments? Locate their reminisces and diaries and read their first-hand accounts of their experiences using POW and military history websites.

EPILOGUE

Women have consistently shown they are able fighters for their nations and beliefs. Since the emergence of the myth of the Amazon Penthesilea and subsequent eras, women have fought in ground combat and at sea. The ideal Amazon, part of a legendary race of female warriors, was believed to be a fictitious role only a goddess and not a human woman could fill. Courage and physical ability were the stuff of masculinity, not femininity. The reality was that such women did exist and were expert archers, field warriors, and cavalry. It took modern DNA research to show that among the Scythians who lived from 900 to 200 BC, fierce horse-riding women were buried with the same military honors as men. Storylines of Amazonian types remained stuck in ancient history until the rise of colonialism became an impediment to the peoples of the African continent. The general public was largely unaware there were African Amazons, but they had existed internally since before the Portuguese established a presence in the 1480s.

In the 19th century, colonial wars increased in number and severity to conquer and exert total and permanent control over African territories and their populations. The Western interlopers, mainly the nations of Portugal, France, and Great Britain, faced the largest contingent of female Amazons in history. Of those women who fought, the most formative were the Dahomey female bush fighters who trained and lived in Benin. Other African Amazons also fought and led military organizations before the Dahomeys. Queen Amanirenas ruled the Kingdom of Kush in Northern Africa and led an army of 30,000. Queen Nzinga Mbande from the Southern African Kingdom of Ndongo fought enemy tribes and was a talented military strategist. Yaa Asantewaa, Queen of the Ashanti Empire in Southern Ghana, called upon her women to fight like men until the last of them fell on the battlefield. The

282 Epilogue

legend that women could not handle battles' psychological and physical temperament was put away for all time with the world knowing of the Dahomey example. Or so it might seem. The stories in this book from the 19th century onward showed this not to be the case. Just as with the first wave of suffragism and the Women's Civil War, females have had to continue to fight in legislative halls and on the streets to become combatants because they were banned from these roles legally. Not until 2013 in the United States was the Combat Exclusion Policy for women rescinded. It was the first significant change in women's military integration since President Harry Truman passed the 1948 Women's Armed Services Integration Act, which allowed women to serve in non-combat positions with appropriate ranks and pay similar to men.

Women were ostracized for wanting to enlist during wartime and were not considered believable candidates for military service in a period in which, nearly every year of the 20th and 21st centuries, a form of conflict arose someplace in the world – many of the events limited or completely disallowed women's inclusion. Women's roles in military history are cyclical, with blockages, fighting for inclusion, acceptance, plateau, and back to regeneration as they seek new responsibilities. This cycle has existed globally, and because of tenacity, the only nation excluding women from combat today is Mauritania in northwestern Africa. More equitable but unequal treatment regarding what positions women can serve and their pay and promotional abilities has occurred in North America, Australia, India, and Russia. Myanmar, Israel, Eritrea, Libya, Malaysia, North Korea, Peru, and Tunisia are nations that conscript women. When Marion Olds served in the US Navy, women were automatically expelled if they married or became pregnant, and there was a cap on the number of women per service branch who could become officers. Using the United States as an example, the military demographic dashboard has shifted drastically. Women comprise 17.3 percent of the active-duty force and 21.4 percent of the National Guard and Reserves. Thirty-eight percent have a college education, and almost 30 percent are single parents, with the same percentage being married with children. Fifty-seven percent identify as White, 25 percent as Black, 6 percent as Asian, and 7 percent as multiracial or share an Indigenous background. Six percent identify as LGBT out of 1.3 million total service members. Data from NATO shows the share of female active-duty personnel in its member states ranges from 20 percent in Hungary, 16 percent in France, 12 percent in Germany, 11 percent in the United Kingdom, seven percent in Poland, less than one percent in India, and less than half a percent in Turkey.

Roles for female navalists since the time of Artemisia have drastically changed. Women serve and lead on all forms and sizes of combat vessels above and below the water line. The first submarine commander in the world, Norwegian Solveg Krey, took command of a Kobban class diesel submarine in 1995. Women serve aboard ballistic missile submarines and guided-missile submarines. A more significant proportion are specialty-rated enlisted personnel. Twenty-five females are actively serving among 268 US active duty and reserve admirals. Michelle Howard became the first Black woman to command a US Navy combatant ship and was the first woman to be promoted to four-star admiral. She was selected for the second-highest position in the ableist and largest global Navy as Vice Chief of Naval Operations. Admiral Howard served as a member of the Joint Chiefs of Staff, a body of the top senior uniformed leaders within the Department of Defense. Three days into her new job as head of a US Navy task force charged with countering piracy, she led the successful rescue attempt to free merchant vessel *Maersk, Alabama,* overtaken by four Somali pirates in the Somali Basin.

Boudica's and other historical fighters' battle strengths as charioteers, cavalry, sword fighters, siege shapers, and hand-to-hand combatants, have expanded into other realms as new warfare tools emerged. In Israel and Russia, women participated in contemporary ground combat as snipers, tank drivers, and artillery experts beginning in World War I. There have been numerous female Israeli Defense Force commanders who have held combat leadership roles. Women were employed in full combat for the first time for all three years of the Palestine War beginning in 1947. As within the saga of Penthesilea's demise at the hands of Achilles and the rapes and lashings of Boudica, male treatment of female troops has remained brutal in some instances. After Arab troops were caught abusing female soldiers' corpses on the battlefield, the Israeli cabinet voted to withdraw them from the front lines of combat until 2000, when the Caracal Battalion was formed. Its name comes from a species of cat whose sexes appear the same. Over 2000 women snipers enlisted in the Red Army, becoming the terrors of the Eastern Front in World War II. Lyudmila Pavlichenkoput announced, "We mowed down Hitlerites like ripe grain." She is among the deadliest snipers of all time, credited with 309 kills.

Female engagement teams were formed by the United States Marine Corps in Afghanistan in 2009. All were volunteer members chosen on maturity and the ability to build trust-based relations with Afghan women while troops were on patrol. To be selected for the teams, women had to be exceptionally physically fit, notable in their level of sound judgment, dependability, endurance, and courage. The US Army followed with its Lioness program of women who worked with special operations troops during the Iraq War. Women needed to prove they had extreme mental and physical toughness again when the Army rescinded its all-male policy in 2015 to open the role of Army Ranger to women. Of those who entered the training modules, five made the grade and earned the right to wear the coveted tan beret. Each destroyed the falsehood that women did not have the strength and endurance required on the battlefield by dispelling the nagging question: "Can you lift

284 Epilogue

a 200-pound man?" Even though these myth busters succeeded, a report released by the Army Special Command in 2023 stated they were kept from missions because of benevolent sexism and rejected from leadership positions because "dibs" on jobs were handed to males first.

Other service members have been retained as prisoners of war since the Allied Army and Navy nurses were captured in World War II in the Pacific and Europe. Today, they make the media headlines, secure book contracts, and appear as paid speakers and on TV shows, which would have been unbelievable to the nurses who spent four years imprisoned by the Japanese and Germans. During debriefs, they were told to keep their mouths shut as a duty to the men who failed to protect them. A majority of American women captured were White. Today, the racial and sexual orientation of the services has changed drastically from prior generations. More than 30 countries and many NATO members allow gays and lesbians to serve. Draconian laws such as Venezuela's Military Code of Justice still punish consensual same-sex conduct with up to three years imprisonment. The justification for criminal action is based on a code of cowardice and crimes against military decorum.

Four of the best-known female prisoners of war from the recent past are flight surgeon Army General Rhonda Cornum, who was shot down on a search and rescue mission during the Gulf War; Army Specialist Shoshana Johnson, the first Black female prisoner of war in the US military who was captured during Operation Iraqi Freedom; Hopi Tribal member Lori Piestewa, who died in an ambush in southern Iraq; and Private First Class Jessica Lynch, who was captured and recovered in a dangerous mission from hospital US special operations forces, including the Army Special Forces, Joint Special Operations Task Force 121, Air Force Pararescuemen, Army Rangers, Navy SEALS, and Marines in the spring of 2003. Similar cross-participant daring rescue missions were undertaken to release the Allied nurses in the Pacific. One Air Force flight nurse, Reba Zitella Whittle, who was imprisoned with the Luftwaffe, was released through third-party mediations with the International Red Cross just as there were mediations to free Marion Olds and her nurses early in the US entry into World War II. A differentiator with prisoner internments today has been that one section of the world was at war, not the entire globe, the imprisonments were shorter in duration, and access to tracking technology and human information networks that can locate the individuals far surpasses anything that existed in the past.

An additional note should be made about military air power, as this is not covered in this volume. Women went on to prove their mettle in the age of Flight when Turk Sabiha Gokcen, an adopted daughter of Ataturk, President of the newly formed Turkish Republic, trained in parachuting and gliding and was allowed to enroll in specialty training in military aircraft at the age of 23. She went on to fly 8000 hours and 32 combat missions – just another female who challenged traditional boundaries. In Russia, during World War II, the all-female Night Witches flying squadron of the 588th Night Bomber Regiment was formed under the leadership of Major Marina Raskova, who, like Mabel St. Clair Stobart, was rebuffed for her idea of women serving on the front lines of war. Her perseverance resulted in the formation of a unit of women who flew the Polikarpov PO-2, an all-weather craft used in low-cost ground attacks, liaison duties, and aerial reconnaissance. The regiment collected 23,627 sorties at the Battle of Caucasus, Kuban, Crimea, Belarus, Poland, and German offensives. They dropped over 2000 tons of bombs and 26,000 incendiary shells. Two hundred and sixty-one women served in the regiment. Women would continue contributing as wartime aerial experts such as jet, helicopter, bombing, and transport craft operators. Since 1963 and the space flight of Russian Cosmonaut Valentina Tereshkova, they have expanded their flight reach into space.

The number of female military characters in pulp comics and video games has ballooned. New roles and a different ethnic mosaic have arisen in carica-tures. Lady Jaye is a covert operations specialist. Amanda Blake Waller is a black espionage and federal law enforcement agent whose backstory is as a widow who escaped the Chicago Cabrini Green housing projects with a son and daughter after her husband was murdered. Danielle (Dani) Moonstar is a fictional Northern Cheyenne superhero based on real-life women like Buffalo Calf Road Woman who fought in the Battle of the Rosebud or Apache Lozen, who was known for her bravery, could ride and shoot, and was a trusted ally of Apache Chief Geronimo. The character of Major Carol Danvers is a military superhero jet-fighting ace. Currently, Ms. Marvel, Kamala Khan is represented as a Muslim Pakistani American who can shape-shift her body. Mystique is a proficient espionage agent and an expert in hand-to-hand com-bat and digital information technology. What has not changed is that all are drawn as sexual icons, except Amanda Waller, portrayed in tight-fitting knee-length professional attire and of average weight. The majority are still de-picted in what illustrators call the broken back position, an anatomy-defying distortion of an arched back, buttocks, and a posture that is impossible to attain in real life unless the spine has been severed. They usually sport reveal-ing spandex and plunging necklines and share a common physical attribute of tiny waists and overly ample bosoms.

As societal acceptability for women serving in war has risen, the toy mar-ket has begun to create more female military characters. Like other artifacts of material culture, toys mimic changing attitudes and values. Businesses have started to market dolls, puppets, games, and figurines that duplicate the numerous roles women have taken on as military professionals. There is a 36-piece pink (or green) plastic BMC female soldier playset and a GI Joe Hasbro Classified Series of Lady Jaye Action Figures with realistic mul-tiple accessories. There is an Army medic Barbie and a Marine Corps dress blue Barbie. Tiny Tots Boutique makes personalized "Itty Bitty Soldiers."

286 Epilogue

Funko POP will make a female military doll for all services and all races. There is a limited-edition paper doll set with female characters from military stories spanning 40 years and including all military branches. Small bronze and stone sculptures are available for purchase around the 100-dollar level. Proud Army wife T-shirts are being replaced with T-shirts claiming I'm not the veteran's wife; I'm the Veteran.

Sculpted female images remain minuscule. It was not until the late 20th and early 21st centuries that there was an increase in the commissions for more busts, statuettes, bronzes, and iconic representations. Statuary statistics in the United States are alarming. There are only 300 statues of real women in the United States compared to over 5000 real men, making women's remembrances a mere 1.2 percent in the category of public sculpture. A Vietnam memorial to women did not appear in the United States until 1993. It took two decades to bring the work into the public arena. In Kansas, at Army Camp Fort Leavenworth, the first monument honoring an all-female African American battalion was erected in 2019. The first women of color military exhibit appeared in 2021 at the Women's Memorial in Washington, D.C.

John W. Mills, whose mother was a World War II fire service member, sculpted a moving monument in London to honor the over seven million women who lent their services during World War II. Six hundred and fifty thousand of those honored were military members. The statue, erected in 2005 and unveiled by Queen Elizabeth II, was well behind the timeline in its creation of honoring women since nearly all Allied nations had existing national monuments honoring women's contributions to the war effort. It stands 22 feet high with 17 individual sets of clothing and uniforms around the sides, symbolic of the hundreds of different jobs women undertook. Among the 21 reproductions are the Women's Royal Naval Service uniforms, Royal Air Force, Red Cross nurses, air wardens, female police, and the Women's Land Army. The clothing appears to hang on wall pegs in either a state of readiness or as a memorial to a job completed. Do the items await the return of those who left them to be donned as soon as needed, or are they now closeted for the last time to be walked away from toward a new day?

In 2021, one of the most inspirational anti-monument statues raised relative to women's equality was *Glorieta de las mujeres que luchan* (The Glory of the Women's Struggle). Originally called "Anti-monument, We Want Us Alive," the piece is a feminist militant guerilla sculpture raised in Mexico City to promote justice for violence against women. The group convened at the Christopher Columbus roundabout in a "deeds, not words" daring move to overtake the public edifice. They installed a purple wooden woman with her arm raised and the word justice carved down her back. It was dedicated to "those women throughout the country who have faced violence, repression, and revictimization for fighting against injustice." The area is a focal point for marches, protests, and civil actions. On the fences below the plinth were placed men's names who fought for feminist injustices.

If women did obtain a rare art commission to produce war art, they received different monetary stipends than men and were relegated to shorter commission times. The largest body of war art representing women is their work on the Homefront because this is where their chief duties lay. There have been few active-duty female war artists, with the highest number appearing during major global conflicts as replacements for male artists who volunteered to fight. Nurses have been painted more than any other military women because these jobs were where they were allowed to serve legally. Very few could name a female counterpart to the male artists described. Those who have represented war in art have tended to avoid portraying battle conditions principally because they were not allowed near battles. War art is not just frontline scenes. It is the totality of creative responses across all societies, including the civilian viewpoint. What women artists have left to posterity are more of the social and personal histories associated with conflict. This makes their contributions important for adding a more rounded picture and a broader perspective of the totality of war. Much of their production involved unofficial portraits, the inside of war factories, agriculture, hospital wards, military tribunals, mass graves, recuperating and damaged people, street life, and post-destructive scenes.

Major museums like the Imperial War Museum in London have held outstanding exhibits related to women, war, and art. Internationally recognized museums have fashioned women-centric exhibits. In 2016, the Imperial War Museum exhibited 33 photographs, and 11 three-minute short films from British photographer and filmmaker Nick Danziger's collection entitled "Eleven Women Facing War." Eight conflict zones were represented: Bosnia, Kosovo, Israel, Gaza, Hebron West Bank, Sierra Leone, Colombia, and Afghanistan. The Metropolitan Museum of Art in New York City generated "100 Years of the Great War Through the Eyes of Four Female Artists." The Tate Museum produced "Women, War and Social Change." At the National Museum in Belgrade, an exhibit of war photographer Nadezda Petrovic, deemed "The Most Important Serbian Female Painter of the Period," can be downloaded online. The Fridman Gallery in New York City presented works of female artists who fled the war in Ukraine. In the Voloshyn Gallery in Kyiv, an exhibit honored women and war with their photography, paintings, and modern art. The Metropolitan Museum of Art presented "One Hundred Years of the Great Wars Through the Eyes of Four Female Artists." Smaller venues are also beginning to show exhibits tied to women and war. At Florida State University, an installation asked, "In what way do women have agency in war?" Its emphasis is on the Ukrainian war with Russia. It won a media award for the top ten best art exhibitions in 2022.

288 Epilogue

From out-of-this-world idealized pulp figures of modern times to mythical characters from centuries past, from space to under the sea, strides are continually being made by women breaking down barriers in service to their countries. Since it has only been within the last few decades that more attention has been paid to them through the use of art and artifacts, there is hope that through these two critical avenues of recounting their narratives, their stories and accomplishments will be more permanently represented equally to the attention that has been paid to their male counterparts. There is an immense suppressed population of women whose stories have yet to be told. Stories about art and artifacts are imperative for future generations to come physically face-to-face with women's extraordinary achievements.

BIBLIOGRAPHY

"1913 Cat and Mouse Act," UK Parliamentary Archives # HL/PO/PU/1/1913/3&4G5c4 Cat and Mouse Act first page – UK Parliament.

"Amazons Prove to Be Real Warriors, Artistic and Archeological Finds in Italy Vindicate Legends of Virgil, War Chariots and Armor, Contents of Tombs in Belmonte Necropolis Show that Women Fought in Armies," *New York Times*, Aug. 21, 1910, p. 64, ProQuest Historical Newspapers.

"Baseball Clubs Organized Among Amazons of Dahomey," *Chicago Daily Tribune* (1872–1972), Apr. 2, 1905. ProQuest Historical Newspapers.

"Boudicea-Boudicca," War Memorial Register, Imperial War Museums, Boadicea – Boudicca | War Imperial War Museums (iwm.org.uk).

"Coast, (The) Slave, and the American Squadron," *New York Times*, Mar. 5, 1862, p. 2, ProQuest Historical Newspapers.

"Commodore Wilmot's Visit to the Kingdom of Dahomey," *The Sydney Morning Herald*, Sep. 3, 1863, p. 3. Trove Search Engine. 03 Sep 1863 – COMMODORE WILMOT'S VISIT TO THE KING OF DAHOMEY. – Trove (nla.gov.au).

"Crystal Place the Famous Amazons, Natives of Dahomey," *The Pall Mall Gazette*, May 19th (n.y.) ProQuest Historical Newspapers.

"Dahoman Amazons Their Reckless Daring and Bravery in Battle," *The Chicago Tribune*, Jul. 20, 1890, p. 27, ProQuest Historical Newspapers.

"Dahomey Amazons in London, From the London Chronicle," *The Washington Post*, (1877–1922), May 29, 1903. ProQuest Historical Newspapers.

"Dahomey Amazons to Visit Europe-From the Pall Mall Gazette," *New York Times* (1857–1922), Oct. 23, 1890. ProQuest Historical Newspapers.

"Dahomeyan Amazons, Warriors and Witch Doctors from the Jardin d' Acclimation, Amazons of Dahomey," *Le Petit Journal*, n.d. ProQuest Historical Newspapers.

"Dahomeyans Revel in Cruelty, the Savage African Tribe Which Delights to Kill and Torment," *Chicago Daily Tribune* (1872–1922), Jun 13, 1892, ProQuest Historical Newspapers.

290 Bibliography

"Enormalies of the Slave-Trade, From the West African Herald," *New York Times,* Nov. 28, 1860, p. 2. ProQuest Historical Newspapers.

"Famous Amazons, The, Who Took Part Last Week in a Battle with the French, Killed on the Battlefield," *The Washington Post,* May 7, 1890. ProQuest Historical Newspapers.

"Fighting in Africa, French Engage with Both Morocco and Dahomey," *Chicago Daily Tribune,* Apr. 1, 1892, ProQuest Historical Newspapers.

"Fire in the Dahomey Village, Warriors, and Amazons Extinguish It with Hands and Teeth," *Chicago Daily Tribune* (1872–1920), June 8, 1893, ProQuest Historical Newspapers.

"Frederick Martyn in London Answers, Women as Soldiers," *The Washington Post,* May 6, 1917, p. F6, ProQuest Historical Newspapers.

"General Alfred Amedee Dodds (1842–1922) in Dahomey, from '*Le Petit Journal,*'" Illustrated Supplement, Dec. 3, 1892. Image of General Alfred Amedee Dodds (1842–1922) in Dahomey, from 'Le Petit by Meyer, Henri (1841–99) (bridgem-animages.com).

"Grasset de Saint-Sauveur, Jacques, 1757–1810. National Library of New Zealand, (22 items) Grasset de Saint-Sauveur, Jacques, 17... | Items | National Library of New Zealand | National Library of New Zealand (natlib.govt.nz).

"HMS Bonetta (1836) Royal Naval Vessels," HMS Bonetta (pdavis.nl).

"Incidents of the Dahomey War Dol. Dodds Says He Never Saw Black Warriors Fight So Desperately," *Chicago Daily Tribune* (1872–1922). Dec. 18, 1892, ProQuest Historical Newspapers.

"Joseph Mallory William Turner, The Deluge, Exhibited 1805," The Tate Museum, The Deluge, Joseph Mallord William Turner? exhibited 1805 | Tate.

"King (The) of Dahomey's Amazons," *Chicago Daily Tribune,* Jan. 28, 1877, p. 6, ProQuest Historical Newspapers.

"King (The) of the Slave Traders, From the New York Evening Post," *Chicago Press and Tribune,* Apr. 11, 1859, p. 3. ProQuest Historical Newspapers.

"King of Black Amazons Frank G. Carpenter Had the Last Newspaper Interview with Behanzin, the Blood-Thirsty Old Monarch of Dahomey, Just Before He Died-Held as a Prisoner by the French and Kept Under Close Guard for Years," *Boston Daily Globe,* May 3, 1907, p. SM3, ProQuest Historical Newspapers.

Kunz, George Frederick. "Precious Stones and Their Lore." *The Lotus Magazine* 6, no. 5 (1915): 223–33. http://www.jstor.org/stable/20543625.

"Mr. Francis Dodd," *The Times.* Mar. 10, 1949, p. 7. The Times Digital Archive (gale.com).

"Original (The) Suffragettes. Race of Amazons Who Fought Like Men and Had an Army Entirely of Their Own Sex," *The Washington Post,* Sep. 4, 1910, p. M1. ProQuest Historical Newspapers.

"Paris Salons (1673-Present)," Art Institute of Chicago Paris Salons (1673–present) | The Art Institute of Chicago (artic.edu).

"Pisindelis," *Encyclopedia, Science News & Research Reviews,* Academic Accelerator. Pisindelis: Most Up-to-Date Encyclopedia, News & Reviews (academic-accelerator.com).

"Renaissance Portrait Medals from the Robert Lehman Collection," Exhibition December 19, 2016–May 29, 2017," The Met, Portrait Medals: History and Production Processes | The Metropolitan Museum of Art (metmuseum.org). "Pisanello and the History of the Renaissance Medal."

"The History of the Academia de San Luca, c. 1590–1635: Documents from the *Archivio di Stato di Roma,*" National Gallery of Art, Intro (nga.gov).

"The Women of Weinsberg and other legends of Aarne-Thompson-Uther type 875 translated and edited by D. L. Ashliman," 2009–2011. The Women of Weinsberg (The Wives of Weinsberg): Folktales of Type 875* (pitt.edu).

"West Coast of Africa, The Slave-Trade – A Stupendous Human Sacrifice," *New York Times*, Aug. 27, 1860, p. 8, ProQuest Historical Newspapers.

"When Dahomey's Female Warriors Led a Counterattack Against French Forces," *HISTORYNET*, Sep. 5, 2006. When Dahomey's Female Warriors Led a Counterattack against French Forces (historynet.com).

"Whipped an Army of Women, The King of Dahomey's Amazons Defeated by a French Force," *The Washington Post*, Mar. 7, 1890, p. 1, ProQuest Historical Newspapers.

"Women and the Crusades," Women and the Crusades (knighttemplar.org) *OPCCTS – The Knights Templar North America*.

"Women as Warriors, Dahomey to Fight the French Invaders with Amazons," *Chicago Daily Tribune*, Aug. 14, 1892, p. 33, ProQuest Historical Newspapers.

"Women Fought in Battle Against Foreign Legion More Deadly than the Male According to Frederick Martyn Who Served in the Famous French Command Adventures with a Woman Pirate and Others in China," Article 18 – No Title, *New York Times*, Jan. 7, 1912, ProQuest Historical Newspapers.

"Women's Suffrage, the Struggle for the Right to Vote," National WWI Museum and Memorial, Women's Suffrage | National WWI Museum and Memorial (theworldwar.org).

"World's Fair Chicago, 1893, A Fair to Remember," n.d. The 1893 World's Fair in Chicago – Chicago's 1893, Worlds Fair (worldsfairchicago1893.com).

"You Could Smell a Slaver Five Miles Down Wind: The Unsavory Recollections of a Self-Made Merchant of Black Ivory Describe the Old Slave Trade," *New York Times (1923-)*, Jul. 22, 1928, p. 51, ProQuest Historical Newspapers.

Adam, H., and A. D. Galinsky. "Enclothed Cognition." *Journal of Experimental Social Psychology* 48, no. 4 (2012). https://doi.org/10.1016/j.jesp.2012.02.008. Enclothed cognition (utoronto.ca)

Adams, Maeve E. "The Amazon Warrior and the De/construction of Gendered Imperial Authority in Nineteenth-Century Colonial Literature." *Nineteenth-Century Gender Studies* no. 6.1 (Spring 2010).

Addison De Wolf Gibbs, Julia. *Arts and Crafts in the Middle Ages: A Description of Mediaeval Workmanship in Several Departments of Applied Art, Together with Some Account of Special Artisans in the Early Renaissance*. Scotts Valley California: Create Space Independent Publishing Platform, 1908. Release Date: Apr. 19, 2006 [eBook #18212] Project Gutenberg Ebook Arts and Crafts in the Middle Ages E-text prepared by Robert J. Hall & Chapuis, Julien.

Ade Ajayi, J. F., and Robert Smith. *Yoruba Warfare in the Nineteenth Century*. Cambridge, England: Cambridge University Press, 1964.

Adedze, Abenyega. "The Amazons of Dahomey," May 29, 2020 https://doi.org/10.1093/acrefore/9780190277734.013.274.

Aeschylus. *The Persians* (produced 472 BC), The Internet Classics Archive | The Persians by Aeschylus (mit.edu).

Akinjogbin, I. A. "The Oyo Empire in the 18th Century – A Reassessment." *Journal of the Historical Society of Nigeria* 3, no. 3 (1966): 449–60. http://www.jstor.org/stable/41856706.

Al, B. "Cretan Religion in Relation to Greek Religion." *Mnemosyne* 12, no. 3 (1944): 208–22. http://www.jstor.org/stable/4427070.

Alonso, Harriet Hyman. "Peace and Women's Issues in U.S. History." *OAH Magazine of History* 8, no. 3 (1994): 20–25. http://www.jstor.org/stable/25162961. Pp. 20–22.

Alonso, Harriet Hyman. "Review of *Women (and Others) as Movers and Shakers in Pre-World War I Europe and the United States*" by David S. Patterson. *Diplomatic History* 35, no. 1 (2011): 81–83. http://www.jstor.org/stable/24916402.

292 Bibliography

Alpern, Stanley B. *Amazons of Black Sparta (2ⁿᵈ Ed). The Women Warriors of Dahomey.* Manhattan, NY: NYU Press, Apr. 11, 2011.

Anderson, Louisa Garrett. "The Papers of Louisa Garrett Anderson 1879–1943," Ref. GB 106 7LGA, London: Women's Library Archives, Joint Information Systems Committee, United Kingdom. Papers of Louisa Garrett Anderson – Archives Hub (jisc.ac.UK).

Antliff, Mark. "Cubism, Futurism, Anarchism: The 'Aestheticism' of the 'Action d'art' Group, 1906–1920." *Oxford Art Journal* 21, no. 2 (1998): 99–120. http://www.jstor.org/stable/1360616.

Aperghis, G. "Athenian Mines, Coins, and Triremes." *Historia: Zeitschrift Für Alte Geschichte* 62, no. 1 (2013): 1–24. http://www.jstor.org/stable/24433621.

Armstrong, Meg. "'A Jumble of Foreignness': The Sublime Musayums of Nineteenth-Century Fairs and Expositions." *Cultural Critique*, no. 23 (1992): 199–250. https://doi.org/10.2307/1354195.

Atkins, Annette. "Dressing for Success, Suffrage Style." *Minnesota History* 67, no. 3 (2020): 140–45. https://www.jstor.org/stable/26977819.

Atsma, Aaron J. New Zealand *Epic Cycle, Fragments, Classical Texts Library,* Theoi Project, 2000, EPIC CYCLE FRAGMENTS – Theoi Classical Texts Library.

Auble, Cassandra. "The Cultural Significance of Precious Stones in Early Modern England," University of Nebraska (2011). The Cultural Significance of Precious Stones in Early Modern England (unl.edu). Accessed 1 Apr. 2022.

Aurélia Masson-Berghoff (ed). *Statues in Context: Production, Meaning and (Re)Uses.* Vol. 10. Leuven, Belgium: Peeters Publishers, 2019. https://doi.org/10.2307/j.ctv1q26tr1.

Babac, Dusan. *The Serbian Army in the Great War, 1914–1918.* Amherst, MA: Helion and Company, Apr. 21, 2016.

Babelon, Jean. "The Medal in Art and Society." *Journal of the Royal Society of Arts* 103, no. 4961 (1955): 782–92. http://www.jstor.org/stable/41364760.

Baker, Phil. *Austin Osman Spare: The Life and Legend of London's Lost Artist.* London: Strange Attractor, Jan. 1, 2010.

Baker, Phil. *Austin Osman Spare: The Occult Life of London's Legendary Artist.* Berkeley, CA: North Atlantic Books, 2014.

Baldwin, Agnes. "Symbolism on Greek Coins." *American Journal of Numismatics (1897–1924)* 49 (1915): 89–194. http://www.jstor.org/stable/43589909.

Ball, Hugo, and Gerhardt Edward Steinke. The Life and Work of Hugo Ball (Founder of Dadaism), Mouton The Hague Paris, 1967.

Baranyi, Anna. "Traditional and Avant-Garde Bartók Medals in Hungarian Art." *Studia Musicologica Academiae Scientiarum Hungaricae* 40, no. 1/3 (1999): 85–93. https://doi.org/10.2307/902554.

Barr, Jr. Alfred H. *Cubism and Abstract Art, Painting, Sculpture, Constructions, Photography, Architecture, Industrial Art, Theater, Films, Posters, Typography.* New York, NY: The Museum of Modern Art, 1936.

Barton, Thomas W. *Victory's Shadow: Conquest and Governance in Medieval Catalonia.* Ithica, NY: Cornell University Press, 2019. http://www.jstor.org/stable/10.7591/j.ctvfc54nx.

Bay, Edna G. "On the Trail of the Bush King: A Dahomean Lesson in the Use of Evidence." *History in Africa* 6 (1979): 1–15. https://doi.org/10.2307/3171738.

Baylen, J. O. "Politics and the 'New Journalism': Lord Esher's Use of the 'Pall Mall Gazette.'" *Victorian Periodicals Review* 20, no. 4 (1987): 126–41. http://www.jstor.org/stable/20082281.

Bearman, C. J. "An Examination of Suffragette Violence." *The English Historical Review* 120, no. 486 (2005): 365–97. http://www.jstor.org/stable/3490924.

Beazley, J. D. "Achilles and Polyxene: On a Hydria in Petrograd." *The Burlington Magazine for Connoisseurs* 28, no. 154 (1916): 137–39. http://www.jstor.org/stable/860265.

Beazley, John Davidson. *Development of the Attic Black-Figure, Revised edition*. Berkeley, CA: University of California Press, 1986. http://ark.cdlib.org/ark:/13030/ft1f59n77b/.

Beete, Paulette. *Creativity and Persistence: The Art that Fueled the Fight for Women's Suffrage*. Washington, D.C.: National Endowment for the Arts, 2020.

Bierschenk, Thomas. "The Creation of a Tradition: Fulani Chiefs in Dahomey/Bénin from the Late 19th Century." *Paideuma* 39 (1993): 217–44. http://www.jstor.org/stable/40341663.

Bland, Sydney R. "Never Quite as Committed as We'd Like, The Suffrage Militancy of Lucy Burns." *Journal of Long Island History* 17, no. 2 (1981): 15–17.

Blier, Suzanne Preston. "The Path of the Leopard: Motherhood and Majesty in Early Danhomè." *The Journal of African History* 36, no. 3 (1995): 391–417. http://www.jstor.org/stable/182468.

Boardman, John. "Exekias." *American Journal of Archaeology* 82, no. 1 (1978): 11–25. https://doi.org/10.2307/503793.

Bohm-Duchen, Monica. *Art and the Second World War*. Princeton, NJ: Princeton University Press, 2014.

Bois, Yve-Alain, and Thomas Repensek. "Francis Picabia: From Dada to Pétain." *October* 30 (1984): 121–27. https://doi.org/10.2307/778301.

Boldane-Zelenkova, Ilze. "Displaying Otherness: Does the Space Matter?" *Journal of Ethnology and Folkloristics* 16, no. 2 (Dec. 24, 2022): 219–38.

Bom, M. M. "The Lay Sisters of Saint John of Jerusalem." In: *Women in the Military Orders of the Crusades. The New Middle Ages*. New York, NY: Palgrave Macmillan, 2012. https://doi.org/10.1057/9781137088307.

Boon, Troy. *Youth of Darkest England: Working-Class Children at the Heart of Victorian Empire*. New York, NY: Routledge, 2005.

Bourgault, Sophie, and Rebecca Kingston (eds). *Christine de Pizan, The Book of the City of Ladies and Other Writings*. Indianapolis, IN: Hackett Publishing, 2018.

Bourke, Joanna. *War and Art: A Visual History of Modern Conflict*. London: Reaktion Books, 2017.

Bowra, C. M. *The Sewanee Review* 64, no. 3 (1956): 498–507. http://www.jstor.org/stable/27538559.

Brainard, Alfred P. "Polish-Lithuanian Cavalry in the Late Seventeenth Century." *The Polish Review* 36, no. 1 (1991): 69–82. http://www.jstor.org/stable/25778547.

Bremmer, Jan N., and Andrew Erskine (eds). *The Gods of Ancient Greece: Identities and Transformations*. Edinburgh University Press, 2010. http://www.jstor.org/stable/10.3366/j.ctt1r236p.

Brett, Maurice V. *Journals and Letters of Reginald Viscount Esher*. London: Ivor Nicolson & Watson, Ltd, 1934.

Bridges, Roy. "The Visit of Frederick Forbes to the Somali Coast in 1833." *The International Journal of African Historical Studies* 19, no. 4 (1986): 679–91. https://doi.org/10.2307/219140.

Britannica, T. Editors of Encyclopaedia. "Alfred-Amédée Dodds." *Encyclopedia Britannica*, July 14, 2023. https://www.britannica.com/biography/Alfred-Amedee-Dodds.

Britannica, T. The Editors of Encyclopaedia. "Caffaro Di Caschifellone". *Encyclopedia Britannica*, Jul. 27, 2023. https://www.britannica.com/biography/Caffaro-di-Caschifellone. Accessed 27 Dec. 2023.

Brown, Michelle. *Understanding Illuminated Manuscripts: A Guide to Technical Terms*, Revised Edition (Looking At). Los Angeles, CA: J Paul Getty Museum; Second Ed, Dec. 4, 2018.

294 Bibliography

Brulé, Pierre, and Antonia Nevill. *Women of Ancient Greece*. Edinburg, UK: Edinburgh University Press, 2003. http://www.jstor.org/stable/10.3366/j.ctt1r25hx.

Bugge, Alexander. "Costumes, Jewels, and Furniture in Viking Times." *Saga-Book* 7 (1911): 141–76. https://www.jstor.org/stable/48611663.

Bullen, J. B. "Renaissance Portrait Medals." *The Metropolitan Museum of Art Bulletin* 7, no. 3 (1912): 49–54. https://doi.org/10.2307/3252739.

Bunche, R. J. *The Journal of Negro Education* 8, no. 2 (1939): 209–12. https://doi.org/10.2307/2292577.

Burton, R. F. "The Kong Mountains." *Proceedings of the Royal Geographical Society and Monthly Record of Geography* 4, no. 8 (1882): 484–86. https://doi.org/10.2307/1800716.

Burton, Richard Francis. *A Mission to Gelele, King of Dahome, In Two Volumes*. London: Tinsley Brothers, 1864.

Byles, Joan Montgomery. "Women's Experience of World War One: Suffragists, Pacifists and Poets." *Women's Studies International Forum* 8, no. 5 (1985): 473–87. https://doi.org/10.1016/0277-5395(85)90078-0.

Cahill, Cathleen D. "Epilogue: Remembering and Forgetting." In *Recasting the Vote: How Women of Color Transformed the Suffrage Movement*, 262–78. Chapel Hill, North Carolina: University of North Carolina Press, 2020. http://www.jstor.org/stable/10.5149/9781469659343_cahill.24.

Campbell, Ballard. "Comparative Perspectives on the Gilded Age and Progressive Era." *The Journal of the Gilded Age and Progressive Era* 1, no. 2 (2002): 154–78. http://www.jstor.org/stable/25144294.

Campbell, Olivia. *Women in White Coats: How the First Women Doctors Changed the World of Medicine*. New York, NY: Park Row, Mar. 15, 2022.

Carney, E. D. "Women and Dunasteia in Caria." *The American Journal of Philology* 126, no. 1 (2005): 65–91. http://www.jstor.org/stable/1562184.

Carpenter, Rhys. "Dynamic Symmetry: A Criticism," *American Journal of Archeology* 25, no. 1 (Jan–Mar 1921): 18–36. https://www.jstor.org/stable/i221771.

Carter Olson, C. S. "'To Ask Freedom for Women': The Night of Terror and Public Memory." *Journalism & Mass Communication Quarterly* 98, no. 1 (2021): 179–99. https://doi.org/10.1177/1077699020927118.

Cassidy, Kim. "Jewels of Denial: A Look at British Suffrage Jewelry," Apr. 16, 2020, The Frick Museum, Jewels of Denial | The Frick Pittsburgh.

Cassius, Dio. *Roman History*. Chicago, IL: University of Chicago (Bill Thayer website editor) LacusCurtius • Cassius Dio's Roman History (uchicago.edu) URL: tinyurl.com/CasDioWPT.

Cassius, Dio. *Roman History, Volume VIII: Books 61–70*. Translated by Earnest Cary, Herbert B. Foster. Loeb Classical Library 176. Cambridge: Harvard University Press, 1925.

Catlos, Brian A. Review of "Caffaro, Genoa and the Twelfth-Century Crusades." Translated by Martin Hall and Jonathan Phillips. *Comitatus: A Journal of Medieval and Renaissance Studies* 45 (2014): 218–19. https://doi.org/10.1353/cjm.2014.0003.

Caws, Mary Ann. *Manifesto: A Century of Isms*. Stamford, CT: Griffin Books, Dec. 1, 2000.

Chamberlin, Christopher. "Bulk Exports, Trade Tiers, Regulation, and Development: An Economic Approach to the Study of West Africa's 'Legitimate Trade.'" *The Journal of Economic History* 39, no. 2 (1979): 419–38. http://www.jstor.org/stable/2118946.

Chaudoin, E. "Extract from the Illustration," 26 July 1890. *Les Africains*. Tome X, Editions, J. A., 1978, p. 250.

Bibliography 295

Chenault, Rachel L. "The Celtic Queen Boudica as a Historiographical Narrative." *The Gettysburg Historical Journal* 19, Article 6 (Sep. 2020). The Celtic Queen Boudica as a Historiographical Narrative (gettysburg.edu)

Chibnall, Marjori. *The Ecclesiastical History of Orderic Vitalis, Vol 2 Books III and IV*, Oxford, UK: Clarendon Press, 1991.

Chibuife, Vivian. *Dahomey, and the Slave Trade: The Real Story of the Slave Trade in Dahomey vs. The Woman King (Black History Series)*. Anambra, Nigeria: Independently Published, Oct. 4, 2022. IAVN 13 979-8356113413.

Childs, William A. P. "Lycian Relations with Persians and Greeks in the Fifth and Fourth Centuries Re-Examined." *Anatolian Studies* 31 (1981): 55–80. https://doi.org/10.2307/3642758.

Church, John Alfred, and William Jackson Brodribb (translation). *The Annals by Tacitus Written 109 A.C.E.* Cambridge: MIT Classics online, 1994.

Clark, Evans. "Woman Suffrage in Parliament. A Test for Cabinet Autocracy." *The American Political Science Review* 11, no. 2 (1917): 284–309. https://doi.org/10.2307/1943988.

Clement, Russel T. *Les Fauves: A Sourcebook*. Westport, CT: Greenwood Press, 1994.

Clifford, Carrie Williams, and Cathleen D. Cahill. "The Problem of the Color Line." In *Recasting the Vote: How Women of Color Transformed the Suffrage Movement*, 121–30. Chapel Hill, NC: University of North Carolina Press, 2020.

Clutton-Brock, A. "The Post-Impressionists." *The Burlington Magazine for Connoisseurs* 18, no. 94 (1911): 216–19. http://www.jstor.org/stable/858608.

Cobbs, Elizabeth. "Fighting on Two Fronts: World War One, Women's Suffrage, and John Pershing's 'Hello Girls.'" *South Central Review* 34, no. 3 (2017): 31–47. https://www.jstor.org/stable/26410811.

Collins, Hugh E. L. *The Order of the Garter 1348–1461: Chivalry and Politics in Late Medieval England*. Oxford: Oxford University Press, July 2000.

Comena, Anna. *Alexiad*, Fordham University Medieval Sourcebook online (English translation) From original translation Elizabeth A. Dawes, London, 1928. Internet History Sourcebooks: Medieval Sourcebook (fordham.edu).

Corbey, Raymond. "Ethnographic Showcases, 1870–1930." *Cultural Anthropology* 8, no. 3 (1993): 338–69. http://www.jstor.org/stable/656317.

Cornebise, Alfred Emile. *Art from the Trenches: America's Uniformed Artists in World War I*. College Station, TX: Texas A&M Press, 1991.

Costa, Emilia Viotti da. "The Portuguese-African Slave Trade: A Lesson in Colonialism." *Latin American Perspectives* 12, no. 1 (1985): 41–61. http://www.jstor.org/stable/2633561.

Crouch, David, and Jeroen Deploige. "Taking the Field: Knighthood and Society in the High Middle Ages." In *Knighthood and Society in the High Middle Ages*, edited by David Crouch and Jeroen Deploige, 1–26. Leuven, Belgium: Leuven University Press, 2020. https://doi.org/10.2307/j.ctvbtzmj5.5.

Cudny, Waldemar, and Hakan Appleblad. "Monuments and their Functions in Urban Public Space." *Norwegian Journal of Geography* 73, no. 5 (2019): 273–89 https://doi.org/10.1080/00291951.2019.1694976.

Cupic, Simona. "The Interpretation of Female Bodies as a Projection of Identity: The Orient, the Balkans or Something Else?" *Anthropology of East Europe Review* 20, no. 1 (2022): 87–94. Indiana University Scholar Works. https://scholarworks.iu.edu/journals/index.php/aeer/article/view/390.

Curtenius Roosevelt, Anna. "The Rise and Fall of the Amazon Chiefdoms." *L'Homme* 33, no. 126/128 (1993): 255–83. http://www.jstor.org/stable/40589896.

Cvetkovic, Dragon. "Beta Vukanovic Babette Bachmayer 1872-1972," Beta Vukanović Babette Bachmayer 1872–1972 – YouTube.

296 Bibliography

D'Agata, Anna Lucia, and Antoine Hermary. "Ritual and Cult in Crete and Cyprus from the Third Millennium to the First Millennium BC: Towards a Comparative Framework." *British School at Athens Studies* 20 (2012): 273–88. http://www.jstor.org/stable/23541213.

De Lorris, Guillaume, and Jean de Meun (translator Frances Horgan). *The Romance of the Rose (Oxford World Classics)*. Oxford: Oxford University Press, 2009.

de Saint-Sauveur, Jacques Grasset. "Tableau of the PrincipalPeoples of America (Tableau des principaux peoples de l'Ajmerique) 1798," The Met, Jacques Grasset de Saint-Sauveur | Tableau of the e Principal Peoples of America (Tableau des principaux peuples de l'Amérique) | French | The Metropolitan Museum of Art (metmuseum.org).

Dean, Sidney. "Ringing out the Middle Ages: Landsknecht Mercenaries Lead Europe into the Renaissance." *Medieval Warfare* 1, no. 2 (2011): 12–17. https://www.jstor.org/stable/48577837.

Decker, John R. "Aid, Protection, and Social Alliance: The Role of Jewelry in the Margins of the *Hours of Catherine of Cleves*." *Renaissance Quarterly* 71, no. 1 (2018): 33–76. https://www.jstor.org/stable/26560746.

Decker, Sarah Ifft. *The Fruit of Her Hands: Jewish and Christian Women's Work in Medieval Catalan Cities*. University Park, PA: Penn State University Press, 2022. https://doi.org/10.5325/jj.5233100.

Deknatel, Frederick B. "The Thirteenth Century Gothic Sculpture of the Cathedrals of Burgos and Leon." *The Art Bulletin* 17, no. 3 (1935): 243–389. https://doi.org/10.2307/3045586.

Deming, Dorothy. *Ginger Lee War Nurse*. New York, NY: Dodd Mead & Company, 1942.

Dewald, Carolyn, and John Marincola (eds). *The Cambridge Companion to Herodotus*. Cambridge: Cambridge University Press, 2006.

Dinsmoor, William B. "The Mausoleum at Halicarnassus: I. The Order." *American Journal of Archaeology* 12, no. 1 (1908): 3–29. https://doi.org/10.2307/496853.

Dodd, Francis. *Admirals of the British Navy*. London: Country Life and George Newnes Ltd, 1917.

Dodd, Francis. *An Operation for Appendicitis at the Military Hospital, Endell Street, London. Chalk Drawing by Francis Dodd, 1920*. [1920]. Colored chalk on paper, sight 30.6 x 26.5 cm. <a href="https://wellcomecollection.org/">Wellcome Collection</a>.

Dow, Arthur Wesley. "Modernism in Art." *The American Magazine of Art* 8, no. 3 (1917): 113–16. http://www.jstor.org/stable/23934265.

Dragnich, Alex N. "Leadership and Politics: Nineteenth Century Serbia." *The Journal of Politics* 37, no. 2 (1975): 344–61. https://doi.org/10.2307/2128998.

DuBois, Ellen. "The Radicalism of the Woman Suffrage Movement: Notes toward the Reconstruction of Nineteenth-Century Feminism." *Feminist Studies* 3, no. 1/2 (1975): 63–71. https://doi.org/10.2307/3518956.

Dumenil, Lynn. "Women's Reform Organizations and Wartime Mobilization in World War I-Era Los Angeles." *The Journal of the Gilded Age and Progressive Era* 10, no. 2 (2011): 213–45. http://www.jstor.org/stable/23045158.

Duncan, John. *Travels in Western Africa in 1845 and 1846 in Two Volumes Comprising a Journey from Whydah through the Kingdom of Dahomey to Adofoodia in the Interior*. London: Richard Bentley Press, 1847.

Duram, James C. "A Study of Frustration: Britain, the USA, and the African Slave Trade, 1815–1870." *Social Science* 40, no. 4 (1965): 220–25. http://www.jstor.org/stable/41885111.

Dyson, Hannah. "The 'Antis': Minnesota Women Opposed to Female Suffrage." *Minnesota History* 67, no. 3 (2020): 163–68. https://www.jstor.org/stable/26977824.

Eisenman, Stephen F. "The Intransigent Artist or How the Impressionists Got Their Name." In *Critical Readings in Impressionism and Post-Impressionism: An Anthology*, edited by Mary Tompkins Lewis, 1st edition, 149–61. Oakland, California: University of California Press, 2007. https://doi.org/10.2307/jj.8501295.10.

Elias, Ann, Ross Harley, and Nicholas Tsoutas. "Introduction." In *Camouflage Cultures: Beyond the Art of Disappearance*, edited by Ann Elias, Ross Harley, and Nicholas Tsoutas, vii–x. Camperdown, Australia: Sydney University Press, 2015. http://www.jstor.org/stable/j.ctt1bh4b60.4.

Eller, Cynthia. "Matriarchy and the Volk." *Journal of the American Academy of Religion* 81, no. 1 (2013): 188–221. http://www.jstor.org/stable/23357881.

Eller, Cynthia. "Matriarchy and the Volk." *Journal of the American Academy of Religion* 81, no. 1 (2013): 188–221. http://www.jstor.org/stable/23357881.

Ellis, A. B. *The Land of Fetish*. London: Chapman and Hall, 1883.

Ellis, Douglas, Ed Hulse, and Robert Weinberg (eds). *The Art of the Pulps: An Illustrated History*. San Diego, CA: IDW Publishing, Oct. 24, 2017.

Fagbohoun, Louis, and Cathy Vieillescazes. "Cultural Heritage Objects of Wourthern Benin: Plant Dyes and Exudates Used in Their Confection," Chapter from the edited volume, *Heritage*, Daniela turcanus-Carutiu (ed). Sep. 9, 2020, EBOOK 978-1-83881-926-2.

Farrokh, Kaveh. *Shadows in the Desert: Ancient Persia at War*. Oxford: Osprey Publishing, 2007.

Fay, Sidney B. "Bismarck's Welfare State." *Current History* 18, no. 101 (1950): 1–7. http://www.jstor.org/stable/45307677.

Finn, Howard. "Modernism and the Suffragette Prison Narratives." *Key Words: A Journal of Cultural Materialism* 18, no. 3 (2000): 94–108. https://www.jstor.org/stable/26920224.

Fitzroy, Yvonne. *Scottish Nurses in the First World War with the Scottish Nurses in Roumania and a History of the Scottish Women's Hospitals*. Driffield: Leonaur Ltd, Dec. 2015.

Forbes, Archibald. *Battles of the Nineteenth Century, Vol 2: With about 320 Illustrations and 80 Plans*, reprint, 2018. London, UK: Forgotten Books, ISBN 0282511237

Forbes, Frederick E. *Dahomey, and the Dahomans; Being the Journals of Two Missions to the King of Dahomey and Residence in His Capital in 1849 and 1850*. London: Longman, Brown, Green and Longmans, 1851.

Forgey, Sarah. "Art in the Trenches: The World War I Paintings of Samuel Johnson Woolf." *Army History*, no. 95 (2015): 26–31. http://www.jstor.org/stable/26300397.

Forss, Amy Helene. "Introduction." In *Borrowing from Our Foremothers: Reexamining the Women's Movement through Material Culture, 1848–2017*, 1–12. Lincoln, NE: University of Nebraska Press, 2021. https://doi.org/10.2307/j.ctv21fqjp5.5.

Forss, Amy Helene. "Parading Their Colors." In *Borrowing from Our Foremothers: Reexamining the Women's Movement through Material Culture, 1848–2017*, 33–48. Lincoln, NE: University of Nebraska Press, 2021. https://doi.org/10.2307/j.ctv21fqjp5.7.

Forss, Amy Helene. "Silently Disobedient." In *Borrowing from Our Foremothers: Reexamining the Women's Movement through Material Culture, 1848–2017*, 49–62. University of Nebraska Press, 2021. https://doi.org/10.2307/j.ctv21fqjp5.8.

Franklin, Margaret. "Boccaccio's Amazons and Their Legacy in Renaissance Art: Confronting the Threat of Powerful Women." ("Boccaccio's Amazons and Their Legacy in Renaissance Art – JSTOR") *Woman's Art Journal* 31, no. 1 (2010): 13–20. http://www.jstor.org/stable/40605235.

298 Bibliography

Fratantuono, Lee. "The Penthesilead of Quintus Smyrnaeus: A Study in Epic Reversal." *Wiener Studien* 129 (2016): 207–31. http://www.jstor.org/stable/24752775.

Freville, G. "Dahomey-Expo Paris 1900," Worldfairs, 1900. Expo Paris 1900 | Dahomey | French Colonies (worldfairs.info).

Fussell, Paul. *Uniforms Why We Are What We Wear*. Boston, MA: Houghton Mifflin, 2002.

Gambash, Gil. "Servicing the Mediterranean Empire: Non-State Actors and Maritime Logistics in Antiquity." *Mediterranean Studies* 25, no. 1 (2017): 9–32. https://doi.org/10.5325/mediterraneanstu.25.1.0009.

Garcia-M., Anna Gutiérrez. "The Exploitation of Local Stone in Roman Times: The Case of North-Eastern Spain." *World Archaeology* 43, no. 2 (2011): 318–41. http://www.jstor.org/stable/41308500.

Garrett, Miranda, and Zoe Thomas. *Suffrage, and the Arts: Visual Culture, Politics, and Enterprise*. Camden, NJ: Bloomsbury Visual Arts, 2020.

Garrido I Valls, Josep-David. *Ramon Berenguer IV*, Rafael Dalmau (ed). Catalonia: Self-Publisher, Apr. 1, 2014.

Garrihy, Andrea. "Falling Heads, Raised Arms and Missing Persons: Thornycroft Studio Practice." *Sculpture Journal* 15 no. 1 (June 2006) Gale Academic OneFile, Falling heads, raised arms and missing persons: Thornycroft studio practice – Document – Gale Academic OneFile.

Geary, Patrick J. *Women at the Beginning, Origin Myths from the Amazons to Virgin Mary*. Princeton, NJ: Princeton University Press, Feb. 19, 2006.

Georges, Pericles B. "Saving Herodotus' Phenomena: The Oracles and the Events of 480 B.C." *Classical Antiquity* 5, no. 1 (1986): 14–59. https://doi.org/10.2307/25010838.

Gies, Joseph, and Frances Gies. *Women in the Middle Ages: The Lives of Real Women in a Vibrant Age of Transition*. New York, NY: Harper Collins e-books, Nov. 30, 2010.

Gillespie, Caitlin C. "Introduction." In *Boudica: Warrior Woman of Roman Britain*, Women in Antiquity. New York, NY, 2018; online edn: Oxford Academic, 21 June 2018. https://doi.org/10.1093/oso/9780190609078.003.0001. Accessed 27 Dec. 2023.

Gilman, Sander L. "Black Bodies, White Bodies: Toward an Iconography of Female Sexuality in Late Nineteenth-Century Art, Medicine, and Literature." *Critical Inquiry* 12, no. 1 (1985): 204–05. http://www.jstor.org/stable/1343468.

Ginovart, J. Luis I, A. Costa-Jover, S. Coll-Pla, and R. Miralles-Jori. "Non-invasive Techniques for the Assessment of Masonry Structures: Experiences in the Pillars of a Gothic Apse." In *Structural Analysis of Historical Constructions-Anamnesis, Diagnosis, Therapy, Controls*, Van Balen, and Verstrynge (eds). London: Taylor and Francis Group, 2016.

Godley, A. D. (translation). *The Histories of Herodotus*. Pontiac, MI: Scribe Publishing, 2018.

Goldman, Bernard. "Women's Robes: The Achaemenid Era." *Bulletin of the Asia Institute* 5 (1991): 83–103. http://www.jstor.org/stable/24048288.

Goodier, Susan. "Antis Win the New York State Campaign, 1912–1915." In *No Votes for Women: The New York State Anti-Suffrage Movement*, 67–92. Urbana-Champaign, IL: University of Illinois Press, 2013. http://www.jstor.org/stable/10.5406/j.ctt2ttdcb.7.

Gordon, Ann. *The Selected Papers of Elizabeth Cady Stanton and Susan B. Anthony. An Awful Hush, 1895–1906*. New Brunswick, NJ: Rutgers University Press, 2013.

Graham, Sally Hunter. "Woodrow Wilson, Alice Paul, and the Woman Suffrage Movement." *Political Science Quarterly* 98, no. 4 (1983): 665–79. https://doi.org/10.2307/2149723.

Grant, Kevin. "British Suffragettes and the Russian Method of Hunger Strike." *Comparative Studies in Society and History* 53, no. 1 (2011): 113–43. http://www.jstor.org/stable/41241735.

Graves, Robert. *The Greek Myths*. London: Penguin Books, UK, 1955.

Green, Barbara. "From Visible Flâneuse to Spectacular Suffragette? The Prison, the Street, and the Sites of Suffrage." *Discourse* 17, no. 2 (1994): 67–97. http://www.jstor.org/stable/41389369.

Green, Nicholas. "Dealing in Temperaments: Economic Transformation of the Artistic Field in France during the Second Half of the Nineteenth Century." In *Critical Readings in Impressionism and Post-Impressionism: An Anthology*, edited by Mary Tompkins Lewis, 1st edition, 31–47. Oakland, CA: University of California Press, 2007. https://doi.org/10.2307/jj.8501295.6.

Greene, T. Whitcombe. "German Medallists of the Sixteenth and Seventeenth Centuries." *The Numismatic Chronicle and Journal of the Numismatic Society* 8 (1888): 145–53. http://www.jstor.org/stable/42682590.

Greenwell, W., and Canon Greenwell. "On Some Rare Greek Coins." *The Numismatic Chronicle and Journal of the Numismatic Society* 10 (1890): 20–32. http://www.jstor.org/stable/42679615.

Grethlein, Jonas. "How Not to Do History: Xerxes in Herodotus' 'Histories.'" *The American Journal of Philology* 130, no. 2 (2009): 195–218. http://www.jstor.org/stable/20616180.

Guliaev, Valeri I. "Amazons in the Scythia: New Finds at the Middle Don, Southern Russia." *World Archaeology* 35, no. 1 (2003): 112–25. http://www.jstor.org/stable/3560215.

Gutiérrez, Anna. "The Exploitation of Local Stone in Roman Times: The Case of North-Eastern Spain." *World Archaeology* 43, no. 2 (2011): 318–41. http://www.jstor.org/stable/41308500.

Haan, Francisca de; Daskalova, Krasimira; and Loutfi, Anna (January 2006). *Biographical Dictionary of Women's Movements and Feminisms in Central, Eastern, and Southeastern Europe: 19th and 20th Centuries*. ISBN 9789637326394.

Hacker, Barton C. "Women and Military Institutions in Early Modern Europe: A Reconnaissance." *Signs* 6, no. 4 (1981): 643–71. http://www.jstor.org/stable/3173736.

Hadaway. "Developments in the Art of Jewellery." *Journal of the Royal Society of Arts* 56, no. 2881 (1908): 287–97. http://www.jstor.org/stable/41337952.

Hall, Richard C. *The Balkan Wars, 1912–1913 Prelude to the First World War*. Abingdon: Routledge, 2000.

Halsall, Paul. "Medieval Sourcebook: Anna Comnena: The Alexiad," Fordham University Sourcebooks, Nov. 20, 2023. Internet History Sourcebooks: Medieval Sourcebook (fordham.edu).

Hambidge, Jay. *Dynamic Symmetry: The Greek Vase*. New Haven, CT: Yale University Press, 1920.

Hambidge, Jay. *The Elements of Dynamic Symmetry (Dover Art Instruction)*. Mineola, NY: Dover Publications, 1967.

Hannah, Robert. "An Astean Ancestry: Sources for Multi-Level Compositions." *Mediterranean Archaeology* 2 (1989): 65–71. http://www.jstor.org/stable/24666624.

Hanson, John H. "The Aesthetics of Futurism." *The Comparatist* 7 (1983): 19–28. http://www.jstor.org/stable/44366696.

Harms, Ernst. "The Psychology of Clothes." *American Journal of Sociology* 44, no. 2 (1938): 239–50. http://www.jstor.org/stable/2768730.

Harper, Ida Husted (ed). *The History of Woman Suffrage*, illustrated with copperplate and photogravure engravings *in six volumes* volume vi 1900–1920. National American Woman Suffrage Association, 1922. Pp. 729–38.

Harper, Ida Husted. "Woman Suffrage throughout the World." *The North American Review* 186, no. 622 (1907): 55–71. http://www.jstor.org/stable/25105981.

Bibliography

Hawkins, Mike. "What's in a Name? Republicanism and Conservatism in France 1871–1879." *History of Political Thought* 26, no. 1 (2005): 120–41. http://www.jstor.org/stable/26221728.

Hazlehurst, Cameron. "Asquith as Prime Minister, 1908–1916." *The English Historical Review* 85, no. 336 (1970): 502–31. http://www.jstor.org/stable/563193.

Heilbrunn, Gunther, and Paul Anthony Rahe. "Meet the Spartans." *The National Interest*, no. 152 (2017): 83–92. https://www.jstor.org/stable/26557432.

Helion, Jean. *They Shall Not Have Me, The Capture and Forced Labor and Escape of a French Prisoner in World War II*. New York, NY: Arcade, June 3, 2014.

Herodotus. *Delphi Complete Works of Herodotus (Illustrated) Delphi Ancient Classics Book 12)*. East Sussex: Delphi Classics, 2013.

Herodotus. *The History*. Translated by George Rawlinson. Full Text of Herodotus Volume I & II. New York, NY: Dutton & Co., 1862. Archive.https://archive.org/stream/herodotus00herouoft/herodotus00herouoft_djvu.txt.

Higgins, Lisa Cochran. "Adulterous Individualism, Socialism, and Free Love in Nineteenth-Century Anti-Suffrage Writing." *Legacy* 21, no. 2 (2004): 193–209. http://www.jstor.org/stable/25679506.

Hilton, Alison. "From Abramtsevo to Zakopane: Folk Art and National Ideals in Russia and Eastern Europe." *Russian History* 46, no. 4 (2019): 241–61. https://www.jstor.org/stable/26870021.

Hingley, Richard, and Christina Unwin. *Boudica: Iron Age Warrior Queen*. London: Hambledon Continuum, New edition, Aug. 21, 2006.

Ho, Cynthia. "Communal and Individual Autobiography in Christine de Pizan's 'Book of the City of Ladies.'" *CEA Critic* 57, no. 1 (1994): 31–40. http://www.jstor.org/stable/44377130.

Hodgson, Natasha R. "Conclusion." In *Women, Crusading and the Holy Land in Historical Narrative*, 25:236–45. Martlesham, Suffolk UK: Boydell & Brewer, 2007. http://www.jstor.org/stable/10.7722/j.ctt81mst.16.

Hodgson, Natasha R. "Women in the History of Crusading and the Latin East." In *Women, Crusading and the Holy Land in Historical Narrative*, 25:36–52. Boydell & Brewer, 2007. http://www.jstor.org/stable/10.7722/j.ctt81mst.11.

Hoepker, Karin. "Frederick Douglass's 'The Heroic Slave' – Risk, Fiction, and Insurance in Antebellum America." *Amerikastudien/American Studies* 60, no. 4 (2015): 441–62. http://www.jstor.org/stable/44071920.

Hooton, E. R. *Prelude to the First World War: The Balkan Wars 1912–1913*. Stroud, UK: Fonthill Media, Oct. 19, 2014.

http://www.jstor.org/stable/10.5149/9781469659343_cahill.11.

https://jstor.org/stable/community.24843254.

Hulse (ed). *The Art of Pulp Fiction: An Illustrated History of Vintage Paperbacks*. San Diego, CA: IDW Publishing, illustrated edition, Sep. 7, 2021.

Humphries, Michael. "'Perfectly Secret and Perfectly Democratic': Lord Esher and the Society of Islanders, 1909—14." *The English Historical Review* 127, no. 528 (2012): 1156–79. http://www.jstor.org/stable/23272742.

Huscroft, Richard. "The Matron's Tale: Nicola de la Haye and the Defence of England." In *Tales from the Long Twelfth Century: The Rise and Fall of the Angevin Empire*. New Haven, CT: Yale, 2016; online edn.

Hutton, I. *With a Women's Unit in Serbia, Salonika, and Sevastopol*. London: Williams and Norgate, 1928.

Jackson, Leona. "I Was on Guam." *The American Journal of Nursing* 42, no. 11 (1942): 1244–46. https://doi.org/10.2307/3415546.

James, E. O. "The Nature and Function of Myth." *Folklore* 68, no. 4 (1957): 474–82. http://www.jstor.org/stable/1258206.

Janson, H. W. *19ᵗʰ Century Sculpture*. New York, NY: Harry N. Abrams Inc, 1985

Jarrett, Christian. "Introduction 'Enclothed Cognition' How What We Wear Affects How We Think," The British Psychological Society Cognition and Perception, Mar. 1, 2012. Introducing "enclothed cognition" – how what we wear affects how we think | BPS.

Jeal, Tim. "Introduction: A Contradictory Hero." In *Livingstone: Revised and Expanded Edition*, 1–4. New Haven, CT: Yale University Press, 2013. http://www.jstor.org/stable/j.ctt32bm79.6.

Jeal, Tim. "The Last Journey: 1872–1873." In *Livingstone: Revised and Expanded Edition*, 365–81. New Haven, CT: Yale University Press, 2013. http://www.jstor.org/stable/j.ctt32bm79.29.

Jewell, William. *The Golden Cabinet of True Treasure*. London: John Crosley, 2011.

Johnson, Lily. "Boadicea and Her Daughters, Statue," History Hit, Boadicea and Her Daughters Statue – History and Facts | History Hit, Mar. 23, 2021.

Johnson, Marion. "News from Nowhere: Duncan and 'Adofoodia.'" *History in Africa* 1 (1974): 55–66. https://doi.org/10.2307/3171760.

Jones, Adam. "My Arse for Akou, A Wartime Ritual of Women on the Nineteenth-Century Gold Coast," *Cahiers d'Etudes Africaines* 33, no. 13 (1993): 545–66. https://www.jstor.org/stable/4392492.

Jones, Gilbert E. "The Position of the Anti-Suffragists." *The Annals of the American Academy of Political and Social Science* 35 (1910): 16–22. http://www.jstor.org/stable/1011239.

Jones, Janey. *The Edinburgh Seven: The Story of the First Women to Study Medicine*. Barnsley: Pen and Sword History, June 30, 2023.

Jones, Mark. "The Medal as an Instrument of Propaganda in Late 17th and Early 18th Century Europe PART 2." *The Numismatic Chronicle (1966–)* 143 (1983): 202–13. http://www.jstor.org/stable/42665176.

Jordan, David Starr. "The Ways of Pangermany." *The Scientific Monthly* 4, no. 1 (1917): 27–40. http://www.jstor.org/stable/22612.

Joseph, Nathan, and Nicholas Alex, "The Uniform a Sociological Perspective," *American Journal of Sociology* 77, no. 4 (Jan 1972): 719–30. http://www.jstor.com/stable/2776756.

Josten, C. H. "Elias Ashmole, F.R.S. (1617–1692)." *Notes and Records of the Royal Society of London* 15 (1960): 221–30. http://www.jstor.org/stable/531041.

Jovanov, Jasana M. "Cyril Kutlik and Early Modernism in Serbia," Translated to English, Academia.edu. (99+) Kiril Kutlik i počeci moderne umetnosti u Srbiji/ Cyril Kutlík and Early Modernism in Serbia | Jasna M Jovanov – Academia.edu.

Jovanović, M. "The Heroic Circle of Serbian Sisters: A History." *Serbian Studies: Journal of the North American Society for Serbian Studies* 24, no. 1 (2010): 125–39. https://doi.org/10.1353/ser.2012.0011.

Justin's History of the World, Extracted from Trogus Pompeius. Translated by John Selby Watson (1804–84), (G. Bell, 1876) a work in the public domain placed online by Roger Pearce at Tertullian.org. ToposText.

Kandinsky, Wassily. *Concerning the Spiritual in Art*. Garden City, NY: Dover Publications, June 1977. ISBN 0486234118

Kanter, Emmanuel. "Concerning the Amazons," *New York Times (1923–)*, Jan. 16, 1927, p. X14, ProQuest Historical Newspapers.

Katagiri, Nori. "Drawing Strategic Lessons from Dahomey's War." Air University, initially in *ASPJ Africa & Francophonie*, 3rd Quarter, 2012. katagiri_e.pdf (af.edu).

Kea, R. A. "Firearms and Warfare on the Gold and Slave Coasts from the Sixteenth to the Nineteenth Centuries." *The Journal of African History* 12, no. 2 (1971): 185–213. doi: 10.1017/S002185370001063X.

Kendrick, Ruby M. "'THEY ALSO SERVE': THE NATIONAL ASSOCIATION OF COLORED WOMEN, INC." *Negro History Bulletin* 17, no. 8 (1954): 171–75. http://www.jstor.org/stable/44214997.

Kern, Kathi. "'A Great Feature of the General Uprising': The Revising Committee and the Woman's Bible." In *Mrs. Stanton's Bible*, 135–71. Ithica, NY: Cornell University Press, 2001. http://www.jstor.org/stable/10.7591/j.ctv5qdj6z.9.

Kern, Kathi. "Introduction." In *Mrs. Stanton's Bible*, 1–13. Itaca, NY: Cornell University Press, 2001. http://www.jstor.org/stable/10.7591/j.ctv5qdj6z.5.

Kern, Kathi. "'The Bigots Promote the Sale': Responses to the Woman's Bible." In *Mrs. Stanton's Bible*, 172–222. Ithica, NY: Cornell University Press, 2001. http://www.jstor.org/stable/10.7591/j.ctv5qdj6z.10.

Kesler, R. L. "The Idealization of Women: Morphology and Change in Three Renaissance Texts." *Mosaic: A Journal for the Interdisciplinary Study of Literature* 23, no. 2 (1990): 107–26. http://www.jstor.org/stable/24780630.

King (ed). "The Crystal Palace and Great Exhibition of 1851." *British Library Newspapers*. Detroit, MI: Gale, 2007.

Kissinger, Henry A. "The White Revolutionary: Reflections on Bismarck." *Daedalus* 97, no. 3 (1968): 888–924. http://www.jstor.org/stable/20023844.

Koehler, Robert. "Painting of the Nineteenth Century in Germany." *Fine Arts Journal* 34, no. 11 (1916): 579–608. https://doi.org/10.2307/25587423. Pp. 585–88.

Kohler, Timothy A., et al. There were more significant post-Neolithic wealth disparities in Eurasia than in North America and Mesoamerica. *Nature* 551 (2017): 619–622. https://doi.org/10.1038/nature24646.

Konečni, Vladimir J. "The 'Golden Section' as Aesthetic Idea and Empirical Fact." *Visual Arts Research* 30, no. 2 (2004): 75–86. http://www.jstor.org/stable/20715354.

Kriger, Colleen E. *Cloth in West African History (African Archaeology Series)*. Walnut Creek, CA: Alta Mira Press, June 2, 2006.

Krippner, Monica. *The Quality of Mercy: Women at War, Serbia 1915–1918*. London: David and Charles, 1980.

Kroeber, A. L. "Frederic Ward Putnam." *American Anthropologist* 17, no. 4 (1915): 712–18. http://www.jstor.org/stable/659986.

Kunst, and Ambiente. Manufactory for Bronze Sculpture and Statues, "Manufacturing of our Bronze Statues," Dresden, Manufacturing of our Bronze Statues – Art Bronze Sculptures (art-bronze-sculptures.com).

Kuper, Hilda. "Costume and Identity." *Comparative Studies in Society and History* 15, no. 3 (1973): 348–67. http://www.jstor.org/stable/178260.

Lance, Keith Curry. "Strategy Choices of the British Women's Social and Political Union, 1903–18." *Social Science Quarterly* 60, no. 1 (1979): 51–61. http://www.jstor.org/stable/42860512.

Larsen, Timothy. "Epilogue: Forgetting and Remembering." In *Christabel Pankhurst: Fundamentalism and Feminism in Coalition*, NED-New edition, 139–42. Suffolk, UK: Boydell & Brewer, 2002. http://www.jstor.org/stable/10.7722/j.ctt14brvj4.11.

Law Trecker, Janice. "The Suffrage Prisoners." *The American Scholar* 41, no. 3 (1972): 409–23. http://www.jstor.org/stable/41208790.

Law, Robin. "Dahomey and the Slave Trade: Reflections on the Historiography of the Rise of Dahomey." *The Journal of African History* 27, no. 2 (1986): 237–67. http://www.jstor.org/stable/181135.

Law, Robin. "Further Light on John Duncan's Account of the 'Fellatah Country' (1845)." *History in Africa* 28 (2001): 129–38. https://doi.org/10.2307/3172211.

Law, Robin. "Royal Monopoly and Private Enterprise in the Atlantic Trade: The Case of Dahomey." *The Journal of African History* 18, no. 4 (1977): 555–77. http://www.jstor.org/stable/180832.

Law, Robin. "Slave-Raiders and Middlemen, Monopolists and Free-Traders: The Supply of Slaves for the Atlantic Trade in Dahomey c. 1715–1850." *The Journal of African History* 30, no. 1 (1989): 45–68. http://www.jstor.org/stable/182694.

Law, Robin. "The Amazons of Dahomey." *Paideuma: Mitteilungen zur Kulturkunde* 39 (1993): 245–60. https://www.jstor.org/stable/40341664.

Law, Robin. "The Slave-Trader as Historian: Robert Norris and the History of Dahomey." *History in Africa* 16 (1989): 219–35. https://doi.org/10.2307/3171786.

Leighten, Patricia. "Response: Artists in Times of War." *The Art Bulletin* 91, no. 1 (2009): 35–44. http://www.jstor.org/stable/20619654.

Lenman, Robin. "A Community in Transition: Painters in Munich, 1886–1924." *Central European History* 15, no. 1 (1982): 3–33. http://www.jstor.org/stable/4545947.

Levine, Edward M. "Abstract Expressionism: The Mystical Experience." *Art Journal* 31, no. 1 (1971): 22–25. https://doi.org/10.2307/775629.

Levy, Raphael. "The Daily Press in France." *The Modern Language Journal* 13, no. 4 (1929): 294–303. https://doi.org/10.2307/315897.

Lewer, Debbie. "Hugo Ball, Iconoclasm and the Origins of Dada in Zurich." *Oxford Art Journal* 32, no. 1 (2009): 17–35. http://www.jstor.org/stable/25650841.

Lewis, Danny. "These Anti-Suffrage Postcards Warned Against Giving Women the Vote," *Smithsonian Magazine*, July 19, 2016. These Anti-Suffrage Postcards Warned Against Giving Women the Vote | Smart News | Smithsonian Magazine.

Lewis, Mary Tompkins. "Introduction: The Critical History of Impressionism: An Overview." In *Critical Readings in Impressionism and Post-Impressionism: An Anthology*, edited by Mary Tompkins Lewis, 1st edition, 1–20. Oakland, CA: University of California Press, 2007. https://doi.org/10.2307/jj.8501295.4.

Llewellyn-Jones, Lloyd. "In and Out of Imagination: Locating the Women of Achaemenid Persia," Cardiff University Lecture Series, Iran Heritage Foundation Prof. Lloyd Llewellyn-Jones: 'Locating the Women of Achaemenid Persia' (youtube.com).

Lluís i Ginovart, Josep, and Agustí Costa Jover. "Design and Medieval Construction: The Case of Tortosa Cathedral (1345–1441)." *Construction History* 29, no. 1 (2014): 1–24. http://www.jstor.org/stable/43856060.

López, María Isabel Rodríguez. "Victory, Triumph, and Fame as the Iconic Expressions of the Courtly Power." *Music in Art* 37, no. 1/2 (2012): 9–23. http://www.jstor.org/stable/24420190.

Lubin, David M. *Grand Illusions: American Art and the First World War.* Oxford: Oxford University Press, 2016.

Lucchesi, Emilie Le Beau. *This Is Really War: The Incredible True Story of a Navy Nurse POW in the Occupied Philippines.* Chicago, IL: Chicago Review Press, 1st edition. May 7, 2019.

Luxenberg, Alisa. "Originality and Freedom: The 1863 Reforms to the École des Beaux-Arts and the Involvement of Léon Bonnat." *Nineteenth-Century Art Worldwide* 16, no. 2 (Autumn 2017). https://doi.org/10.29411/ncaw.2017.16.2.3.

MacGaffey, Wyatt. "Commodore Wilmot Encounters Kongo Art, 1865." *African Arts* 43, no. 2 (Su 2020): 52–53. URL: https://www.jstor.org/stable/20744843.

Malcomson, Robert. "The Sad Case of Sir George," *Naval History Magazine, Feb. 2020, Vol. 24, No. 1.* The Sad Case of Sir George | Naval History Magazine – Feb. 2010, Vol. 24, Number 1 (usni.org).

Malin, James C. "Carlyle's Philosophy of Clothes and Swedenborg's." *Scandinavian Studies* 33, no. 3 (1961): 155–68. http://www.jstor.org/stable/40916341.

Mancoff, Debra N. *Woman's Art Journal* 11, no. 1 (1990): 42–45. https://doi.org/10.2307/1358388.

304 Bibliography

Manderson, Desmond. "Bodies in the Water: On Reading Images More Sensibly." *Law and Literature* 27, no. 2 (2015): 279–93. https://www.jstor.org/stable/26770753.

Manlin, James C. "Emanuel Swedenborg and His Clothes Philosophy." *Scandinavian Studies* 33, no. 2 (1961): 45–67. http://www.jstor.org/stable/40916327.

Mansback, S. A. *Modern Art in Eastern Europe, From the Baltic to the Balkans, ca. 1890–1939*. New York, NY: Pratt Institute, 2001.

Marc, Franz, and Wassily Kandinsky. *The Blaue Reiter Almanac*. Boston, MA: Da Capo Press, Mar. 1989 (reprint) ISBN:0306803461

Marino, Kelly. "We Protest the Unjust Treatment of Pickets, Brooklyn Suffragist Lucy Burns, Militancy in the National Women's Part, and Prison Reform, 1917–1920." *Lond Island History Journal* 28-1, Pingback: 2020. Stonybrook.edu.

Marion, Jennifer. "Historic Heteroessentialism and Other Orderings in Early America." *Signs* 34, No 4 (2009) 981–1003.

Martin, Thomas R. *Ancient Greece*. New Haven, CT: Yale University Press, 2013. http://www.jstor.org/stable/j.ctt32bm98.

Martyn, Frederic. *Life in the Legion: Amazon Warriors from Dahomey, from a Soldier's Point of View*. New York, NY: C Scribner's Sons, 1911.

Marwick, Arthur. "War and the Arts – Is There a Connection? The Case of the Two Total Wars." *War in History* 2, no. 1 (1995): 65–86. http://www.jstor.org/stable/26004405.

Matheolus. English translations of excerpts from *The Lamentations of Matheolus*, Misogyny Unlimited theabsolute.net, n.d. The Lamentations of Matheolus (theabsolute.net).

Matheolus. *The Lamentations of Matheolus*. Paris: Emile Bouillon, 1892 (in French).

Mayor, Adrienne. *The Amazons: Lives and Legends of Warrior Women across the Ancient World*. Princeton, NJ: Princeton University Press, 2016.

McCammon, Holly J. "Stirring up Suffrage Sentiment: The Formation of the State Woman Suffrage Organizations, 1866–1914." *Social Forces* 80, no. 2 (2001): 449–80. http://www.jstor.org/stable/2675586.

McCormack, Catherine. *Women in the Picture, Women Art and the Power of Looking*. London: Icon Books Ltd, May 6, 2021.

McCracken, Penny. "Sculptor Mary Thornycroft and Her Artist Children." *Woman's Art Journal* 17, no. 2 (Autumn, 1996–Winter 1997): 3–8. https://www.jstor.org/stable/1358460. Accessed 29 Dec. 2023.

McRae, Elizabeth Gillespie. "Caretakers of Southern Civilization: Georgia Women and the Anti-Suffrage Campaign, 1914–1920." *The Georgia Historical Quarterly* 82, no. 4 (1998): 801–28. http://www.jstor.org/stable/40583906.

McWhinnie, H. J. "Influences of the Ideas of Jay Hambidge on Art and Design," *Computers Math. Applic.* 17, no. 4-6 (1989): 1001–1008.

Meretskaya, Yu S. "Roman Circle: German Formalism Influence on the Anton Azbe's Pedagogical Method, Russian State University for the Humanities. https://philosophy.rsuh.ru/jour/article/view/241?locale=en_US.

Middleton, J. C. "'Bolshevism in Art': Dada and Politics." *Texas Studies in Literature and Language* 4, no. 3 (1962): 408–30. http://www.jstor.org/stable/40753524.

Millard, Charles W. "Fauvism." *The Hudson Review* 29, no. 4 (1976): 576–80. https://doi.org/10.2307/3850497.

Miller, Ian. "A History of Force Feeding: Hunger Strikes, Prisons and Medical Ethics, 1909-1974," Palgrave Macmillan, Basingstoke, UK, Aug. 2016. The National Library of Medicine US government.

Miller, Ian. "Forcible Feeding and the Cat and Mouse Act: One Hundred Years On, June 19, 2013, OUPblog Oxford University Press Forcible feeding and the Cat and Mouse Act: One hundred years on | OUPblog.

Milliken, William M. "Four Stone Models for German Medals." *The Bulletin of the Cleveland Museum of Art* 44, no. 6 (1957): 118–21. http://www.jstor.org/stable/25142217.

Minty, Nancy. "Painting for Peace: Art Exposes the Cruelty of War," JSTOR.org, Oct 13, 2022, Painting for peace: Art exposes the cruelty of war – About JSTOR.

Moffitt, John F. "'Fighting Forms: The Fate of the Animals.' The Occultist Origins of Franz Marc's 'Farbentheorie.'" *Artibus et Historiae* 6, no. 12 (1985): 107–26. https://doi.org/10.2307/1483239.

Moore, G. "Julian Meissonier and the Salon Julian." *Fortnightly Review, May 1865–June 1934* 48, no. 283 (1890). ProQuest

Moore, Wendy. "The Medical Suffragettes." *The Lancet, Perspectives The Art of Medicine* 391, no. 10119 (Feb. 3, 2018): 422–423.

Moore, Wendy. *No Man's Land: The Trailblazing Women Who Ran Britain's Most Extraordinary Military Hospital during World War I.* New York, NY: Basic Books, Apr. 2020.

Morka, Mieczysław. "The Beginnings of Medallic Art in Poland during the Times of Zygmunt I and Bona Sforza." *Artibus et Historiae* 29, no. 58 (2008): 65–87. http://www.jstor.org/stable/40343650.

Morrison, Susan Signe. "Margaret of Beverley (c.1150–c.1214/15): Fighting Crusader." In *A Medieval Woman's Companion: Women's Lives in the European Middle Ages*, 74–82. Oxford, UK: Oxbow Books, 2016. https://doi.org/10.2307/j.ctvh1dnb3.13.

Morton-Williams, Peter. "A Yoruba Woman Remembers Servitude in a Palace of Dahomey, in the Reigns of Kings Glele and Behanzin." *Africa: Journal of the International African Institute* 63, no. 1 (1993): 102–17. https://doi.org/10.2307/1161300.

Murray, Flora. *Women as Army Surgeons: Being the History of the Women's Hospital Corps in Paris, Wimereux and Endell Street, September 1914–October 1919.* Cambridge: Cambridge Library Collection-History of Medicine, Apr. 2014.

Murtala, M.L., M. Hamza, and A. Lawal. "Recognition of the Place of Women in 19th Century African Warfare: A Study of the Amazons of Dahomey." *Lajohis Lasu Journal of History and International Studies* 4, no. 1 (2022). www.lajohis.org.ng.

Myers, Nicole (ed), Katherine Rothkopf (ed), Anna Katherine Brodbeck, et al. Cubism in Color: The Still Lifes of Juan Gris, Dallas Museum of Art, Apr. 20, 2021.

Myres, J. L. "Homeric Art." *The Annual of the British School at Athens* 45 (1950): 229–60. http://www.jstor.org/stable/30096756.

Natalis, Alexandre. *Historia Ecclesiastica. Ed. Omnium Novissima Opera Et Studio C. Roncaglia* (English translation). Charleston, SC: Nabu Press, 2011.

Nelle, Patrick. "Benin's 30m-tall Amazon Statue Honors the Women Warriors of Dahomey," Aug. 16, 2022, Bella Naija, Benin's 30m-tall "Amazon" statue honors the women warriors of Dahomey | BellaNaija.

Nelson, Lynn H. "The Kings of Aragon." In *The Chronicle of San Juan de La Pena: A Fourteenth-Century Official History of the Crown of Aragon*, 16–40. Philadelphia, PA: University of Pennsylvania Press, 1991. http://www.jstor.org/stable/j.ctv512w38.7.

Nelson, Lynn H. "The Kings of the Crown of Aragon." In *The Chronicle of San Juan de La Pena: A Fourteenth-Century Official History of the Crown of Aragon*, 53–104. Philadelphia, PA: University of Pennsylvania Press, 1991. http://www.jstor.org/stable/j.ctv512w38.9.

Newberry, Jo Vellacott. "Anti-War Suffragists." *History* 62, no. 206 (1977): 411–25. http://www.jstor.org/stable/24410789.

Nicholson, Helen J. *Women, and the Crusades.* Oxford: Oxford University Press, May 23, 2023.

306 Bibliography

Nimura, Janice P. *The Doctors Blackwell: How Two Pioneering Sisters Brought Medicine to Women and Women to Medicine.* New York, NY: W.W. Norton & Company, 1st edition, Jan. 19, 2021.

Nord, Jason. *The Silent Sentinels.* Lincoln: Equality Press, 2015.

Norman, Elizabeth. *We Band of Angels, The Untold Story of American Nurses Trapped on Bataan by the Japanese.* New York, NY: Pocket Books, Oct. 29, 2013.

Nosch, Marie-Louise, and Henriette Koefoed. "Introduction and Acknowledgements." In *Wearing the Cloak: Dressing the Soldier in Roman Times,* edited by Marie-Louise Nosch, 10: v–viii. Oxford, UK: Oxbow Books, 2012. https://doi.org/10.2307/j.ctvh1ds7f.3.

Nunez-Franklin, Brianna. "Democracy Limited: The Prison Special Tour of 1919," National Park Service, Democracy Limited: The Prison Special (U.S. National Park Service) (nps.gov).

Nym Mayhall, Laura E. "Domesticating Emmeline: Representing the Suffragette, 1930–1993." *NWSA Journal* 11, no. 2 (1999): 1–24. http://www.jstor.org/stable/4316653.

O'Byrne, E. K. "Finger Rings." *The Irish Monthly* 45, no. 528 (1917): 393–96. http://www.jstor.org/stable/20504824.

Oakley, John H. "Greek Vase Painting." *American Journal of Archaeology* 113, no. 4 (2009): 599–627. http://www.jstor.org/stable/20627620.

Oakley, John H. *The Greek Vase Art of the Storyteller.* London: British Museum Press, 2013.

Offhaus, Sarah Ruth. "The Negro Exhibit at the Pan-Am," Buffalo Rising, "The Negro Exhibit" at the Pan-Am – Buffalo Rising.

Oksanen, Eljas. "Knights, Mercenaries and Paid Soldiers: Military Identities in the Anglo-Norman Regnum." In *Knighthood and Society in the High Middle Ages,* edited by David Crouch and Jeroen Deploige, 71–94. Leuven, Belgium: Leuven University Press, 2020. https://doi.org/10.2307/j.ctvbtzmj5.8.

Orr, Megan. "Ladylike in the Extreme: The Propogandism of Sarah Forbes Bonetta, Britians, 'African Princess,'" " BYU Scholars Archive Student Works, 12-2021. Ladylike in the Extreme: The Propogandism of Sarah Forbes Bonetta," Britain's "African Princess" (byu.edu).

Overbeck, John C. "Tacitus and Dio on Boudicca's Rebellion." *The American Journal of Philology* 90, no. 2 (1969): 129–45. https://doi.org/10.2307/293422.

Pankhurst, Christabel. *Unshackled the Story of How We Won the Vote.* London: Hutchinson, 1959.

Pankhurst, Emmeline. *Freedom or Death.* Glasgow: Good Press, 2020.

Pankhurst, Emmeline. *My Own Story.* Westport, CT: Praeger, June 4, 1985, Reprint.

Pankhurst, Emmeline. *Suffragette My Own Story the Origins of the Suffragettes.* London: Hesperus Press, reprint 2015.

Panofsky, Erwin. *Meaning in the Visual Arts.* Chicago, IL: University of Chicago Press, 1983.

Pantelić, Bratislav. "Nationalism and Architecture: The Creation of a National Style in Serbian Architecture and Its Political Implications." *Journal of the Society of Architectural Historians* 56, no. 1 (1997): 16–41. https://doi.org/10.2307/991214.

Park, Jihang. "The British Suffrage Activists of 1913: An Analysis." *Past & Present,* no. 120 (1988): 147–62. http://www.jstor.org/stable/650925.

Pasler, Jann. Composing the Citizen, Music as Public Utility in Third Republic France, Chapter 12 "The Dynamics of Identity and the Struggle for Distinction," pp 643–694. University of California Press, Oakland, CA, July 2009.

Pastorello, Karen. *New York History* 99, no. 3/4 (2018): 484–87. https://www.jstor. org/stable/26908721. Book Review of *Gilded Suffragists: The New York Socialites Who Fought for Women's Right to Vote*, by J. Neuman.

Patrick, Manning. "The Technology of Production in Southern Dahomey, c. 1900." *African Economic History*, no. 9 (1980): 49–67. https://doi.org/10.2307/ 3601387.

Paul, Alice, and Amelia R. Fry. *Conversations with Alice Paul: Woman Suffrage and the Equal Rights Amendment: Oral History Transcript/and Related Material, 1972*. Open Library: Andesite Press, Aug. 21, 2017.

Peniston-Bird, C. M. *War in History* 8, no. 4 (2001): 483–85. http://www.jstor.org/ stable/26013914.

Perloff, Marjorie. "'Violence and Precision': The Manifesto as Art Form." *Chicago Review* 34, no. 2 (1984): 65–101. https://doi.org/10.2307/25305249.

Pfanner, Toni. "Military Uniforms and the Law of War." *International Review of the Red Cross* 86, no. 853 (2004): 93–123.

Philips, F. Carter. "Greek Myths and the Uses of Myths." *The Classical Journal* 74, no. 2 (1978): 155–66. http://www.jstor.org/stable/3296798.

Phillips, Jonathan. *The Second Crusade: Extending the Frontiers of Christendom*. New Haven, CT: Yale University Press, 2010.

Phillips, Jonathan, and Hall, Martin (eds). *Caffaro, Genoa and the Twelfth-Century Crusades*. London, UK: Ashgate, 2013.

Pilossof, Rory. Review of *"Guns Don't Colonise People…": The Role and Use of Firearms in Pre-Colonial and Colonial Africa*, by John Lamphear, William K. Storey, Jeff Guy, and Joseph P. Smaldone. *Kronos*, no. 36 (2010): 266–77. http:// www.jstor.org/stable/41056654.

Plutarch. "Moralia. On the Malice of Herodotus," Loeb Classics Library. LCL 426 PLUTARCH, Moralia. On the Malice of Herodotus | Loeb Classical Library (loeb-classics.com).

Plutarch. *Parallel Lives of Noble Grecians and Romans*, MBS Library Micro Book Studio. Plutarch PARALLEL LIVES OF NOBLE GRECIANS AND ROMANS (documentacatholicaomnia.eu).

Poirer, J. (translated by G. F. Nafzinger). *The Dahomey Campaign (1892–2894) Originally published in 1895, this work covers the French response to attacks and slave raids by the King of Dahomey against French allies in what is modern Benin. It is a detailed account of colonial warfare in the late 19th century. Today, Dahomey is known as Benin*. West Chester: Nafziger Collection, 2015.

Polyaenus. *Strategems*, Attalus translations online. Polyaenus: Stratagems – translation (attalus.org).

Polyaenus. *Strategims*, Book 8(b), Chapters 26–71. Adapted from the translation by R. Shepherd (1793) Attalus, Polyaenus: Stratagems – Book 8(b) (attalus. org).

Popham, Hugh. *The FANY in Peace and War: The Story of the First Aid Nursing Yeomanry 1907–2003*. Barnsley: Leo Cooper, 2003. ISBN 085052934 4.

Preston Blier, Suzanne. "Animalia: The Natural World, Art, and Theory," On the Human, n.d.Animalia: The Natural World, Art, and Theory « On the Human (nationalhumanitiescenter.org).

Price, Dorothy, and Christopher Short. "Introduction: Why Does Der Blaue Reiter Still Matter?" In *German Expressionism: Der Blaue Reiter and Its Legacies*, edited by Dorothy Price, 1st edition, 1–14. Manchester, UK: Manchester University Press, 2020. http://www.jstor.org/stable/j.ctv1384308.6.

Pritchard, Jack. "Gropius, The Bauhaus And The Future." *Journal of the Royal Society of Arts* 117, no. 5150 (1969): 75–94. http://www.jstor.org/stable/41370286.

308 Bibliography

Proctor, Alice. *The Whole Picture, the Colonial Story of the Art in Our Museums and Why We Need to Talk About It*. London: Octopus, 2020.

Pugh, Martin D. "Politicians And The Woman's Vote 1914–1918." *History* 59, no. 197 (1974): 358–74. http://www.jstor.org/stable/24409414.

Pullen, Richard Popplewell, and Charles Thomas Newton. *Halicarnassus: The History and Legacy of the Ancient Greek City and Home to One of the Seven Wonders of the World* (1861). Sacramento, CA: Creative Media Partners, 2015.

Quinault, Roland. "Asquith's Liberalism." *History* 77, no. 249 (1992): 33–49. http://www.jstor.org/stable/24420531.

Rade, R. Babić. "Nadežda Petrović – A Female Painter and a Nurse" (PDF). *Istorija Medicine* 10 (2008): 1. Archived (PDF)

Ray, Jonathan. *The Sephardic Frontier: The "Reconquista" and the Jewish Community in Medieval Iberia*, 1st edition. Manchester, UK: Cornell University Press, 2006. http://www.jstor.org/stable/10.7591/j.ctt7v6p8.

Rentzou, Effie. "Messy Internationalism: Dada, Anarchism, and Picabia's Group Portraits." In *Concepts of the World: The French Avant-Garde and the Idea of the International, 1910–1940*, 97–152. Christchurch, NZ: Northwestern University Press, 2022. https://doi.org/10.2307/j.ctv2rcnqh7.7.

Reynolds, Gordon M. "*Cross purposes: Frankish Levantine perceptions of gender and female participation in the crusades, 1147–1254*," Master's Thesis University of Canterbury, 2017. Cross purposes: Frankish Levantine perceptions of gender and female participation in the crusades, 1147–1254 – Medievalists. net.

Richter, Gisela M. A. "Red-And-Black Glaze." *Nederlands Kunsthistorisch Jaarboek (NKJ)/Netherlands Yearbook for History of Art* 5 (1954): 127–36. http://www.jstor.org/stable/24705257.

Richter, Gisela M. A. "The Pheidian Zeus at Olympia." *Hesperia: The Journal of the American School of Classical Studies at Athens* 35, no. 2 (1966): 166–70. https://www.jstor.org/stable/i207987.

Robb, John. "Prehistoric Art in Europe: A Deep-Time Social History." *American Antiquity* 80, no. 4 (2015): 635–54. http://www.jstor.org/stable/24712796.

Robert, Krisztina. "Gender, Class, and Patriotism: Women's Paramilitary Units in First World War Britain." *The International History Review* 19, no. 1 (1997): 52–65. http://www.jstor.org/stable/40108083.

Robinson, Jane. "Pilgrimage of Greats: Why the March of the Suffragists Should Be Commemorated." *TLS. Times Literary Supplement*, no. 5993 (9 Feb. 2018): 16. *Gale Literature Resource Center*, link.gale.com/apps/doc/A634971445/LitRC?u=anon~fb5cc518&sid=googleScholar&xid=05f8b643. Accessed 2 Oct. 2024.

Rodini, Elizabeth. "The Language of Stones." *Art Institute of Chicago Museum Studies* 25, no. 2 (2000): 17–104. https://doi.org/10.2307/4113058.

Rollyson, Carl. "A Conservative Revolutionary: Emmeline Pankhurst (1857–1928)." *The Virginia Quarterly Review* 79, no. 2 (2003): 325–34. http://www.jstor.org/stable/26440996.

Romney, Rebecca. "The Story Behind Richard F Burton's Pilgrimage to Media and Mecca," Bauman Rare Books website, Aug. 12, 2013.The Story Behind Richard F. Burton's Pilgrimage to Medina and Mecca – Bauman Rare Books.

Ross, David. "Mid-Nineteenth Century Dahomey: Recent Views vs. Contemporary Evidence." *History in Africa* 12 (1985): 307–23. https://doi.org/10.2307/3171725.

Rouille, Guillaume. *Handbook of the Images of Renown*, 1553. Public Domain Internet Archive.org, 1553. Lausanne: University of Lausanne, Google-idf5FDAAAAcAAj.

Rubin, William. *Picasso and Braque: Pioneering Cubism*, 1st edition. New York, NY: Museum of Modern Art, Sep. 1, 1989.

Rupprecht, Anita. "'All We Have Done, We Have Done for Freedom': The *Creole* Slave-Ship Revolt (1841) and the Revolutionary Atlantic." *International Review of Social History* 58 (2013): 253–77. https://www.jstor.org/stable/26394646.

Sammons, Jeffrey T., and John H. Morrow Jr. "Horace Pippin: World War I Soldier, Narrator, and Artist." *Pennsylvania Legacies* 17, no. 1 (2017): 12–19. https://doi.org/10.5215/pennlega.17.1.0012.

Santesso, Aaron. "The Literary Animal and the Narrativized Zoo." *Modern Fiction Studies* 60, no. 3 (2014): 444–63. https://www.jstor.org/stable/26421739.

Saunders, David, and Norman Saunders. "Field Guide to Wild American Pulp Artists," Catalog (pulpartists.com). The site was last updated in September 2023.

Scarinci, D. "Medals are Sculpture For Everyone." *Sculpture Review* 69, no. 1 (2020): 24–26. https://doi.org/10.1177/0747528420926813.

Scholarship Online, Sep. 22, 2016. https://doi.org/10.12987/yale/9780300187250.003.0010. Accessed 27 Dec. 2023.

Schubert, Gudrun. "Women and Symbolism: Imagery and Theory." *Oxford Art Journal* 3, no. 1 (1980): 29–34. http://www.jstor.org/stable/1360176.

Schutz, Alexander H. "'The Lamentations of Matheolus' and the Basic Tempo of Villon's Testament." *Studies in Philology* 47, no. 3 (1950): 453–59. http://www.jstor.org/stable/4172936.

Sciacca, Christine. *Illuminating Women in the Medieval World*, 1st edition. Las Angeles, CA: Paul Getty Museum, June 20, 2017.

Selz, Peter. "The Aesthetic Theories of Wassily Kandinsky and Their Relationship to the Origin of Non-Objective Painting." *The Art Bulletin* 39, no. 2 (1957): 127–36. https://doi.org/10.2307/3047696.

Shaw, Margaret T., Felicia Keesing, and Richard S. Ostfeld. "Herbivory on Acacia Seedlings in an East African Savanna." *Oikos* 98, no. 3 (2002): 385–92. http://www.jstor.org/stable/3547179.

Shiff, Richard. "Art History and the Nineteenth Century: Realism and Resistance." *The Art Bulletin* 70, no. 1 (1988): 25–48. https://doi.org/10.2307/3051152.

Sifakis, G. M. "'ILIAD' 21.114-119 AND THE DEATH OF PENTHESILEA." *Bulletin of the Institute of Classical Studies*, no. 23 (1976): 55–57. http://www.jstor.org/stable/43646137.

Simcha, Lev-Yadun. "Does the Whistling Thorn Acacia (Acacia drepanolobium) Use Auditory Aposematism to Deter Mammalian Herbivores?" *Plant Signaling & Behavior* 11, no. 8 (2016): e 1307035. https://doi.org/10.1080/15592324.2016.1207035.

Simmons, Sherwin. "Advertising Seizes Control of Life: Berlin Dada and the Power of Advertising." *Oxford Art Journal* 22, no. 1 (1999): 119–46. http://www.jstor.org/stable/1360686.

Simmons, William E. "Myth of the Amazons Revived by War: Fable Tells of Nations of Women Warriors They Fought Against Greeks at Troy and Built Cities," *Boston Daily Globe*, Sep. 16, 1917, p. 53, ProQuest Historical Newspapers.

Skertchly, J. A. *Dahomey as it is: Being narrative of eight months' residence in that country, with a full account of the notorious annual customs and the social and religious institutions of the Ffons; also, an Appendix on Ashantee, and a Glossary of Dahoman Words and Titles.* London: Chapman and Hall, 1874.

Slater, Candace. "Visions of the Amazon: What Has Shifted, What Persists, and Why This Matters." *Latin American Research Review* 50, no. 3 (2015): 3–23. http://www.jstor.org/stable/43670307.

Small, R. C. "Crusaders' Castles of the Twelfth Century." *Cambridge Historical Journal* 10, no. 2 (1951): 133–49. http://www.jstor.org/stable/3021083.

310 Bibliography

Smith, A. K. "'The Woman Who Dared': Major Mabel St Clair Stobart." In: A. S. Fell, and I. Sharp (eds). *The Women's Movement in Wartime*. London: Palgrave Macmillan, 2007. https://doi.org/10.1057/9780230210790_10. 'The Woman Who Dared': Major Mabel St Clair Stobart | SpringerLink

Somigli, Luca. "Strategies of Legitimation: The Manifesto from Politics to Aesthetics." In *Legitimizing the Artist: Manifesto Writing and European Modernism 1885-1915*, 29–92. Toronto, ON: University of Toronto Press, 2003. http://www.jstor.org/stable/10.3138/j.ctt130jvhd.5.

Southard, Belinda A. Stillion. "Militancy, Power, and Identity: The Silent Sentinels as Women Fighting for Political Voice." *Rhetoric and Public Affairs* 10, no. 3 (2007): 399–417. http://www.jstor.org/stable/41940153.

Spare, Austin Osman, and Jake Dirnberger. *The Pocket Austin Osman Spare*. Norwell, MA: Trident Business Partners, Jan. 22, 2020.

Spare, Austin Osman. *Earth Inferno*. London: Cooperative Printing Society, 1905.

Spare, Austin Osman. *Ethos: The Magical Writings of Austin Osman Spare Micrologus, the Book of Pleasure, the Witches Sabbath, Mind to Mind and How by a Sorcerer*. Open Library: I-H-O Books, (5th printing) Jan. 1, 2001.

Speidel, Michael Alexander. "Dressed for the Occasion: Clothes and Context in the Roman Army." In *Wearing the Cloak: Dressing the Soldier in Roman Times*, edited by Marie-Louise Nosch, 10: 1–12. Oxford, UK: Oxbow Books, 2012. https://doi.org/10.2307/j.ctvh1ds7f.4.

St Cyr, Cassondra, Anne Peterson, Taylor Franks. National Woman's Party Project, Chapter 4, (2015). *Mapping American Social Movements Through the 20th Century*.

Stahl, Alan M. "The Classical Program of the Medallic Series of Louis XIV." *The Princeton University Library Chronicle* 76, no. 1–2 (2015): 267–87. https://doi.org/10.25290/prinunivlibrchro.76.1-2.0267.

Stanley, Monica M. *The Stobart Nurses: Accounts of British Volunteer Nurses during the First World War – My Diary in Serbia April 1, 1915–Nov. 1, 1915*. Driffield: Leonaur Ltd, Sep. 2014.

Steiner, Christopher B. "Another Image of Africa: Toward an Ethnohistory of European Cloth Marketed in West Africa, 1873–1960." *Ethnohistory* 32, no. 2 (1985): 91–110. https://doi.org/10.2307/482329.

Stobart, Mabel Annie Boulton. *War, and Women, from Experience in the Balkans and Elsewhere*. London: G. Bell & Sons, Ltd, 1913.

Stobart, Mabel. *The Flaming Sword in Serbia and Elsewhere*. London: Hodder and Stoughton, 1916.

Stone, Becky. "Jewels for Votes for WOMEN: Let's Talk Suffragette Jewelry," Diamonds in the Library, Oct. 24, 2016. Jewels for votes for women: Let's talk suffragette jewelry. (diamondsinthelibrary.com).

Stoneman, Richard. *Xerxes A Persian Life*. New Haven, CT: Yale University Press, Aug. 15, 2015.

Strauss, Barry. *The Battle of Salamis, The Naval Encounter That Saved Greece and Western Civilization*. New York, NY: Simon and Schuster, June 29, 2004.

Strauss, Barry. *The Trojan War: A New History*. New York, NY: Simon and Schuster, Sep. 2006.

Strom, Sharon Hartman. "Leadership and Tactics in the American Woman Suffrage Movement: A New Perspective from Massachusetts." *The Journal of American History* 62, no. 2 (1975): 296–315. https://doi.org/10.2307/1903256.

Struckmeyer, Myra. "Female Hospitallers in the Twelfth and Thirteenth Centuries, Dissertation University of North Carolina, Chapel Hill, 2006. Female_hospitallers_in_the_twelfth_and_thirteenth_centuries.pdf

Tacitus, Publius Cornelius. *Tribes of Ancient Britain and Germany*. Bob Carruthers (ed). Barnsley: Pen and Sword Books, 2013.

Tacitus. *The Annals, The Histories* (Bill Thayer website editor). Chicago, IL: University of Chicago, LacusCurtius • Tacitus (uchicago.edu) URL: bit.ly/TacitusLCx

Tarn, W. W. "The Fleet of Xerxes." *The Journal of Hellenic Studies* 28 (1908): 202–33. https://doi.org/10.2307/624607. P. 2.

Terborg-Penn, Rosalyn. *African American Women in the Struggle for the Vote, 1850–1920.* Bloomington, IN: Indiana University Press, 1998.

Thanhauser, Sophie. *Worn A People's History of Clothing.* New York, NY: Vintage, Jan. 10, 2023.

The Annual Report of the Museum for 1921. *Museum of Fine Arts Bulletin* 20, no. 117 (1922): 9–10. http://www.jstor.org/stable/4169804.

Thompson, Georgina. "Iranian Dress in the Achaemenian Period: Problems Concerning the Kandys and Other Garments." *Iran* 3 (1965): 121–26. https://doi.org/10.2307/4299565.

Thompson, James M. (ed). "Introduction." In *Twentieth-Century Theories of Art, xi–xii.* Montreal Quebec: McGill-Queen's University Press, 1990. http://www.jstor.org/stable/j.ctt1cd0kz3.4.

Thornycroft, Elfrida, and Thomas Thornycroft. *Bronze and Steel. The Life of Thomas Thornycroft, Sculptor and Engineer.* Shipston-On-Stour: King's Stone Press, 1932.

Title History of the Boadicea group [by T. Thornycroft] erected 1902 [on the Victoria embankment], Thomas Thornycroft, Compiled by L. Priddle, 1902.

Toit, L. A. du. "Tacitus and The Rebellion of Boudicca." *Acta Classica* 20 (1977): 149–58. http://www.jstor.org/stable/24591531.

Torres, Tereska. *Women's Barracks (Femmes Fatales)* reprint. Manhattan, NY: The Feminist Press at CUNY, May 1, 2005.

Toynbee, J. M. C. "Roman Medallions: Their Scope and Purpose." *The Numismatic Chronicle and Journal of the Royal Numismatic Society* 4, no. 1/4 (1944): 27–44. http://www.jstor.org/stable/42663365.

Trent, Sydney. "Battle for the Ballot, the Black Sorority that Faced Racism in the Suffrage Movement but Refused to Walk Away," *The Washington Post*, Aug. 8, 2020. Deltas: Black sorority faced racism at a suffrage parade in Washington in 1913 – Washington Post.

Trotsky, Leon. "Art and Politics in Our Epic," first published by *Partisan Review*, June 18, 1938. Source: Fourth International, March–April 1950, 11:2. Pp. 61–64.

Tucker, Paul. "Monet and the Challenges to Impressionism in the 1880s." In *Critical Readings in Impressionism and Post-Impressionism: An Anthology*, edited by Mary Tompkins Lewis, 1st edition, 227–50. Oakland, CA: University of California Press, 2007. https://doi.org/10.2307/jj.8501295.15.

Turpin, John. "Art History and Art Criticism: Incompatible Partners?" *The Maynooth Review/Revieú Mhá Nuad* 5, no. 2 (1979): 15–24. http://www.jstor.org/stable/20556934.

Twomey, Lauren. "The Story of Lucy Burns," Independent Research Study, Shippensburg University, Microsoft Word – LB Research Draft 12:15 Post Edit.docx (ship.edu).

Tyler, Linda. "From Ghillie Suit to Glittering Kowhaiwhai – Contemporary New Zealand Artists Deploy the Camouflage Aesthetic." In *Camouflage Cultures: Beyond the Art of Disappearance*, edited by Ann Elias, Ross Harley, and Nicholas Tsoutas, 115–26. Camperdown, NSW: Sydney University Press, 2015. http://www.jstor.org/stable/j.ctt1bh4b60.13.

Urban, William. "The Teutonic Knights and Baltic Chivalry." *The Historian* 56, no. 3 (1994): 519–30. http://www.jstor.org/stable/24448704.

Vandrei, Martha. "'A great deal of historical claptrap': Heroine of Empire." *Queen Boudica and Historical Culture in Britain: An Image of Truth*, The Past and Present Book Series. Oxford, 2018; online edn, Oxford Academic, July 19, 2018. https://doi.org/10.1093/oso/9780198816720.003.0006. Accessed 27 Dec. 2023.

312 Bibliography

Vandrei, Martha. "A Victorian Invention? Thomas Thornycroft's 'Boadicea Group' And The Idea Of Historical Culture In Britain." *The Historical Journal* 57, no. 2 (2014): 485–508. http://www.jstor.org/stable/24529056.

Vandrei, Martha. "Queen Boudica, A Life in Legend, A pagan queen, an unruly woman and a valiant warrior avenging her daughters: Boudica has lived a varied afterlife in British history. Why is the ancient queen of the Iceni such an enduring figure?" Sep. 18, 2018. Queen Boudica, A Life in Legend | History Today.

Vannan, Elanor M. "The Queen of Propaganda: Boudica's Representation in Empire." *The Arbutus Review* 12, no. 1 (2021). https://doi.org/10.18357/tar121202120187.

Verbruggen, J. F. "Women in Medieval Armies." In Rogers, Clifford J., Kelly Devries, and John France (eds). *Journal of Medieval Military History: Volume IV*. Suffolk, England: Boydell & Brewer, 2006, pp. 119–36. http://www.jstor.org/stable/10.7722/j.ctt81ntp. https://www.jstor.org/stable/10.7722/j.ctt81ntp.10.

Vincent, Susan. "5. Queen Elizabeth: Studded with Costly Jewels". *Sartorial Politics in Early Modern Europe: Fashioning Women*, edited by Erin Griffey. Amsterdam: Amsterdam University Press, 2019, pp. 115–138. https://doi.org/10.1515/9789048537242-008.

Vinson, Alexandra H. "Short White Coats: Knowledge, Identity, and Status Negotiations of First-Year Medical Students." *Symbolic Interaction* 42, no. 3 (2019): 395–411. https://www.jstor.org/stable/26760904.

Virgil. *Aeneid*. Cambridge: Harvard University Press Loeb Classics online, 2023.

Von Bothmer, Dietrich. *Amazons in Greek Art, Oxford Monographs on Classical Archeology*, 1st edition. Oxford: Clarendon Press, Jan. 1, 1957.

Von Lkeist, Heinrich. *Penthesilea*. New York, NY: Harper Collins, 1998.

Vondeling, Johanna E. "The Manifest Professional: Manifestos and Modernist Legitimation." *College Literature* 27, no. 2 (2000): 127–45. http://www.jstor.org/stable/25112518.

Walker, Andrew. "From Private Sermon to Public Masterpiece: J. M. W. Turner's 'The Slave Ship' in Boston, 1876–1899." *Journal of the Museum of Fine Arts, Boston* 6 (1994): 4–13. http://www.jstor.org/stable/20519760.

Wallinga, H. T. "The Trireme and History." *Mnemosyne* 43, no. 1/2 (1990): 132–49. http://www.jstor.org/stable/4431893.

Ward-Jackson, Philip. "Expiatory Monuments by Carlo Marochetti in Dorset and the Isle of Wight." *Journal of the Warburg and Courtauld Institutes* 53 (1990): 266–80. https://doi.org/10.2307/751351.

Way, A. S. (trans.). *Quintus Smyrnaeus the Fall of Troy*, Loeb Classic Library, Vol. 19. London: William Heinemann, 1913.

Webster, Graham. *Boudica: The British Revolt against Rome AD 60*. New York, NY: Routledge, 1999.

Weems, Jason, and Alexander Nemerov. *The Art of World War I*. Philadelphia, PA: Pennsylvania Academy of Fine Arts, Nov. 6, 2016.

Weisinger, Herbert. "'A Very Curious and Painstaking Person' Robert Graves as Mythographer." *Midwest Folklore* 6, no. 4 (1956): 235–44. http://www.jstor.org/stable/4317604.

Wells, Helen. *Cherry Ames, Chief Nurse: Book 4*. New York, NY: Springer Publishing Company, Nov. 22, 2005.

Wells, Helen. *Cherry Ames, Flight Nurse Book 5*. New York, NY: Springer Publishing Company, June 30, 2020.

West, Gilbert. *The Institution of the Order of the Garter. A Dramatic Poem*. London: R. Dodsley, 1742.

Wheeler, Charles. "English Sculpture: Style and Materials." *Journal of the Royal Society of Arts* 93, no. 4695 (1945): 398–409. http://www.jstor.org/stable/41362159.

Wilberforce, W. "On the Abolition of the Slave Trade A Letter on the Abolition of the Slave Trade; Addressed to the Freeholders and Other Inhabitants of Yorkshire." In *Introduction*. London: Luke Hansard and Sons, 1807.

Willette, Jeanne. "French Artists During the Great War: Braque, Part One, arthistoryunstuffed, French Artists During the Great War: Braque, Part One | Art History Unstuffed.

Williamson, Claude C. H. "Chivalry." *The Irish Monthly* 47, no. 552 (1919): 330–39. http://www.jstor.org/stable/20505321.

Wills, Mary. "Abolition at Sea." In *Envoys of Abolition: British Naval Officers and the Campaign against the Slave Trade in West Africa*, 15–40. Liverpool, UK: Liverpool University Press, 2019. https://doi.org/10.2307/j.ctvsn3p4h.7.

Wills, Mary. "Officers' Contributions to Britain's Anti-Slavery Culture." In *Envoys of Abolition: British Naval Officers and the Campaign Against the Slave Trade in West Africa*, 167–90. Liverpool, UK: Liverpool University Press, 2019. https://doi.org/10.2307/j.ctvsn3p4h.12.

Wills, Mary. "Officers' Commitment to the Anti-Slavery Cause." In *Envoys of Abolition: British Naval Officers and the Campaign against the Slave Trade in West Africa*, 69–96. Liverpool, UK: Liverpool University Press, 2019. https://doi.org/10.2307/j.ctvsn3p4h.9.

Winsor, Mary. "The Militant Suffrage Movement." *The Annals of the American Academy of Political and Social Science* 56 (1914): 134–42. http://www.jstor.org/stable/1011988.

Woods, H. Charles. "The Balkans, Macedonia, and the War." *Geographical Review* 6, no. 1 (1918): 19–36. https://doi.org/10.2307/207447.

Xu, J., R. Zhang, and S. Yang. "Earrings Culture of Ancient Chinese Han Nationality and Its Aesthetic Evolution." *Art and Design Review* 10 (2022): 455–66. doi: 10.4236/adr.2022.104036.

Y, Dr. "Description of King Behanzin's Army on 13 March 1890," *Great Civilizations, Great Moments Great People!*, Apr. 27, 2020. African Heritage Blog, Description of King Behanzin's Army on 13 March 1890 – African Heritage (afrolegends.com).

Zahniser, J. D., and Amelia R. Fry. *Alice Paul: Claiming Power*. Oxford: Oxford University Press, 2014.

Zupnick, I. L. "The Social Conflict of the Impressionists. Zola's Opinions versus Evidence in Portraits." *College Art Journal* 19, no. 2 (1959): 146–53. https://doi.org/10.2307/774121.

ART AND ART PERIODS ADDENDUM

An excellent resource on the major movements in art: Stephen Farthing (ed), *Art the Whole Story*, Thames, and Hudson, 2020.

An interactive global timeline of art history can be found in the Metropolitan Museum of Art, Heilbrunn Timeline of Art History by period and geographical region. Chronology | Heilbrunn Timeline of Art History | The Metropolitan Museum of Art (metmuseum.org).

All definitions are taken directly from Internet sources such as art museum websites, art encyclopedias, and ArtStory.

Abstract Art   Approximate date: 1910–Present. Use of shapes and colors, forms, and markings rather than visually realistic depictions of something. Notable artists: Wassily Kandinsky, Piet Mondrain, Joan Miro, Frantisek Kupka, Yves Klein, Gerhard Richter, Helen Frankenthanthaler, Cy Twombly, Lee Krasner, Kazimir Malevich, Mark Rothko, and Hilma of Klint. Book: Michael Taylor, *Inventing Abstraction*, 1910–1925, Jan 31, 2013, The Museum of Modern Art NY.

Art Academies   Approximate date: 1563, *Accademia del Disegro* Florence, Italy–Present. Artist-run organizations that provide professional education and increase their professional standing. Notable academies: *Accademia de San Luca*, Rome, *Ecole des Beaux-Arts*, Paris, The Paris Salon, Royal Academy of Arts, London, *Academie Julian*, Paris, Slade School of Fine Art, London, Bauhaus, Germany. Book: Nikolaus Pevsner, *Academies of Art: Past and Present*, Cambridge University Press, 2014.

Avant-garde   Approximate date: 1850s. Any person, artwork, or art movement that breaks with the norm of the era is innovative and pushes boundaries. Includes all art forms. The term was borrowed from the French military advance guard that moved ahead of the main army. Has become synonymous with modern art. Book: *Art Attack: A Short Cultural History of the Avant-Garde*, Clarion Books,

Art and Art Periods Addendum **315**

April 20, 1998. Numerous artists are considered avant-garde across many generations for introducing new art approaches. French artist Gustave Courbet is a notable first.

Bauhaus Movement   Approximate date: 1919–1933. The core objective was a radical concept to reimagine the material world to reflect the unity of the arts. It was composed of a utopian craft guild that combined architecture, sculpture, and painting into one creative expression. Book: *Bauhaus: 1919–1933*, Bauhaus-archiv Berlin, Magdalena Droste. Taschen America LLC, 2019.

Black Figure Pottery   Approximate date: Greece, Mid-7th–5th centuries BCE. A painting technique where the flesh of the image is portrayed in black using an outline, filling the outline with refined clay to turn the figures dark. Details were carved into the clay deep enough so the red clay color would emerge. Notable black figure artists: Exekias, Amasis Painter. Books: Robert Slade Folsom, *Attic Black Figured Pottery*, Jan 1, 1975, Noyes Press. Joan R. Mertens, How to Read Greek Vases (The Metropolitan Museum of Art), Jan. 18, 2011, MET NY.

Blue Rider Group   Approximate date: 1911–1914. Created by artists Russian Wassily Kandinsky and German Franz Marc, it was a short-lived German Expressionist Group founded in Munich. Artists attracted to the group shared an interest in expressing art through spiritual and symbolic dimensions of color and abstract forms. Notable artists: Wassily Kandinsky, Franz Marc, Paul Klee, August Macke, Marianne von Werefkin, and Alexej von Jawlensky. Book: Franz Marc and Wassily Kandinsky (eds), *The Blaue Reiter Almanac*, reprint, Da Capo Press, March 1989.

Bronze Casting   Approximate date: About 2500 BC, Asia lost wax casting. The oldest known bronze sculpture is the *Dancing Gril*, found in modern-day Pakistan. The Greeks were the first to master life-size bronze statues – pouring molten bronze into a hollow mold to create a sculpture or object. Methods include lost wax, ceramic shell, and sand casting. Notable bronze statues: The Bronze David, Boxer at Rest, Little Mermaid, Manneken Pis, Bronco Buster, The Charioteer of Delphi, L'Homme Qui Marche I, The Statue of Unity, The Thinker, and L'Homme Au Doigt. Book: Carol Mattusch, *Enduring Bronze: Ancient Art, Modern Views*, J Paul Getty Museum, June 15, 2014.

Caricature Art   Approximate date: 16th century. Synonymous with satirical art is usually a figurative drawing or pen-and-ink portrayal of a person that distorts or exaggerates certain features but retains a recognizable likeness and is often used to ridicule public figures. Notable artists: Al Hirschfeld, Isaac Cruikshank, Carlo Pellegrini, Kate Carew, Pier Leone Ghezzi, Andre Gill, Alexander Sarukhan, Honore Daumier, James Gillray, Thomas Nast, and Emile Cole. Book: Feaver William, *Masters of Caricature from Hogarth and Gillray to Scarfe and Levine*, Alfred A. Knopf, First American edition, Jan. 1, 1981.

Chromoluminarism   Approximate date: 1884. Also called divisionism. Using individual dots or patches of color that form optical interactions on a painting. Book: *Georges Seurat: The Art of Vision*, Michelle Foa, Yale University Press, 2015.

Classical Art   Approximate date: 8th century BCE–5th century CE. A reference term to the artistic styles of ancient Greece and Rome. Characteristics associated with classical art vary and may include appeal to the intellect, restrained emotion, perfection, structural clarity, emphasis on form, and proportion. Notable artists: Nicolas Poussin, Annibale Carracci, Claude Lorrain, Jacques Louis David, Jean Auguste Domingue Ingres, and Anton Raphael Mengs. Book: Mary Beard and John Henderson *Classical Art: From Greece to Rome (Oxford History of Art)*, Oxford University Press, 2001.

316 Art and Art Periods Addendum

Coinage Art Approximate date: First millennium BC–Present. Applying aesthetic components to rounded pieces of metal produced by a legal or government authority as money. Notable historical examples: King Alyattes of Lydia and the Lydian Lion, Princess Hermodike I standardized currencies, Pisanello Renaissance commemorative coin maker, Isaac Newton, milled coins, George T. Morgan, US Mint, Roman Booten hobo nickels, *Art in Coinage*, B. T. Batsford, Jan. 1, 1955.

Constructivism Approximate date: 1915–1940. This art movement, which arose primarily in the Soviet Union and Germany, was known for its abstractions, geometric forms, and alliance with visual propaganda for the communist and socialist revolutions of Eastern Europe. Recognized for stark and harsh angularizations and minimal use of the color continuum, the movement's primary aim was to reflect the harshness of industrial society and urbanization. Notable artists: Eli Lissitzky, Alexander Rodchenko, Varvara Stepanova, El Lissitzky, Sophie Taeuber-Arp, Hans Richter, Kazimir Malevich, Lyubov Popova, and Theo van Doesburg. Book: Stephen Bann, *Traditions of Constructivism*, Hatchett Books, Mishawaka, IN, 1990.

Cubism Approximate date: 1907–1914. One of the most influential art styles introduced in the 20th century. This painting style uses geometric forms and realigns them within two-dimensional space while contrasting multiple points of view. Notable artists: Pablo Picasso, George Braques, Fernand Leger, Robert and Sonia Delaunay, Juan Gris, Marcel Duchamp, Albert Gleizes, and Jean Metzinge. Book: Anne Gantefuher-Trier, *Cubism*, TASCHEN, Dec. 8, 2015.

Dadaism Approximate date: 1916–mid-1920s. An informal international movement in Europe and North America was organized around the time of the outbreak of World War I. Proponents of the movement produced satirical and nonsensical forms of art as a reaction to the horrors and folly of war. Notable artists: Francis Picabia, Hugo Ball, Max Ernst, Hannah Hoch, Kurt Schwitters, Raoul Hausmann, Marcel Duchamp, Man Ray, Jean Arp, and Hans Richter. Book: Deitmar Elger, *Dadaism*, TASCHEN, Feb. 15, 2016.

Engraving and Etching Approximate dates: engraving as a formal art form: 15th century, etching as a formal art form, 1513. Engraving is an intaglio printmaking process that uses sharp instruments to cut lines into a hard surface that will hold ink. Etching uses a form of acid or inorganic oxide to cut into unprotected parts of a metal surface. Notable etchers: Albrecht Durer, Hendrik Goltzius, Hieronymus Cook, Edgar Degas, Ferdinand Bol, Joan Miro. Notable engravers: Johannes Gutenberg, Robert Doisneau, Constant Dutilleux, Luke Fildes, Jacob de Gheyn III, John Greenwood, and Emily Sartain. Book: Arthur Mayger, *A Short History of Engraving and Etching For the Use of Collectors and Students With Full Bibliography, Classified List, and Index of Engravers*, Reprint Wentworth Press, Aug. 27, 2016.

Exhibitions, Art, and Expositions Approximate date: First modern public exhibition 1760. First international exposition 1851. Art exhibitions were organized to allow artists to show their studio work before a public buying audience. Artists' reputations were built and lost as a result of public opinion. Notable exhibitions: The Salon des Refuses, 1863; The First Impressionist Exhibition, 1874; The Armory Show, 1913; Exhibition Internationale su Surrealisme, 1938. Expositions, known as World's Fairs, were large global gatherings organized to showcase science, industry, and cultural achievements. Notable expositions: Society for the Encouragement of Arts, Manufacturers, and Commerce, 1760; The Great Exhibition, 1851; Exposition Universelle, 1889; Centennial Exhibition, 1876; Philadelphia Centennial Exposition, 1876. Books: Paul Greenhalgh, *Fair World: A History of World's Fairs and Expositions* *from London to Shanghai 1851–2010*, Papadakis Dist A C; Aug. 16, 2011. Nickolaus Pevsner, *Academies of Art Past and Present*, reprint Cambridge University Press, Aug. 14, 2014.

Expressionism Approximate date: 1905–1920. A form of art that arose in Germany and Austria that uses extreme angles, flat forms, bold colors, and distortions in viewpoint, arising from the anxieties of modern life. Notable artists: Ernst Ludwig Kirchner, Edvard Munch, Jackson Pollack, Franz Marc, Paul Klee, Wassily Kandinsky, Erich Heckel, August Macke, Mark Rothko, Helen Frankenthaler, and Vincent van Gogh. Book: Norbert Wolf, *Expressionism*, TASCHEN, Dec. 2015.

Fauvism Approximate date: 1905–1910. The first avant-garde movement that arose in France in the early 20th century was the first group of artists to break away from impressionism and traditional methods of perception. Their work often utilized bold brushwork and vibrant colors. Rather than painting with a brush, artists would use paint directly from the tube. Notable artists: Henri Matisse, Maurice de Vlamink, Derain, Kees van Dongen, Charles Camoin, Henri Charles Manguin, Othon Friesz, Jean Puy, Louis Valtat, Andre Derain, Georges Roudult, and Georges Braque Raoul Dufy. Book: Dita Amory and Ann Dumas, *Vertigo of Color: Matisse, Derain, and the Origins of Fauvism*, TASCHEN, Metropolitan Museum of Art, Oct. 24, 2023.

Futurism Approximate date: 1909–1914. An art movement that originated in Italy that emphasized representing the dynamism of technology, industrialization, and violence arising in Europe. Common themes were cars, airplanes, industrial cities, and youth. Notable artists: Marcel Duchamp, Goncharova, Filippo Marinett, Lyubov Popova, Mario Sironi, Umberto Boccioni, Carlo Carra, and Kazimir Malevich. Book: Geert Buelens (ed), *The History of Futurism, The Precursors, Protagonists and Legacies*, Lexington Books, Aug. 31, 2012.

Golden Mean Art Approximate date: 300 BCE. Based on the golden ratio, an irrational number with an approximate value of 1.618 was used to divide lines and rectangles aesthetically pleasingly. Notable artists include Leonardo da Vinci, Sandro Botticelli, Vincent van Gogh, Salvador Dali, and Leonardo da Vinci. Book: Gyorgy DOczi, *The Power of Limits Proportional Harmonies in Nature, Art and Architecture*, Shambhala (1st ed), Oct. 11, 2005.

Illuminated Manuscripts Approximate date: 4th century BCE. These manuscripts were handwritten books with decorative artwork within the document's body. Gold and silver were often used on pages made of animal skin. A majority of manuscripts were produced in religious settings and for wealthy patrons. Notable artists include Herman, Paul, and Jean Limbourgh. Book: Christopher De Hamel, *A History of Illuminated Manuscripts*, Phaidon Press, Sep. 26, 1997.

Impressionism Approximate date: 1867–1886. Anonymous Society of Painters, Sculptors, and Printmakers, etc., launched it. It is governed only by independence from the official annual jury Salon. Diverse approaches. Modern life. Style short brushstrokes, unblended colors, emphasis on effects of light, and barely conveyed forms. Notable artists: Pierre-August Renoir, Berthe Morisot, Paul Cezanne, Mary Cassat, Camille Pissarro, Edgar Degas, and Edouard Manet. Book: Norbert Wolf, *Impressionism: Reimagining Art*, Prestel, Oct. 3, 2023.

Jewelry The approximate date is 3000–400 BC. Personal ornamentation worn on the body usually includes items for the neck, head, fingers, arms, wrists, and ankles. Notable modern jewelers include Tiffany & Co., Cartier, Boucheron, Van Cleef & Arpels, Buccellati, Harry Winston, and David Webb. Book: Maren Eichorn-Johannsen, Adelheid Rasche, Astrid Bahr, and Svenia Schneider (eds), *25000 Years of Jewelry*, Prestel (New ed), Oct. 19, 2021.

318 Art and Art Periods Addendum

Lithography Approximate date: 1796, commercialized around 1820. As a substitute for engraving and etching, the lithography process is more straightforward and versatile due to its ability to produce rapid and cheap reproductions. A method using stone, zinc, or aluminum as a base where the base's inked and uninked sections are at the same level. Designs are drawn or painted with greasy ink or crayons and moistened with water. Notable artists: Henri de Toulouse-Lautrec, Alphonse Mucha, John L. Magee, and Henri Matisse, Book: Alois Senefelder, Honore Daumier, Sonia Delaunay, Piere Bonnard, Joan Miro, John James Audubon, Marc Chagall, and Francis Flora Bond Palmer, *The Invention of Lithography*, Aug. 24, 2018, Forgotten Books reprint.

Manifestos Approximate date: 1886–Present. Public declarations describing motives, viewpoints, and intentions of an art movement. Notable manifestos (hundreds exist): The Foundation and Manifesto of Futurism, Dada Manifesto, Against Traditionalist Venice, Der Blaue Reiter Almanac, Rayonists and Futurists: A Manifesto, Cerebrist Art, Cubism Futurism and Suprematism, Dada Manifesto, The Realistic Manifesto, Manifesto of DeStijl, and Manifesto of the Constructivist Group. Book: Alex Danchev, *100 Artist Manifestos from the Futurists to the Stuckists*, Penguin, 2001.

Medallions and Medals Approximate date 1400s–Present. Medals are small portable items, usually made of metal, with a design on one or both sides. Medallions are large medals traditionally given as an award or commemoration. Notable artist: Pisanello. Book: Eugene F. Fairbanks, *Medals, Medallions, and Reliefs: Created by Avard Avard T. Fairbanks*, Create Space Independent Publishing Platform, Apr. 26, 2018. Book: *Lincoln Financial Foundation Collection, Medals and Medallions*, Creative Media Partners, LLC, Reprint Sept. 2021.

Stanley Lane POOLE, Coins and Medals: Their Place in History and Art, Jan. 1, 2022, Gyan Publishing House, Jan. 1, 2022.

Modern Art Approximate date: 1860–1975. Experimental art challenged the long-held concept that art should realistically depict the world. Pablo Picasso, Salvador Dali, Frida Kahlo, Jeff Koons, Andy Warhol, Vincent van Gogh, Jean-Michel Basquiat, Yayoi Kusama, Claude Monet. Jackson Pollock, and David Hockney. Book: Elizabeth C. Mansfield and H. Harvard Arnason, *History of Modern Art*, Pearson (7th ed), Dec. 12, 2022.

Modernism Approximate date: Late 19th to mid-20th century. It was a period in art punctuated with experimentation and rejection of traditional or accepted ideas. Vibrant colors, bold brushstrokes, abstractions, and forms and shapes were familiar to the period. Book: *Modern Art and Modernism A Critical Anthology*, Francis Frascina and Charles Harrison (eds), Bold Type Books, 1983.

Monuments and Statues Approximate date: 2500 BC–Present. Form of sculpture that honors a person or event. Notable Sculptors: Donato di Niccolo di Betto Bardi, Michelangelo Buonarroti, Gian Lorenzo Bernini, Antonio Canova, Auguste Rodin, Constantin Brancusi, Pablo Picasso, and Robert Smithson. Book: Antony Gormley and Martin Gayford, *Shaping the World: Sculpture from Prehistory to Now*, Thames and Hudson, Nov. 17, 2020.

Naturalism Approximate date: Renaissance, 1820s–1880s. The painting movement involved humans and other subjects being painted in their natural habitats and social settings. Book: *Rousseau and Naturalism in Life and Thought*, Legare Street Press, 2022.

Neoplasticism Approximate date: 1917–1931. Avant-garde art theory employed by Dutch artists from the DeStijl group. Color, line, and form in painting were used in their purest, most fundamental state. Only primary colors and non-colors, squares and rectangles, and straight and horizontal or vertical lines were combined. Book: *Piet Mondrian a Life*, Hans Janssen and Piet Mondrian, Ridinghouse/Kunstmusem Den Haag, The Hague, 2022.

Non-Figurative (Non-objective Art) Approximate date: 1919–Present. A work of art that unrealistically distorts form and figure may be a design, shape, or color with no representation of a natural object or reality. Notable artists: Wassily Kandinsky, Piet Mondrian, Nuam Gabo, Mark Rothko, Elaine de Kooning, Kasimir Malevich, Jackson Pollock, and Pablo Picasso. Book: Tracey Bashkoff, Don Quaintance, John G. Hardt (authors) and Karole Vail (ed), *The Museum of Non-Objective Painting: Hilla Rebay and the Origins of the Solomon R. Guggenheim Museum*, Guggenheim Museum, Aug. 31, 2009.

Occultism Approximate date: 16th century–Present. Magic and occult art are closely related to religion but oppose formal religious doctrines and scientific approaches. Much of this art is devoted to animism, astrology, and fetishism. Notable artists: Austin Osman Spare, Kurt Seligmann, Majorie Cameron, Pamela Colman Smith, Rosaleen Norton, and Lon Milo DuQuette. Book: Gabriyell Sarom, *The Art of Occultism & Inner Exploration (The Sacred Mystery)*, Independently published, Dec. 27, 2018.

Orphism Approximate date: 1910–1913. Also called orphic cubism, it is an offshoot of pure cubism focusing on pure abstraction and bright colors. Notable artists: Robert Delaunay, Sonia Terk Delaunay. Book: Virginia Spate, *Orphism: The Evolution of Non-Figurative Painting in Paris, 1910–1914 (Xzoford Studies in the History of Art and Architecture)*, Oxford University Press, Jan. 24, 1980.

Pointillism Approximate date: Mid-1880s–1890s. It appeared after the Impressionist period and is also called Neo-impressionism or Divisionism. Using a highly accomplished pictorial technique and dabs of color allows the viewer to see a complete landscape, portrait, or seascape from a distance. Book: *Ways of Pointillism: Seurat, Signac, Van Gogh*, Klaus Albrecht Schroder (ed), Hirmer Publishers, 2017.

Postcard art Approximate date: 1869–1915. Thin or thick paper carding, usually rectangular, that often has blank art on one side is intended for writing and mailing without an envelope. Notable artists: There have been hundreds of postcard artists. Book: Lydia Pyne, *Postcards: The Rise and Fall of the World's First Social Network*, The University of Chicago Press, 2021.

Printmaking Approximate date: Han Dynasty 206 BC–Present. Includes woodcutting, etching, engraving, and lithography. Transfers images from a template onto another surface, allowing numerous iterations of the same image. Notable artists: Leonardo da Vinci, Rembrandt van Rijn, Edvard Munch, Henri Matisse, Pablo Picasso, MarcChagall, Andy Warhol, Salvadore Dali, Roy Lichenstein, David Hockney, and Bansky. Book: Donald SaffandDeli Sacilotto, *Printmaking: History and Process.*

Pulp Magazine Art Approximate date: 1896–1960s. Art created for the covers of inexpensive fiction magazines. Notable artists include Margaret Brundage, Austin Briggs, Robert McDinnis, Everett Kinstler, Rolf Armstrong, and Normal Saunders. Tom Lovell, Leo Morey, Tom Lovell, and Amos Sewell. Book: Douglas Ellis, Ed Hulse, and Robert Weinberg (eds), *The Art of the Pulps, An Illustrated History*, IDW Publishing, Oct. 24, 2017.

Purism Approximate date: 1918–1925. Movement that reduced subject matter to the relationships of geometric angles and shapes aimed to infuse mechanical and industrial subject matter in the work. Taking everyday objects and distilling them into aesthetically pleasing shapes and forms. Notable artists: Amedee Ozenfant,

320 Art and Art Periods Addendum

Charles Edourart Jeanneret (Le Corbusier), Joseph Csaky, Ivan Llium, and Peter Blume. Book: Carol S. Eliel, Francoise Ducors, Tag Gronberg, and Lesprit Nouvea, *Prusim in Paris 1918–1925*, Los Angeles County Museum of Art, 2001.

Realism   Approximate date: 1850–1930. An un-cohesive group of artists rejected Romanticism and generally expanded the concept of what constituted art. Rather than painting grand history and allegory, these artists painted real-life events at all levels of society. Notable artists: Gustave Courbet, Edouard Manet, Jean-Francois Millet, and James Whistler. Book: Brendan Prendeville, *Realism in 20th Century Painting (World of Art)*, Thames and Hudson, Oct. 17, 2000.

Red Figure Pottery   Approximate date: Period 1: 530–480 BCE; Period 2: 480–323 BCE. A form of vase painting usually of heroic scenes that used foreshortening to present decorative scenes. Decorations were first outlined in black, and the figures were left red. Notable artists include Epictetus, Euphronius, Euthymides, Onesimus, Douris, and Brygos Painter. During the 2nd period of pottery scenes, artists used yellow-brown, gold, and blue. Book: Robert Slade Folsom, *Attic Red-Figured Pottery (Noyes Classical Studies)*, Jan. 1, 1976, Noyes Data Corporation/Noyes Publications, 1976.

Romanticism   Approximate date: 1800–1850. Both an artistic and intellectual movement originating in Europe. Sense and emotions, not reason and order, are equally important in experiencing the natural world, supernatural and mysterious, imagination, and the subconscious. Book: William Vaughan, *Romanticism and Art*, Thames and Hudson (2nd Revised ed), Sep. 1, 1994.

Spiritualism   Approximate date: Renaissance–Present. Using non-programmed approaches to creativity, such as automatic drawing or precipitation – using human hands during a séance in the belief spirits can guide creativity. Popular subject matter of the genre has been transcendency, mystical, and cosmic themes. Notable artists: Piet Mondrian, Georgiana Houghton, Anna Mary Howitt, Hilma af Klimt, Salvadore Dali, and Rene Magritte. Book: Charlene Spretnak, *The Spiritual Dynamic in Modern Art: Art History Reconsidered, 1800 to the Present*, Palgrave Macmillan (2014th ed), Oct. 23, 2014.

Stone Engraving   Approximate date: Prehistoric–Present. Using a hard implement to change rock forms into desired images as simple as letter carving or as complex as intricate sculptures. Notable artists: Constantine Seferlis, Benvenuto Cellini, Lorenzo Ghierti, and Carvers of Escolasticas, Book: Dj Garrity, Nicola Pisano, Giovanni Pisano, Jacopo della Quercia, Auguste Rodin, Marcel Duchamp, and Hans Arp, *Stone: A Legacy and Inspiration for Art*, Black Dog Press, Nov. 22, 2011.

Suprematism   Approximate date: 1913–1919. Reduction in the art to its most fundamental geometric forms – the square, the cross, and the circle – were austere and cerebral. Notable artists: Kazimir Malevich, Alexander Rodchenko, El Lissitzky, and Olga Rozanova. Book: Paricia Railing, *Kazimir Malevich: Suprematism: 34 Drawings (1920)*, Artists Bookworks; reprint Aug. 29, 2018, and Gilles Neret, *Kazimir Malevich 1878–1935: And Suprematism*, TASCHEN, May 9, 2017.

Surrealism   Approximate date: 1924–1966. Primarily, it was a literary movement experimenting with automatic writing and utilizing the subconscious to produce unexpected, uncanny, and unconventional artworks. A primary influence was the free association theories of Sigmund Freud and the political ideas of Karl Marx. The basis of the movement was a reaction against cultural and political upheaval. Notable artists include Max Ernst, Andre Masson, Joan Miro, and Man Ray. Book: Whitney Chadwick, *Women Artists and the Surrealist Movement*, Thames and Hudson, revised Nov. 23, 2021.

Symbolism Approximate date: 1886–1900. A reaction to rationalism and materialism in Western Europe promoting the validity of pure subjectivity and ideas over realistic renderings of the natural world. Artists partially returned to the expressivity of the Romantic artisans of the early 19th century. Notable artists: Paul Gauguin, Albert Aurier, Gustave Moreau, Puvis de Chavannes, Odilon Redon, Eugene Carriere, Arnold Bocklin, and Edward Burne Jones. Book: Michelle Facos, *Symbolist Art in Context*, University of California Press, Mar. 31, 2009.

INDEX

abolitionism 7, 103, 108, 109, 111, 133, 134, 153, 313; Collier, Sir George Ralph and 108; *HMS Creole* and 108; JWM Turner and 108, 134, 290

Achaemenid 28, 29, 31, 33–35, 40, 45, 298, 303

Achilles 6, 9–12, 14, 16–19, 22–23, 283, 293

Addams, Jane 157, 158, 159, 160, 163, 183n

Aeschylus 45, 149, 235, 291; *Seven Against Thebes* and 149, 235; Theban women and 149

Africa Squadron 107, 134

African American 280, 286; Appo Cook Helen and 150, 151, 180n; Colored Women's League (CWL) and 150; Delta Sigma Theta Sorority and 152; Iris Calderhead and 152; jailing and 152; National Association of Colored Women NAWC and 151; suffrage and 150, 151, 152, 187

Albert, Prince 52–54, 56–57, 69

Allender, Nina 174

Amazons 12–14, 19, 21, 24–26, 84; Dahomey women as 1, 6–8, 97–98, 102, 109, 110, 112, 118, 121–122, 126–129, 136, 138–139, 289; Penthesilea as 1, 5, 6, 7, 10–20, 21, 22, 23, 26, 281, 283, 298, 309, 312; scientific evidence and 21, 26

America(ans) 1, 16, 17, 21n, 56, 99, 118, 119, 120, 121, 129, 150, 152, 156, 157, 159, 16, 163, 164, 171, 174, 175, 204, 208, 227, 259, 261, 264, 266, 267, 269, 271, 272, 273, 274, 280, 284, 285, 286

Anatolian region 27–48

Anderson, Elizabeth Garrett 152, 236, 238

anthropologists 109, 118

anti suffragism 143–145, 150, 178n, 180n, 199, 298; Abbott, Lyman and 145; Jewel, Josephine and 145, 179n; Kendrick Johnson, Helen and 147, 179n, 180n; beliefs about suffragism and 147; book *Woman and the Republic, A Survey of the Woman-Suffrage Movement in the United States, and A Discussion of the Claims and Arguments of Its Foremost Advocates* and 147; description of 147; Theban women and 149

army 3, 14, 35, 36, 38, 64, 65, 85, 95, 100, 102, 112, 116, 117, 120, 156, 195, 199, 210, 235, 258; Army nurse corps 158, 260, 261, 266, 269; British 7, 18, 56, 92, 159, 197, 198, 230, 233, 234, 236, 237, 239; French 120, 193; Genoese 79; German, Imperial 224, 227; Greek 12, 14; Moorish 84; Ottoman 194; Persian

35, 46n; Red 255, 256; Roman 64, 130n; Salvation Army 118, 157, 158; Serbian 7, 196, 202, 204, 205, 216n, 218; United States 3, 158, 259, 270, 283

art: history of 32, 68, 88, 136, 191, 211, 212, 243, 244, 245, 247, 255, 275, 309, 311, 313, 314; iconography and 22, 40, 44, 48, 128, 298; illustrations and 31, 57, 124, 126, 137, 139, 209, 231, 258, 260; *Lady of the Black Horse* 6, 190, 209; *Luncheon on the Grass* 252, 275n; manifestos and 222, 243, 252, 254, 279, 312, 318; *Operation at Endell Street Hospital* 220; paintings and 1, 5, 11, 75, 192, 209, 218, 224, 227, 229, 231, 232, 233, 238, 253, 255, 265, 287; periods and 314–321; Serbian and 193–195; sexualization and 8, 128; *The Slave Ship* 108

art movements: abstractionism 17, 192, 193, 194, 222, 223, 227, 228, 232, 254, 275, 314, 315, 316, 318, 319; Arts and Crafts Movement 164, 195; Bauhaus 224, 244, 275, 307, 314, 315; Blue Rider Movement (*Der Blaue Reiter*) 192, 244, 315; Chromoluminarism 225, 315; Cubism 192, 212, 223, 225, 256, 292, 305, 316, 318, 319; Dada 226, 227, 228, 244, 245, 246, 293, 303, 304, 308, 309, 318; Dadaism 223, 228, 246, 292, 316; Fauvism 192, 194, 195, 209, 212, 222, 232, 225, 226, 243, 304, 317; Futurism 222, 243, 244, 254, 256, 275, 292, 299, 317, 318; Impressionism 195, 211n, 212n, 194, 256, 275n, 297, 299, 303, 311, 316, 317, 319; Modernism 185n, 195, 213n, 221, 222, 225, 243n, 244n, 246n, 275n, 296, 297, 301, 310, 318; Neoclassical 17, 54; Pointillism 222, 319; Post Impressionism 211n, 212n, 297, 299, 303, 311; Realism 17, 53, 55, 124, 195, 211n, 217, 233, 256, 309, 320; Renaissance 25n, 41, 44n, 90n, 165, 177n, 229, 252, 255, 258, 275n, 290, 291, 294, 296, 297, 302, 318; 320; Romanticism 53, 256, 320; Suprematism 318, 320; Surrealism 223, 243n, 256, 276n, 316, 320

art technique 53, 68n, 77, 100, 141, 192, 195, 218, 222, 230, 252, 253, 254, 315, 319

Artemisia I 5, 6, 7, 28, 31, 33, 34, 35, 40, 41, 42, 44n, 46n, 47n; Caira and 39, 42

Artemisia II 31, 34, 41

artifact 1, 4, 5, 6, 8, 26, 32, 33, 75, 95, 100, 110, 117, 119, 140, 174, 175, 285, 288; clothing as 1, 4, 5, 33, 34, 41, 45n, 53, 85, 94, 95, 96, 97, 103, 105, 106, 120, 122, 129, 164, 165, 170, 234, 273, 274, 286; costume as 6, 11, 95, 96, 124, 129, 130n, 165

artists: Azbe, Anton 195; Bachmayer, Babette 195, 213n, 295; Ball, Hugo 223, 226, 227, 228, 245n; Beckman, Max 225, 244n; Braque, Georges 193, 212n, 225; Breton, Andre Robert 255, 256, 276n; Brundage, Margaret 258, 277n; Cassatt, Mary 192; Cezanne, Paul 222, 317; Cvetkovic, Natalija 195, 218, 295; Delaunay, Robert 316, 318, 319; Degas, Edgar 192, 265, 316, 317; Deming, Dorothy 260, 261, 296; Derain, Andre 225, 224n, 317; Dodd, Francis 7, 220, 230, 233, 234, 238, 242, 296; Duchamp, Marcel 316, 317, 320; Flack, Dorothy 258, 277n; Gauguin, Paul 321; Gleizes, Albert 224, 225, 226, 244n; Gropius, Walter 224, 244n, 307; Kandinsky, Wassily 193, 195, 212n, 223, 224, 225, 227, 228, 243n, 301; Kutlic, Kiril 195, 301, 213n; Macke, August 224, 225, 315; Mackey, Haydan Reynolds 233; Manet, Edouard 252, 253, 265, 275n; Marc, Franz 212n, 223, 224, 225, 315, 317; Marinetti, Fillipo 222, 228, 243n; Marochetti, Carlo Baron 53, 54, 69n, 312; Matisse, Henri 225, 226, 245n, 265, 317, 318; Monet, Claude 192, 212n, 318; Moore, Henry Spencer 194; Pankhurst, Sylvia 154, 231, 232, 247n; Petrovic, Nadezdax 195, 196, 202, 213n; Picabia, Francis 225, 226, 244n; Picasso, Pablo 193, 196, 212n, 244n, 265, 316, 318, 319; Pissarro, Camille 317; Rankin, George James 7, 209, 210; Robinson, Boardman 207; Seurat, Georges 315, 319;

324 Index

Sinzogan, Julien 129; Spare, Austin Osman 223, 229, 230, 239–241; Steinlen, Theophile Alexandre 207; Thornycroft, Mary 68n, 304; Thornycroft, Thomas 6, 50, 52, 67; Turner, JWM 108, 134n; Tutundijian, Leon Arthur 254; Van Doesburg, Theo 254, 276n; Van Gogh, Vincent 317, 319; Von Kaulbach, Willem 31
artworks: Ball, Hugo R. *MUTT, 1917* 227; Beckman, Max *Happy New Year* 225; Beckman, Max *Madhouse* 225; Beckman, Max *The Night* 225; Dodd, Francis, *An Operation at the Military Hospital, Endell Street-Dr. L. Garrett, Dr. Flora Murray, Dr. W Buckley* 205; Kandinsky, Wassily *The Last Judgment* 193; Manet, Edouard, *Le Dejeuner surl'herbe (Luncheon on the Grass)* 252; Osman Spare, Austin *Dame Rachel Crowdy, Principal Commander of the VAD* 238, 239; Osman Spare, Austin *Pastel image of a nurse in uniform at Endell Hospital, a Nurse in a White Lab Coat* 240; Osman Spare, Austin *Pastel Drawing of a Nurse at Endell Street in Outdoor Uniform* 241; Picasso, Pablo *Mother and Child* 265; Rankin, George James *Lady of the Black Horse* 171; Reynolds, Haydan *A Royal Army Medical Corps Bearer Supplying Water to the Front Line* 223; Turner, JMW *The Deluge* 108; Turner, J.M.W. *The Slave Ship* 108, 134n
Ashmole, Elias 83–85, 301
Asquith, H.H. 141n, 155, 166, 168

Balkans 191, 193, 194, 195, 198, 199, 201, 213n, 214n, 217
Ball, William H. 167, 170, 171
Behanzin 115, 125, 127, 131n, 290, 305
Belgrade 195, 196, 200, 205, 287
Berengar IV, Ramon 79; Catalonia women and 78–79; feminine cavaliers and 1, 5, 74–76; sieges of Almeria and Tortosa and 85–87; Second Crusades and 80
Beverly, Margaret 80, 89n
Blake, Sophia Jex 234–236
Bonetta, Sarah Forbes 111, 135n, 306; *HMS Bonetta* and 290; education and 111; marriage and 111–112

Boudica: arts and (plays, music, opera) 55; battle speeches and 65–66; Camulodunum and 60, 62, 63, 64; Celts and 50, 56, 58, 62, 66, 67, 70n, 71n, 143; chariot fighting and 65, 70n, 116; description of 50, 62; druids and 55, 61, 62, 64, 66, 67, 69n; Iceni and 66, 67, 70n, 71n; Londinium and 63, 64; revolt and reasons for 67, 70n, 71n; tactics and 64, 65; ultimate battle and 66; Verulamium and 63; Wattling Road battle and 64, 65, 67, 71n
Brazil 99, 108
Breton, Andre Robert 255, 256, 275n
bronze 50, 51, 53, 58, 60, 68n, 77, 129, 141, 143, 196, 286, 302, 315
Burns, Lucy 152, 153, 172, 181, 293, 304, 311
Burton, Sir Richard Francis 93, 100, 103, 112, 113, 123, 132n, 294

Caesar, Julius 50, 55, 56, 60, 65, 71n
Caffaro 85, 86, 90n
Calderhead, Iris 152
Cassius Dio 60, 61, 62, 65, 71n, 294
castles 6, 78, 79, 80, 81, 88n, 111, 197
Cat and Mouse Act 169, 185n, 197, 289, 304
Catt, Carrie Chapman 153, 159, 160, 175, 183n
cavaliers 1, 5, 74, 76, 77, 82, 90n
Christian(s) 79, 82, 85, 86, 87, 88n, 98, 111, 149, 160, 163, 191
Circle of Serbian Sisters (*Kolo Srpskih Sestara*) 196, 200, 226, 214n
cloth 4, 94, 96, 106, 111, 122, 123, 124, 125, 126, 128, 129, 137n, 138, 143, 302, 310
clothing 4, 5, 33, 34, 41, 45n, 53, 85, 94, 95, 96, 97, 103, 105, 106, 120, 122, 129, 164, 165, 170, 234, 273, 274, 286, 311; caps as 106, 123, 124, 125, 126, 128, 27; chiton as 15; girdle as 13, 105, 106; helmet as 15, 81, 119, 200, 233; robe as 123; sakkos as 30, 41, 42; sashes as 106, 122, 124, 125, 126; shirt as 95, 128, 286; surtout as 105; tunic as 6, 33, 96, 106, 112, 123, 126, 128; waistcoat as 106; wraps as 33
coins 33, 41, 44n, 47n, 60, 316, 318
colonialism 6, 55, 103, 114, 120, 124, 126, 131n, 281

Index **325**

combat 2, 3, 8, 14, 19, 20, 21, 34, 38, 50, 64, 67, 78, 95, 99, 100, 102, 115, 125, 128, 116, 126, 127, 128, 129, 143, 199, 225, 265, 282, 283
Communism(ist) 150, 158, 316, 256
community 24n, 35, 79, 88n, 94, 114, 126, 136n, 141, 149, 151, 152, 174, 176, 211, 213n, 215n, 225, 229, 232, 242, 255
Conches, Isabel of 81
continent(s) 103, 119, 122, 157, 176, 192, 198, 208, 228, 281
costume 6, 11, 95, 96, 124, 129, 130
Cowper, William 50
Cretan 31, 35, 46n
Crystal Palace 69, 118, 120, 241

da Sousa, Francisco Felix 104, 110
Dahomey, Kingdom of: acacia bush and 101, 132; Edo and 99; enslavement and 7, 97, 98, 106, 107, 108, 111, 112, 153, 208, 209; geography and 133n, 294; King Ghezo and 99, 100, 104, 107, 114; sacrifices and 93, 97, 102, 132n
Dahomey Amazons: Adegon, battle of and 114; baseball and 117, 121, 207, 208, 223, 224, 232, 253, 254, 266, 267, 282; bush survival and 102; Cana, battle of and 114, 115; Dogba, battle of and 114, 126, 128, 137n; elephant and alligator hunters 102; fetish and 109, 110, 134n; nomenclature of 99; oaths and 109; officers and deputies and 113; oral histories and 113, 126; *Domnatio memoriae* 114; *Kpanlingan* 114, 135n; recruiting and 100; *Akpadume* and 113; *Fosupo* and 113; *Khe-tun-gan* and 113; *Zokhenu* and 113
Dahomeyan wars 8, 102, 122, 128; First Franco and 118, 126; Second Franco and 115, 120
Damasithymus 38, 39
Darius I 28, 40
daughters 28, 39, 41, 55, 145, 147, 151, 152, 155, 158, 176, 197, 236, 255, 259, 272, 284, 285
De Lay Haye, Nicola 81, 89n, 300
De Lorris, Guillaume 19, 296
De Meun, Jean 19
De Pizan, Christine 19, 25, 77, 293; *City of Ladies, The* and 19

decorative arts 5, 17, 52, 75, 78, 164, 165, 195, 213, 317, 320; artifacts as 140–189
DNA 21, 41, 281
doctors, female 158, 202
Dodds, Alfred-Amedee 115, 120, 135n, 290; *Life in the Legion: From ta Solder's Point of View* and 115
Douce I, Countess of Provence 82
druids 55, 61, 62, 64, 66, 67, 69n
Duncan, John 102, 103, 133n; journeys of 104; Kong Mountain and 103; Mountains of the Moon and 103

education 68n, 111, 132n, 148, 150, 153, 157, 161, 195, 202, 230, 256, 282, 314; medical and: Blake, Sophia Jex and 234; 235, 236; degrees and 200, 211, 236, 265; Edinburgh Seven and 8, 234, 301; female doctors and 152, 158, 202; *Seven Against Thebes* and 235
enclothed cognition 6, 94–96, 291, 301
Endell Street Military Hospital 240, 241, 248n
Escher, 2nd Viscount (Regionald Brett) 196, 197, 199, 200
Exekias 6, 9, 15, 16, 315
exotica 7, 117; Chicago World's Columbian Exposition and 118, 119, 136n; Chicago World's Fair and 112, 136n; London Crystal Palace Exhibition and 118; Paris Hall Exhibition and 118
exposition organizers: Bodinus, Heinrich and 118; Hagenanuer, Friedrich and 142; Hagenbeck, Carl and 118; Pene, Xavier and 119, 122

Fabian Art Society 165
feminine cavaliers 76, 77, 82, 90n
feminism 148, 153, 158, 174
First Aid Nursing Yeomanry (FANY) 214, 307, 196, 197, 198, 199
Fon 97, 101, 114, 119, 122, 123
Forbes, Frederick 102, 103, 105, 109, 110, 134n, 138, 293, 297; Bonetta, Sarah Forbes (Aina) and 111, 135n, 306; education and 110; *HMS Bonnetta* and 290; Queen Victoria and 111; West Africa Squadron and 107, 134n

326 Index

force feeding 127, 140, 166–168, 172, 174, 175, 185n, 236, 304; Ball, William description of 170; court documentation description of 169; data about 169; Holloway Prison and 166, 174, 236; Horsley, Victor and 169; Leigh, Mary description of 166; Lyton, Constance description of 168; Mansell-Moullin, Charles and 169–170; Occoquan Workhouse and 152, 171, 172, 173; Savill, Agnes and 169
Freedom or Death Speech 150, 155, 182, 187, 306
fusiliers 18, 23n

Garrett Anderson, Louisa 6, 7, 211, 220, 230, 236, 237, 249, 292
Genoa 82, 85, 86, 90n, 294, 307
Germany 1, 2, 44n, 72, 80, 81, 145, 153, 160, 165, 191, 195, 196, 201, 207, 208, 223, 224, 232, 253, 254, 266, 267, 282, 314, 316, 317
Ghent, treaty of 107
goddesses 10, 32, 58, 70n; Ares, 13; Belenus 59; Brigid 59; Clonie 14; Dana 58; Harmotome 13; Hippolyta 13, 19, 20, 81; Tomyris 19, 20
gods 11, 14, 21n, 23n, 40, 58, 61, 70n
golden ratio (mean) 10, 15, 16, 17, 21n, 22n, 193, 317; Euclid and 10, 16; Phi and 10, 21n; Phidias and 10, 11
Granville-Wright, Lady Ada Cecile 197
Graves, Robert 18, 23n, 312
Great Britain 1, 8, 59, 60, 71n, 81, 83, 163, 165, 174, 177, 200, 228, 229, 253, 281
Greeks 8, 12, 13, 18, 31, 34, 35, 36, 37, 39, 40, 41, 44n, 46n, 47n, 194, 255, 309, 315
Guam 2, 7, 8, 262, 267, 268, 269, 270, 271, 278n

Hague, The 156, 157, 159, 163, 182n, 246n, 292n, 319
Halicarnassus 10, 31, 34, 28, 41, 45n, 47n, 296, 308
Hambidge, Jay 16–17, 22n, 23n, 299; dynamic symmetry, elements of 16, 17, 22n, 23n, 299
Hangbe, Queen 99, 113, 114
Helion, Jean 254–255, 276n, 300
Hercules 13

Herodotus 20, 24n, 28, 31, 34, 35, 36–39, 40, 41, 43n, 45n, 46n, 47n, 298, 299, 300; *Book seven* and 44n, 45n, 46n; *Book eight* and 38n
Hillman, Alex L. 264–266; colleagues and 264–265
Hospitallers (Maltesers) 2, 79, 81, 83, 89n, 310n
husbands 58, 62, 68n, 80, 81, 149, 154, 157, 165, 167, 169, 170, 195, 198, 204, 255, 258
Husted Harper, Ida 176, 180n, 181n, 299

iconography 22n, 40, 44n, 128–129, 298; Panofsky, Irwin and 32, 33, 47, 306
illustrations 31, 57, 124, 126, 137n, 209, 231, 258, 260, 297
Italian (Italy) 16, 53, 54, 62, 80, 81, 86, 120, 141, 165, 208, 221, 222, 228, 253, 254, 255, 266, 314

Jackson, Leona 263, 269, 278n, 300
Jameson, Anna Brownell 147
Japan(ese) 7, 8, 222, 223, 261, 262, 263, 266, 268, 269, 270, 271, 272–274, 284
jewelry 5, 17, 41, 60, 174, 184n, 186n, 294, 317; armbands as 122, 126, 128, 143, 160; clasps as 33, 165; Dahomey warrior's cowrie shells as 100, 109, 122, 125, 126, 128, 132n; suffragism and 164, 165, 310
Jewish peoples 41, 79, 88n, 163, 188, 231, 258, 265, 277n, 296, 308

Kaulbach, Wilhelm von 31; three step approach and 33
knights 75, 78, 79, 81, 82, 83, 84, 85, 86, 88n, 89n, 91, 167, 291, 306
Knights Templar 75, 79, 81, 83, 88n, 291
kings 5, 7, 14, 19, 28, 35, 27, 38, 39, 40, 58, 62, 79, 80, 83, 93, 97, 98, 99, 100, 103, 104, 105, 107, 109, 110, 113, 114, 115, 121, 123, 124, 125, 126, 127, 131n, 132n, 137n, 138, 142, 196, 197, 234, 235, 289; animalia symbols, and 123, 137n, 307

laboratory coats 94, 95, 96, 99
Lamentations of Matheolus 19
Latin 28, 60, 71, 81, 108, 144, 232, 260

law(s) 5, 6, 8, 16, 17, 61, 75, 83, 85, 90, 97, 107, 134n, 143, 145, 149, 150, 156, 159, 161, 163, 167, 173, 182, 184n, 191, 229, 284, 285, 304, 307
legionnaires 8, 114, 143
legislation 107, 154, 169, 188, 260
lesbianism 260, 277n
Lifeguards, Regiment of 103, 104, 106
Livingstone, David 103, 133n, 301
Lyton, Constance Lady 166, 167, 168, 170, 197

male viewpoint 50, 113, 126, 284; histrionics and 87; misogyny and 18, 304
manifestos 178n, 222, 223, 226, 228, 230, 243n, 245n, 255, 256, 307, 310, 318; Bauhaus Movement Manifesto 224, 244n, 275n, 307, 314, 315; Concrete Art Manifesto 254, 276n; Dada Manifesto 226, 245n, 318; Founding Manifesto of Futurism 222; Manifesto Towards a Free Revolutionary Art 255, 275n, 276n; Southern Manifesto 260; Surrealist Manifesto 255
Mardonius 37, 40
Martyn, Frederick 115, 120, 124, 135n, 290, 291, 304; eyewitness accounts and 114, 115, 117; Franco Dahomeyan wars and 116; Senegalese Tirailleurs and 116
Marxism 221, 232, 255, 256, 272n
medals 6, 95, 96, 141, 143, 170, 177n, 178n, 214n, 268, 269, 290, 292, 294, 301, 305, 318; history and 141–143; Polybius and 142, 178n; suffragettes and 127–128, 174, 197
media 56, 92, 94, 102, 114, 154, 203, 210, 223, 230, 256, 257, 262, 280, 284, 287; journals and newspapers: *Daily Chronicle, The* 120, 230; *Daily Record,* The 203; *Daily Telegraph* 120, 211; *Dundee Courier* 257, 276n; *Evening News,* The 203; *Glasgow Courier* 54; *Hartford Current, The* 155, 182n; *Illustrated World, The* 126; *Izvestia* 256; *Le Petit Journal* 124, 135n, 289, 290; *Le Tour du monde* 125; *London Chronicle* 118, 136n, 219; *Navy Nurse Magazine* 266; *New York Evening Journal,* The 258, 266;

New York Times, The 208; 215n, 216n, 244n, 245n, 259, 266, 277n, 278n; *Omaha Bee* 204; *Partisan Review* 255, 276n, 311; *Pravda* 256; *Punch* 257; 276n; *Speaker, The* 257; *Votes for Women* 168, 203; *Woman King, The* 128, 129, 139, 295
medallions 141; chasing and 141; embossing and 141; Hagenauer, Friedrich and 142; *intaglio* and 141, 316; *repousse* and 141; Weiditz, Christoph and 141
minorities 119, 188, 191
morale 64, 86, 95, 234
Murray, Flora 211, 220, 230, 236, 237, 238, 239, 240, 242, 248, 305
Muslims 6, 7, 85, 86, 92, 112, 285
Mussolini, Benito 253
myths 13, 18, 22n, 23n, 25, 90n, 103, 298, 299, 307

Navy, US 8, 134n, 262, 272, 275, 282, 283
New York City 2, 151, 152, 157, 159, 164, 173, 207, 226, 227, 255, 258, 265, 270, 287
Night of Terror, the 171, 174, 185n, 186n, 294
nursing 3, 160, 167, 176, 196, 200, 202, 208, 217, 260, 261, 262, 263, 266, 267, 268, 269, 270, 271, 272, 274, 275, 279, 284, 286, 287, 297, 306, 310; Baker, Eduard, and impact on 198

occult(ism) 223, 229, 230, 231, 232, 233, 242, 244n, 246n, 247n, 319
Olds, Marion 7, 8, 24, 251, 262, 263, 266, 267, 269, 271, 272, 273, 274, 275, 278n, 282, 284
opinion 38, 40, 124, 132, 147, 158, 161, 176, 316
Order of the Hatchet, the Most Nobel, 74, 76, 77, 87
Ottoman Empire 191, 194, 215n

pacifism 6, 143, 144, 150, 156, 157, 158, 160, 161, 162, 163, 176, 183, 184n, 186n, 187, 156, 207, 294; Theodore Roosevelt and 156, 163, 183n, 184n
Paul, Alice 153, 164, 166, 187, 298, 307, 313

328 Index

painting 15, 16, 17, 22n, 44, 52, 103, 108, 174, 190, 192, 193, 194, 195, 209, 210, 213n, 244n, 245, 252, 254, 256, 265, 292, 302, 305, 306, 309, 315, 316, 317, 319, 320; social commentary as 220–242

Paris 77, 118, 119, 129, 221, 224, 225, 226, 228, 229, 236, 237, 243n, 252, 314, 319, 320

peace 42, 62, 85, 149, 156, 158, 159, 162, 182n, 183n, 184n, 193, 208, 209, 213n, 214n, 216n, 291, 305

peace conference, women's 156, 157, 160, 161, 163; Women's International League for Peace and 164

Penaeus 11

Penthesilea 5, 7, 9, 10, 11, 12, 13, 14, 15, 16, 17, 18, 19, 21n, 22n, 23n, 81, 281, 309; interpretations of 12

Persians 31, 34, 35, 36, 37, 44n, 45n, 291, 295

Pompeius Trogus 33, 43n, 301

portraiture 5, 6, 27, 31, 33, 52, 75, 165, 177, 209, 212n, 214n, 230, 231, 233, 238, 239, 242, 244n, 245n, 287, 290, 294, 308; historical record as 190–219

Portuguese 99, 131n, 259, 281

pottery 5, 9, 11, 15, 16; amphora and 5, 6, 15, 17; Black-figure and 5, 15, 22n, 25, 293, 315; design and 16, 17, 22n, 23n; Red-figure and 11, 12, 15, 320

prisoners of war: Anton, Frank 3; Cobb, Laura Mae 268, 278n; Davison, Maude 267, 268; Fogarty, Virginia 269, 278n; Helion, Jean 254, 276n; Jackson, Leona 263, 269, 278n; Olds, Marion 7, 8, 24, 251, 262, 263, 266, 267, 269, 271, 272, 273, 274, 275, 278n, 282, 284; Schwinn, Monika 1–4; Whittle, Reba Zitella 284, 267; Yetter, Doris 263, 269, 270, 278n

propaganda 1, 70n, 142, 162, 177n, 228, 230, 233, 259, 267, 274, 279, 301, 312, 316

public sculpture 5, 50–69, 69n; assembly and 51; bronze and 51, 53, 58, 60, 67; Boudica, London and 49; Dahomey Amazon, Benin and 129; equestrian and 52

pulp art 5, 7, 8, 251, 257–258, 266, 275n, 27; female artists and 258–261

pulps 257, 262, 264, 265, 266, 277n; *Cherry Ames, Chief Nurse* and 260, 261, 312; *Cherry Ames Senior Nurse* and 260, 261; *Ginger Lee War Nurse* and 260, 261, 296; Hillman, Alex and 264, 265, 266, 277n; industry and 257, 258; penny dreadfuls and 256, 276n; *Sensation* Magazine and 262, 264, 266, 277n; Torres, Tereska and 258, 277n; Free French Forces and 259; *Women's Barracks* and 260, 277n; Wells, Helen and 260

Red Cross, The 130n, 158, 175, 195, 196, 197, 199, 201, 202, 204, 205, 210, 215n, 233, 236, 242, 261, 266, 273, 284, 286

remonstrant 145, 148, 164

river(s) 86, 128; Danube 194, 202; Ebro 76; Lena 85; Niger 104, 121; Nile 103, 112; Queme 126; Thames 50; Yewa 101

Romans 6, 20, 43n, 55, 58, 59, 60, 61, 62, 63, 64, 65, 66, 67, 71n, 102, 143, 255, 307

Rouille, Guillaume 6, 27, 32, 40, 41, 44n, 47; women and 41

Royal Academy of Art(s) 221, 238, 243n, 314

Russia (Russian) 14, 20, 21, 24n, 144, 191, 224, 253, 255, 282, 284, 287

Salamis, battle of 8, 28, 35, 36, 37, 43

Scythians 24n, 25n, 281, 299

sea(s) 5, 7, 8, 10, 19, 28, 35, 36, 38, 40, 41, 44n, 47n, 48, 108, 197, 268, 269, 272, 281, 288; Adriatic 194; Aegean 11; Black 20; Ionian 37; Irish 234; Java 266; Mediterranean 82; Tyrrhenian 11

Sensation Magazine 8, 251, 262, 264, 266, 277n, 278n

Serbia(an) 5, 7, 14, 163, 175, 190, 191, 194, 195, 196, 199, 200, 202, 203, 205, 210, 211n, 213n; army and 202, 204, 205, 209, 210; artists and art and 193–194, 195; *Kirk Kilisse* and 202, 215n; *Kolo srpskih sestara* and 196, 202; retreat and 206–207, 210

Serbian Relief Fund 205, 215n

sexualization 7, 19, 26, 32, 44n, 73, 112, 113, 230, 284, 285
She Dong Hong Beh 109, 110
ships: *Creole, HMS* 107, 108; *Bonetta, HMS* 107, 133n
sieges 6, 7, 8, 79, 80, 81, 84, 85, 90n, 283; Almira and 85; Tortosa and 5, 6, 7, 8, 75, 76, 79, 84, 85–87
Silent Sentinels, the 152, 153, 187, 306, 310
Skertchly, Sydney Barber Josiah (J.A.) 103, 106, 123, 124, 131n, 133n
social change 258, 287
social status 33, 82, 94, 98, 122, 145
socialism 150, 191, 221, 224, 300
Soudan Campaign 198
Spain 75, 76, 77, 79, 87n, 88n, 99, 253, 259
Spare, Austin Osman 223, 229–232, 234, 238, 239, 240, 241, 242, 246n, 319; colleagues and 232; Crowdy, Rachel Dame and 239; Norman, Lady Florence Priscilla and 241, 242
speeches 65, 66, 114, 208, 211n, 154, 155
statuary 50, 51, 52, 58, 68n, 286
statues 10, 11, 40, 49, 50, 51, 52, 53, 54, 56, 57, 58, 64, 67, 68n, 129, 137n
stone: carving and 63, 74, 75, 77, 87; engraving and 5, 6, 11, 74, 75, 77, 87n, 88n; guilds and 77, 88n; history and 75–76; masons and 77; quarries and 76, 82; uses of 33, 51, 59, 75, 78, 141, 166, 196, 286, 298
Stobart, Mabel St. Clair 6, 7, 190, 197, 198, 199, 200, 201, 203, 204, 206, 207, 208, 209, 211, 214n, 215n, 216n, 217n, 285, 310; flying field hospital and 205; French Red Cross and 205; honorary decorations and 210; media coverage and 203–204; retreat and 206–207
storytelling 4, 9, 12, 14, 35, 113
strategy 37, 38, 39, 40, 46n, 73, 117, 136n, 137, 153, 157, 181n, 267, 302
Suetonius Paulinus 60, 64, 65, 71n
suffrage societies: National American Woman Suffrage Association (NAWSA) and 152, 162, 180n, 183n, 299n; National Union of Women's Suffrage Societies (NUWSS) and 153, 158, 159, 162, 175, 180n, 181n, 183n, 236, 299; Women's Social and Political Union (WSPU) and 150,

153, 154, 155, 156, 165, 169, 170, 173, 174, 175, 181n, 208, 236, 302
suffragism 6, 7, 140, 143, 144, 145, 147, 148, 149, 150, 153, 157, 163, 187; clothing and 165; Child and Child and 165; Derry and Tom and 165; Mappin and Webb and 165; Selfridge's and 165; cross country train trip and 175–176; jewelry and 164, 165; picketing and, 152, 161, 171, 172; pilgrimage and 152; political imprisonment and 166, 171; procession and 173; types of suffragism 144; World War I intervention and 175–177
Swindler, Mary 16

Tacitus 60, 61, 62, 64, 65, 66, 70n, 71, 72, 295
Thermopylae, 35, 36, 46n
Thessaloniki, Greece 11
Thornycroft, Mary 68n, 304
Thornycroft, Thomas 6, 49, 50, 51, 52, 53, 54, 55, 56, 57, 58, 67, 68n, 69n, 72; children and 52; critiques and 50, 53, 54; Dickinson, W.B. and 54, 55; *Gallic War* and 55, 56, 60, 70n, 71n; London Great Exhibition and 53; Marochetti, Baron Carlo and 53, 54, 69n
Torch of Tortosa, Order of the Hatchet 74, 76, 84, 90n
Torres, Tereska 258–259, 277n
tribes 18, 21, 57–59, 62, 63, 70n, 72, 99, 101, 102, 281, 310n; Africa and 99, 101, 102, 281; Great Britain and 18, 21, 57, 58, 59, 62, 63, 72, 310
trireme 28, 30, 34, 36, 37, 38, 44n
Trotsky, Leon 255, 256, 267n, 311
Türkiye 11, 14, 21, 85, 255, 282

uniforms 2, 5, 6, 34, 95, 96, 103, 106, 123, 129, 130n, 137n, 173, 193, 200, 267, 286; artifacts as 93–139; Fussel, Paul and 96; Landsknechts and 97; winged hussars and 97; Ghillie suits and 97

Victoria, Queen 52, 54, 56, 69n, 103, 104, 111, 124
Victorian 31, 41, 52, 53, 55, 67, 68n, 69n, 70n, 94, 103, 138, 164, 167, 177, 197, 198, 256, 276n, 293, 312
Virgil 14, 22n, 312

330 Index

war art 189, 193, 195, 225, 232–234, 287, 218, 219, 230, 233, 246n
warriors 5, 6, 14, 17, 20, 25n, 32, 40, 99, 100, 101, 114, 117, 118, 120, 126, 128, 129, 132n, 135n, 136n, 137n, 138, 143, 144, 218, 281; Dahomey of West Africa and 93–139
Wars: Adegon, battle of 114; Artemisium, battle of 28; Balkan Wars 191, 193, 194, 195, 201, 213n, 214n; Dogba, battle of 114, 115, 126, 128, 137n; First Franco Dahomey War 126; Guam, battle of 8; Marathon, battle of 34; Salamis, battle of 35–37, 43; Second Franco Dahomey War 120, 137n; Trojan War 8, 13, 14, 310; women's civil war 140–189; World War I 18, 19, 23n, 56, 142, 156, 161, 163, 175, 183n, 187n, 192, 193, 194, 195, 197, 198m, 202, 204, 217, 222, 223, 224, 226, 232, 233, 242, 248, 249, 253, 256, 258, 268, 283; World War II 5, 7, 8, 92, 231, 238, 242, 253, 256, 258, 259, 265, 269, 271, 277n, 278n, 283, 284, 286
Washington, Madison 107
weapons: boiling oil as 79; bush knives as 109, 114; cavalry as 8, 18, 56, 64, 66, 82, 100, 103, 127, 142, 194, 198, 199, 281; chariots as 8, 23n, 50,

54, 56, 57, 60, 64, 65; clubs as 114; daggers as 21, 31; guns as 82, 102, 105, 119, 126, 128, 206, 228, 272; hand-to-hand combat as 7, 8, 34, 64, 67; machetes as 116, 126, 129; mangonels as 34, 85, 86; rocks and stones as 34, 79, 81, 84, 85, 86, 87, 197; staves as 125
Wells, Ida B. 152
West Africa 7, 103, 107, 109, 118, 119, 125, 133n, 134n, 136, 137n, 313
Wilson, Woodrow 152, 159, 161, 163, 183n
wives 16, 41, 52, 55, 81, 110, 111, 118, 145, 147, 149, 154, 170, 228, 231, 255, 258, 259, 265, 272, 286
Woman's Suffrage Parade Washington, D.C description of 152
Women's Sick and Wounded Convoy Corps 190, 196, 199

Xerxes I 28, 29, 34; Achaemenid Empire and 29, 31, 33, 34, 35, 40, 45n; Artemisium, battle and 28, 35; Salamis, battle and 35–37; Thermopylae, battle and 35, 36; war councils and 37, 40

Zentsuji Prison Camp 270, 273, 274, 278n; treatment and 273–274; types of internees and 273
Zeus 10, 16, 39